The Graphic Communicatio. Handbook

The Graphic Communication Handbook is a comprehensive and detailed introduction to the theories and practices of the graphics industry. It traces the history and development of graphic design, explores issues that affect the industry, examines its analysis through communications theory, explains how to do each section of the job, and advises on entry into the profession.

The Graphic Communication Handbook covers all areas within the industry including pitching, understanding the client, researching a job, thumbnail drawings, developing concepts, presenting to clients, working in 2D, 3D, motion graphics and interaction graphics, situating and testing the job, getting paid, and getting the next job. The industry background, relevant theory and the law related to graphic communications are situated alongside the teaching of the practical elements.

Features include:

- introductions that frame relevant debates
- case studies, examples and illustrations from a range of campaigns
- philosophical and technical explanations of topics and their importance.

Simon Downs is Lecturer in Graphic Communication at Loughborough University, UK. He is Managing Editor of *The Poster – The Journal of Visual Rhetoric in the Public Sphere*, Co-Editor of *Tracey – The Journal of Contemporary Drawing*, one of the authors of *Drawing Now: Between the Lines of Contemporary Art* (2007), and Associate Editor of the *Journal of Technology, Knowledge and Society*. He is a Fellow of the Higher Education Academy, and a member of the Design Research Society's Special Interest Group on Design Pedagogy.

Media Practice

Edited by James Curran, Goldsmiths College, University of London

The *Media Practice* handbooks are comprehensive resource books for students of media and journalism, and for anyone planning a career as a media professional. Each handbook combines a clear introduction to understanding how the media work with practical information about the structure, processes and skills involved in working in today's media industries, providing not only a guide on 'how to do it' but also a critical reflection on contemporary media practice.

The Advertising Handbook
3rd edition
Helen Powell, Jonathan Hardy,
Sarah Hawkin and Iain MacRury

The Alternative Media Handbook
Kate Coyer, Tony Dowmunt and
Alan Fountain

The Cyberspace Handbook
Jason Whittaker

The Documentary Handbook
Peter Lee-Wright

The Fashion Handbook
Tim Jackson and David Shaw

The Graphic Communication Handbook
Simon Downs

The Magazines Handbook
2nd edition
Jenny McKay

The Music Industry Handbook
Paul Rutter

The New Media Handbook
Andrew Dewdney and Peter Ride

The Newspapers Handbook
4th edition
Richard Keeble

The Photography Handbook
2nd edition
Terence Wright

The Public Relations Handbook
4th edition
Alison Theaker

The Radio Handbook
3rd edition
Carole Fleming

The Television Handbook
4th edition
Jeremy Orlebar

The Graphic Communication Handbook

Simon Downs

Routledge
Taylor & Francis Group

LONDON AND NEW YORK

First published 2012
by Routledge
2 Park Square, Milton Park, Abingdon, Oxon OX14 4RN

Simultaneously published in the USA and Canada
by Routledge
711 Third Avenue, New York, NY 10017

Routledge is an imprint of the Taylor & Francis Group, an informa business

British Library Cataloguing in Publication Data
A catalogue record for this book is available from the British Library

Library of Congress Cataloging in Publication Data
Downs, Simon.
   The graphic communication handbook/Simon Downs. – 1st ed.
   p. cm. – (Media practice)
   Includes bibliographical references and index.
   1. Commercial art—Vocational guidance. 2. Graphic arts—Vocational
   guidance. I. Title.
   NC1001.D69 2011
   741.6023–dc22
   2011009220

ISBN: 978–0–415–55737–5 (hbk)
ISBN: 978–0–415–55738–2 (pbk)
ISBN: 978–0–203–80466–7 (ebk)

Typeset in Helvetica and Avant Garde
by Florence Production Ltd, Stoodleigh, Devon

MIX
Paper from
responsible sources
FSC
www.fsc.org   FSC® C004839

Printed and bound in Great Britain by the MPG Books Group

This book is dedicated to Claire Lerpiniere:
a fine design educator without whom this
book would not have been possible;
and to Andrew Chong, an inspirational
graphics educator

Contents

Figures

Tables

Contributors

Malcolm Barnard is a lecturer in visual culture at Loughborough University, UK, where he teaches the history and theory of art and design. His background is in recent French philosophy and sociological theory, and he is the author of *Graphic design as communication* (2005, Routledge), *Fashion as communication* (2002, Routledge), *Approaches to understanding visual culture* (2001) and *Art, design and visual culture* (1998). He is also the editor of *Fashion* (2011, Routledge) and *Fashion theory* (2007, Routledge).

Gui Bonsiepe studied graphics and architecture in post-war Germany before becoming a teacher at the influential Ulm School of Design, Germany, in the 1960s. From 1968 onwards, he worked as a freelance graphic and interface designer, consultant, writer, design theoretician and thinker in Latin America. He is currently Visiting Professor of Integrated Media at the ESDI (Escola Superior de Desenho Industrial, Universidade do Estado de Rio de Janeiro).

Matthew Fray has been working in the printing industry since 1972; as a result, he has seen first-hand the changes from pre-digital to digital and from letterpress to computer set type. His skill set ranges from setting lead type to writing web pages. As a trained educator he has, for over 25 years, passed on this knowledge to generations of graphics workers, always trying to train designers who can work professionally with the people who make their work real.

Ken Garland studied graphic design at the Central School of Arts and Crafts, London, in the 1950s. Before founding his own company, Ken Garland and Associates, he worked as the Art Director of *Design Magazine*. He has spent five decades designing for high-profile clients and political causes, has taught design around the world, including at the Royal College of Art, has lectured graphics students around the globe, has appeared on television and has written key graphics texts, including *Graphics handbook* (1966), *Mr Beck's underground map* (1994) and *A word in your eye* (1996). He is currently Visiting Professor in Graphic Design at Brighton University.

Steve Garner is currently the Professor of Design at the Open University. An acknowledged expert on design thinking, Garner writes extensively on the application of drawing and representation as tools in the design process. His research covers the mental processes that are active in sketching (the *Designing with Vision* project) and the ways in which design can be taught through distance learning (*Atelier-D*). For many years he has served as head of the *Drawing Research Network*, offering guidance and a forum for debate for those interested in drawing research.

Johnny Hardstaff is a director, designer and modern storyteller. He has directed and designed innovative moving-image work across a broad spectrum of both commercial and non-commercial strands of the visual arts. Clients include Radiohead, Sony, Philips, Toshiba, Sony PlayStation and the BBC. Hardstaff's work has been broadcast worldwide and exhibited at major museums of modern art and cultural institutes, including Tate Modern, NFT, ICA, Laforet Museum, Museum of Contemporary Art, Chicago, ACMI, Melbourne, MOMA, San Francisco, and the V&A Museum. Among his most notable works to date are *History of Gaming* and *Future of Gaming*, now inducted into the National Film Archive, the Radiohead film *Like Spinning Plates*, and the 2010 future noir short film *DarkRoom*. Hardstaff is currently a very occasional Visiting Lecturer in Design at the Manchester School of Art.

Steve Seidman is Professor of Communication Management and Design at the Roy H. Park School of Communications, Ithaca College, New York. He is an expert on visual literacy and looks at political propaganda, with a special interest in the visual aspects of campaigning, including design of political posters, T-shirts, yard signs and bumper stickers. He is the author of *Posters, propaganda and persuasion around the world and through history* (2008), a multidisciplinary look at communication media in election campaigns, with an emphasis on posters. Seidman currently serves on the editorial boards of the *Journal of Visual Literacy* and the *International Journal of Instructional Media* and the board of the International Visual Literacy Association.

Karel van der Waarde studied graphic design in the Netherlands at the Design Academy, Eindhoven, De Montfort University and the University of Reading. In 1995, he started a design-research consultancy in Belgium specializing in the testing of information design. Avans University of Applied Sciences, in the Netherlands, appointed him as scholar in Visual Rhetoric in 2006. This research post investigates the development and use of visual communication, with a longer-term aim to support the relations between practice, research and education. Van der Waarde is a Life Fellow of the Communications Research Institute, Melbourne, a board member of the International Institute for Information Design, Austria, and editorial board member of *Information Design Journal, Iridescent, The Poster* and *Visible Language*.

Introduction

This book is called *The graphic communication handbook* not *The graphic design handbook*. Getting names right from the off is important: call it *Pokey Cola*, and it doesn't taste as good; call it a *Plum* computer, and suddenly it's not so glamorous to play with; and, over the course of the twentieth century, the title 'Graphic Design' has often come to mean something narrow, something limited. Something less than the subject's history or its future prospects.

This change has been quite rapid, perhaps sparked by reactions to social change (maybe Jamie Reed's punk graphics scared folk) or technical evolution of old processes to new in computer-aided design and manufacture (CAD/CAM) in the 1980s, or it is possible that the art theorists scared the practitioners with their post-modernist talk. So, where once Saul Bass made films, logos, industrial design and posters, without for a moment doubting that he was a graphic designer, and William Adison Dwiggins *knew* he was a graphic designer (he did invent the term), despite being a publisher, practising calligraphy, writing and making puppets (no lie!), there are people who try and pin graphics down to its most constrained historical basics as communication through print. As you are reading this book, I'm going to assume that you are not one of those people, and that you see what the subject is and can be. I'm going to work from the assumption that you want to be part of a bigger, better world, where graphic communication is big and clever, brave and fun!

This change in meaning has come about because, on one hand, technology has allowed us to design graphics with radically new media that our ancestors in design could never have anticipated, and in response to new social needs that tradition could never have anticipated. By contrast, the narrow view of the possibilities inherent in graphics has come about because people with vested interests in the traditional ways of doing graphics have declared that 'the graphic crafts are the graphic arts are graphic design'. Which is simply not true. Let me explain.

GRAPHIC/ART

The word *graphic* is defined by the O*xford English dictionary* (*OED*) as:

> A. adj. 1. Drawn with a pencil or pen. *Obs*. 2. Of or pertaining to drawing or painting. **graphic arts**: the fine arts of drawing, painting, engraving, etching, etc.; also, the techniques of production and design involved in printing and publishing . . .

The word *art* is derived from the same root word as artifice and artefact. It carries many meanings, but the most applicable from the *OED* are either:

> I. Skill; its display, application, or expression.
> 1. Skill in doing something, esp. as the result of knowledge or practice.

or

> 8. a. The expression or application of creative skill and imagination, typically in a visual form such as painting, drawing, or sculpture, producing works to be appreciated primarily for their beauty or emotional power. Also: such works themselves considered collectively.

As such, we are left with the meaning of the term *graphic art* meaning something like '. . . a person who skilfully makes artefacts with drawing, painting and printing'.

Unfortunately, this interpretation leads to the fine arts confusions, where the term 'graphic' is used to indicate a style, not a process, so that the work of Roy Lichtenstein becomes a 'graphic art work'. **Graphics is not a style!**

The *graphic crafts* are the historic tools and processes we use, and the ways of thought imposed by these tools. However, the process of making graphics is not the same as communicating graphically. So, where lithographically printing a poster is a craft, using that poster to change the world is design. There are historic reasons for certain ways of making being associated with graphics; time moves on, and we must move with it.

The *graphic arts* are a historic social role that goes with the subject. A role with status, a job description that brings us a certain kudos, a profession you can be proud of. Look at the etymology of the words and you have a person who skilfully makes artefacts with drawing, painting and printing.

However, as with all professions, it is in the profession's interests to solidify the status quo, to define what is in the club and what is unforgivable and foreign. Step out of line and you're out of the club.

Graphic design is the logical combination of the two – the arts and the craft – and as such it does a very fine job. Combining the process with its skilful application was a very good way of describing the subject. But, and it is a huge but, the arts and the craft bring with them ways of doing and ways of thinking that don't cope very well with the new. Craft typographic principles don't translate in a predictable way to screen-based media, nor to other cultures. Rules about applying craft print media don't translate very well to interactive animations: the paint drips off the computer screen, for a start.

By contrast, *graphic communication* does not care about history per se, unless that history serves the job. It does not care if its designs fit the status quo, only that they work for the benefit of those who will use them. A graphic communicator does not

How graphics used to be done

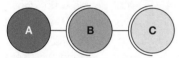

A. The client issues a brief
B. The graphic designer designs a solution
C. The user uses the solution

How graphics should be done

1. The client identifies a need fo a design from all the possible bits of knowledge in the world that they can know. This immediately reduces the options for the design.
2. From this client choice the options are further reduced down through reference to the user's knowledge of the world (which might be different from the client's knowledge, which is why they have their own spur coming from the world knowledge pool).
3. The designer makes a design which is informed by their knowledge of the world and is either workable (go to 4) or not workable (go to 1).
4. The client approves the design. If they don't approve the design it's straight back to 1.
5. If the users can use the design then it's on to 6. If they find the design unusable it's back to 3.
6. Finally the designer sends the design to manufacture and then analyses whay they have learnt from the whole process to help with the next job.

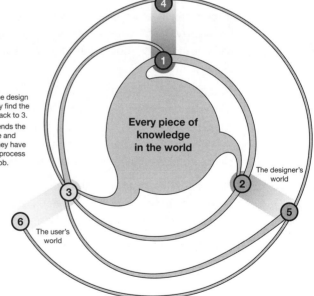

FIGURE 0.1

The traditional model of graphic design was a simple, linear affair; for reasons that are discussed later, the current model gets less linear all the time

have to serve the people with the money and power to make the presses run; it should celebrate the opportunity to play badly, if it makes the world a better place. A graphic communicator will do whatever it takes to get the job done.

Graphic communication is not a way of making, a box of tools, though it uses lots of tools: it is a process of thinking and planning, so that when we do what we have to do, when we make what we need to make, we do it right first time, every time. Graphic communication has a different relationship to those we design for. In the past, graphic designers had to make one person happy: the client. Graphic communicators understand that the client may have the wrong idea about the needs of the user and, by blindly serving the client's wishes, they may be damaging their interests (because, although the client may be happy, the dissatisfaction of the user will mean the client gets no long-term benefit).

I have on my bookshelf at home a copy of Ken Garland's 1966 *The graphics handbook*. It is a wonderful book, full of understanding and enthusiasm. I am always struck by the clarity and insight of Garland's understanding of the subject, but also how the number of ways of graphically engaging with people has grown since his book was published. Designers can do more in 2011 than could have been imagined in 1966.

Beyond the process, graphic communication is knowing that people build identity and meaning in their lives with visual symbols: my colleague Malcolm Barnard will talk more about this in Chapter 11. Graphic communication is understanding that those symbols are real – a matter of life and death – to the user and the user's community. It's about understanding that, if we can work with these symbols, we can speak clearly to our users in ways that they understand as honest and meaningful.

Graphic communication is showing people the things they urgently need to understand, in ways that they can understand. We are like shadow puppeteers: we stand between the candle and the night, casting images that illuminate the world for our viewers. This work will inform, entertain, sell to, protect from, agitate, pacify, clarify, illuminate, bring people together and divide them.

Graphic communication is the process through which we can decode the visual culture of those we need to communicate with; it is the process of planning a response; it is the process of making a solution.

Sometimes, most of the time, this means using tools and processes that have their origins in graphic design. Our DNA is the same as graphic design's, in the same way that your DNA is your parents'. But that doesn't make us the same. We proudly carry a heritage and are in some measure defined by this heritage, but we make ourselves through the things we do.

The philosopher Gilles Deleuze neatly summed up this proposition with his observation that many academics are fond of defining the world in terms of trees and branches (this thing is the child of that thing and the parent of something else, and

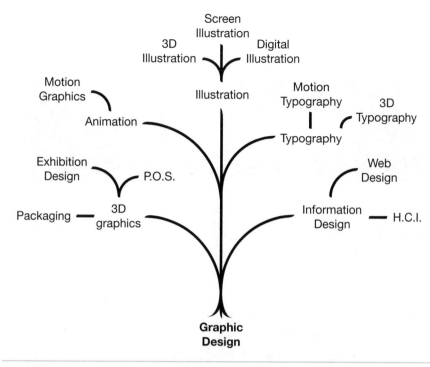

FIGURE 0.2
Graphics as a tree. Everything is distinct; nothing connects. In this diagram, motion typography and animation are completely different branches

is defined by this relationship). 'Not so', says Deleuze: in the case of cultural things (and graphics is certainly a cultural thing), we are like rhizomes. Rhizomes are those knotty masses of root things, where all the parts of the cluster of plants are connected as one organism, sharing and communicating, and yet the tiniest slice, containing the DNA of the whole, can grow into a whole new plant. Deleuze pointed out that this was a smarter model of culture than the tree.

In this model, while all the parts of graphic communication contain bits of graphic design's heritage, and all the parts of graphic communication – from typography to illustration, from HCI to packaging – can stand on their own, they are all interconnected. All the parts support and nourish the whole, while being distinct. So, we will talk about graphic communication (the whole thing), rather than graphic design (the single part).

This book believes that it helps to look at the whole, the twisted mass of connections, the common elements that bring us together, and to downplay the differences. Which is why this is *The graphic communication handbook.*

In this book, we will work through the main stages of a single graphics job: from the first task (getting the job) to the last (making sure you can get another one); taking

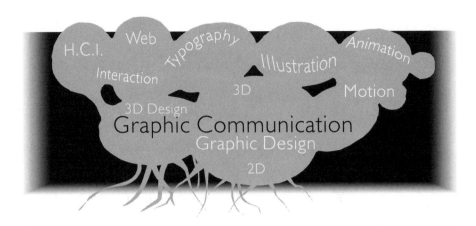

FIGURE 0.3
Graphics as a rhizome

in such popular destinations as briefing, making and the ever favourite, getting paid; and also visiting some less popular but essential destinations such as research, development and self-publicity.

The book is designed to be consulted when you need advice. It was never conceived as a book you will read from cover to cover. (You can if you want. Like Deleuze's rhizome, the parts, while distinct, make a whole.) The handbook was intended to be a reference source to dip into when you need to. If you need to review your plans for putting a folio or CV together, it's there in a form you can reach in and grab.

That said, some of the content of the book is not so easily acquired, and it will require a degree of effort on your part, some thought, *some reading.* The world is complex, and a graphic designer must know the world. An old chum of mine once put it as, 'A graphic designer must be a mini-expert on everything.' This is true of graphic design, and it is even more important for graphic communication. If we don't know the world, all we have is the content of our own head, and that is a terrible position for any designer to be in.

So, there are times when the book will ask, and assume, that you are driving your own studies and practice, because the book cannot do it for you. The book cannot see movies for you or visit clubs; the book cannot travel or read books. These are things you have to do for yourself.

What the book will do is offer you explanations of why doing these things will help you be a better, more imaginative, braver and more exciting designer.

The book is full of facts and it is full of opinions. In writing the book, I have tried to keep the two separate and well marked. If there are disputes about the facts, I'll try and play the debate out for you, but remember: it is always your duty to check and not believe everything that you read.

At the end of your design education, you should be able to do the following things:

1　uncover user and client needs – which may be different from the things they ask for;

2　uncover graphic languages necessary to address these needs – which will be specific to their cultures and their needs;

3　uncover material processes that serve these graphic languages – find the right ways to produce the graphic languages.

The book will offer some pointers that will help you do these things.

Above all, I'd like to thank all the kind people who contributed to the book. You didn't have to, but it would have been dull without you.

NOTE

This book was written using a mix of commercial and OpenSource software as a testament to the maturity of the OpenSource software project:

1　It was written in OpenOffice and LibreOffice. The graphics were made and edited in either the Adobe CS suit or with the OpenSource (and free to use) GIMP, Inkscape and Scribus.

2　It was made on two Macs running OS 10.5 and 10.6, two Ubuntu machines running Ubuntu 9.10 to 10.10 (free to use).

3　Shortage of cash need be no barrier to doing beautiful work.

CHAPTER 1

A step towards the reinvention of graphic design[1]

Gui Bonsiepe

I do not pretend exclusivity of, or paternity over, the proposals presented in this paper; nor do I expect an endorsement of my interpretations of the works consulted.[2]

However, I do claim that the reassessment of graphic design and graphic design education differs from the design conceptions that represent the common-sense understanding of graphic design. I want to draw attention to the fact that I repeatedly had to make use of neologisms and linguistic terms that are generally not related to the discourse of graphic design. This is not the result of pure whim. If we want to reinvent and reconstruct graphic design, we have first of all to create linguistic distinctions capable of grasping a new reality that otherwise would not be understood if we remained bound to standard terminology.

NAME AND JUSTIFICATION OF GRAPHIC DESIGN AS DISCIPLINE

The term 'graphic design' and its corresponding term 'graphic designer' have strong ties with a particular *technology*, i.e. *printing*. Therefore, graphic design runs the risk of not covering new phenomena that result from technological innovations, particularly computers and computerisation. As new concepts arise, such as:

- audiovisual means
- multimedia
- information management

they reveal the limitations of the traditional concept of 'graphic design'. We observe a growth in the domain that has been called *'retinal space'*. This expansion requires a reconsideration of the skills and professional attributions of the graphic designer. This forces us to ponder the convenience of using a new term, recognising the possibility and probability that this is a polemical issue.

It is traditionally understood that the graphic designer is mainly a visualiser, one who organises visual components that are then reproduced with the aid of printing technology. Consequently, among the list of objects of professional action, we find:

- logotypes
- stationery
- book and magazine layout
- advertisements and campaigns
- posters
- packages (labels)
- exhibitions
- displays
- corporate identity systems
- signage systems.

Therefore, I propose to put emphasis on graphic design as information management and link it to the notion of information. Though this concept is far from clear, it would identify the central issue of graphic design today and for the future: information and its organisation. Notions such as:

- information explosion
- information glut
- visual pollution

reveal a set of new issues and problems that the graphic designer should confront.

If there exists a predisposition to consider this possibility, then one can also consider the convenience of using a new name for the specialty: *'information designer'* (or the more compact *'info-designer'*). An info-designer approaches the tasks of efficient communication less from the perspective of visualisation, or 'creation' of images, and more from the perspective of organising information. I propose to shift the role of the graphic designer from translation of information from a non-visual state into a visual state, to the *authorial organisation of information*. This proposal reflects recent changes in technology known under terms such as *hypermedia* and *hypertext*, where the world is seen as a huge data bank, in which the reader is author of the information molecules that he or she collects and establishes connections between. According to this line of speculation, visualisation would be removed from its prima donna position and put into relation to a central question of today: *the organisation of information for effective communication in the most diverse domains, from education to entertainment*.

It is not by chance that the notions of 'education' and 'entertainment' appear together and are put into relation, though generally they are thought of as mutually exclusive. In this way, one would take into account the domain of play (aesthetics) – and 'play' is a more fundamental concept than 'fun', associated with the ephemeral, the superficial and even the frivolous and the individualistic. This reorientation of graphic design also results in liberation of graphic design from its ancillary status in the domain of advertising and promotion. This unlinking does not mean to deny the economic importance of advertising and marketing, but the environmental crisis leads to questions about the ecological viability of a lifestyle and society centred on stimulation of sales and promotion of merchandises (from detergents to political candidates). Particularly in Latin America, with its torn social fabric, the info-designer, through his or her work, might attend to needs less focused on competitive consumption, thus creating a counterweight to a lifestyle that currently only a small segment of society attains.

PROFESSIONAL PROFILE OF THE INFO-DESIGNER

A profile of a profession can be defined with the help of a three-dimensional matrix:

1   concerns that are brought into play by a particular profession and that are addressed under a particular perspective (approach);
2   the objects of professional activity;
3   the competencies (know-how) necessary to act efficiently in a particular domain.

We can use the medical profession as an example. A doctor looks at the human body from the perspective of illness and provides care. Objects of his professional activity include diagnoses, surgical interventions and prescriptions. In order to be capable of producing these objects, he needs knowledge of anatomy, physiology and causes of illness.

The info-designer approaches the domain of communication from the perspective of organising information with the aim of taking possible effective action. With a slight degree of exaggeration, one could say that the final aim of the info-designer is not communication, but effective action. In the same way that a doctor takes care of human illness, the info-designer concentrates his or her attention on what I call 'informational opacity'. The info-designer would be a specialist in articulating information and provides techniques to navigate in a highly complex information universe. Apart from the traditional printed objects, the info-designer would assume responsibility for new groups of communication artefacts that are based on informatics or computers:

- interface design for computer programs;
- design of 'information bodies' (texts in both a metaphorical and broad sense) for formation, instruction and entertainment;
- design of audio-visual means.

To intervene as designer in these new fields that are part of the worldwide process of digitalisation, the info-designer needs the following competencies:

- be capable of selecting and structuring information and building coherent bodies of knowledge;
- be capable of interpreting information and transforming it into objects of the retinal space;
- be capable of understanding in productive terms the interaction between language, graphics, sound and music (in the dimension of time);
- be capable of using computer programs for scripting, illustration, image editing, animation and desktop video, as well as programs for layout and letter design;
- be capable of managing the constitutive elements of the retinal space (colour, texture, size, orientation, contrast, transitions in time, transformation, rhythm, etc.);
- be conversant with the analytical apparatus of visual rhetoric;
- be familiar with theories and techniques required to evaluate the communicational efficiency of design proposals;
- be capable of realising design studies and design research (the cognitive dimension of the design process) and presenting design proposals in a coherent manner;
- manage design projects and companies (taking into account that an info-designer as partner or owner of a design studio is and has to be a manager of a firm).[3]

To this incomplete list, I would add the competencies that are considered standard in the profession and academe:

- open historical formation in the domain of graphics, literature, art, music, science, technology and industry;
- training in the professional aspects, such as contracts, determining fees and professional ethics;
- knowledge of production processes in the domain of info-design and the socio-ecological impact of the work of the info-designer.

CORE CURRICULUM FOR INFO-DESIGN

The list of responsibilities and competencies of the info-designer can be mapped on to a study programme in different ways. The resulting programme would reflect the local conditions and, above all, the interests and experiences of the persons who formulate the programme, i.e. the faculty staff. In opposition to current models of design education, I would emphasise that an up-to-date study programme should include the cognitive domain of the design process. As far as I know, this is not standard practice, though there are certainly attempts in different parts of the world to find a new approach to design education. Perhaps there exists a consensus, particularly in the group of design students, that the central function of a study programme consists in stimulating creativity. Sometimes, designers behave as if they own the monopoly on creativity, an attitude that can be found also in art circles. This attitude seems to me arrogant and obnoxious, and probably has contributed to the counterproductive tendency to set the world of design apart from the rest of the world. Creativity is not a gift of a happy few privileged persons selected by divine providence. Furthermore, it might be more appropriate to talk of competence to innovate. To be competent in innovation implies breaking of routines, and therefore courses devoted to creativity techniques consist basically of a set of recommendations to break routines and taboos. I propose to put the term creativity into the deep freeze for a while.

With regard to the terminology for the various disciplines in a graphic design course, we observe a certain incoherence. For example, what in one programme is called 'visual methodology' is called 'basic design' or 'design fundamentals' in another programme. The content of the design discipline sometimes cannot be deduced from its name. If we use the name of a scientific discipline, for instance, psychology, we don't get a clear idea about its content. For this reason, it might be more appropriate to use more descriptive names to characterise the various course items. To create such a programme, it is necessary to refer to diverse areas of human knowledge and to scientific disciplines that provide the know-how for grounding the work of the info-designer and protect it against the danger of short-sighted pragmatism:

- theories (psychology) of perception;
- theory of language (in particular of speech acts);
- semiotics;
- visual rhetoric;
- cultural history (including art, literature, design, science, technology and industry);
- history of visual communication;
- anthropology of everyday life;
- theories of communication and information;

- philosophy of science;

- applied mathematics (analytical and descriptive apparatus for describing shapes);

- basic concepts of programming and computer science;

- basic concepts of management;

- design theory and criticism, to list but a few.

The description of the precise course content would constitute the future work of the group and provide a point of departure to put graphic-design education on a more grounded and cognitively more demanding base.

NOTES

1   This paper was originally prepared in early 1993 for the Education Project developed in Latin America for ICOGRADA (International Council of Graphic Design Associations). Participants were asked to present their proposals following an outline formulated by the coordinator of the working group, José Korn Bruzzone.

2   Several of the proposals presented in this document have been discussed with colleagues in various regions of Latin America. Other sources that directly or indirectly present new perspectives on graphic design and graphic-design education include: the journal *Visible Language*, particularly the articles of Sharon Helmer Poggenpohl; the publications of the Graphic Design Education Association; the works of Richard Wurman and Ted Nelson; and articles by Victor Margolin.

3   I don't think that it is necessary to revive the old debate regarding aesthetic sensibility. I take it for granted that the concern for aesthetics is intrinsic to design.

CHAPTER 2

Broad knowledge

Clearly, as world citizens, designers are strategically important in terms of the global ecosystem's well-being. Ideally speaking, they should therefore be equipped to discharge this responsibility by being conversant with political, ethical, ecological, technological, economic, and other issues. This is easily said but difficult to achieve.

(John Wood, 'The culture of academic rigour', *Design Cultures* conference, Sheffield University, March–April 1999)

Without knowledge action is useless and knowledge without action is futile.

(Abu Bakr)

In this chapter, we will be looking at why a designer of graphic communications, of any sort, needs to have a broad knowledge of the world and its cultures. An overview on where things fit, how people live and where their cultural, social and political interests lie. We'll look at why this broad knowledge is essential for a designer and not an added extra. Suggestions will be made of ways to gather and make sense of this knowledge.

If we attempt to design without understanding the visual signs and symbols people use to give shape and meaning to their lives, we are like those who drive cars without knowing how they work: sooner or later the fuel runs out, and everything stops.

AN UNCOMFORTABLE TRUTH . . .

We are born into the world innocent, unknowing and empty. As babies, we are born empty of culture, waiting to be filled up with tasty nuggets of cultural experience: obsessions, hobbies, languages, tastes and opinions. Our very sense of what is real, what is possible and what is right is built this way. *Culture* is the thing.

Commonly, when we hear the word culture, we either think of establishment culture – of galleries, of movie premieres, of fat ladies singing opera, of suits – or we think of culture as a synonym of nationality, which is a kind of culture, but not by any means the whole thing.

Others talk of the *multicultural*, which is a little closer to the truth in that it accepts that people have different cultural frameworks. This is a much better way of thinking of culture, but still too conceptually limited. The idea of the multicultural suggests a difference that is clear to see anywhere where a multitude of nationalities live together; you can see this in big cities such as London or New York. Even the most superficially homogeneous cultures, perhaps a small village in Leicestershire or the Punjab, will be host to a multitude of cultures.

Culture is everything that people make, whether they know it or not, whether they intended to make it or not. A graphic work is certainly culture; so is a football chant, a catwalk dress, a hair cut, the way you kiss, the person you kiss, the language you speak to your Mum and the one you speak to your boy- or girlfriend. The plants in our fields and the tiles on our roof are culture.

When you speak to your lecturer, you speak in a different way than you do to your friends. If truth be known, your lecturers speak in a different way to you than they do to their friends – I guarantee it. Each of these small, local 'ways of doing stuff', each 'way of being' is a culture.

You wear a *national culture* that allows you to function in your own country, a *regional culture* and a *local culture* that you wear to mark you out from others in your nation. Beyond that, you will have an identity built on your sex and your ethnicity, which is another culture. You will have a generational identity that is different from that of your parents (and perhaps from that of your brothers and sisters). You will have interests that might reinforce your community identity, but might exist completely outside it: this is yet another culture you are a part of. You are your own multicultural community.

Each of these cultures, deliberately or accidentally, defines itself as a set of codes: what you wear, speak, think, eat, etc., these codes form the basis of communication.

To communicate, scientists and philosophers tell us, designers need to have a model in their head of the people they are intending to talk to. At some level, the designer and the designed for must have access to the same cultural codes. Communication is not, as many older books of graphic design would tell you, a matter of coldly

FIGURE 2.1
Communication is not a matter of forcing our ideas into others' heads. It is an exchange of ideas, a game for two or more

delivering information to others (like a postman who anonymously delivers 'stuff' to you and leaves you to make sense of it); it is about understanding others, so that we can prepare a message using just the right codes to make it seem as natural to them as a greeting from a friend or a hug from a loved one.

To offer a metaphor, older models of communication suggest that the activity should be thought of as the communicator throwing balls (of message stuff) at the viewer until they stick in the viewer's head. The idea is that a graphic communicator will *deliver* a message to the viewer, who has no option to interpret or personalise the meaning. Not only is this explanation incorrect, it seems patronising and more than a little rude.

Current descriptions of communications favour the metaphor of a tennis game, where the communicator and the viewer both volley the message backwards and forwards: communication is commonly described as a *language game* (*Sprachspiel*, in Wittgenstein's original German, if your lecturers ask). The designer needs to be playing the same game as the people he or she is communicating with, or the design will fail. If designers do their job well, it is entirely possible that the user will never consciously consider that they have just been affected by our work. Don't believe me? Consider this:

If we read a novel that is well designed and never consider the act of reading the text, the story just seems to happen in your head. This ability to unthinkingly use books correctly happens because novels are a very specific cultural form, a form that we are familiar with, and they are designed to follow the rules of the form. If I were to make a minor change and reorder the pages to follow the Japanese book form, reading from the back forwards (but still in English), it would now be impossible for the reader unthinkingly to use the novel, because he or she would have to be actively thinking about the act of reading and not the story. In a well-designed piece of graphics, the cultural form hides the communication. A good piece of design becomes invisible, allowing the user to concentrate on the message. In the same way, a piece of video, a fight from the *Bourne* trilogy for example, will have cuts every few frames – cuts that we never notice, because they are arranged so artfully that we are swept up in the action and not seeing the craft.

C@SE STUDY

THE CRYSTAL GOBLET

In 1955, the American typographer and educator Beatrice Warde wrote her book *The crystal goblet: sixteen essays on typography*. In the title essay, 'The crystal goblet, or printing should be invisible', she examined this notion of the designer shouldering the burden by relieving the user of the effort of using the design. The whole essay is printed here because it emphasises many of the points that a good graphic communicator should be considering: a responsibility to make our design serve the user, the duty of a designer to plan, and, while the text gets carried away in places about the fine details of typography, it never loses track of the fact that, without the context provided by the user, the craft means nothing.

Imagine that you have before you a flagon of wine. You may choose your own favourite vintage for this imaginary demonstration, so that it be a deep shimmering crimson in colour. You have two goblets before you. One is of solid gold, wrought in the most exquisite patterns. The other is of crystal-clear glass, thin as a bubble, and as transparent. Pour and drink; and according to your choice of goblet, I shall know whether or not you are a connoisseur of wine. For if you have no feelings about wine one way or the other, you will want the sensation of drinking the stuff out of a vessel that may have cost thousands of pounds; but if you are a member of that vanishing tribe, the amateurs of fine vintages, you will choose the crystal, because everything about it is calculated to reveal rather than hide the beautiful thing which it was meant to contain.

Bear with me in this long-winded and fragrant metaphor; for you will find that almost all the virtues of the perfect wine-glass have a parallel in typography. There is the long, thin stem that obviates fingerprints on the bowl. Why? Because no cloud must come between your eyes and the fiery heart of the liquid. Are not the margins on book pages similarly meant to obviate the necessity of fingering the type-page? Again: the glass is colourless or at the most only faintly tinged in the bowl, because the connoisseur judges wine partly by its colour and is impatient of anything that alters it. There are a thousand mannerisms in typography that are as impudent and arbitrary as putting port in tumblers of red or green glass! When a goblet has a base that looks too small for security, it does not matter how cleverly it is weighted; you feel nervous lest it should tip over. There are ways of setting lines of type which may work well enough, and yet keep the reader subconsciously worried by the fear of 'doubling' lines, reading three words as one, and so forth.

Now the man who first chose glass instead of clay or metal to hold his wine was a 'modernist' in the sense in which I am going to use that term. That is, the first thing he asked of his particular object was not 'How should it look?' but 'What must it do?' and to that extent all good typography is modernist.

Wine is so strange and potent a thing that it has been used in the central ritual of religion in one place and time, and attacked by a virago with a hatchet in another. There is only one thing in the world that is capable of stirring and altering men's minds to the same extent, and that is the coherent expression of thought. That is man's chief miracle, unique to man. There is no 'explanation' whatever of the fact that I can make arbitrary sounds which will lead a total stranger to think my own thought. It is sheer magic that I should be able to hold a one-sided conversation by means of black marks on paper with an unknown person half-way across the world. Talking, broadcasting, writing, and printing are all quite literally forms of thought transference, and it is the ability and eagerness to transfer and receive the contents of the mind that are almost alone responsible for human civilization.

If you agree with this, you will agree with my one main idea, i.e. that the most important thing about printing is that it conveys thought, ideas, images, from one mind to other minds. This statement is what you might call the front door of the science of typography. Within lie hundreds of rooms; but unless you start by assuming that printing is meant to convey specific and coherent ideas, it is very easy to find yourself in the wrong house altogether.

Before asking what this statement leads to, let us see what it does not necessarily lead to. If books are printed in order to be read, we must distinguish readability from what the optician would call legibility. A page set in 14-pt Bold Sans is, according to the laboratory tests, more 'legible' than one set in 11-pt Baskerville. A public speaker is

C@SE STUDY

more 'audible' in that sense when he bellows. But a good speaking voice is one which is inaudible as a voice. It is the transparent goblet again! I need not warn you that if you begin listening to the inflections and speaking rhythms of a voice from a platform, you are falling asleep. When you listen to a song in a language you do not understand, part of your mind actually does fall asleep, leaving your quite separate aesthetic sensibilities to enjoy themselves unimpeded by your reasoning faculties. The fine arts do that; but that is not the purpose of printing. Type well used is invisible as type, just as the perfect talking voice is the unnoticed vehicle for the transmission of words, ideas.

We may say, therefore, that printing may be delightful for many reasons, but that it is important, first and foremost, as a means of doing something. That is why it is mischievous to call any printed piece a work of art, especially fine art: because that would imply that its first purpose was to exist as an expression of beauty for its own sake and for the delectation of the senses. Calligraphy can almost be considered a fine art nowadays, because its primary economic and educational purpose has been taken away; but printing in English will not qualify as an art until the present English language no longer conveys ideas to future generations, and until printing itself hands its usefulness to some yet unimagined successor.

There is no end to the maze of practices in typography, and this idea of printing as a conveyor is, at least in the minds of all the great typographers with whom I have had the privilege of talking, the one clue that can guide you through the maze. Without this essential humility of mind, I have seen ardent designers go more hopelessly wrong, make more ludicrous mistakes out of an excessive enthusiasm, than I could have thought possible. And with this clue, this purposiveness in the back of your mind, it is possible to do the most unheard-of things, and find that they justify you triumphantly. It is not a waste of time to go to the simple fundamentals and reason from them. In the flurry of your individual problems, I think you will not mind spending half an hour on one broad and simple set of ideas involving abstract principles.

I once was talking to a man who designed a very pleasing advertising type which undoubtedly all of you have used. I said something about what artists think about a certain problem, and he replied with a beautiful gesture: 'Ah, madam, we artists do not think —we feel!' That same day I quoted that remark to another designer of my acquaintance, and he, being less poetically inclined, murmured:

C@SE STUDY

'I'm not feeling very well today, I think!' He was right, he did think; he was the thinking sort; and that is why he is not so good a painter, and to my mind ten times better as a typographer and type designer than the man who instinctively avoided anything as coherent as a reason. I always suspect the typographic enthusiast who takes a printed page from a book and frames it to hang on the wall, for I believe that in order to gratify a sensory delight he has mutilated something infinitely more important. I remember that T.M. Cleland, the famous American typographer, once showed me a very beautiful layout for a Cadillac booklet involving decorations in colour. He did not have the actual text to work with in drawing up his specimen pages, so he had set the lines in Latin. This was not only for the reason that you will all think of; if you have seen the old typefoundries' famous Quousque Tandem copy (i.e. that Latin has few descenders and thus gives a remarkably even line). No, he told me that originally he had set up the dullest 'wording' that he could find (I dare say it was from Hansard), and yet he discovered that the man to whom he submitted it would start reading and making comments on the text. I made some remark on the mentality of Boards of Directors, but Mr Cleland said, 'No: you're wrong; if the reader had not been practically forced to read – if he had not seen those words suddenly imbued with glamour and significance – then the layout would have been a failure. Setting it in Italian or Latin is only an easy way of saying "This is not the text as it will appear".'

Let me start my specific conclusions with book typography, because that contains all the fundamentals, and then go on to a few points about advertising.

The book typographer has the job of erecting a window between the reader inside the room and that landscape which is the author's words. He may put up a stained-glass window of marvellous beauty, but a failure as a window; that is, he may use some rich superb type like text gothic that is something to be looked at, not through. Or he may work in what I call transparent or invisible typography. I have a book at home, of which I have no visual recollection whatever as far as its typography goes; when I think of it, all I see is the Three Musketeers and their comrades swaggering up and down the streets of Paris. The third type of window is one in which the glass is broken into relatively small leaded panes; and this corresponds to what is called 'fine printing' today, in that you are at least conscious that there is a window there, and that someone has enjoyed building it. That is not objectionable, because of a very important fact which has to do with the psychology of the subconscious mind. That is that the mental eye

C@SE STUDY

focuses through type and not upon it. The type which, through any arbitrary warping of design or excess of 'colour', gets in the way of the mental picture to be conveyed, is a bad type. Our subconsciousness is always afraid of blunders (which illogical setting, tight spacing and too-wide unleaded lines can trick us into), of boredom, and of officiousness. The running headline that keeps shouting at us, the line that looks like one long word, the capitals jammed together without hair-spaces – these mean subconscious squinting and loss of mental focus.

And if what I have said is true of book printing, even of the most exquisite limited editions, it is fifty times more obvious in advertising, where the one and only justification for the purchase of space is that you are conveying a message – that you are implanting a desire, straight into the mind of the reader. It is tragically easy to throw away half the reader-interest of an advertisement by setting the simple and compelling argument in a face which is uncomfortably alien to the classic reasonableness of the book-face. Get attention as you will by your headline, and make any pretty type pictures you like if you are sure that the copy is useless as a means of selling goods; but if you are happy enough to have really good copy to work with, I beg you to remember that thousands of people pay hard-earned money for the privilege of reading quietly set book-pages, and that only your wildest ingenuity can stop people from reading a really interesting text.

Printing demands a humility of mind, for the lack of which many of the fine arts are even now floundering in self-conscious and maudlin experiments. There is nothing simple or dull in achieving the transparent page. Vulgar ostentation is twice as easy as discipline. When you realise that ugly typography never effaces itself, you will be able to capture beauty as the wise men capture happiness by aiming at something else. The 'stunt typographer' learns the fickleness of rich men who hate to read. Not for them are long breaths held over serif and kern, they will not appreciate your splitting of hair-spaces. Nobody (save the other craftsmen) will appreciate half your skill. But you may spend endless years of happy experiment in devising that crystalline goblet which is worthy to hold the vintage of the human mind.

(London, 1955)

C@SE STUDY

In order to achieve this seemingly natural communication, it is vital to remember that design is not primarily about the satisfaction of the designer but about the needs of those being designed for (we're not fine artists, after all). In design terms, you (the designer) are less important than the user of your design. Sorry about that.

So what do we do about this? How do we move from being a potentially magnificent designer hampered by a narrow view of the world, to being a magnificent designer who does work that people care about.

Over the years, you have become an expert in 'you', 'your locality', 'your local culture'. This is not enough to design well. Without working to acquire a really broad picture of the world, you may find that you lack the knowledge to make designs that connect with people. This is recognised by experts in design thinking and psychology, who talk about two different kinds of knowing. There is information we need for a specific job that is related to specific events (*episodic knowledge*) and there is information we have that gives our world its shape (*general knowledge* or *broad knowledge*).

Let me offer you an example. Do you know the book *Treasure Island*, by Robert Louis Stevenson? If the answer is 'no', then we've just encountered a huge blank area you really need to fill. The book is a very common root of a mass of cultural reference (*Pirates of the Caribbean*, a dozen direct film adaptations – one with The Muppets – and much more), a reference that is unavailable because you don't know the source.

However, assuming you said 'yes', we can go on. The book has a lovely map in it. It shows where the buried treasure is (just like *Pirates of the Caribbean*. See?). It is said that Stevenson invented the whole 'X marks the spot' convention in pirate maps. This map is very much like an uninformed designer's world-view: locally detailed, full of interesting stuff and completely disconnected from the world at large. We know where the treasure is on the island. We just don't know where the island is. In short, the map is completely and utterly useless for finding treasure.

You see, the map so lovingly drawn by Stevenson lacks useful navigational directions. There is no latitude or longitude given for the island. So, although the map (like our uninformed designer) is locally informed, it has no external relationship with anything else, which means we can't get from the local to the global. In story terms, we can never get to Treasure Island, because we don't know where it is. In design terms, a local outlook and lack of broad vision trap a designer on an island of his or her own ignorance.

The treasure map is the equivalent of episodic knowledge. It is the good stuff we need to find the treasure, once we know the location of the island. The knowledge to get to the island is general knowledge. An example might be found in designing for a client in another country. To get to the fine detail that will allow us smoothly to insert the client's product into the users' heads, we first need to know enough about the culture of the country to look in the right places.

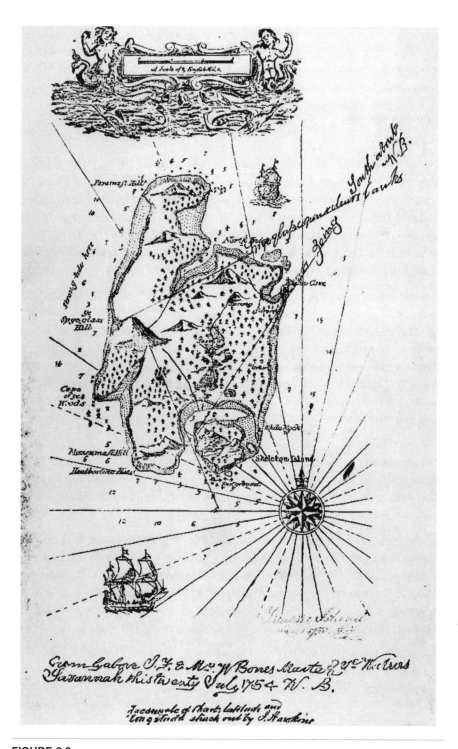

FIGURE 2.2
Treasure Island treasure map

Researchers are largely in agreement that problem-solvers (including designers) cannot generate solutions without having a range of different types of knowledge at their disposal. Having broad knowledge is like having a school atlas. It shows the whole world, but in absolutely no detail. We might be able to use it to show where we're going on holiday, but not to plan a trip. It shows London but not Loughborough (not a bad thing some people would say), shows the Dominican Republic but not my garage.

Most of the time, we have no need of local detail (like my garage), just the broad detail. But, by knowing the broad detail, such as knowing that the Dominican Republic is in the Caribbean, we can find other sources that allow us to zoom in on the specific detail when we have a need. For example, I like Korean food and I know that New York has a compact and vibrant Korean district. Knowing this, I can locate the district. Finding the district makes finding a Korean restaurant simple. Being ignorant of the existence of the district means I don't get dinner.

Consider a design job that requires our design to suggest modern Japanese design influences. If we know that *manga* is a Japanese variant of the comic book, a fusion of traditional *Ukio-e* prints and Western 'funnies' (general knowledge), then we can drill down to the specific forms that mark its internal differences. Knowing the difference between *shōnen* (comics for young girls), *seinen* (comics for young boys) and *seijin* (comics for adults), we can selectively use the correct graphic styles from the correct source materials for appropriate purposes, avoiding an embarrassing, *Japanese style* pastiche. Ignorance of the first nugget of information means we could never get to the good stuff.

Without wanting to labour the point, I'd like to make a plea on behalf of design lecturers everywhere: I'd like to make a plea for a war on ignorance. No matter how good their skills are, no matter how hard they work, ignorant designers are bad designers, and we don't need any more bad designers.

Why is this *broad knowledge* not included in Chapter 5, 'Researching the job'? Both activities are clearly research. The difference is that acquiring broad knowledge should be an everyday activity for a designer. It is not a matter of putting time aside in a project to understand the place of the project in the world; that would be episodic knowledge. It should be a daily activity, on a par with brushing your teeth (you could skip a day or two, but people would start to notice and avoid you).

How do we accumulate 'broad knowledge'? Let's list some of the ways. This is not intended to be a definitive list, but a sample that can act as a guide for your own personal exploration. It is intended to be a provocation.

FIRST-HAND SOURCES

A first-hand source of information is one that we can experience directly.

CLICHÉ - TAKING THE EASY SHOT

Theorists in the realm of emergence talk of a 'fitness landscape', a virtual realm that describes all of the possible solutions in terms of their fitness as answers to a specific problem.

So, if you start from any point on a fitness landscape, there will be low areas that are easy for you to get to (but equally easy for everyone else to get to as well): the low areas represent easy solutions. There will be high areas that are close by (still pretty easy to get to): these represent better solutions that need more effort to get to; and there will be distant peaks that are quite hard to scale: the highest peaks are the killer solutions every designer dreams of finding.

But let's not forget that we are talking about an ideas space. In idea terms, the low areas are seen as pretty ineffective solutions, or solutions that are close to what you started with; the peaks are strong solutions, with the closer peaks being good solutions that refine thoughts you already have; and the farthest, the highest peaks, are ideas having genuine novelty.

This is relevant to designers because it describes the way we work. It describes our responses to the culture around us. If we start from a cultural low point (ignorance), we have to work harder to reach any of the idea peaks. If we only know our own local cultural terrain, we will be unaware of the great ideas over the horizon. We won't even know that a great solution exists.

OK so far?

However, as the fitness landscape is an emergent phenomenon, each change or input from us changes the whole landscape. Design we do today changes the way everybody sees the world tomorrow (remember, 'culture is feedback'). In a way, by scaling that peak, we lower it for everyone else, making it accessible. What was high is now low. Equally, culture that is neglected becomes a very hard peak to climb. So, although today we might (vaguely) know that an Oedipus complex is the male version of an Electra complex, most people are unlikely to know the names of their respective mother and father. What was once such a cultural commonplace that Freud used it as a cultural shorthand (cliché) for mental conditions becomes an obscure fact in a general-knowledge quiz.

Our training places us at a very specific place on the fitness landscape of culture. Globally, designers have common ways of looking at things:

e.g., a magazine will tend to have a grid, text and images. Working back from this place to a position from which we can access the rest of the landscape is not easy; it requires work.

Would it be unfair to suggest that, on a fitness landscape, the low-level, easy-to-access stuff is cliché? This is the material on the cultural landscape that everybody sees, that everybody knows, the song on every lip, our local cultural environment. This applies equally to the materials and techniques we use to materialise our work.

When we operate as designers, we venture on to a landscape that represents the total sum of all cultural forms in the world. I suspect that many of us are quite lazy in our explorations; we take day-trips to the closest, nearest peaks. In design terms, we are often flabby day-trippers in plastic macs, when we should be hard-bodied, free climbers of the imagination.

Talking to people

Try and mix with people who do not share your background. Ask them questions about their experience of the world. You do not have to accept what they say. You do not have to pass judgement on the honesty or value of their responses; just knowing the things that people care about is helpful. Learn to listen and remember. If you are designing for a club of UFO watchers, you do not need to believe in UFOs to do the work, but you do need to understand the beliefs of those you are designing for. This is an *unstructured qualitative* research approach.

A more structured approach could be to apply an ethnographic or phenomenological method (see Chapter 5). Here, we would spend time among people and see how they live. This is probably overkill for getting a general feel of the world, but would certainly be useful if you went to work overseas.

The designer provides a focus (an object, a subject, etc.) for the conversation and asks the users to talk about their experience of it. Do this often enough and you start to build a quick and dirty map of people's attitudes to the world they live in. The important point is to get into the habit of asking for, and responding to, the beliefs of others. We do not have to buy into these belief systems, but we need to understand that the people that we design for *will*.

Travel (abroad or at home)

Not necessarily gap-year beach holidays to Thailand, but travel in general. There is nothing quite as effective at making you understand how narrow your own attitudes are than travelling to a place where the people are different. Cross the US border into Canada and look at the packaging: it has French on it. Take a ferry to the Netherlands and see what they eat at breakfast (strangely familiar), or fly to Japan and sample a traditional Japanese breakfast (strangely disturbing). Did you know that some people put mushy peas on their chips? Learning that others are different *denaturalises*[1] our own understanding of the world, making us look twice and question our assumptions.

Go for a walk and travel at home

Difference isn't automatically a case of nationality. The world is rich in distinct communities, locally and overseas. Discover them. See what people care about. If you normally drive, take a bus; if you take buses, walk. Be part of the world.

Start collecting

Pick up interesting stuff wherever you find it. If you can't grab it, photograph it. For example, I have some nice sweets from the Asian-Pacific Rim, and included among them is a sweet packet shaped like an old-fashioned box of matches. The box carries the print of a boy on it. To get a sweet, you have to slide the inner tray out. In doing so, you activate a tab that causes the boy to moon at you. This tells me something about humour in Japan.

Follow your obsessions, and, if you don't have one, get one

How will you create interesting designs if you have no interests? Every good designer I have ever met has personal interests (Johnny Hardstaff has about a million obsessions, many quite odd).

SECOND-HAND SOURCES

A second-hand source is one that has been passed to us by someone else.

Access at least two contrasting news outlets every day

Know what is happening on your planet – news outlets are not without prejudice. They have strong points of view; they represent strong vested interests. Because of this, you need to get a parallax view[2] of the same events. So, reading a left-wing newspaper and a right-wing website reveals these prejudices. Get into the habit of asking why the news that is chosen to be reported on has been chosen. Ask why certain news outlets maintain certain points of view. Ask why newsreaders wear suits, and sports journalists wear suits, except for the female presenters on Sky. Be curious.

- Wikinews (http://en.wikinews.org/wiki/Main_Page) is an interesting project and manages to be both global in scope and local in focus by being a user-created wiki. It is, of course, free to use.

- Newsvine (www.newsvine.com/) is also worth adding to your RSS feed. It tends to be more US-centred than Wikinews, but is still a valuable news source and free as well.

- The BBC maintains the largest online news reporting presence in the world at http://news.bbc.co.uk/. CNN has a presence at www.cnn.com/, and, for a contrasting, but still English-language, view of our planet, you can do a lot worse than look at Aljazeera, the independent Arab news agency at http://english.aljazeera.net/.

- Your own country's national newspapers will tend to have websites that are free (for the moment) to access. In the United Kingdom, we have the *Guardian* (www.guardian.co.uk/), the *Independent* (www.independent.co.uk/) or the *Telegraph* (www.telegraph.co.uk/). News International has started to charge for access, so that *The Times*, excellent newspaper that it is, is no longer free to read online (www.timesonline.co.uk/tol/news/).

- The United States has the *New York Times* (www.nytimes.com/), the *Wall Street Journal* (http://online.wsj.com/) and *USA Today* (www.usatoday.com).

Join a film library or cinema club

Discover the world through the eyes of great artists and designers. Online film libraries commonly carry tens of thousands of titles: go crazy and see something that will never be found playing at your local multiplex. It no longer matters where you come from, be it the middle of the country or an inner-city estate: if you get a postal delivery you can see the finest (and maddest) films ever made. You will often find that your tutors may have an online list of 'must see' movies. If not, just nag them to tell you the names of a choice few gems.

Join a public library – read a book

Books, especially novels, represent a direct route into someone else's head. They inform us how people think. You can be a Japanese samurai or French factory worker through the power of a book. Books are a powerful way to experience the grandeur and madness of the world and its people. (Thanks to Mike Davidson, an excellent graphics educator, for pointing this out to me. He's a very smart man.)

Get books online, for free

There are online resources of copyright-free books that you can save and read at your leisure. My favourite is Project Gutenberg (www.gutenberg.org/), which carries 30,000 free texts, including many world classics, from Richard Burton's

MY FILM LIST

This is the film list my students get sent. It is very personal and intended to be provocative:

2001: A Space Odyssey (1968)

A Clockwork Orange (1971)

A Night at The Opera (1935)

Akira (1988)

Alice (Svankmajer) (1988)

Amélie (2001)

Annie Hall (1977)

Anything by Laurel and Hardy

Apocalypse Now (1979)

Batman – The Dark Knight (2008)

Barry Lyndon (1975)

Battleship Potemkin (1925)

Black Narcissus (1947)

Blade Runner (1982)

Brazil (1985) or anything by Terry Gilliam

Breakfast at Tiffany's (1961)

Bullitt (1968)

Casablanca (1942)

Chinatown (1974)

Cinema Paradiso (1988)

Citizen Kane (1941)

Come and See (1985)

Donnie Darko (2001)

Dr. Strangelove (1964)

Easy Rider (1969)

Fanny and Alexander – Part 1 (1982)

Fantasia (1940)

Farewell My Concubine (1993)

Fargo (1996) or anything by the Coens (except The Lady Killers)

Fight Club (1999)

Fitzcarraldo (Herzog)

Funny Face (1957)

Get Carter! (1971)

Inception (2010)

It's a Wonderful Life (1946)

Jean de Florette/Manon des Sources (both 1986)

Kung Fu Hustle (2004)

Léon (1994)

The Man With a Movie Camera (1929)

Metropolis (1927)

North by Northwest (1959)

Nosferatu (1922)

Pinocchio (1940)

Prospero's Books (1991)

Rebel Without a Cause (1955)

Rosemary's Baby (1968)

Scanners (1981)

Seven Samurai (1954)

Singing in the Rain (1952)

Sleeper (1973)

Solaris (1972)

Some Like it Hot (1959)

South Park: Bigger, Longer and Uncut (1999)

Soylent Green (1973)

Spirited Away (2001)

Taxi Driver (1976)

Tetsuo (1989)

The Big Sleep (1946)

The Godfather (Parts 1 & 2 only) (1972 & 1974)

The Good, the Bad, and the Ugly (1966)

The Hairdresser's Husband (1990)

The Royal Tenenbaums (2001)

The Seventh Seal (1957)

The Singing Detective (1986)

The Thing (1982)

The Usual Suspects (1995)

The Wild Bunch (1969)

THX1138 (1971)

Time Bandits (1981)

Touch of Evil (1958)

Un Chien Andalou (1929)

Unbreakable (2000)

Wings of Desire (1987)

The Book of the Thousand and One Nights to the horror works of H.P. Lovecraft. They even format books to be read on your phone.

Listen to talk radio

Find a station that you wouldn't normally listen to, something rich in talk, and leave it playing while you work. Radio programmes are vast stores of opinion about things people care about. Radio programmes are (relatively) cheap, in that they can be made with a smaller financial outlay than a TV programme. Nowadays, Internet radio programmes focus on all sorts of minute and personal obsessions.

THEORY

> Expertise in design is understood as *the possession of a body of knowledge and the creative and analytical ability to extract, analyse and apply that knowledge.* . . . design is categorised as an 'adaptive expertise', within the framework of the 'non-routine activity' of designing as designers adjust to the design task by utilising their knowledge which they adapt to the current tasks.
>
> (Popovic, 2004; author's emphasis)

To understand a design problem, we must first understand the nature of the people we design for; we must understand their culture. Beyond reasons of politeness, why is this true?

The design theorist Richard Buchanan talks of the design problem being 'a *quasi-subject matter*, tenuously existing within the problems and issues of specific circumstances', by which he means that the design problem, as a subject, is defined by the demands of specific times and spaces. What is a design problem for one client is a non-issue for another. The people involved in a situation make both the problem and the solution, and both the problem and solution are entirely local to the stakeholders in a particular design problem. Buchanan says: 'For example, a client's brief does not present a definition of the subject matter of a particular design application. It presents a problem and a set of issues to be considered in resolving that problem.' This way of thinking about the relationship between design problems and user culture was named *wicked problems*.[3]

Buchanan writes:

> Design problems are 'indeterminate' and 'wicked' because design has no special subject matter of its own apart from what a designer conceives it to be. The subject matter of design is potentially universal in scope, because design thinking may be applied to any area of human experience.
>
> (Buchanan, 1992)

This talk of 'special subject matter' may appear to be one of those intellectually clever, but pointless, turns of phrase that make academics happy, but it is, in fact, making a very important point. If we think about music rather than design, the special subject matter of music is the music itself: the harmonies, the rhythm, the melodies. Music is the plan, the performance, the reproduction and the reception. If we think about design, what do we have? The production processes? Not really: processes come and go – they have different values in different times and places. Design has no special subject matter of its own, because design is planning and then making. Design can incorporate music (and film, print, cake, dance or any other form of culture that works), which is both the joy of design and the problem.

Wicked problems were defined by their author, Horst Rittel, as follows:

1 Wicked problems have no definitive formulation, but every formulation of a wicked problem corresponds to the formulation of a solution

Rittel means that, in order to express the problem, the project stakeholders (client, user and designer) will have already moved a long way towards working out the solution, or at least towards the sort of approach that might yield a solution. They will have set the boundaries inside which success or failure will be defined. For example, in designing the London Underground (Tube) map, Harry Beck had moved a long way towards the final design solution by realising that an underground map does not have to show a clear relationship to features of the surface geography.

2 Wicked problems have no stopping rules.

In mathematics, it is said that some problems have *stopping rules*. The problem 2 x 2 = ? has an end. In the final step, we get an answer, and the problem is done. This is not true of all problems. Design rules are not like this; we get to a point where we change things (improve sales, lower rates of heart disease, mobilise public interest), but we very rarely end the problem. Designs change the social world for the people who use our designs; we don't stop the wider world producing problems.

For example, when Jock Kinneir and Margret Calvert designed the spine of British transport signage, they made the very best job of providing a clear and consistent graphic language for road users that they could. Of course, this wasn't the end of the process, however, as road conditions change meaning, so that additions, changes and amendments are still happening today.

3 Solutions to wicked problems cannot be true or false, only good or bad

The solution will not be universally true or false; our solution will not be received the same way by everybody, but it will be a working solution, one that is either invalid for the people we are working with (bad) or useful for them (good). This will be the measure by which we can assess the value of our solutions. Once again, having a broad overview of the world will make designing an effective graphic piece possible.

4 In solving wicked problems, there is no exhaustive list of admissible operations

This one is very important for us as graphic communicators. Graphic communicators start a job with all options on the table for consideration. They have no material or process limits. They paint, they video, they dance and they sing (but only if singing and dancing are the right solution). Graphic communicators don't charge into a job knowing how the job will end before they have started, nor do they mark any process as being off-limits without a good reason. The form of the job should stem naturally from the demands of the job.

5 For every wicked problem, there is always more than one possible explanation, with explanations depending on the *Weltanschauung* of the designer (a German term, meaning 'view of the world')

Absolutely. Never believe that, because your carefully planned solution is 'X', that a solution 'Y' is inherently wrong. Our preconceptions about the job (which come from our world-view) define the *conceptual horizon* for the job.[4] As we can't see beyond the horizon, any alternative solutions that might work quite well are hidden from us. This is why we need a wide world-view: the more we experience, the wider our pool of responses, and the wider our pool of responses, the broader our conceptual horizon.

Any designer could create a witty design piece about your home town, possibly a reasonable design response about your nearest big city. I'm guessing that designing a piece about Timbuktu would be a job over the conceptual horizon (with apologies to readers from Mali).

6 Every wicked problem is a symptom of another, 'higher-level', problem

This is inherently a difficult position for designers to understand. Our design problems (and solutions) don't exist in isolation from the rest of the world. The problems we are brought in to solve exist as problems before the client realises they need our help in finding a solution. If we need to design a bilingual document, the design problem (two languages, different quantities of text generated by different line lengths from different word lengths) comes from a higher-level problem (people in different countries speak different languages).

7 No formulation and solution of a wicked problem have a definitive test

There is a class of mathematical (and biological and social) problem called *halting state problems*, in which you can't know if the problem will reach a solution after a defined number of steps without actually running the problem. Life has been defined as a halting state problem: we don't know how it will work out until we live it. Wicked problems in design fall into this category, as we can never know if the solution works

CONCEPTUAL HORIZON

Weltanschauungen (world-views) are real. People from inside one *weltanschauung* will literally not be able to see someone else's point of view. I call this limit to a person's world-view the *conceptual horizon*.

Black holes are surrounded by an area of warped space–time called an event horizon. This is the point beyond which nothing, including light, can escape. Any events that happen beyond the event horizon are by definition unknowable; there is no way that they can have any effects back in the universe, and so, effectively, it is as if they had never happened.

In the same way, we all carry around personal event horizons in the mind, a set of assumptions about the world that blind us to anything happening beyond our assumptions. It is as if they had never happened.

Now, I'm not saying this in an elitist spirit. Everyone has what I call a conceptual horizon: a place where their mind cannot go, cannot imagine, cannot conceive of anyone else going, that place where, when we hear of others going to it, we say: 'I don't know what they were thinking of', 'I don't know how anyone could have done that', 'It's beyond human comprehension'. In fact, what we're doing is admitting that we have reached the edge of our conceptual horizon.

In Figure 2.3, we have Anna and Bob. Both have working views of their worlds, but both have views that do not connect in any way with the other. More than this, neither can see beyond the conceptual horizon to each other, or the area unknown to both of them. It is as if the other, together with the world in between, simply does not exist. In terms of communication, it is as if Habermas's normative consensus is absent. Anna and Bob cannot even have an argument: they lack the common framework needed to have one.

What can we do about this?

Simply speaking, we talk to each other. In talking to each other, we don't have to accept the other's views; we just need to know what the other believes and accept the existence of this belief. Extending our general knowledge of the world feeds our horizons. By acting this way, we extend our own conceptual horizon in much the same way that black holes expand: through a slow absorption of the universe around us.

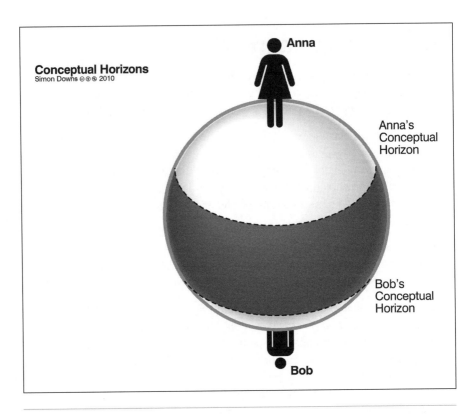

Conceptual Horizons
Simon Downs ⊜①⑨ 2010

Anna

Anna's
Conceptual
Horizon

Bob's
Conceptual
Horizon

Bob

FIGURE 2.3
The conceptual horizon

until we try it. There are no simple short cuts, there are no specified design approaches that will always work, no rules that, if obeyed, will grant design wishes.

8   Solving a wicked problem is a 'one-shot' operation, with no room for trial and error

Even when you have achieved a solution that you and the other stakeholders believe works, you cannot be sure that the same solution will work if you try it again for a different client or user. More than this, by succeeding in your job, the job becomes part of the world and, in doing so, changes the world. If it fails, it closes that design approach for you in the future. Either way, your 'one shot' has changed the rules of the game.

9   Every wicked problem is unique

The circumstances that define a wicked problem are a unique set of possible problems, every single time. This means that each design problem should be approached afresh, every time. Superficial similarities should be not be taken as short cuts; take the time and design properly, because the problem will never actually be the same.

10 The wicked problem-solver has no right to be wrong – they are fully responsible for their actions

Ah, the sting in the tail! There are no excuses in solving wicked problems, no 'I didn't know that was going to happen that way'. You are responsible for the effects your design has on the world. This is not a moral judgement, merely a statement of fact. The advertising designer who promotes a car as a fast-driving speed machine is responsible if people who like to drive fast buy the car and live out their fantasies by driving fast.

For us, this all means that engagement with the world is the only way forward. Wicked problems are (if we remember) wicked because each is unique and defined by the social origins of the problem. This means that, in conducting the briefing process, we *must* fully include the stakeholders in the briefing process: they are part of both the problem and the solution. We are just outsiders looking in.

In this, we share much with ethnographers, those social scientists who study people and culture through their artefacts and the rituals they build around their use. As designers, we use a broad, general knowledge of the world to gain access to the episodic knowledge we need for the job.

I once heard the design theorist Malcolm Barnard say, 'If graphic design is about anything, it is about culture.' Victor Margolin agrees, noting that:

> The concept of a culture of design, . . . reinforces the point that design is an activity which is defined to some degree by the social milieu in which it operates. Therefore we cannot conceive of any theory of design that is independent of a theory of society.
>
> (Margolin, 1989, p. 7)

Graphics is not, at its core, a craft subject. Where we were once shaped by printing presses, we now have access to the tools of any of the other art and design disciplines. Unlike sculptors, we are not defined by bronze, plaster and stone. Unlike textile designers, our work is not defined by thread and yarn, warp and weft. Jewellers work in precious metals and stones. Photographers work with light. Graphic communicators work with culture and the artefacts created by culture.

A traditional graphic designer (with his or her emphasis on skilful application of craft) might well take all of this discussion of theory as some sort of elitist attempt by academics to kidnap the subject, but I would like to make a counter-argument based on some very real-world design facts. According to the British Design Innovation (BDI) survey for 2008, the design industry in the United Kingdom earned £3.4 billion of income in that year. Almost a quarter of this income (£0.8 billion) was from overseas income. If you are a designer happy to limit your working range to your home culture,

EXAMPLE

So, while hair is not in itself culture (it is part of our biological make-up),
what we do with our hair most definitely *is*. Take a look at the collection
of hair culture in Figure 2.4. Each is distinct enough to tell its own story.
This is not an accident, but is instead a clue to a hidden meaning that is
intended to be communicated through these styling choices. Each
combination of choice and hair is an *artefact*, a thing that is made, not
natural (it didn't grow that way), not innocent (without *intent*, without an
underlying reason). When we make things, we have a reason to do so
(not necessarily a world-shaking reason such as curing cancer or saving
the planet, but simple, personal reasons such as 'it looks good', 'it
matches my eyes' – a reason nonetheless).

So, unlike hair, which is a natural object, the hairstyle, as an artefact, has
a reason behind it. As designers of communication, we need to know
this reason. Why? Because the person beneath this hairstyle has thought
the style important enough to spend time and resources to create it.
What is important to them must be important to us, if we want to
communicate with them. Understanding this style choice (and the others
that go with it) gives us a wonderful way into a person's world of private
meanings. In classic *semiotics*, this artefact would be said to be a
signifier, an object that carries a meaning. The artefact (our hair style)
would be said to be in two parts: *the sign* – the actual object or symbol
– and *the signified* – the meaning carried by the styled hair. In our
example, the signified can usefully be thought of as the combination of
the hair as an artefact and the meaning carried by the artefact.

FIGURE 2.4
Hair culture

the one you know intimately and grew up in, you have just lost a quarter of your income. A designer from one region, nationality or ethnicity who disregards the differences in others will find users' inner worlds a closed book. A male designer who refuses to learn from women, or a female designer who has no interest in finding out what men care about, cannot communicate with half the world. Whole sections of the design industry will be closed off from them. No designer can afford to work from the limited contents of their own head. Design without an external context does not work. Designers working this way will not only be poor designers, they will also be poor.

The digital theorist Lev Manovich says that, 'we live in remix culture';[5] this is doubly true for graphic designers. The culture of others is our medium, the stuff we work with. In order to 'remix', we need to be aware that there are media out there to work with and understand that these media carry meaning for those we design for (possibly the folk who pay us, but absolutely those who will be using our design; they are often different people). If we fail to listen to the user, and insist on designing from our limited stock of pre-existing knowledge, no matter how great our practice and digital skills are, our work will seem false and shoddy to the people it was designed for.

The German social philosopher Jürgen Habermas has written on the subject of communication, and his writings have informed this chapter. Habermas notes that, 'As soon as we start communicating, we implicitly declare our desire to reach an understanding with one another about something. If consensus – even about a difference of opinion – can no longer be reasonably expected, communication breaks down.' So, in order to communicate (at all, in any way), there needs to be a consensus.

Habermas goes on to lay out a series of four conditions that will allow communication to happen (Habermas says, 'run smoothly') and to be read as honest:

1   Communication happens if both the shared, matter-of-fact, meaning of the communication and the communication's underlying implied meaning are clear to both parties. For instance, if someone in a club leans on the bar and asks another club goer whether 'they come here often?', they are probably not asking for precise details about the other's club attendance but might well be trying to chat them up (however badly). If this shared understanding is not there, at least one of the clubbers is in for a disappointing and confusing time. A good piece of graphic design uses elements with meanings that can be agreed on by the intended user. The first time I saw the US traffic sign 'Bike Xing', I was deeply confused. I was simply not the intended audience – I did not share a common visual culture.

FIGURE 2.5
Bike Xing

FIGURE 2.6
Stripes as signs: double yellow lines; double red lines; Adidas stripes; an admiral's rank stripes

In Figure 2.6, we have a number of uses of parallel stripes as graphic devices. If any of the messages they communicate is not clear to you, then Habermas would say you are not sharing a meaning with the designer (Habermas, 2007).

2   Communication happens if both parties recognise that there is truth in the communication (Habermas says 'recognise the truth of the proposition stated within the speech act'). Habermas is not saying that the communication is always true (lies can be communication too), but that the communication contains elements that both parties can agree truly mean the same thing. For example, a travel company called Blue Skies is not promising blue skies with every holiday. No customer would expect that to be true, but users would share a common understanding that the name related to a 'common truth' that people want good weather on holiday. If we named our travel company Green Skies or Pink Skies, people would expect a different kind of experience. One might suit a specialist travel agent for the gay community, the other an eco-tour firm. Guess which is which?

FIGURE 2.7
Overlapping meaning in signs: Fed Ex: promising speed through the arrow; East-German crossing signal showing urban man; toilet sign, supposedly stripped of cultural meaning; a green traffic light – a universal sign?

3   Communication happens if both parties accept that the communication fits the normal range of meaning that such a communication would be expected to fulfil (Habermas says, 'acknowledge the normative rightness of the norm that the given speech act may be regarded as fulfilling'). For instance, the range of symbols used to represent airports or railway stations is wide, but tend to use representations of planes or trains in some way or another (see Figure 2.8). This concept is so common that its operation is almost

FIGURE 2.8
Planes and trains

invisible, except when artists and designers deliberately play against it to make a point. No one ever notices a clothes peg, unless, like Claes Oldenburg, you make it one hundred times the normal size, build it out of steel and place it in downtown Philidelphia. The thing that makes Oldenburg's *Clothespin* noteworthy is the lack of 'normative rightness'.

FIGURE 2.9
Claes Oldenburg's *Clothespin*

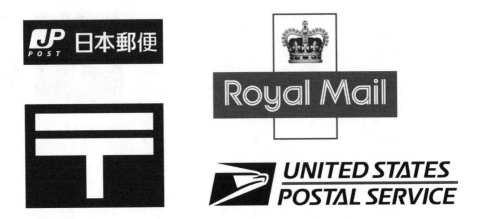

FIGURE 2.10
Postal logos: JP Post; UK Royal Mail; U.S. Postal Service

This is not to say that designers must always work within existing conventions; designers often have reasons for working outside existing cultural meaning, creating designs that might be interesting or fun but don't work by fitting within an existing range of meaning. For example, the logo of the UK postal service has, as far as I can tell, no connection, historic or cultural, with the delivery of post. However, it still functions tolerably well as an identifier of the postal service, because the citizenry of the United Kingdom has, through past experience, learned to interpret the sign as belonging to the company. In other words, the designer has shifted the burden of decoding, of knowing what the design means, from him- or herself to the user: forcing the user to put in the work of making meaning.

Unfortunately, if the user comes fresh to a design, without the chance to build familiarity with it and lacking a cultural point of reference, he or she has no chance to identify or understand the design. I once needed to post a card in Japan and I had to go online and look up the logo for JP Post (the Japanese Post office); it turned out it was the large building across the street from my hotel – I'm not from Japan, and the logo was not part of my culture, and so I didn't stand a chance. By contrast, the U.S. Postal Service has, through television and film, become part of my culture, and so I recognise it when I see it. This is what Habermas means by 'acknowledging the normative rightness'.

4   'Do not cast doubt on the sincerity of the subjects involved' (Habermas, 2001, p. 448). This last point is so clear, it is quoted as written. A visual communication with a design that is not read as honest by users will be ignored. So often, communications intending to change behaviour are read as false, because the combination of the visual language being used and the person using it is utterly implausible. Leong Chen of the University of

New South Wales, a design researcher into HIV/AIDS campaigns, has found that campaigns designed by the gay community are much better at affecting attitudes to sexual behaviour than those designed by governments. The gay community read the campaigns designed by those in the know (who understood the appropriate imagery) as being sincere and worth paying attention to.

Having a broad view of the world allows us to see the shape of the world for our client. It allows us to see ways into a job that we would otherwise miss.

NOTES

1   Jacque Derrida's term for understanding that in culture nothing is natural, everything means something.
2   A term from astronomy that describes how two different views of an object allow you accurately to measure its position.
3   By Horst Rittle, in 1973.
4   The *conceptual horizon* is my term for the limit of things we can conceive of. Our experience of the world determines our ability think of new solutions. In the same way that we cannot know what is beyond the horizon because it is hidden from us, we cannot imagine that which we don't know.
    A person who has experienced the colour black and seen a swan can conceive of a black swan, even if they have never seen one. A person who has never experienced 'black' cannot conceive of a black swan. If I were to talk of a *2 terahertz xchotle* ('2 terahertz' being a 'colour' of infrared light, and the 'xchotle' being something I invented for the sheer fun of it), you have a named concept that exists beyond the conceptual horizon. We simply don't have a picture in our heads.
5   Lev Manovich, *Generation Flash*, Manovich@ucsd.edu www.manovich.net/DOCS/generation_flash.doc.

CHAPTER 3

Getting your first job and pitching

This book is intended to follow the path of a typical graphic design job. So, in the previous chapter, we looked at the sort of knowledge an informed world citizen and designer needs to have at his or her fingertips in order to be fit to practise. In this chapter, we are going to look at the most important part of the whole graphic-communication job cycle: getting a job.

Let's first think about what you mean by 'a job'. You will have to make choices that will define the sort of companies and organisations you will work with and for,[1] choices that will define how you approach a company and how you prepare yourself.

The traditional designer's working life was a simple and direct thing and would have made a very short and sharp chapter that would have read as follows:

1 Leave art school.
2 Get a job.
3 Retire.
4 Die.

There were optional extras, such as 'get married', 'have kids', 'lose your mind' and 'wander the world like Kane',[2] but the generalities were fairly similar. This is no longer the case.

Digital technologies and economic change have acted (for good and bad) like a forest fire. The whole stately and ordered design ecosystem of the predigital era was burnt to the ground and has regrown into a lush but disordered mess. This mess allows for rich pickings and tasty surprises, but, like any jungle, it does not suit the casual tourist, only the prepared adventurer.

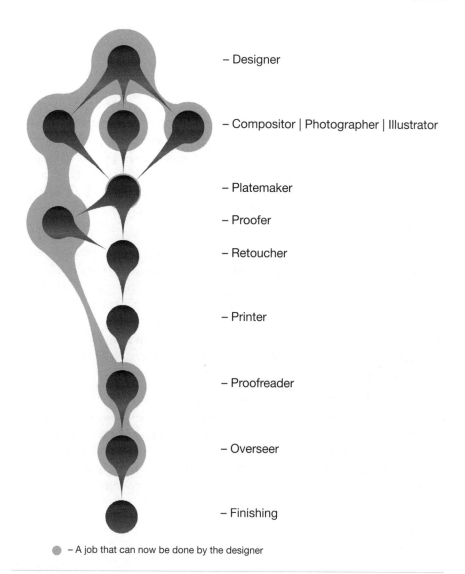

- Designer

- Compositor | Photographer | Illustrator

- Platemaker

- Proofer

- Retoucher

- Printer

- Proofreader

- Overseer

- Finishing

- A job that can now be done by the designer

FIGURE 3.1
The predigital print chain. Matthew Fray of Loughborough University.

Figure 3.1 shows the distinct jobs that made up a typical printshop before digitisation. The brown area shows the jobs that can now be done on a computer by the designer. Some jobs are heavily embedded in the designer's world (broad margins); some are marginally possible (narrow margins), but the total number of people working on the job has dropped from ten to four or five.

The Mac, as a tool, allows a small group of designers to move a staggering mass of design tasks around in a way that previously required some serious manpower. Simple functions such as design templates in DTP programs such as Adobe InDesign or QuarkXPress remove whole layers of traditional working practice and the jobs that serviced these practices. Gone forever in a puff of smoke was the tiresome task of cut and paste, and the layout artist who did it; as well as the compositor, and the proofer, and the proofreader, and many other variations. In some ways, this absence is a good thing: these could be tedious and dull jobs for the graphic professionals doing them. Nevertheless, it was still someone's job: a job that is now gone for good. As a young designer, in the early 1990s, I once saw a predigital designer crying, as the new technology destroyed their practice and stole away their job.

In contrast to the state of affairs in the design industry before the Mac, design companies today tend to be massive and diverse (such as Wolf Olins or R/GA), small and nimble (such as Airside or Neighbour) or sole operators (such as Johnny Hardstaff). The digital revolution has made it possible for the small to band together on a job-by-job basis and compete with the big, while the mid-sized companies have all of the costs of the massive (offices in world capitals, lots of staff that cost you money whether you are earning or not), but without the savings that both the massive and the small enjoy.

You can see from Figure 3.2 that the proportions of large and small companies remain moderately stable year on year. The very largest companies are steadily employing a little over 9 per cent of the designers (average 9.17 per cent), while the companies employing ten or fewer people are over seven and a half times as common (at an average of 70.33 per cent). It is unlikely that a designer will have the luxury of working in one company for the whole of his or her career. The designer of the future works in networks.

We can see that the old model of graphics, if not dead, is changing. You may be lucky and get a job for life, but I doubt it. A designer in any of the fields of visual communication – photography, graphics or illustration – will have to have an entrepreneurial attitude towards work and not leave it to chance.

So how do you find a job? Are you even sure that you want a 'job'? Perhaps you want to be a freelance (very exciting, very scary), or part of a design cooperative (exciting and fun with the right friends; not as scary as going it alone). These career opportunities are not mutually exclusive. You can work for a company during the day; you might freelance in the evenings on personal work; you might even work up a client base so big that you need to bring in partners to cope. Each of these ways of working asks you to prepare your case for employment in different ways. The folio for a prospective employer is not the same as that for a specific client. Study the market, know the people you are pitching to and take it seriously, because, no matter how fresh out of college you are, luck can smile on you, and you can find yourself doing the job.[3]

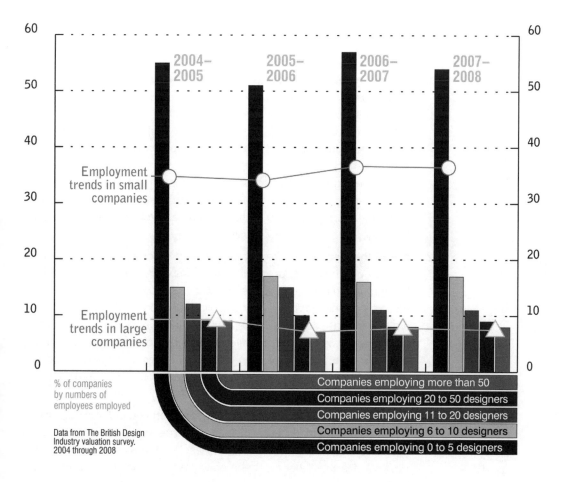

FIGURE 3.2
The BDI's Industry Valuation Survey

The first thing to remember is that you're not alone: there are organisations out there that exist to help put together your creativity with an industry hungry for bold new ideas, and I'm not talking about agents and employment bureaux (though they perform a valuable service). On your behalf, I went and talked to some of the people who can help you out.

This book has been written in Britain, but there will be organisations in your own country that will do the same job.

In the United Kingdom, there are a pair of organisations that are strongly involved in bridging the gap between student designers and the industry. They are not the only groups that do this, but, in my experience, they are the most professional and the most helpful. They are D&AD (Designers and Art Directors) and the

YCN (Young Creatives Network). The main message is that finding employment should be treated like any other graphic design job. You need to:

1   **Research your audience**. In this case, the audience is the company you want to work for. What are the company's values? Not just their product but the ethos and identity of the company. What they stand for and what they will not stand for. When approaching each potential employer or client, you should adapt your portfolio, your approach, your dress and even your grooming to be a fit for the organisation. Research tends to show that people running interviews start with the assumption that they want to employ you and then, through the interview process, discover reasons why they don't want to work with you. A little up-front research will give you the ability to dodge the pitfalls in an interview.

2   **Know the people**. You're not dealing with a company in the interview. I know point 1 was about knowing 'the company'. The company will be a background presence, but the company is also people. So do some research on the company's people. Who founded it? Who runs it? What are their outside interests? Be prepared and tailor your work to those people doing the interviewing. It is absolutely no use turning up at a general graphics agency with a portfolio of image-based work for multimedia, if the guy conducting the interview is an expert on typography for packaging. Know the people and make yourself personally relevant to them.

3   **Aim at companies that do work that you wish you did**. It is very difficult to fake enthusiasm in design. The job requires us to put in so much of ourselves that, if you don't love (or at least like) the work you are asked to do, your design will not fly. So be brave and approach companies whose work excites you.

4   **Tailor your initial contact method to the results of your research**. Speak to the potential organisation through a graphic language they will appreciate. I trained and worked as an illustrator/graphic image-maker. I also did interactive media work, some animation, was a design consultant for a well-known merchant bank, did some editorial and club flyers and, on one occasion, I even designed a trophy for an awards ceremony. Each of these roles required that I pitched in a different way. Each pitch required a different means of contact (letter, email, phone, etc.), a different way of showing my work (folio, show reel, electronic folio, web-based folio, etc.), and even different ways of dressing. (Pitching in the headquarters of a merchant bank is totally different from pitching to the music industry. Get the dress code wrong and you are just not going to be taken seriously.) Know your audience and treat their opinions with respect. If this sounds like you are selling out, then I would suggest that you consider the kind of work you are aiming to do. If you are offended by working with merchant bankers, then don't.

FINDING A JOB

For the book, I spoke to Rhiannon James, the Senior Manager for Education & Professional Development at D&AD. Rhiannon showed typical kindness and clarity in answering my questions about getting a job. Her answers meshed surprisingly closely with my own experience in industry.

I started by asking Rhiannon for her opinions on preparing yourself for the task of finding a job: things to do before you send mail and start phoning. She recommended that you 'know your audience. Without a doubt you must be ready to conduct research every time'. She stressed how important it was to, 'express and communicate an interest in the company. Know the work that they do and be prepared to talk about it.' It is simply bad manners to do anything else.

We moved on to the matter of how you even know the right places to look for a potential job. Rhiannon recommended research into:

- **Schemes and placements** (both things that D&AD can help with). You are not alone. You represent a valuable resource for a design company. They need to find you. This means that many companies will have formal schemes, or be partnered with organisations such as D&AD or the YCN. Do some research; know your schemes.

- **Read the trade press**. Not only does the trade press carry job adverts, but it is full of industry news. So, if your favourite design company has picked up a four-year contract with a major broadcaster to provide design services, the odds are good that they might well be hiring. Knowing your industry turns news from an interesting diversion into a guide for employment.

- **Follow design blogs**. This is exactly the same deal as reading the trade press, except the information will be faster, newer and more current. And you can write back to ask questions.

- **Be aware**. This is so vital to the task of finding a job that Rhiannon repeated it several times, but it's a really important repetition. You are a designer: you have to be able to walk the walk, *and* talk the talk. It is pointless being a design genius if you have no idea what industry does, who does it, or what the industry's social role is. If a potential employer starts to ask you questions about the industrial sector they're in, you need to be able to talk to them: it's your job.

Interestingly, Rhiannon noted that, 'illustrators are different; they need to get noticed'. While completely accepting Rhainnon's point about illustrators, I'd point out that many graphics people will be entering parts of the industry where they need to be noticed. Graphic designers of motion or web-based work will need to exercise creative thinking. Do competitions, do free work for high-profile causes, be like the ladies and gentlemen at ShellsuitZombies and stage events.

C@SE STUDY

PORTFOLIOS

Before I graduated, back in the days of paper and card, we were given a lecture on portfolios. In those days, portfolios were the only logical method of showing people your work. Some people (those with money to burn) loved the idea of cards as well, the principle being that you would send people your work printed on postcards, they would like what they saw and give you a job; it never worked for me.

In this portfolio talk, we were told about the colour of card we should use, the size of the portfolio we should carry and the number of sheets in the portfolio. The answers were apparently:

- colour = black, mid-grey or white
- size = A4 or A3
- number of sheets = ten sheets, twenty sides.

Looking back, I can see the wisdom of the advice, but it was never put in a context that explained why the advice worked. This meant that, when computer-aided graphic communication came along, a whole generation of designers had to rethink, relearn and invent new ways of getting work.

The context of the black/grey/white, A4/3, ten/twenty rule was this: coloured artwork looks better against a monochrome background. Perceptual effects mean that the colour of the background affects the perceived colour of the image it surounds. So, a white, grey or black background will allow the work to be visually read properly.

The size of the portfolio was a simple piece of ergonomics. Art directors'/senior designers' (i.e. the people evaluating your work) desks could accommodate an open A4 or A3 folio, where an open A2 or bigger folio is effectively a hang-glider and tends to start destroying a studio. Smaller than A4, and the work becomes cramped.

The limit of ten sheets, twenty sides is a piece of psychology. Twenty sides hold enough work to demonstrate ability and are short enough not to bore the pants off the designer doing the viewing and long enough to create a narrative about the designer's sensibility, ambition and world-view.

Looking back, I can see that this advice worked, because, like all good graphic communication, the answers we need to do the job right are provided by knowing the user. The choice of mounting materials and number of sheets is about client psychology; the scale of work is about social factors (office size).

Although the actual rules are less relevant than they were, the things they tell us about the relationship between junior designers and potential employers are very useful.

The most direct connection is between background colours. This works equally well on web and screen as it does on paper. A designer who frames his or her video with a pink frame runs the risk of distracting the viewer from the movie, and will certainly introduce a perception of a greenish cast on the movie.

We can move on by thinking about the size of a show reel or screen-based samples. In the matter of show reels, look at the 'standards' for video, and think about the media you will be working from. A full 1080p video will *not* stream a DVD properly (it will stutter and jerk, if you are lucky); 720 may well stream off the web, if you have access to a streaming server and a fast web connection. A 640 x 480 pixel movie should play well across most connections, but it's kind of cramped as a way of showing off your masterpiece. A 320 x 240 pixel movie is sufficient for most mobile phones, but forget any kind of detail. The choice is yours to make, based on what you know of your potential employer. If you are showing video to a client, a good-quality USB 2.0 flash drive should be able to show your video without problems.[4] That said, however, perhaps it might make more sense to send them a link to your Vimeo site, so that they can see your work before you even get there. Once again, we are looking at the designer having to understand the user: in this case, the potential employer. The technology is fun, but people being able to appreciate it is vital.

In the same way, the graphic language used in presenting your design should be sympathetic and attractive to the particular audience. There are no set rules, except make it easy for your prospective client to like your work.

I would suggest that the rule about twenty sides of work still makes a lot of sense, but perhaps we could redefine it for a digitally literate audience. It would typically take less than five minutes to view twenty pieces of work. This makes good social sense when pitching your work. People in the design industry are always busy. This isn't an affectation; a design company that's not busy won't need to see you in the first place, because it won't need any extra help. A busy designer will be able to spare five minutes to see your work; ten minutes is asking a lot; asking for someone to spend half an hour in the working day to love your work is just silly. So, you need to break your work down into packets that can be easily absorbed in short sittings. This is doubly true of the web, where all sorts of figures about attention span are bandied about (one minute or less is the common figure, though I cannot find the origin of the figure). Whatever the truth, it is clear that, if you design a site that requires a busy designer to go down through six layers of pages and takes five minutes to access, the site will actively discourage them from contacting you to give you work. Keep it brief and to the point.

Make your work easy to access, clearly labelled to help viewers understand what they are expected to do, and clearly signposted to help them find their way around. This is not only true of screen-based media, it is true of any presentation you will make to a potential employer. If you are presenting print design, it is still a very good idea to make the context clear. If you have some excellent visuals, put them in context. A logo is nice; a logo together with it in use on the side of a van, on a website, on stationery or on a poster is better. Help yourself by helping the viewer to see what you need them to see.

Don't ever put anything into a presentation (on screen or in the world) that distracts the viewer from loving your work. Don't use tricky media if they serve no good purpose.

Last, use a medium that people can access.[5] My advice would be a FAT 32 flash memory stick (which is pretty much every memory stick you can buy in a supermarket). Such devices will work on Mac, PC and Linux computers. Apple iPods, iPhones and SmartPhones could potentially carry your work, but I wouldn't rely on them, as they use proprietary software that might not be present on the host machine. On your flash drive stick have a Mac and a PC copy of your presentation (if you only have one, you can guarantee that it will be the wrong one). Then, test your presentation on both operating systems. Even if you use something 'cross-platform' such as HTML, PDF or MPEG 4 for presenting your work, there will be differences in playback. Be safe and check. Take more than one version of the job in different formats: do not assume that the audience will have your chosen form of technology. Then, having done all that, slip an emergency DVD-ROM version of your work into your bag. Even if everything goes wrong, you can leave the DVD with them.

INTERVIEWS AND PITCHES

This will be brief. Make sure that you have everything you need for the interview before you leave home. Dress appropriately (once again, research your client and make a guess based on their corporate culture). Limit your conversation at interview to answering the questions asked and go deeper in unpacking the answer if asked. Let the interviewer or client you are pitching to lead the discussion.

When you are pitching, your pitch should be a single strand of narrative, a strand that is designed to respond to the client need, showing how your solution is the most logical way of achieving the desired end. Don't get distracted; keep to the narrative strand. Once again, make the pitch brief and clear; if the client wants to know more, you can go deeper.

Make sure that you have material to leave with the client at the end of the pitch. You must be able to leave a business card (or equivalent): this is your lifeline to the client. Once again, base your card design on the principle of making it easy for the user to read your details and contact you. Have some samples that you can leave, or some other way for the client to review your work. This can be as simple as some prints, a DVD perhaps, or as complex as setting up a password-protected online folder (with a platform such as Apple's MobileMe, DropBox or YouSendIt).

Note: If you do leave a digital sample, do make sure that the sample is a low-resolution sample, preferably in Adobe's Acrobat format, as you can allow viewing but deny the ability to copy, edit or print. This may seem a little paranoid, but your work is your intellectual property, it is your livelihood. It must be protected.

Try to find out when you will hear from the client: set a definite time and date if possible. If you don't hear by the appointed time, send a polite email asking for a decision and also setting a time a couple of days in the future, when you will phone if you don't hear from them. If you still hear nothing, you can assume that the pitch has not been a success. Be gracious about it: it happens to the best of us, and there is always next time.

To review:

- It is all about the clients and the users.
- All design decisions, from media to your haircut, should be designed to make a single coherent narrative about the job you want to do.
- Make it as easy for the client to love your work as you can. Don't include any distractions: no bells or whistles that will stop the client seeing your quality.

WORK PLACEMENTS (SOME WORDS OF ADVICE)

Work placements are an invaluable opportunity. Every young graphic student should try and get at least one. So let's look at the current state of play in work placements.[6]

A work placement is an opportunity for a company to see what talent is out there and to gain a benefit from working with this talent. The young designer gets the benefit of real experience in a real industrial context. The company normally does this so that it can fill a position with a known quantity, a student or young designer that they can trust. These work placements might run for up to three months.

The usual arrangement is that the student or recently graduated designer does low-level work, perhaps sitting in on a client meeting or two, and generally gets some experience of the design field. The employers get some labour – not free labour, not slave labour – but some labour exchanged for experience. Employers will sometimes cover expenses for such things as accommodation or travel; wages are unlikely. It is important to note that no young designer should ever be asked to give their labour for more than three months: if a company likes you enough to use your work for more than that time, they should pay; if they don't like what you do, why would they keep you around? If you are ever unsure and need advice, contact your graphics association or the relevant trades union for your industry.

Finally, there are formal, structured placement opportunities (placement years or placement semesters) that are governed by legal agreements with the educational institution. These agreements will ensure that the student gets a fair educational experience from the placement: such agreements are tightly controlled and will be monitored by your educational institution. They will place a burden of care on the employer; the work produced will also be subject to review by the institution. Any design student on a placement year will have to demonstrate that he or she has used the opportunity to its fullest.

Without wanting to worry you, some people will take the attitude that work placements fall outside employment law. This is not true: you have full employment rights. Anyone working for someone else deserves rest, a safe working environment and to be treated appropriately. If you encounter a bad situation during a placement, you need to:

- **Tell your current or previous educational institution**. Even if you've left education, the institution needs to know about the company, so that it can advise other students against work placements there.
- **Get legal advice**. Consider alerting the authorities, the local industry trade association or the relevant trades union. If you have suffered a problem, it is likely that others have too.
- **Keep a record of the problem** – times, dates and events.
- **Leave**.

Remember that very few design placements ever cause problems, and most offer a genuine benefit to the young designers involved.

NOTES

1   The old idea that a graphic communicator's natural home is within a money-making *company* is not necessarily true; there is much work to be done in campaigning social activism, community service or in a mixed environment with commercial practice. Just look at the work of Bruce Mau.
2   This is a genuine quote from a friend of mine, made before he left his job and started walking east across Europe.
3   My first big freelance job came from a contact in a bigger design firm needing me to join in to make up numbers in a pitch to a huge, international company. The clients clearly liked what they saw, because they went with me. I'd only just gone freelance.
4   A good quality memory stick/flash drive should have a transfer speed of about 27 megabits per second, which is much lower than needed to transfer digital video. Do an experiment and try to play some 1080p video off a flash drive.
5   One of the saddest things I've ever seen was at a job interview, where the guy who went before me had brought his show reel in one format (Quicktime, if I remember correctly) on one medium. The interview team (he told me when he left) had neither a drive that would support his media nor Quicktime on their PC. In my satchel, I had a CD-ROM that had my show reel as Flash (Windows and Mac), Quicktime, AVI and a self-running Windows and Mac

application. I had also brought a thing called a Zip drive (an old USB-drive technology) and a Macbook. The moral of the story is simple: don't place the burden of supplying the right technology on the interview panel or clients you are pitching to; take responsibility and take work in a way they can access.

6   Work placements also offer some serious potential for abuse, not only in graphic design but in any area of employment where many people are desperate to get into a small number of jobs. For example, the fashion industry has a very patchy record when considering job placements. Some companies are excellent employers, but some have business models that depend on a continual supply of young designers, who will work for months at a time, doing long days, in poor conditions, just so they can put a fashion house on their CV. Although this is not the common state of affairs in graphic design, some disturbing tales have come to me from other sectors of the graphic-communication arena.

CHAPTER 4

Knowing your client
Fixing the brief

Ask stupid questions.

(Bruce Mau, *Incomplete manifesto for growth*)

Bruce Mau's quote is such a wise piece of advice for designers, I am tempted to leave the rest of the chapter blank. In design, it is extremely counter-productive to assume that either you or the client has any of the answers to hand. Forming a design brief is a learning process for both parties.[1] The worst experience I ever had as a designer came at the hands of a client who, with the best possible intentions, had no idea of what they wanted me to do for them: through being utterly clueless, these charming folk, who I had worked with before, made my life a living hell for the duration of the job.

It would be untrue to say that I was blameless. I made mistakes: I made the mistake of not understanding that my client had no idea what was going on and, most of all, of not understanding that they lacked an aim (they didn't know what they wanted to happen if my job turned out 100 per cent successful). I didn't understand that clients are, as W.A. Dwiggins (the inventor of the term *graphic artist*) once put it, 'know-everything-yet-know-nothings' (Dwiggins, 1941). The client knows the issues, concerns and no-go areas in his or her own world with a lover's intimate detail, but knows nothing of the issues in ours, and it is up to us to bridge this gap. The brief is that bridge.

The problem job was to create a visual identity for a conference. I had the name of the conference and a verbal briefing consisting of 'You are an artist. Do what you feel', and that was that. Over several weeks, I struggled to uncover anything more

FIGURE 4.1
Bridging the gap

meaningful: I never did. In truth, there was nothing more to know; the clients simply *didn't know* what they wanted. I suspect they thought that graphics and design were a magic wand that conjures meaning from mist (what, in 1941, Dwiggins called 'art-varnish': the quality of expecting design magic to be painted on to a stale biscuit to make it a cream cake).

At that stage, I should have sat down with them and talked the job out, but they were in another country, and it was in the days before Skype, so instead . . .

. . . I completed nine versions of the job to the point that they could have gone to press. I'm not sure that the client was ever really happy. In the end, we both simply grew too tired to work on it any longer.

This chapter is intended to save your lives by making sure that this never happens to you. This chapter is about understanding the difference between what the client thinks they want and what they actually need. It is about pinning down the problem for the client and, in doing so, helping the client to form a clear brief.

Later in the chapter, we will look at some of the theory around the problem of 'problems': how you define them, and how you agree with your clients that there is an issue there at all, which is an important point, as it is entirely possible that a client may believe (because of their experience) that the problem looks like *this* (because the clients know their product), when in reality it looks like *that* (because the way the product is actually used is different from the way the clients believe it's used).

'Know-everything-yet-know-nothings', remember?

ADVICE

The kind of research talked about in the previous chapters, combined with that discussed in the next chapter, can be applied to investigate clients; to understand their *world-view*; to understand the problems in their world; to understand their strengths; to understand their joys and fears; to understand their prejudices and those things they will not even talk about. This may sound a little daunting (and perhaps just a bit like stalking, but in a good way), until you realise that:

1   Whatever the qualities of the job we produce at the end, good or bad, if the client isn't happy, we don't get paid. You must clarify with the client what exactly they want to happen at the end of the job, what the *victory conditions* are. We can't guarantee that the client will love the work we design; we can't guarantee the job will actually work. We *can* guarantee that we have addressed the problem.

2   The client is likely to be an expert on the area you are designing into. They will carry huge quantities of *explicit knowledge*.[2] But there may well be issues that they simply will not talk about: issues that may need to be addressed for a successful resolution to be reached. Don't forget that clients are people too, and, like all people, they will have their own conceptual horizon: there will be parts of the world that they are simply blind to. This can be frustrating, but these absences of knowledge are almost as informative as the explicit knowledge. If you discover something about the user's relationship to the client's business that the client was unaware of, you have just given your work a real shot in the arm.

3   The client is important, but we should remember that he or she is part of a larger system, including users and general culture, fashion and trends, production technologies and material reception, which we are designing for. As part of the system, they will carry *implicit knowledge*[3] that you need to have to do the job. They will not know that they have this knowledge, but it is essential for us to draw it out.

Take a simple example of a design brief to create soup packaging. If we take the project at face value, and don't question the client further, we can say 'soup packaging = tin cans' and leave it at that.

If we make some very basic enquiries, we might find that the soup is intended for the Indian market. Fine, we now know that we might have to leave space in our design for at least two official languages (Hindi and English) and perhaps up to eight recognised languages. That makes things a bit trickier to design for, but we can still do it.

We sit down and talk to the client for a bit and we find out that, although their current business is selling soup to the domestic market, they're looking to make future sales to the Indian military. Now fully informed, we can make some design decisions that move us away from labels on tins and move us towards high-tech Mylar pouches of soup, with dual-use labels that serve both civilian taste and military requirements.

However, until we observe soldiers and civilians actually cooking in the real world, see their lives and observe the unspoken (implicit) ways in which they actually prepare food, we can't really design for them. If we take the time, we face a more interesting challenge and help our clients make those dreams of military contracts a reality.

TO DESIGN, WE NEED TO KNOW . . .

Let's start with some definitions of knowing. First, knowledge is not the same as belief. Philosophy tells us that knowledge has three components, sometimes called *justified true belief*. I find it helps to understand these three concepts if we take the three terms in reverse order.

3   **Belief**: philosophers tell us that we can't know something we don't actually believe in; e.g., if I don't even believe the walls of my house are made of chocolate, it is impossible for me to *know* that my house is made of chocolate.

2   **Truth**: philosophers tell us that we can't know something that is untrue; e.g., if I say that I believe you, the reader, are made of marshmallow, a thing that cannot be true even if I believe it to be, then it cannot be knowledge.

1   **Justification**: finally, philosophers tell us that we need an element of justification for our true beliefs to be held as knowledge. In this context, we're not talking about typographic justification, but about proof. For example, if I believe that you like to eat marshmallows dipped in chocolate, which might well be true, as I can see an empty pack of chocolate marshmallows in your hand and have the added justification of seeing smears of chocolate around your mouth, then I might be said to have knowledge of your taste in sweets. The sweet packet and chocolate smears justify my beliefs as knowledge.

To complicate the issue, in social, cultural and graphic communication terms, this *knowledge* will be quite local. What is held to be true in San Diego will not necessarily be held to be true in Shanghai or Southend. Local beliefs will frame the bits of the world we hold truths about, and those truths will be about local cultural conventions, so that the justifications of those truths will only be applicable inside local cultures.[4]

Don't make the mistake that, because these local truths are local, they will still be regarded as TRUE. If you design something that is true for you but defies a local truth for the users, they will not be happy, they will not love the design, they will not see it as a solution; they may not even understand what it is.

This has been explicitly acknowledged in industrial design, where they talk about *user-centred design*. For graphic communication, this user-centredness means understanding how the *user* knows his or her world. This, in turn, means understanding the person who actually makes use of our design, not the person commissioning it. For example, the London Underground map was commissioned by London Transport, but used by passengers: pleasing the commissioning agency is important for getting paid; serving the user is vital for making the job work. User-centred design makes the user's knowledge the central resource for design.

'User-centred design is a design methodology that utilizes users as a designing resource to increase understanding of the user' (McDonagh-Philp and Lebbon, 1993).

For example, many good draughtsmen believe that complex variable lines, lines that are worked over in a dynamic way, will indicate both movement and closeness to the viewer (generally held to be true). There are informed rationales about the brain interpreting high levels of detail as closeness, and this would appear to be true in certain cultures – ours, for example. I could not honestly claim that this was true everywhere, but, as I'm not designing for everywhere, just one group or culture at a time, I don't care. All we need to know as designers is that this specific use of line is good enough for here and now.

Going further, there is *explicit knowledge*, which is knowledge we know we know. For example, we explicitly learn to drive a car. We learn which order we use the controls in for which effects, when to do this and when to do that. This is explicit knowledge, things we know that we know. This is what briefings from clients will be made up of. Things they *know* to be *true* in their *local* context.

Over time, explicit knowledge is applied in a wider context, one formed of experience and trials of your explicit knowledge played out against the real world; repetition of this kind of knowledge in the world changes it. So, in our car analogy, we explicitly know that applying the brake in wet conditions slows the car less than in the dry. Until we've tried it a couple of hundred times, however, under different road conditions, we don't make the connection between the patterns of weather and braking that makes us good drivers. Through this process of application and testing of explicit knowledge, it becomes implicit: something we know without knowing. Although we have the knowledge in our head as facts, we no longer have to consider it as a distinct and separate set of facts every time we use it – we just use it. For example, we move from walking to running without consciously considering the act or the surface we are moving on. Watch a child learn to walk: they consider every step, and still they fall. Yet, by adulthood, we adjust our movements for concrete, mud, sand or ice without considering every step. The knowledge is there, but we apply it without even knowing that we possess it.

FIGURE 4.2
Beardsley's *Pierrot and Columbine*

GETTING TRICKY WITH A LINE

In this example of an endpaper by the Victorian illustrator Aubrey
Beardsley (Figure 4.2), we can see the effect of different line weights and
detail being played with by a master.

See how Beardsley sketches in the background hills with low-level detail
but with a line of consistent width. The detail gets richer and the lines
less consistent in weight, the closer to the viewer they are. Where
confusion could arise, in the telegraph pole for example, extra detail is
added to make it pop out.

To make this work, Beardsley must have possessed a good working
knowledge of the viewers' culture and of their perceptual frameworks.
As simple and charming as this image looks, it is a deeply sophisticated
piece of work by a designer who knew the people for whom he
worked.

For the people who own it, implicit knowledge often carries the flavour of 'everybody knows that!'. By its nature, we're not conscious of sitting down and learning implicit knowledge; it seems magically to arrive, without help. This is particularly true in cultural matters (see Derrida, below). The very daily facts of life that are so obvious and everyday to our clients that they would not think of mentioning them are often the key to making our designs seem real and honest in practice. We absolutely have to get this kind of information if we can. This applies equally to knowing the user.

However, user knowledge is not the same as client knowledge. This is one of the dark secrets of design that no one likes to talk about. Clients, whether corporate, charitable, government, political or anti-governmental, enable our work. Even if we are working pro bono (Latin: 'for the good', a contraction from pro bono publico: 'for the public good', meaning free or charitable work), the client will be paying for materials and production, and so our natural urge is to design for the person with the wallet. The client, however, may well know the world in ways that the user doesn't. Think about it for a moment. A government agency asking a designer to design a leaflet for the long-term unemployed is, by definition, not itself unemployed. How accurate is its information likely to be? The experience and world-view of its members of staff will be massively different: their graphic languages will be different.

Hence, the dirty secret: much of design is design for the client, not design for the user, because the user isn't sitting in the room during briefings, doesn't have our phone numbers and isn't paying us. Therefore, it's up to you as a designer to formulate your own response. The last time I designed for the user not the client, the art director (who I'd worked with for years) noted that the users loved the design, but I was never to go 'off reservation' again. My advice is always to talk to both groups. If you can improve on the client's ideas by listening to the user, do it.

What can we actually do about this knowledge gap? Well, the answer is simple to say and harder to do. You talk to people in ways that allow you to discover something useful about their worlds. Here are some suggestions.

1 We go to them; they don't come to us

If your client visits you, their reactions and the answers they give will not be the answers they will give in their world. Don't believe me? Ask yourself if you speak in the same way to your friends as you do to your grandparents. Humans change their behaviours for the society in which they find themselves. If we go to them, that forces us to do the changing; it forces us to have an empathetic relationship with the client.

This is part of what cyberneticians[5] call *second-order cybernetics*. In the early 1970s, the cybernetics world realised that observers are not, as had been assumed, outside the thing they are observing. By setting up a situation where we can observe something – a community, a company, it doesn't matter – we alter the thing we observe. We become part of the system we intended to observe. The more artificial we make this observation, the more we change the thing we observe. We cannot avoid some degree of interference, but, by following some simple principles, we can minimise it and get some good-quality information.

So, you visit the client, dressed and acting in a way that doesn't draw attention to your status as an outsider (people are less open around outsiders). Try and meet your clients in an environment of their choosing, where they feel comfortable (as much as you can, without putting yourself at risk). Ask open questions.[6] Listen a lot. Speak a little. Ask what the important items or symbols are for the group. Ask them open questions about these symbols. Don't interrupt. Record what you can at the time. Discuss what you've found out with a friend when you get home (as a form of debriefing).

We want the client to feel comfortable. Comfortable people open up to you.

2   Ask the client to explain, as clearly as they can

- **What they want you to do for them**. A client may have unrealistic expectations about your ability to change the world for them. I can't think of a design solution that would make the oil industry or banking look good at the moment. If the client wants the impossible, help them adjust their expectations to something that can be achieved. It may be that the assignment is not even a graphics job at all: perhaps it is a PR job, or product design. In that case, you can either decline the job, or offer to work with the other professionals as a team to tackle the problem.

- **What they will do for you in return**. Some clients want the world for a penny. It is always better to find this out early. Designers are enthusiasts who will often work for peanuts. Many clients will exploit this. Don't let it happen to you. If you are worth using, you are worth paying for.[7]

- **What they would like the results to be at the end of the job**. This is key. Many clients go into a meeting with both a plan and the results of the plan fixed in their head. This may well be the right way forward, but then again it may just be a plan in their head. You need to help them separate out their preconceptions from what they want the job to do. If you can get a clean fix on the client intentions you know where you stand.

- **What their expectations are about the form of the job** (i.e. is it a TV commercial or a website?). Many clients have a specific medium in mind when they come to you (in fact, because of the nature of the business, it is a dead certainty that they will). Be clear on what you are being asked to make.

- **What resources they will be putting into the job**. Now, the resource bit is tricky, because it links up with, but is not exclusively about, fees. We'll address the fees issue further on in the book, but the issue of resources is not really a fees issue at all (you may be working for a design company, be on a wage and have no direct hand in negotiating the money side of the job). In practice, we're talking about the resources the company is going to put at your disposal to get the job done:

- Are they doing research for you?
- Are they going to assign a company contact to whom you can direct questions?
- Are they sending an employee to accompany you, for example out to chauffeur you around to company sites? (This was done for me twice; it was nice.)
- Will someone be made available to introduce you to the company's customers, clients or workers on the ground? This is important: I sparked a wild-cat strike in Cambridge once, because no one had thought to tell the works' trades unions I was coming, and they thought I was a company spy watching them.
- Will the company give samples, access to stock or contacts with their partner companies?
- Will the company help you out with material resources or special equipment? I've had clients buy specialist software for me to do specific jobs.

It is worth clearly addressing these issues at the beginning, because you are very unlikely to be dealing with someone who writes design briefs for a living, and, once the job is running, it is often too late to go back and check.

3   Ask the client to record as much of this draught specification on paper as they can

This serves two purposes. The first is that it will form part of the working agreement between you. Through their explaining what they need you to do, both parties can consider their obligations to the other. Second, the act of putting thoughts down on paper forces the writer to clarify his or her intentions, and, in doing so, may highlight problems in the future.

Respond by offering sketches to the client to confirm your understanding. The process of recoding his or her written ideas as images (with your additions, changes and improvements) is a great way of checking that you share an understanding.

Beyond these 'must-ask', explicit-knowledge questions, there will be all sorts of nuggets of implicit knowledge that the company doesn't know it knows, which can be uncovered with the right questions.

4   Engage the client in conversation designed to draw him or her out

By all means, go into your briefing sessions with some prepared questions, but make them the sorts of question that allow the client to wander, to reminisce and to elaborate. So, if you ask, 'Tell me when the company was founded?', the answer

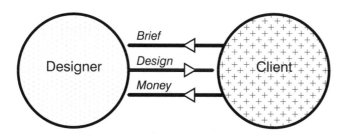

FIGURE 4.3A
The old relationship between designer and client

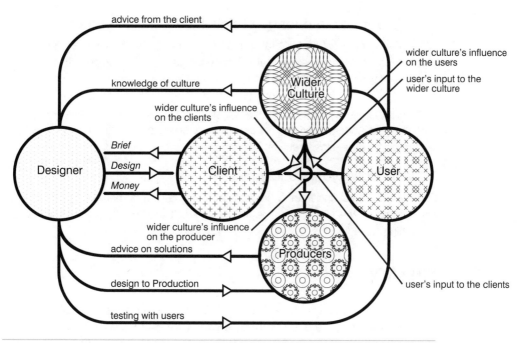

FIGURE 4.3B
The new relationship between client and designer

is a fact. The question offers little room to expand. If you ask, 'Tell me how the company has changed from its foundation to now?', this will allow the client to talk and talk and talk and, in doing so, to feed you all sorts of interesting information about the history, composition and society of the company.

As an aid to the client's and user's narratives, ask them to bring in objects that they feel are associated with the problem. These objects can be pretty much anything, as long as the user strongly identifies with the object, because we will use the object as a prompt to get them to talk. A designer working on building-site safety signage might ask site workers to bring in objects that they associate with site safety and talk about them. By comparing the stories told, we might well stumble upon some common strands that tell us how the workers think about safety.

Tip: If you can talk to the admin staff, do. Admin staff are the glue of the company, almost literally. They connect the boss of bosses with the shop-floor workers. If you ask them nicely, they will tell you the right people to talk to and the right questions to ask.

5 If anything comes up in your questioning that you are not sure of, ask the client

Don't pretend to know stuff you don't. Be honest; check your details; make sure that both you and the clients share a common understanding of the job.

6 Ask to speak to a range of stakeholders in the project

Weiden + Kennedy (W+K) tell a tale about working with Honda. They talk about visiting, not just the executives, but also their engineers. In discussion with the engineers, they found out that Honda had designed a series of very economical engines. They did this with the express intention of changing the hateful practice of wasteful engines into a virtuous practice of lean engines. This was the origin of W+K's 'Hate something, change something' TV campaign. Getting in there and asking questions lead to excellent design practice.

7 Write down your conclusions

Once you feel you understand enough of the issues, write them down, show your conclusions to the client, and see if they agree. If they don't, you've just learned something new.

THEORY

If we are honest, there is probably no such thing as a single, best-possible solution to creating a brief. There are probably a million different ways of formulating each and every problem we will engage with, each with the ability to affect the way we do our job. So, in reality, the role of the brief is not to define the single, best, world-beating formulation of the problem. Rather, it should be understood as being 'the best we're going to get here and now' and 'a formulation of the problem that we can all agree on', the last point being the most important. We are, in fact, reducing the huge number of possible design responses to achieve a single working plan (what the social theorist Nicholas Luhman calls *complexity reduction*, but more of this later).

If a client comes to a designer, it is a tacit admission that:

1 they know that there is a problem that their current resources cannot deal with;

2 they believe that you might be able to bring resources into play that are different enough to deal with the problem.

(That said, they may not be comfortable with this admission (which is why it is tacit), and so we should always be gracious.) They might be wrong: there may be no solution; in fact, there might not even be a problem. This is why we write a brief: to discover what we can, in fact, do.

There are several agreed elements to problems:

Structuredness

How well defined and organised is the definition of the problem? A classic 'well-structured' problem would be a maths problem such as: $2 + 2 = ?$. Everything you need to solve the problem is given to you in the problem, including the method by which you will be getting your answer (the '+' sign). All you have to do is apply a previously learned formula, and the answer slots right in (and no, I'm not going to give you the answer). Finally, structured problems 'have knowable, comprehensible solutions where the relationship between decision choices and all problem states is known or probabilistic (Wood, 1983)' (from Jonasson). In other words, you can see what the bits do and see how they work.

By contrast, we deal with complex and fuzzy problems: 'how can I sell this car?'; 'how can I encourage teenagers to engage in safe sex?'; 'how can I make this text legible to pensioners?'. These problems have some common characteristics (after Jonasson, Rittel and Coyne):

- **They have elements that are unknown, or not known with confidence (all).**

  If the client knew the exact make-up of the design solution, why would he/she need you? However, a review by the parties involved in a job can bring these unknown or uncertain elements to light.

- **They are often what are known as *wicked problems* because they have 'no definitive formulation, but every formulation of a wicked problem corresponds to the formulation of a solution' (Rittel).**

  As discussed in the previous chapters, models of previous successful approaches can serve as a kind of map for continued success, but cannot be relied on to act as a formula for continued success.

- **They 'possess multiple solutions, solution paths, or no solutions at all' (Jonasson).**

  The last part of the previous sentence should scare you: there are some design problems that have *no design solution*. We're going to lose, no matter what we do. Watch out for these jobs and avoid them if you can. A good briefing process can alert you to this sort of job cropping up. If you get through the briefing process and still are not sure what is being asked of you, withdrawing gracefully might be a good idea. (However, if you are incredibly self-confident, you might tempt fate by doing it anyway.)

- **'There is no exhaustive list of admissible operations' (Rittel).**

  There are no means, processes or approaches that are automatically on or off the table for discussion. Getting the brief right gives us our material options: the semantic values that make one medium or technology appropriate derive from the same community or society of users that the job is intended for. A good brief makes these decisions easy.

- **'For every wicked problem there is always more than one possible explanation, with explanations depending on the *Weltanschauung* (view of the world) of the designer' (Rittel).**

  Our solutions, however effective, will be solutions driven by our personalities. We can't escape this fact, but, if we have a broad working knowledge of the world, our work will benefit from having the widest and most exciting material to feed it. The brief allows us to play our preconceptions off against those of the clients and users. The challenge will increase our range of options.

- **'Solving a wicked problem is a "one shot" operation' (Rittel).**

  We cannot keep recycling the same solution and hope that it will work. It won't happen (despite what some advertising agencies think)! By making a successful piece of work, we have changed the rules of the game. Every time we reuse the same approach it will give diminishing results.

- **'The real problem-solving activity involved with solving ill-structured problems is providing a problem with structure when there is none apparent (Simon, 1973)' (from Jonasson).**

  This is very important to remember. By structuring the problem in a way that all the stakeholders can agree on, we are, by default, structuring the solution. As Jonasson says:

  > Just what is a problem? There are only two critical attributes of a problem. First, a problem is an unknown entity in some situation (the difference between a goal state and a current state). Those situations vary from algorithmic math problems to vexing and complex social problems, such as violence in the schools. Second, finding or solving for the unknown must have some social, cultural, or intellectual value. That is, someone believes that it is worth finding the unknown. If no one perceives an unknown or a need to determine an unknown, there is no perceived problem. Finding the unknown is the process of problem solving.

Complexity

How tangled is the problem? Do you have the resources (time, energy and commitment) to untangle the problem? The complexity of a job is the result of the number of elements in it, and the number of ways these elements can interact.

A really simple job, that is well defined, has few elements and few permutations. If we are asked to design a timetable for a single bus route that only runs a few times a day, in a single language, we have a (relatively) simple design task. The number of permutations will be quite forgiving of our design choices.

By contrast, if the job is to design a timetable for five buses in Seoul (the capital of South Korea), in Korean, English and Pinyin Chinese (Seoul public transport

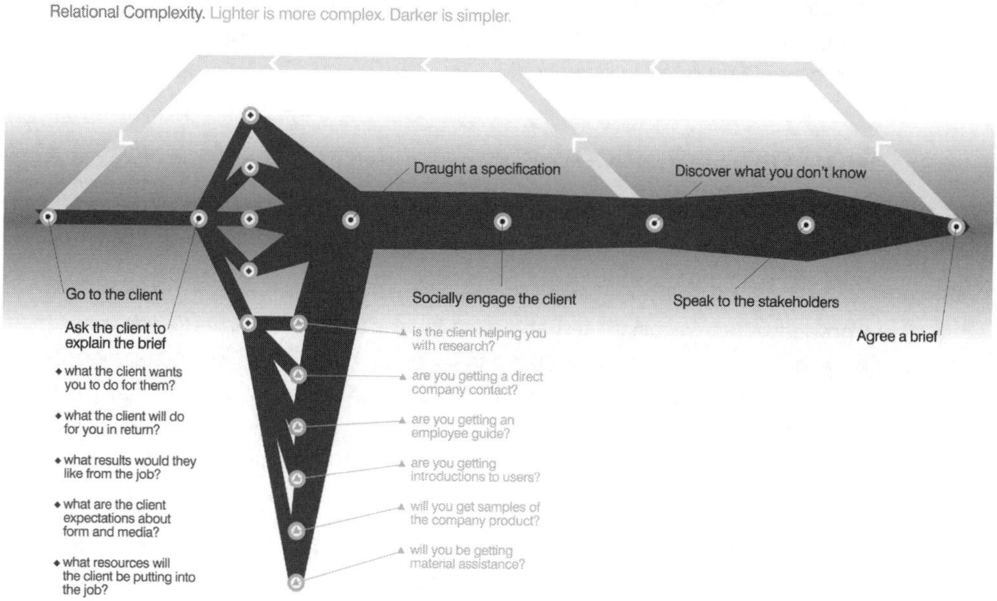

Relational Complexity. Lighter is more complex. Darker is simpler.

Draught a specification   Discover what you don't know

Go to the client   Socially engage the client   Speak to the stakeholders

Ask the client to explain the brief

♦ what the client wants you to do for them?

♦ what the client will do for you in return?

♦ what results would they like from the job?

♦ what are the client expectations about form and media?

♦ what resources will the client be putting into the job?

▲ is the client helping you with research?

▲ are you getting a direct company contact?

▲ are you getting an employee guide?

▲ are you getting introductions to users?

▲ will you get samples of the company product?

▲ will you be getting material assistance?

Agree a brief

FIGURE 4.4
How the complexity of the job changes over time

Note: In **Figure 4.4**, the distance from the centreline indicates the level of complexity, with the area at the centreline being low in options and simple, whereas the pure white areas at the edges are a mass of options caused by the number of choices available to the designer and client. If the briefing process has gone well, there should be a small number of elements (choices) at the beginning and the end, with bulges in the middle showing open options and choices to make.

information is frequently trilingual), with buses that run every twenty minutes during business hours, we have (at least) 270 distinct sets of times to accommodate in our design – a much more complex task.

This is called in the literature *relational complexity* (English, 1998), a measure of the number of possible links (relations) between elements in a brief. Jonasson tells us that the problem here is that an increase in relational complexity is explained very simply as having to think about more things, using more of the brain's available power. Eventually, we occupy all our thoughts just trying to keep up.

There are several ways to tackle this complexity: you can draught in more people (but this sometimes turns an already complex job into an organisational nightmare) or you can spend more time on the job (great, if time isn't an issue), but, perhaps, the best solution is to attempt to work with the client and user to reduce the complexity of the job in person. In the timetable example above, working with the client to make five separate timetables, rather than one, mother-of-all-timetables, is probably the best alternative. Complexity is always part of the design process, but, by working on the brief with the client, we can help ourselves.

Domain specificity

How local is the problem and, perhaps more importantly, how local is the knowledge needed to solve the problem? The word 'domain' is used in its academic sense, meaning a land or a world. It carries similar meanings to world-view.

Knowledge, as we discussed above, is local. Different domains (lands, or worlds) have different ways to understand the world. A surgeon's understanding of the meaning of the word 'clamp' is different from a farmer's or a carpenter's. The same word covers different contexts, different ideas. The same is true of every society and culture on the planet. What will seem familiar will often mislead an unprepared designer into making assumptions that will damage his or her work.

You can walk through the doors of a company and, by crossing the threshold, enter into an entirely new world. A financial-industry client slipped the words 'small cap' into a brief once. From the tone of voice, I knew this was significant, but, to be honest, all I could think of was my Dad (who is fond of flat caps). By admitting my ignorance and asking for an explanation, I found we were talking about 'small capitalised companies or stocks', i.e. a company with only a small amount of money behind it. This knowledge explained a lot about the brief. Without the input of the client, I would have been lost.

To be blunt, we don't know enough on our own to solve the design problem represented by the job. Jonasson puts this very clearly:

> Another strong predictor of problem-solving skills is the solver's level of domain knowledge. How much someone knows about a domain is important to understanding the problem and generating solutions.

FIGURE 4.5
A clamp is a clamp is a clamp!

This is why we work with the client (and, if possible, the user) to define the brief. They know (perhaps unconsciously) what we need to know to understand the problem and formulate a solution. We, the designers, have no local knowledge, but we do know how to extract local knowledge and put it to use.

To sum up, clients, designers and users will have distinct world-views: world-views that will often cause confusion if not addressed through a formal process, which is what the brief does. If the process works well, it reduces the complexity inherent in the job by removing unhelpful options, by clarifying viable approaches and by ensuring that everyone is operating with the same information.

NOTES

1   Remember Horst Rittel's first definition of a wicked problem: 'Wicked problems have no definitive formulation, but every formulation of a wicked problem corresponds to the formulation of a solution.' Getting the formulation is the trick.
2   Explicit knowledge is made up of things that we know that we know; things that we have placed in our own world-view in a structured way; e.g. learning to drive is about gaining explicit knowledge. We gain a set of procedures that we consciously work through to drive, though over time this knowledge becomes implicit, as we stop thinking about it and just drive.

3   Implicit knowledge is made up of things that we don't know that we know; things that we act on, respond to, but often don't have a structured understanding of. Take, for instance, your native language: you will use it without being aware of the underlying rules (though through education you may become so).

4   Remember, Horst Rittle's rule number 3: 'Solutions to wicked problems cannot be true or false, only good or bad' and number 5: 'For every wicked problem there is always more than one possible explanation, with explanations depending on the *Weltanschauung* of the designer.'

5   Scientists who study information flows, including communications.

6   An *open question* is one that encourages the person being asked to answer with an opinion, an emotional response or from their knowledge, not just answer with a 'yes' or a 'no'.

7   I cannot emphasise this enough. If you can't find it in your heart to ask for more money for yourself, think of the other designers. If you charge too little, you are devaluing other jobs, both for yourself and your peers.

CHAPTER 5

Research

Just the sound of it will send a chill down the spine of any self-respecting graphics student; surely design is about doing not thinking? Graphics is about the blending of 'inspiration', craft practice and talent – right?[1]

Well yes, in a way, but not in this simplistic way. Graphic designers and communicators aren't born with a reservoir of inspiration that they draw on throughout their lives and that one day will run down, leaving them incapable of doing another job. Let's look at this 'inspiration' argument and take it apart, piece by piece.

DOING

Make no mistake: doing is the fun bit of design. No one ever got into design because they wanted to do some more research or run off another sheet of roughs. The doing in any activity is the reason we do it. A mountain climber climbs for joy of being out there on a mountain, hanging around, 300 metres up, over certain death. However, the mountain climber who rates the doing more highly than the planning will be facing certain death in any number of very real and painful ways.

What we're seeing here is a confusion between aims and objectives. Aims are the thing we want to do. Objectives are the ways we can make the aims work. Using the examples of mountain climbing and graphics, we can see that the aim is, respectively, the desire to get up that mountain or to answer the brief. The objectives in climbing would be: the route, the training, the equipment, the supplies, the plan and the people we climb with. The graphics equivalent would be understanding the social environment, having the right trained skills, being able to lay our hands on the right kit, using the right materials and having the industrial contacts to make the whole job fly.

The visible, fun part is the objective. The important part in graphics is the aim. This might seem cold and clinical, lacking in romance and artistic credibility, but don't forget the very word design means having a plan.[2] A designer without the plan, however beautifully they work, is simply an artworker.

Doing is the reason we want to be designers, not the way in which we design. Without the knowing, however, the doing is pointless. The question then becomes: how do we understand the job well enough to be able to enjoy the doing? This is one of the problems that research aims to solve.

A REAL-WORLD REASON FOR NOT BEING AN ARTWORKER IN THE TWENTY-FIRST CENTURY

There are two reasons for not entirely relying on your skills (the 'doing' part) in your graphic practice. The reasons are China and India. The design industries in these countries are strong. The graduates of their design schools are strong and skilful – I've had the privilege of teaching many of them at post-graduate level. However, graphic communication is a practice based on social and cultural understanding: you need to know the community to design for the community.

So, while an artworker in Shanghai (and there are '10,000 design organizations employing approximately 100,000 people' in Shanghai[3]) can do the business, creating lovely artwork, because the actual manufacture of, for example, a shoe box or a menu is not a terribly culturally specific piece of design, once the logo, type design and style have been defined (by a senior designer in the West), this kind of low-level design/artworking will go to countries where designers get paid much less than their Western peers.

This is not a matter of opinion or speculation; it is happening now. Artworkers in India and China are now doing work for Western businesses, not just in graphics, but in all parts of the design world.

So, if you are looking for a long life as a graphic communicator, artworking is not the way to go. This part of the industry is shrinking, in the way industrial print in the United Kingdom did, and for the same reasons. However, you can get a shot at this life in design by being the brain of the design process not the hands, the person who devises the plan and then issues the instructions.

INSPIRATION, CRAFT AND TALENT

Before I lead you into design research hows, whats and wherefores, I'd like to consider how the traditional notions of design – inspiration, craft and talent – fit with a notion of design informed by research.

Inspiration

It's that personal spark that allows us to see connections and dream dreams that other people can't. A designer without inspiration is a robot: a mechanical zombie carrying out the instructions of others without personal involvement. I know this for a fact: I was employed as one for about three months in the early 1990s (my job title was Pixel Monkey).

But (and this is a gigantic 'BUT'), inspiration needs both the information to be inspired by (the broad knowledge of the last chapter and the research process of this one) and the means to assess the value of the inspiration (the development process of the next few chapters). Many of the most horrible atrocities of the last century were acted out by people who were driven by inspiration. Pure inspiration is like lightning: beautiful to watch from a distance, of no practical use and uncomfortable to stand next to.

How do we uncover the information that we need to harness our inspiration? Continuing the lightning metaphor, information is like a lightning rod – it channels the inspiration. Inspiration is a lovely idea but a poor tool to rely on. When inspiration runs out, we say that a person is 'blocked', unable to imagine creatively. Artists get blocked all the time, and it is a terrible thing; a designer should never get blocked. Design, as an activity, isn't fuelled by personal inspiration, but by knowledge of the world. If we run out of knowledge, we can always go out and find some more. A real designer can't be blocked, just badly informed.

Craft practice

Craft practices have genuine value, and it would be foolish to deny it, but, in order for them to be effective, they need to be located in a particular time and place. A classical orchestra is a beautiful living museum of craft technologies (the manufacture of the instruments, the skills of the musicians, the dress, the performance, the location and social ritual are magnificent), and as a museum it functions very well. However, you can't dance to it at a party – it wouldn't fit in your living room for a start; it requires huge financial backing, which means that it is entirely associated with wealth and class; it is craft made flesh through the efforts of the musicians; and it only makes sense within this narrow social context.

Craft functions in a space carved out by a culture. When the culture changes, the value of the craft to society changes. The graphic crafts are just like the orchestra.

Placed in the right cultural context, they are both effective and beautiful; taken next door, to the wrong context, they are meaningless. A good designer understands this. The typographer Matthew Carter (possibly the greatest living type designer) was a classically trained craft designer and a punch-cutter too. Technological changes that threw other designers into confusion have done nothing but demonstrate that Carter is a craftsman of skill and wit, who knows that craft is nothing without an understanding of the society it sits within. He has survived and flourished because he has always taken his craft as a starting point to serve the social context. Carter has designed some of the most classically beautiful fonts for print (Galliard is lovely), but is also at home designing a font for a telephone directory (Bell Centennial) or for your computer (Skia, Tahoma and Verdana). As designers, we have to serve society, moving on as it moves; we cannot be the classical orchestra of the visual world. Which raises the question, 'How do we understand the social world well enough to be able to use the right craft in the right way?'

Talent

This is a sensitive issue. We all got into design, as students, professionals or educators, because in the beginning we were talented. We all had family and friends who would coo over our childish scribblings and tell us how clever we were.[4] The sense of talent becomes part of our make-up, a sign of who we are. At times, it seems that to deny a person's talent is to insult them, their family and their whole upbringing.[5]

Well, talent alone is not enough and never was. Talent is probably enough to get you on to a degree course, and then it's exhausted. At this point, you find yourself among a cohort of equally talented students, and your talent is exposed for what it really is: an entry ticket to a very competitive world. You become a talent among talents. The question is: how do you show the difference between your talent and the rest?

To succeed, you have to be able to show that your talent is valuable and relevant. You have to be able to build a bridge between your talent and the world, a bridge that can carry your talent to those people who will use the fruits of your talent as it changes their world. To make this happen, you have to understand those people, and to see what use they might make of your talent. In this way we make our talent shine.

All of these concepts – doing, inspiration, craft practice and talent – are the charismatic and sexy parts of design, the parts that mark us out as special, the parts we want to be associated with us. None of these does the work on its own: all require information and understanding from outside to work. Which brings us back to that terrible word, research.

In this chapter, I'm going to show why research is not just about books, but that a good research process is fun, useful, problem-solving not problem-causing, and the heart of design as an activity.

DEFINITIONS OF RESEARCH (HOW WILL I KNOW I'M DOING IT WHEN I DO IT?)

Research is any activity that changes your relationship to the object you are studying. Trying every pizza shop in a five-mile radius of your university is research (just don't try to get a government grant to do it), because, in trying the pizzas, you learn the neighbourhood and find the best pizza around: you have been changed.

People associate research with reading. Reading books is only research if this reading enables you to change your thinking processes and your perspective on the subject of the book. If the reading just adds to a store of knowledge, but fails to change your ability to act, then it is scholarship not research. The same is true of writing: writing is not research unless it changes the author's and the reader's relationships to the object of study.

An example from outside design might run like this: imagine you come home one night and find a burglar in your home. You take a photo on your mobile phone and say to yourself, 'That was interesting!', and go to bed. The event has been recorded, you know about it, but the event has not changed your relationship to the object of study (the burglar in your house). You leave the process of being burgled better informed, but without learning a thing.

If, by contrast, you enter your house, see the burglar, scream 'Thief, thief!', phone the police and the next day install a burglar alarm and get a big, fierce dog named Fang, then you are doing research. Something has happened to you, and you've considered what that 'something' means. You've related this new information to your existing knowledge of the world and come to an informed conclusion that allows a new course of action. Through interaction with your object of study, you have been changed; the research has made a difference; your personal relationship with the idea has changed.

As designers, we would be rightly dismissive of any scientist who made a discovery about the world but wouldn't change their theories in the face of the discovery. Equally, we would be concerned about those who insisted that their personal beliefs about the world should override any evidence about the world as it actually is. Strangely enough, this very sort of behaviour is often seen as perfectly acceptable in the arts and in design. We are frequently encouraged to allow our personal feelings and gut instincts to define our creative responses (back to inspiration). This is not constructive. Everything designers do should be informed by knowledge of the world, because, when we get down to it, we design for others, and the others we design for will only act on messages that they feel are meaningful and real.

If we say that inspiration and creativity are like a hot fire, a flame that transforms everything it touches, then knowledge is the fuel. Through research, we can throw piles of knowledge on to the bonfire of inspiration and set our creativity alight. Those designers who want to work entirely on the basis of the resources in their heads are like people trying to get warmth and light from a single burning match. It burns out all too swiftly, leaving them cold and in the dark.

Inspiration is problematic, because it is a process with internal origins that are manifested externally. However, our personal knowledge is too local and too partial. The act of training to think like a designer puts us in a mental place where we don't think like other people, as pointed out by Donald Norman:

> Designers have become so proficient with the products that they can no longer perceive or understand the areas that are apt to cause difficulties. Even when designers become users, their deep understanding and close contact with the device they are designing means that they operate it almost entirely from know-ledge in the head. The user, especially the first-time or infrequent user, must rely almost entirely on knowledge in the world.
>
> (Norman, 2002)

The more time designers spend in the company of other designers, the more socially disconnected we become from people who are not designers. To be effective, we need to occupy the head space of those we design for.

The design researchers McDonagh-Philp and Lebbon write – about product designers in the original text, but it's true of graphics folk too – that the

> design fraternity consists generally of a sub-culture of individuals with similar backgrounds, gender and age. It is unreasonable to expect a designer to have experience and understanding of all user types within the shifting demog-raphy. Designers need to employ a variety of methods to fill their knowledge gap and gain the empathy required to deal with user groups outside their own experience.
>
> (McDonagh-Philp and Lebbon, 1993, p. 35)

Research bridges the gap between the designer who has the skills and the user who holds the knowledge we need to apply them.

The next stage up from the designer who designs entirely from the inside of his or her head is the graphic designer who believes that stacks of pictures sourced from the Internet constitute research. This is a phenomenon that every design lecturer is profoundly annoyed by. It is a kind of research, but a very weak kind. Enter a search term in Google or Bing and you are getting a kind of snapshot of the subject. It will be shallow and jointly defined by the search term you enter and the most com-mon responses to that search term. At its most effective, it will give you a very shallow knowledge of the subject. To make search engines work, you need to know the right terms to enter in the first place: information that you have to get from other sources.

In following a design brief, your research absolutely should not just be work-sheets or sketchbooks stuffed full of printouts from the web (think of the poor trees). Gathering information is key, and, while a thick book of printouts and photos might make your lecturer happy (it won't really, trust me on this) and will definitely give you a warm fuzzy feeling of having made a start on the job, it won't tell you anything unless you employ some of the following:[6]

1   **First-hand research**: Talk to the people who inhabit the world you are interested in. Take your Internet pictures to the community and ask them what they mean. Look at the community's artefacts and see what the community thinks about them, what do they mean? For example, if you want to know what is important to a community, read their own, internally directed media (not what others say about them, but what they say about themselves). Designing for the Metropolitan Police means reading their magazines, talking to their officers and listening to their jokes. By accessing cultural resources generated for a community, by that community, about the community, we get quick access to what the community feels. We learn something of their interests, obsessions and fears. This research gives us terms that we can use in other research – possibly as a web search, possibly in conversation with the user – but it gives us the foundation on which we can build.

2   **Personal testimony**: Get your clients or their users to tell stories or make mood boards about their understanding of the issue we are designing for. This is another way to build a reference framework for the defining elements of a user's graphic language. The stories users tell us are not in themselves important, but the ways they tell them, the common elements that they use, even things such as the rhythm the story has, will be information that designers can use. The trick is not just to take one sample, but to take five or six and look for commonalities. If something crops up across the range of testimony, it is probably important in that culture. If it is important to the culture, it will be something we can use as a tool to communicate with the user.

3   **Words**: Ask a community of users to give you five words that are mean-ingful in describing the community. Then, ask them to rank these words in order of importance. If you find a common ranking, or even some elements that are persistently high or low, you have something useful. You can then get the users to comment on their rankings, which will provide more infor-mation about hidden themes within their society. This is a fun game to play with students doing other art and design degrees at your institution. Go and ask the textile designers to list five terms that describe textiles; then ask fine artists to list five terms that describe the arts. Once they have finished ranking and describing, you should have some fascinating insights into their views of themselves and what they do.

4 **Analysis**: Analysis is where you make your personal responses to the material you have gathered as a way of uncovering hidden information. So, as you stick your material on to your design sheet or sketchbook, you should be considering the material, seeing if it sparks any associations with you and with the other material. Do the images or text make you think of anything? Do they connect with other research materials you have gathered for the project?

These questions can be addressed by seeing if you could divide the research you have gathered into categories:

- **Spread your research out** in a way that allows you to see it all at the same time – text, images, audio or video recordings – spread it all out and see if any common themes arise. If you are researching football and you hear people talking about strange combinations of numbers, '4–2–4, 4–4–1–1 or 4–4–2', and in your material research of artefacts see that there is a footy magazine called *FourFourTwo*, you might reasonably think you are on to something.

- **Place your research into clusters** (you can use Post-it notes) based on themes, concepts or ideas. First, the number of notes in any one cluster will tell you something by the size of a cluster. A huge cluster surrounded by a bunch of tiny ones tells you that the big cluster represents something of value to the users. If there are no, or almost no, clusters, this tells you that, either the users have no beliefs, or that your research has not been rich enough. The latter is more likely than the former.

- **Make physical connections between the themes the piles represent**: draw them, stretch string between them, join them with tape – it doesn't matter. What matters is that you are visualizing the relationships, the flow of meaning between the themes. Does the theme in one pile (e.g. 4–4–2) proceed from the theme in a second (e.g. meat pies)? By combining these themes together, we should start to get ideas popping into our head, semantically relevant links that we can use. I'm now thinking of photographing ten pies, arranged in a classic 4–4–2 formation, an image that I think would be meaningful and fun for football fans.[7]

5 **Responding**: Don't just let those lovely connections and ideas rot in some dusty corner of your mind and forget about them: *draw*! Make connections, sketch, write, respond to the material and let it change your mind. If the material fails to spark a response in you, if you don't find yourself itching to comment on it with words or sketches, it's probably weak material, and that tells you something.[8] Now start drawing. Don't stop to worry about the quality, the size, shape or form; just get the ideas down and move on to the next piece of found research.

6 **Example**: Nick Livesey discusses his use of sketchbooks at: www.youtube. com/watch?v=n90cBEjr1jU. Here, we can see some of his research and

development process for the title sequence of the movie *Hannibal*. So, although *Hannibal* is a film (which some of you might not think of as being graphic design), it is also worth remembering that Nick is a trained graphic designer, and his process includes first-hand research in the form of drawings and photos, found (second-hand) imagery and inspirational material. All of which is elegantly drawn together to develop a creative response to the material: a graphic response. He has successfully moved from having a personal point of inspiration to creating a title sequence that successfully informs us about the film we are about to watch.

7   Once you have compiled this material and responded to it on paper (with some nice little seeds of ideas sprouting away on paper), it is time to consider a **second, more focused round of research**. You see, by now you should have a pretty good working knowledge of a thin slice of the user culture you are looking at. You should know which pies the football fan recognises as 'real football pies' and which ones will just look silly. You should now be in a position where you can gather some focused, meaningful, visual research.

One example is the research work undertaken by students developing personal responses to a live packaging design project for Benson Box. The project brief asked that the students design packs for the delivery of emergency medical aid for disaster zones. To fulfil the brief, the students had to research and understand the following:

- The mechanics of packaging design, including a knowledge of which materials are generally used for packaging and why. In addition, they needed to know which materials are used for special purposes, e.g. (i) military-grade consumables and (ii) emergency and survival packaging. The two are different, and understanding this difference is important. The students also needed to add knowledge of how these materials would be processed, printed, stored and fabricated. The students were very lucky to be fully supported by the brief's industrial partners, who made presentations, answered questions and pointed the students in the right directions.

Through having the 'client' on hand, the students were able to get a very real understanding of the nature of the job and the existing boundaries of the field. Some students chose a very respectful approach; others set out to break the rules (including a pair who decided to design for a Zombie Apocalypse.)

This information about the existing industrial and material processes defined the material and process boundaries of the project. Defining boundaries is important to any project, if for no other reason than they tell you when you can, or must, break them to get the job working right. In addition to the important material and production boundaries of the job, the students had to understand the social dimension. The social aspect defines and overrides all other considerations in a design. If the social dimension asks that you break the boundaries of the material constraints, by using an odd, excessive or novel material, then you do it.

For example, the cost of the perfume itself is often a minor part of the entire product. The packaging is designed to plug into cultural notions of wealth, beauty, excess and glamour.[9] As such, the packaging must be over the top, otherwise it is bad packaging, no matter how crazy the material choices are.

So, the students had to understand the visual languages of emergency and disaster. There are many existing international symbols for use in disaster, emergency and hazard. It is debatable how 'universal' universal visual languages are, and so the students had to research existing standard visual languages, regional alternatives, local symbols and the possible biological roots of these languages. This could have made for some very dull research, but the students understood that you read these dry facts and immediately move on to working out personal responses to the facts. This interpretation does a couple of things for the intelligent design student: it fixes the fact in your head by making you think of a visual response, and it forces you, in designing a response, to consider how this new nugget of knowledge fits in with those you already have.

The students looked at existing design and visual culture, not just for emergency applications, but for all the sorts of application that will help a user, in pain and distress, immediately understand that they are looking at an object that can help them.

Initially, this meant gathering existing visual cultural objects that were significant to that culture in indicating 'emergency' and 'medicine'. This formed a fairly typical student scrapbook. The students then started to make text and image notes about the images, and to compare and contrast the different approaches to the design task used. These comparisons allowed them not just to collect the material, but to understand the material in a way that helped them to use this knowledge in their own projects.

More than fifty students took part in the project, and the work produced was extremely diverse. Although not all of it worked perfectly, it was all brave, full of imagination and designed with the confidence that the students' designs could be used by real people. This is the confidence that comes from a good research process.

RESEARCH THEORIES

> Design research can fashion singularities that allow theory to morph into practice and come back through the wormhole as something entirely new. Design research creates a place to braid theory and practice to make the work stronger.
> (Peter Lunenfeld, 'Preface: The design cluster', in Brenda Laurel (ed.),
> *Design research: methods and perspectives*, p. 10)

This quote is entirely true (if expressed in a scarily flowery way). Practice (the doing part) without research (the thinking and assessing part) is like giving a toddler a bag of Smarties and a hammer: something will certainly happen, but probably not in a productive way. Unfortunately for any design student actually intending to be a designer (as opposed to a design researcher, design academic or design teacher), the real gems of research knowledge are often written in ways that are not easily accessible and are held in places that are not the natural habitat of designers. Instead, we are exposed to 'design books', which are often not books about design (having a plan, doing the job, solving the problem), but are records of pre-existing work stripped of its functional context.[10]

There are many interesting ways to think about research for a design professional. I'll suggest a few useful places to look, but first I'll offer a few observations, general rules that may help you in the future to pick and choose ways forward.

'People make culture, and culture makes people.' This is an excellent starting point. If we remember that culture, all the things we surround ourselves with, express ourselves with and use to construct our identities with, is not natural but made by people, then we can see that the smart way of understanding our clients and end-users will be arrived at both through looking at their artefacts but also through asking them what they mean.

We don't need to discover a global truth about the world to make our jobs work; we need to discover the small, local truth about the people who will be using our designs. In the examples below, we can see road signs from the United States, Great Britain, Germany and Japan: each has been designed to be the best possible road sign, each works beautifully, but only in their local culture.

Each of the signs is excellent in its own place and time, because the designers had to intimately appreciate the specifics of the culture that would use the signs, and not some theoretical set of global rules that would work for everybody. Technically, that is because the signs and the culture the signs operate in are 'socially constructed', things made by a society to serve a function in that society. If we know the society and the culture of the society, we are halfway home to a good design.

Now, this way of treating the whole world as lots of tiny little worlds, not one big one, will seem at odds with the way the sciences are portrayed in the media, and I'm not about to get into the argument about science in the media, but I would like to take a quick diversion and talk about two opposing views of the world. Many of the qualities attributed to the sciences are what philosophers call positivist models of the world. These views suppose that global rules can be discovered and measured and provide a progress towards a point where all can be known. In opposition are constructivist models of the world, in which the combinations of things make and remake the world. In a constructivist world-view, there are no overriding rules that are equally true everywhere (Lyotard's metanarratives). For them, the world can never be known completely, because the processes that make up the knowledge are dynamic and continually remaking themselves.

I am frankly not qualified to say one or other of these views is correct, but I would note that the constructivist understanding of social research is ideally suited to the needs of graphic designers, communicators and other workers in the swamp we call culture. For designers, the useful research methods are likely to be those framed by the society being studied. As early as the Second World War, the US Army Air Force instituted studies that asked open questions about combat missions from the people who flew the missions. They understood that, when something went wrong in a combat mission, the number of factors involved meant a positivist approach to discovering the problem was destined to failure (if a life is lost in air combat, we may never be able to nail down the contributory factors: enemy action, stress, engineering failures, weather, etc.). Simply put, the truth of the matter cannot be determined. On the other hand, if accident prevention is your aim, a constructivist model of research is more helpful.

To quote from the 1946 USAAF Aviation Psychology Program Research Reports (as quoted in Flanagan's 'The critical incident report' (1954)):

> Essentially, the procedure was to obtain first-hand reports, or reports from objective records, of satisfactory and unsatisfactory execution of the task assigned. The cooperating individual described a situation in which success or failure was determined by specific reported causes.
>
> This procedure was found very effective in obtaining information from individuals concerning their own errors, from subordinates concerning errors of their superiors, from supervisors with respect to their subordinates, and also from participants with respect to coparticipants.

In other words, the psychologists asked people to tell them what worked and what didn't and compared the results. By allowing the people on the ground to set the agenda, the researchers found out more than if they had imposed a set of ideas from on high. This realisation led directly to a type of psychological investigation called critical incident technique (CIT). CIT is important in recognising that the truth about an event is created by the people involved in it, not from an outside observation. CIT is still used in hospitals when a patient suffers a medical accident. In addition to the legal process of deciding blame, the hospital will run through a CIT review, so that it can learn what went wrong and stop it happening again.

THE TRUTH

the truth

For graphic and other visual communicators, it does not matter what THE TRUTH is: that special truth that is the same everywhere, every time and in every society; what matters for us is the truth: that small slice of the world as understood by the community we are designing for. This is the special genius that CIT brought into play – the knowledge that observers (us), who will not know the things they need to know, can find them out from the user we design for.

By contrast, we look at the alternative, a top–down intervention, where experts tell people what is happening in their lives and how their world works. I will use briefly selected writings addressing the issue of desirable functions in typography to demonstrate that the rules, as laid out for us by informed practitioners as daily guides to typographic practice, are not 'truths', but are manifestations of locally acceptable beliefs. In the following section, one possible principle for distinguishing belief from knowledge is proposed.

In 1935, Herbert Bayer demonstrates a clear awareness of the social construction of legibility:

> much has been written about the legibility of type, oculists can offer no definitive proofs, because their experiments are influenced by habits to which patients are accustomed. For example, it is found that old people with bad eyesight often read complicated gothic type more easily than clear roman type, because they are used to the former.
>
> (Bayer, 1999, p. 61)

In 1993, De Lange tells us that:

> With normal primary school readers, and under normal reading conditions, sans serifs and romans can be regarded as equally legible. Serifs do not appear to affect legibility, as measured by the tests employed in this study. The authors are of the opinion that it is not necessarily serifs or the lack thereof that increase or decrease legibility. It is rather a complex interaction of known and unknown factors that affect a subject's reading performance and the legibility of reading material. Subject-matter, the readers' interest in the material, intellectual ability, and their emotional and physical condition, can all play a role in reading performance.
>
> (De Lange et al., 1993, p. 246)

By 2001, Bernard et al. find the position reversed in elderly people:

> Serif fonts, however, were generally preferred less than the sans serif fonts. Third, there was essentially no difference between the computer fonts and the print fonts. Thus, in light of these results, it is recommended to use 14-point sized fonts for presenting online text to older readers. However, a compromise must be made in deciding which font type to use. If speed of reading is paramount, then serif fonts are recommended.
>
> (M. Bernard et al., 2001, p. 2)

Here, we have three statements about legibility in type. Some or all of them could plausibly be valid in specific circumstances; all are written with honest intent. How are we to know which is valid? The simple answer is we go and ask the potential users.

There are many ways to do this. In the half-century following the invention of CIT, many methods of conducting research into people's socially constructed values have arisen.[11] One that has been shown to have a distinct value for graphics is ethnography. Ethnographers are a special class of anthropologist who devise ways of understanding people and their cultures. Ethnographers tell us that, if we drag our users into a lab and run tests on them, they won't react in the same way they do in the real world. More than this, they tell us that, even if we use hidden cameras and secret microphones, we'll still end up influencing the final results.

Ethnographers have given us a small and perfect truth that graphic communicators really should remember: we learn about a community, a culture or a society by participating with it. Professor Sarah Pink notes, in her book *Doing visual ethnography*:

> I shall define ethnography as a methodology; as an approach to experiencing, interpreting and representing culture and society that informs and is informed by sets of different disciplinary agendas and theoretical principles. Rather than a method for the collection of data, ethnography is a process of creating and representing knowledge (about society, culture and individuals) that is based on the ethnographer's own experience.
>
> (Pink, 2007, p. 22)

This passage contains important truths about research for graphics. We must 'experience' and 'interpret', then 'represent' and 'inform'. We work from that which we have experienced about another's culture. To find the truth about a culture, we have to go to that culture. The closer we can get to becoming a part of the target culture, the truer the information we can get about that culture. Figure 5.1 is a traffic island from a village near my hometown. The traffic island itself is a standard British model, white, to give the maximum contrast, and low, so that people don't damage their cars when they drive over them. However, in June 2010, someone painted a large red cross on this and several other ones. What could the meaning be in this strange outbreak of vandalism? Does it help you answer the question if I tell you that the World Cup was about to happen? Being part of the local culture, I got the implication and so understood the message being made. If you were an outsider, would the message have been clear? I had experience, so I could interpret. With this knowledge, I could make other representations through which I could inform. Without it, I would have seen a random piece of vandalism.

People still like dealing with people. We can find out a little about a culture by looking in from the outside through a computer monitor, but the subtleties of that culture will escape us: we will not only be tourists gawping at the major tourist sites, while missing the back streets, but we'll be the kind of smug, dumb tourists everyone

FIGURE 5.1
An English traffic island

hates, who go home having learned nothing new and complain about the food. This is one of the reasons that, in a world of high-speed video communications (such as Skype), I still find myself writing this paragraph on a crowded plane, flying back from a working trip to Spain (true!). I could have done much of my business (giving a talk on research) across the web, but establishing a real connection still means meeting people in the flesh, seeing how they live and work and immersing yourself in their world. Nothing else will do.

Ethnographers have spent much of the last half-century working to reduce the intrusive presence they impose on the people they observe. In the past, this has meant hidden cameras, video systems and the growing realisation that the most effective method is simply spending time with people.[12]

While ethnographers can afford to spend weeks or months slowly becoming part of those societies they wish to understand, designers generally can't: our jobs run to tighter timescales. However, in truth, we generally don't require the kind of detailed scientific detail the ethnographers do. By borrowing from the ethnographic toolkit, a new generation of design researchers is starting to develop tools that give us a good enough set of results to allow us to design with confidence.

I would like to start with the 'MootSpace' method, developed by the British design democrat Alastair Fuad-Luke. Doesn't that last sentence sound weird? Design democrat? What does that mean? In simple terms, it means a designer using design as a tool to enable people in their lives (the intention of modernist design), through methods that are informed and led by the people being designed for (not the modernists' way at all – they liked to tell people what they needed). In many ways, democratic design is similar to user-centred design, in that the design process is informed by the user. However, user-centred design has scientific overtones of experimenting on users and then designing on them that Fuad-Luke's approach doesn't.

FUAD-LUKE'S MOOTSPACE

MootSpace starts with the principle that the members of the user group, and we are talking about a group, know the shape of their own world. As such, they are in the best place to know what the problems are in their world. It offers a simple-to-use set of tools to get the individuals in the group talking to the group, and to get the group to decide what is important to the group (Fuad-Luke calls this process 'co-design', because neither the designer nor the users is boss: both parties are cooperating with each other to reach a common goal). At no stage does MootSpace discover universal (or even broad) information for us to work with. What it does do is generate a working agreement that we can work with.

In an ideal world, Fuad-Luke is looking towards an entire infrastructure of planning and debating sites, but I'm going to talk about a very reduced set of the greater whole: the simple process a designer can go through to find out what the needs of a particular group are.

For the process you need: the group; a facilitator (can be the designer, might simply be a trusted stakeholder in the group); a flip chart or similar large pad of paper; and some markers. Chairs would help, but this will still work if everybody just sits on the floor. Then:

- The users sit in a circle, and the facilitator stands with the flip chart.
- The facilitator asks the group members to discuss the issue they're concerned with.
- After the group has had a good run at discussing the issue, the members give the facilitator some keywords for the issue. The facilitator writes them down on the flip chart so that everyone can see them.
- The facilitator now draws a huge circle on a new page. The group's keywords are placed around the circumference of the circle (the order doesn't matter).
- The group members are asked to point out words and concepts that are linked. The links are made by drawing a line between the words.
- The words that link with the highest number of concepts are the ones that a designer needs to concentrate his or her attention on in designing for the group.

YEE'S EXPLORER CARDS

This is a methodology developed by Dr Joyce Yee of Northumbria University specifically to get quick cultural data from small groups of people at a low cost. Technically, it is part of a social-science methodology called elicitation, which works by getting people to weave their stories around culturally meaningful props. It shows many similarities with Fuad-Luke's MootSpace, in that it is a system that works because it is founded in engagement with the stakeholders. The rules of the design game are drawn up by the players.

This version of the game is derived from Dr Yee's paper (written with Louise Taylor) for the DeSForm 07[13] conference, where I had the pleasure of trying it out. The paper '"Are you a Delia or a Chantelle?" Engaging stakeholders in branding exercises' defines the following stages:

- A brand audit. In the case outlined in the paper, the client was a company, but even in this case it was important to establish how the company was regarded. For our purposes, this would be the equivalent of establishing the pre-existing visual culture of the group as it is manifested.

- The owners of the company were asked to generate 'a broad pool' of keywords that they believed expressed the nature of the company. These keywords were grouped into categories called elements. These elemental categories are broad groups of concepts that are relevant to the company being studied: things the designer needs to know about the client to understand them. In this experiment, they were: positioning statement, corporate purpose, mission statement, brand culture and brand personality. They would be different for your project.

- Cards were made up that carried these keywords and were supplemented with sets of picture cards.

- A researcher then dealt a stakeholder with a set of cards from one element, and the stakeholder was then asked to select five and rank them in a way that made some sort of sense to him or her. The user would be asked to explain the rankings: this provides the useful data a designer needs. The cards have just acted as a prop.

- The user would also be asked to select one of the picture cards, which could in theory be almost anything that would arouse an emotional response. Dr Yee's project used: celebrities, animals and environments. Once again, the cards are not significant in themselves; what are significant are the choices the users make and the way that they explain these choices.

- The explanation is very important. The users should be given as much support and emotional space as is possible to explain themselves; they should be encouraged to weave as complex a story as they can, because the details that they add will often be the most significant.

- Once again, we are looking for significant details and common themes emerging from a group of users thinking about the same thing.

Dr Yee sums up the advantages of using explorer cards as follows:

- Ease of use, requiring no additional training for designers or participants.
- Pragmatic, rapid and cost-effective way of eliciting intangible information.
- Visible, explicit and engaging process that encourages inclusivity and empowerment among the stakeholders.
- Data collected in the form of ranked keywords and images allowed quick analysis and interpretation into design concepts.
- Ranking stage of the card-based consultation helped stakeholders to focus on primary ideals that characterised their aspirational brand identity.

As such, this method is an excellent way into a user group's culture when time is short.

CULTURAL PROBES

Perhaps the granddaddy of these methods (at least in design terms) is the cultural probe.[14] Designed by Gaver et al. in 1999, the cultural probe is the result of an EU-funded project intended to look 'at novel interaction techniques to increase the presence of the elderly in their local communities'. The rationale for the project was exactly the same as the one I describe above: knowing a community, not forcing bad design upon it; getting information from the users that they didn't know they had. The authors talk about their hopes for the project:

> Understanding the local cultures was necessary so that our designs wouldn't seem irrelevant or arrogant, but we didn't want the groups to constrain our designs unduly by focusing on needs or desires they already understood. We wanted to lead a discussion with the groups toward unexpected ideas, but we didn't want to dominate it.
>
> (Gaver et al., 1999, 'Cultural probes', Interactions, January & February, p. 22)

The probes themselves were a range of found or constructed materials designed to provoke responses and invite participation. So, unlike a questionnaire, where the only response possible is to answer the question, and, if the question is not relevant to the user's life, then everybody's time has been wasted, the culture probe does not specifically know what answers it wants; it only hopes to engage with the user in a way that draws out useful (but often unexpected) information. The probes contained 'packages of maps, postcards, and other materials'. The postcards had questions on the back, but not direct questions, such as 'what colour should a phonebook be?', but more open and abstract questions, such as 'Please tell us a piece of advice or insight that has been important to you'. The postcards were pre-addressed and stamped, so that users could return them in their own time.

In the same way, the maps were intended to be props to evoke discussions and personal responses. So, although some maps were of the locality, others were of the whole world. The world maps had stickers, and the respondents were asked to put them on places where they had been; the local maps were accompanied by questions about the user's relationship to the area, asking such things as: where they would meet people, where they could find space to be alone or where they would like to go but couldn't.

Along with the maps and the postcards, the users were given disposable cameras with a list of questions/prompts written on the back. The prompts ran to questions asking for photos of things such as: your home; what you will wear today; the first person you see today; something desirable; something boring.

As mentioned before, this project was intended to probe the feelings of the elderly towards their communities and was carried out before the explosion of personal digital devices. A designer wishing to launch a cultural probe for his or her own project might usefully look for different prompts. For example, if we were investigating children, we might use things that are part of a child's world-view. Instead of the postcards, we might use stickers to make places and scenes in answer to the questions. Instead of the world maps, we might use photos of the local environment to allow them to draw on or imagine themselves in. The camera task could be left in but might be achieved through their parents' mobile phones. The important part of launching a culture probe is to shape the probe so that you can get relevant information from it.

All three of these methods have been deployed as ways of uncovering users' cultural secrets and making them partners in the act of designing for a community. All of them are moderately easy to deploy, but try and work within the following guidelines:

1   Make sure you have the permission of the community to work with it, both the explicit permission of the community leaders and the implicit permission of the members of the community.

2   Run a small-scale pilot study before you get into the main one. If you take some time to run a pilot (on a couple of people) to make sure the main study will work, you will discover all sorts of small flaws in planning and organization, which will save you a mass of time in the long run.

3   Choose a method or mix of methods that will be suitable for the group you are studying.

4   Fully explain to the people you are working with what is about to happen, what you aim to find out, who is behind the project (disclosure) and what the information will be used for. At that stage, give them the chance to back out.

5   Share your conclusions with the users at the end. They have a right to know. Beyond politeness, this step is essential, because your conclusions (once you have done your design) may be off. Showing the final work to your users can tell how off it is, before you commit to a full production run.

NOTES

1   This is a direct quote from a graphics lecturer I know. I gave a little talk about research in graphics, and he asked if there was a space for 'inspiration'. Of course there is. But the question we need to be able to answer is, 'Is the inspiration a smart inspiration or a dumb inspiration? Informed or ignorant?'

2   A good case can be made about this being a fundamental difference between the arts and design. The linguistic root of the word 'art' is the same as 'artefact', 'artificer' and 'artificial': all of which are about making. By contrast, 'design' as a concept is rooted in having a plan, an idea that will serve an intention. This is a remarkably fundamental difference; it allows us a certainty about our work: designers can tell if our output is working.

3   Bruce, Margret and Daly., Lucy, 'International evidence on design', for the DTI, p. 34, available at: www.bis.gov.uk/files/file21906.pdf.

4   There is some interesting information about the 10,000 hour rule and childhood encouragement. It has been suggested that adult encouragement to our childish selves makes us practise more, which makes us 'talented'. A study by K. Anders Ericsson (*The scientific study of expert levels of performance: general implications for optimal learning and creativity*) has mapped the skill of a musician to years of practice from childhood (the 10,000+ of practice). It is not unreasonable to expect a similar effect in those in the visual cultural world. Early encouragement to repeatedly practise our drawing and making skills is contributory to our later choice to become a designer.

5   Which is why, when designers insult one another, they tend to start with insulting their lack of talent.

6   The methods described below are a mishmash of constructivist social-research methods. Their scientific validity will be low, but they are intended to represent a quick and dirty working toolkit of methods to swiftly dig down to the gross values of a user-group, not to perform world-changing scientific research. These methods tend to be qualitative methods, which means they can function with small sample sizes (five or more) but will generate lots of data to analyse. As such, they are probably more suited to graphics, where a designer could spend a small amount of time in the field gathering data and a lot of time in the studio making something of it. Some are quantitative methods, which rely on much larger groups to work (thirty or more) but provide sets of data in neater forms that can be analysed more easily.

7   Which I am not.

8   Mainly, that you need to try again.

9   The *Guardian* estimated that the cost of the perfume is sometimes only 3 per cent of the end cost (see: www.guardian.co.uk/world/2010/jun/13/katie-price-perfume-india-pragati, 13 June 2010). Packaging comes in at

about 17 per cent, marketing at about 25 per cent (source: *Challenges* magazine, 2006). The semantic value completely outweighs the material value of the product.

10   I confess I own a lot of these books. I love them.

11   If you are interested, I would suggest you look up some material on *grounded theory*, which is explicitly based on the principle of users leading the way in investigating problems in their own worlds. However, there are too many versions and opinions about grounded theory to include it here.

12   To find out more, read Sarah Pink's excellent book, *Doing visual ethnography*.

13   Design and the Semantics of Form and Motion, a research organisation associated with the Design Research Society.

14   The name is intended to invoke the spirit of space probes, not the other kind.

CHAPTER 6

The visual design of election campaign posters

Steven A. Seidman

INTRODUCTION

Inevitably, changes in the worlds of art and graphic design effected changes in political-poster design. Eighteenth-century political broadsides used capital letters and bold, large type for emphasis, and occasionally included visuals. Currier and Ives produced lithographic portraits of presidential candidates and banner-posters that were used in US election campaigns in the nineteenth century. Political illustrators, especially Thomas Nast in post-Civil War America, created woodcut images that became symbols of political parties and even countries: the Democratic Party's donkey; the Republican Party's elephant; Uncle Sam for the United States; and John Bull for England. The lithographic posters designed in France by Henri de Toulouse-Lautrec in the 1890s, to promote the Moulin Rouge and other cafes, were influenced by Japanese woodcuts and featured large, bright areas of primary colours and silhouettes (Haill, 1998). The political posters in the next decades sustained many of these developments, which also incorporated innovative typography.

Poster artists depended increasingly on compelling imagery, composition and colour, minimizing text. This was in order better to convey political and other promotional messages. German graphic designers produced posters with stylish lettering and figures and dominant visuals. The poster designs of Hans Rudi Erdt and Ludwig Hohlwein, during the First World War, were reminiscent of the pre-war work of Edward Penfield (and other graphic designers loosely classified under the art nouveau style), in that their illustrations were simplified by a lack of details, with a plain background, flat areas of colour and original lettering and imagery. Similar developments were evident in the posters of other countries, including those designed for election

FIGURE 6.1
Albert Hahn, 'Vote Red!' (1918), the Social Democratic Workers' Party, The
Netherlands. Courtesy of the International Institute of Social History.

campaigns. A 1918 campaign poster for the Social Democratic Workers Party in The Netherlands (Figure 6.1), for example, included embellished letters, a capitalist octopus with flourished tentacles, and broad colour areas (particularly the red shirt of a worker fighting the tentacles of 'anarchy', 'war', and 'famine') against a plain yellow background.

After the First World War, the ideas of the Bauhaus school, the Dada movement and constructivism in Europe influenced a generation of graphic designers. Photo-montage, compelling colour, simplified shapes and creative typography were present in political posters. In addition, Impressionism continued to exert an influence on political-poster designers. Other art movements, such as cubism, surrealism, futurism, expressionism, art deco, social realism and psychedelic and op art had an impact on political-poster designs as well. The styles of the past can still be seen in election campaign posters today. The design of a poster advertising Democratic candidate Barack Obama's visit to Germany in July 2008, for example, was quite similar to those produced in the 1920s and 1930s by Bauhaus artists, such as Nico Schrier of the Netherlands. These designs boasted strong, clear sans-serif typefaces and used diagonal lines and lettering to increase the dynamism of the composition, as well as employing one dominant image. This focused the viewer's attention on a key visual, limiting competing elements that could distract.

The main trends in poster design for most of the twentieth century (and beyond) were simplification and stylisation. These trends were apparent in posters that advertised products and services, political causes and candidates among them. Most advertising firms sought to present their products to appeal to an audience effectively and deliver the message quickly and clearly. This is particularly important in a modern world in which people are 'increasingly bombarded with messages', according to John Hegarty (1998, p. 223). Poster designers tried to conceive distinctive styles and powerful visuals, used text sparingly and arranged elements to attract attention. A Swedish poster merely had to state 'Ford 1936' below graphic depictions of a new car model and a trail of circles to advertise the product (Figure 6.2). Simplified sans-serif type (seen in the Ford advertisement), which could be more easily read at a distance by people on the go (in cars and on foot), became more common in posters, along with the inclusion of a central image. The dual trends of simplification and stylisation became more and more evident, particularly after the Second World War. A poster issued to support environmentalist Brice Lalonde's campaign for the presidency of France in 1981, for example, featured a single stylised drawing of a tree and a few sans-serif capital letters. As Maurice Saatchi said, 'in great advertising, as in great art, simplicity is all . . . [with] simple themes, simple messages, simple visual images' (Quoted in Goldman, 1997, p. 332).

'Designers are all salespeople selling visually', according to graphic designer Mike Salisbury (2000, p. 46), and a political product can be presented, using positive imagery, so that it will be appealing to voters. The symbols and graphic techniques that have been used in one country are often appropriated by political-poster designers in others: the Statue of Liberty was featured in a Romanian election poster;

FIGURE 6.2
J. Olséns, 'Ford 1936' (1936), Ford Motor Company. Courtesy of Library of Congress, Prints and Photographs Division, reproduction number LC-USZC4–5867.

FIGURE 6.3
'Blessed with victory' (c.1979), The Islamic Republican Party, Iran. Courtesy of the
Hoover Institution Archives, Poster IR 56, Poster Collection.

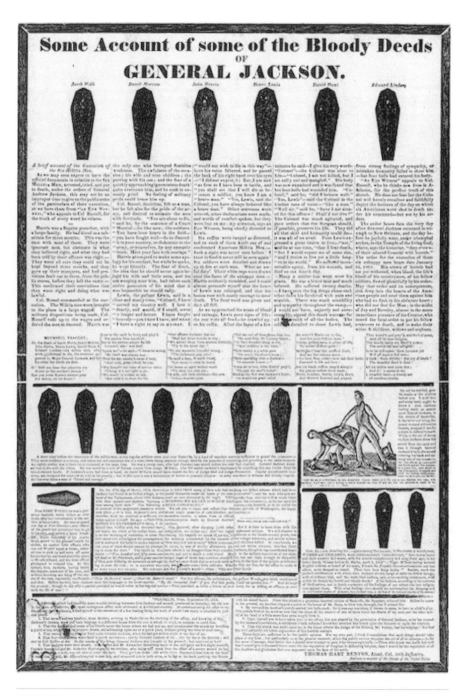

FIGURE 6.4

'Some account of some of the bloody deeds of General Jackson' (1828). Courtesy of Library of Congress Prints and Photographs Division, reproduction number LC-USZ62–43901.

in a Russian campaign poster, a presidential candidate protectively wraps his arms around a pair of children and a dog napping nearby – a scene influenced by paintings by Norman Rockwell. The 'V' symbol – used to signify either 'victory' or 'peace' – has been used in many election posters, for example: in the United States by Democrats for the Humphrey–Muskie ticket in 1968; in Iran by the dominant Islamic Republic Party in the decade after that country's revolution (Figure 6.3); and in Mexico by the Fox campaign in 2000.

The visual images of the rows of coffins in 1828 broadsides – designed to damage Andrew Jackson (Figure 6.4) – followed by those of General William Henry Harrison on horseback, Ulysses S. Grant in a work apron, William Hancock as a rooster, William McKinley standing on a gold coin and Warren Harding in front of a giant American flag, in election posters and prints in the United States, must have had a great impression on the voters before radio, television and the Internet made printed matter a less valuable campaign tool. The same was true in other countries. In Great Britain, for example, voters observed on election posters an apron-clad Henry Campbell-Bannerman in a kitchen and Herbert Asquith on a horse branded 'British Constitution', as well as such scenes as workers ramming the door of the House of Lords. In France, prints of the first Napoleon on a rearing horse were distributed by his nephew Louis during election campaigns in the 1860s.

THE INFLUENCE OF ADVERTISING

Political-poster designers have employed many of the techniques that seem to have worked in the advertising world to draw attention to and sell products: the use of symbols, shapes, colour, eye contact, perspective, simplicity, image manipulation and both positive and negative visual imagery (as well as the inclusion of slogans).

The visual images that were generated for the posters and billboards that advertised both products and candidates could be imposing: a good example is Howard Chandler Christy's idealized rendition of Warren G. Harding, with the candidate dramatically raising one hand and holding an American flag with the other. There were only two words accompanying the image: 'America First!' An advertisement for Palmolive soap, commissioned by Albert Lasker (who coordinated Harding's campaign around the same time), had also featured artwork by another prominent illustrator, Coles Phillips. In the advert, Cleopatra dominated the design as much as Harding did, along with another slogan: 'The oldest of toilet requisites'; the name of the product, presented in large, distinctive type, conveyed that, 'the beautiful of Ancient Egypt . . . chose Palm and Olive Oils [as] their most important toilet requirements' (just as Harding chose 'America First!').

Campaign posters started to become more stylised and simplified in the early years of the twentieth century, as had posters that advertised products such as automobiles and motion pictures, and services such as railways and electric utilities. Most of the election posters were quite simple indeed, showing a photogravure,

FIGURE 6.5
'Pay heed to me . . . Vote DC' (1953), the Christian Democracy Party, Italy. Courtesy of
the Hoover Institution Archives, Poster IT 216, Poster Collection.

photographic or drawn portrait of the candidate, and a few well-chosen words. By the 2004 US campaign, one poster was so 'bare bones' that all it contained were the letter 'W' and '2004' and a colour photograph of President George W. Bush. The use of a 'W' with serifs was a very modern and corporate tactic, because, as Dadich (2004) pointed out, 'Americans are conditioned to equate visual brevity with success and power' (p. A19). Occasionally, the imagery is sexual – a common advertising approach used to get attention. Figure 6.5 is a 1953 Italian Christian Democracy Party (DC) poster, which includes only a photograph of an attractive woman touching a button on her blouse, presumably to open it, and looking alluringly at the audience, with a simple slogan: 'Pay heed to me . . . Vote DC'.

Advertising firms, when brought into the political sphere, sometimes take competitive advertising to new heights (or lows, depending on your outlook) when devising negative poster attacks. One such campaign was developed for the British Labour Party in 1970. It depicted key Conservative leaders – in a poster entitled 'Yesterday's men (they failed before!)' – as shady, incompetent, belittled businessmen by representing them as clay figures, lit from below (but seen from above), against a dark background, to make them seem 'sinister' and 'unworthy'.

Election posters are designed to capture attention for a party or candidate. This is the case not only for the voters passing the posters, but also for the mass-media audiences who see them in newspapers and on televised newscasts, which also help publicize commercial products and services. This is especially true for those election posters that are striking in design and/or visually outrageous. One such poster, issued by the British Labour Party in 2001, caricatured opposition leader William Hague sporting Margaret Thatcher's hairdo; another was distributed by the German Green Party/Alliance 90 coalition in 1990 and targeted feminists by making a nude statue and comic 'Groucho Marx' nose, moustache and eyeglasses, placed over a male statue's genitals, the focal points.

Logos are usually developed for a political campaign. These can play on voters' emotions and help establish the candidate's brand – just as for consumer products. The Obama campaign's logo, for example, was designed to get voters' attention and to make them feel good about the candidate, with its imagery evoking feelings of pride in country, the 'heartland', and optimism: its blue 'O' stands for the candidate; the red stripes symbolize the flag and patriotism; the red-and-white stripes further represent farmland; the white centre of the 'O', rising over the horizon of the stripes, appears to be a sunrise, denoting 'a better tomorrow'.

MANIPULATION OF VISUAL ELEMENTS

Designers of election posters have tried to accomplish their objectives by distorting figures, such as showing Jews with huge noses and obese bodies in Nazi election posters in post-First World War Germany, or by more subtly manipulating visual images (evident in US posters promoting Gerald Ford and Barack Obama, which

FIGURE 6.6

'Who loves freedom' (c. 1917), the Soviet Revolutionary Party, Russia. Courtesy of the Hoover Institution Archives. Poster RU/SU 729, Poster Collection.

presented the candidates from below, so that viewers would perceive them as more imposing – the opposite approach to that taken in 'Yesterday's men').

The goal of the political-poster designer is to attract, and simplify the message for, an audience. Icons are very important visual elements. Such symbols as flags, raised fists and birds (particularly eagles and doves) have been adopted, for generations, in many societies. For example, an eagle perched on a flag displaying the party's logo dominated a poster distributed by the victorious Soviet Revolutionary Party during the 1917 Constituent Assembly election campaign in Russia (Figure 6.6). A poster issued by the Alliance Fatherland and Freedom Party during the 1993 election campaign in Latvia featured an oak tree, a traditional national symbol of 'strength' and 'unity' (Stukuls, 1997).

In general, the formats of the election posters produced in the United States until the early twentieth century were often indistinguishable, with most – regardless of party designation – displaying sober portraits of the candidates, eagles, flags or shields, and some cornucopias. The parties in many other countries around the world have continued to produce conventional designs that are similar to those of the opposition, including candidates (now smiling) and a logo in their posters. In Great Britain, however,

FIGURE 6.7
'Ah-Bian step down!! This will save Taiwan and give hope to the people!' (2004).
Taichung City Election General Headquarters for Lien Chan/James Soong [printed on
the poster]. Courtesy of Stanley Rosen.

design similarities have been less apparent, and, when opponents are shown, they are frequently lampooned. One poster, issued by the Conservative Party in 1997, titled 'New Labour, new danger', depicted Tony Blair with demonic, red eyes; others in the campaign included 'New Labour, new taxes' (which had a purse with red eyes) and 'New Labour, no Britain' (featuring a white flag). In Taiwan, a candidate for president in the 2004 election was compared in a poster to Saddam Hussein and Osama bin Laden (Figure 6.7). In positive posters, depictions of family scenes, as well as portraits of members of such target groups as college students and senior citizens, have also been exhibited in some countries' campaign posters.

The selection of visual elements to be integrated into a design frequently depends on whether or not the poster is authorized by a campaign or created independent of it. 'Official' campaign posters, particularly in the United States, typically feature only large logos that are also used on bumper stickers, badges, letterheads and other material. In recent American elections, all parties have employed stylised designs that are often little more than giant corporate-type logos, devoid of photographic portraits and issues. Their posters are quite similar, with stylised flags and sans-serif letters dominant against a blue background.

However, some candidates attract the support of artists who create unauthorized designs that are unconventional – sometimes posted in 'guerilla-marketing' fashion, meaning they were put up illegally in a variety of places. As these creations are posted online, they also spread virally. Two such artists are Shepard Fairey and Ray Noland, both of whom were pro-Obama, and who incorporated radical imagery into their designs to promote his election in 2008.

Fairey stated that his Obama designs were influenced by Soviet Constructivist posters, in fact (Hartman, 2008). Shapiro (2008), referring to Fairey's idealised portraits of Obama (as well as those by Russian artists of Soviet dictators), wrote that they all depicted 'the leader, face illuminated by "holy" light, look[ing] off to the horizon and see[ing] the truth that is not available to his mere mortal followers, who must look up to his image' (paragraph 1). The image that Fairey created of Obama may be 'revolutionary', but it is much more subtle than the Cuban posters showing raised rifles and fists. It is a simplified portrait of the candidate, with light and patriotic colours enveloping him, with the blue a lot lighter and softer than on the American flag. However, the depiction of Obama as a 'visionary', looking into the distance, has been evident in past posters, including those for Jimmy Carter and even Adolf Hitler.

Noland, in his poster 'The dream', also shows Obama – bathed in light – gazing into the distance, with a sun and rays as a backdrop. The iconography is religious, but similar to some Chinese posters of Mao Tse-tung. Suns have been used in many election posters in a number of countries, including France, Germany, Great Britain, Iran, Italy, Japan, Poland and Taiwan. Some examples are as follows: British Liberal posters in the latter part of the nineteenth century depicted past prosperity, when their party was in power, as rays of sunshine, in contrast to the gloomy economic situation under the Conservatives; a 1991 Solidarity poster featured a flower with the sun in its centre, symbolizing a new beginning in Poland; a 1972 poster for US Democratic presidential candidate George McGovern showed the sun breaking through the clouds, along with the slogan 'A little light in a cold world'.

The McGovern campaign was the last presidential effort that excited artists in the United States before the explosion of artistic support for Obama. N. Schneider, for example, designed a series of McGovern posters, all of which were colourful,

FIGURE 6.8
Ron English, 'Abraham Obama' (oil on canvas, 24 inches x 36 inches, 2008).
By permission of Ron English.

exuberant and stylised: one was dominated by a drawing of a leafy tree, accompanied by the phrase 'A time to grow in a world of permanent change'. In 2008, some artists created similar imagery that symbolised the themes of Barack Obama. One, Scott Hansen, also used a stylised tree in a poster. The tree grows out of the Obama logo, with people joining hands around it. As in McGovern's campaign, 'change' is a keyword, along with 'hope' and 'progress'.

Another 'guerilla artist' who fashioned an iconic image of Obama was Ron English, who fused the candidate's features with those of the revered nineteenth-century US president, Abraham Lincoln (Figure 6.8). English's poster, along with those of Fairey and others, helped build excitement for Obama's campaign, particularly among young voters.

VISUAL DESIGN PRINCIPLES AND ELECTION POSTERS

In recent election campaigns, political parties have often authorised stylised poster designs that have emulated those that have proven to be successful in the advertising world. Good brand management for a candidate or a party, as manifested in posters and other media, is characterised by visual imagery that is both powerful and appealing, along with simple slogans and logos that resonate with voters and their emotions.

Political marketing consultants have sought to present messages to the voters quickly, clearly and appealingly. Accordingly, they have had their poster designers devise distinctive styles, paying careful attention to font selection; employ powerful, emotion-laden visuals and slogans; and arrange elements to attract attention. Lasker understood this and made sure that Harding was shown only with a flag, looking directly at the voters, against a neutral grey background. This principle is known as 'figure/ground', or the brain's 'ability to separate elements based upon contrast' (Fulks, n.d., paragraph 2). He also had Harding establish 'eye contact' to get the viewers' attention and make his candidate seem more compelling, and had him hold the flag's cord to enhance the impact. This was an application of the principle of 'proximity'. It also helped bring about 'unity' – by linking the two dominant visual elements together. Furthermore, the flag and Harding are about equal in visual weight and distribution in space, ensuring that symmetrical 'balance' is achieved (see McClurg-Genevese, 2005, paragraphs 9, 10). Additionally, bold type and an exclamation mark were used to emphasise the verbal message of 'America first!' Finally, the illustrator drew Harding making the 'V' symbol to proclaim visually that he was for 'peace'.

Hitler and his poster designers also realized the importance of following visual design principles. German voters could easily identify Nazi election posters and broadsides – in competition with dozens of other posted visual stimuli – as red was usually the dominant colour, and large swastikas were featured in them. The Nazis' designs were

FIGURE 6.9
Mjölnir (Hans Schweitzer), 'Our last hope: Hitler' (1932), The Nazi Party, Germany.
Courtesy of the Hoover Institution Archives. Poster GE 792, Poster Collection.

generally effective because their themes commanded the attention of the target audiences, who were presented with simple graphic images and symbols that directly communicated both messages of hate and hope. An example of such a poster is shown in Figure 6.9, with its stylised depiction of unemployed workers and the message 'Our last hope: Hitler', in bold, sans-serif type.

It was understood by most designers of election posters that textual messages had to be brief and sloganised, and that elaborate lettering and artistic renderings had to be avoided generally, as they would distract the audience from focusing on the primary message. Modern poster designers usually have chosen sans-serif typefaces, which became more popular after the first quarter of the twentieth century.

The main poster design for John McCain, the Republican candidate for US president in 2008, used Optima Bold – described as 'classic, elite and just a bit old-fashioned' by Simon Daniels, a typography manager at Microsoft (quoted in Tschorn (2008), paragraph 8). It is also the font that was used for the names displayed on the Vietnam Veterans Memorial in Washington DC (Tschorn, 2008). McCain, of course, is perhaps the most famous Vietnam War veteran. Optima Bold is a strong, unique typeface that helps convey what the campaign managers want to about the candidate: that he is a leader who is 'principled', 'experienced', 'exceptional', 'tough', and a 'maverick'. The basic McCain design has good contrast (with white lettering on a blue background) and is dominated by the Republican's name. It has a star and a gold line that symbolise his military background, but, unlike most US election posters, it lacks the usual red, white and blue colours. Good election campaign posters in the United States – typically giant logos today – are part of good image management, and the McCain design succeeds well enough, despite its failure to include all the colours of the flag.

CONCLUSION

Promoters generally demand simplicity and compelling visuals, text, composition and colours for posters advertising their products, because their goal is 'to get the message across quickly and convincingly to the potential market', according to Horn (1976, p. 9). As Tom Purvis, a prominent poster designer in Great Britain in the 1920s and 1930s, pointed out, 'The most valuable asset of a well designed poster is its shock value. By shock value I mean its kick, strength, visibility, immediate readability' (quoted in Cole and Durack, 1972, p. 20). Effective election campaign posters get the attention of the voters, deliver a targeted message simply and clearly, and may even help motivate people into supporting a candidate and/or party. The inclusion of dominant and compelling visuals (often symbolic), bold colour and effective type can be crucial to accomplish these goals.

MY DESIGN WORK FOR CND

Ken Garland

The first piece of graphic design I did for the movement was not for the Campaign for Nuclear Disarmament (CND) itself, but for a breakaway movement, the *Committee of 100*, dedicated to a more vigorous protest than CND and chaired by the aged philosopher, Bertrand Russell.

In the autumn of 1961, I was asked to undertake a Quad Crown poster (30 × 40 in/762 × 1016 mm) by a fellow designer, Robin Fior, and I had about a week to do it. The main display of this poster was to be in the London Underground; several hundred sites had been booked for this with London Transport. It was in three colours: black, khaki green and red. I used the red solely for the word 'resistance'. When London Transport saw the printed poster they rejected it, because they thought the word 'resistance' suggested the use of violence, which was against their policy. So we reprinted the poster without the red printing but made instead a set of self-adhesive strips, just with the word 'resistance'.

On the night after the reprinted posters went up, eager volunteers went down to all the underground sites and pasted on the 'resistance' slips. As far as I recall, there wasn't a single word of protest from London Transport.

When the general secretary of CND, Peggy Duff, saw this poster, she immediately contacted me and asked if I would do the graphics for the CND Easter march for 1962. I agreed with pleasure, and the first result was the Double Crown poster (30 × 20 in/762 × 508 mm), printed in vast numbers, and in black only, an economic and stylistic decision that was sustained throughout all my work for the movement. Peggy was delighted with the design (she was probably my most appreciative client of all time) and warned me to get ready for more commissions.

Not long after the printing of the first poster, she came round to my home one evening and said we had just four days to produce a Quad Crown poster for the same event: a demand that, had it come from one of my commercial clients, would have received a flat 'no way'; but, with Peggy, you got on to it without delay. As she watched, I laid a number of the Double Crown posters we'd already printed and overlapped them to look as though they were a close array, as in a packed march. Peggy said, 'yes, great idea – let's go on that!', and we went. The resulting poster was well received by all concerned, and I was very proud of it. I still am.

In 1963, I designed two posters, one of which was replicated in a leaflet. Peggy said she would produce half a million copies (though I was never sure if this happened). The subject was an idea of mine, in which a little girl was seen looking out of a window. The text read, in part:

> Early one morning, my daughter woke and looked out of the window to see the dawn. She did it every day. It always seemed a magical thing to her that the sun came out of the earth every morning to fill the air with warmth and light. The day quickened for her in those few moments when the great globe of the sun sprang from the dark horizon. It was a secret world she shared with no one else in the world. But the great globe that sprang from the horizon on this particular morning was not the one she had seen and welcomed so many times before.

And so on. Many people told me they were moved by the words and the photograph, which was indeed of my own daughter. Afterwards, I had a slightly uneasy feeling about the poster-cum-leaflet, because I had not asked my daughter's permission to use her photograph.

I also had an uneasy feeling about another graphic contribution to CND. In the same year, 1963, I proposed that we make a large number of banners in black cloth pinned to long poles, on to which were to be stencilled various messages in large letters. On one side of the banner would be the name of the local CND branch; on the other side would be words or short phrases such as 'Disarmament', 'Against NATO', 'Disengagement'. They were to be carried on the march from Aldermaston to Hyde Park. Because all the banners were in identical material, of identical length, on identical poles, and with the lettering executed in identical size and style, they had an overwhelming effect, especially when we diverged from the route of the march to 'invest' Windsor Castle with them. My reason for unease was that, in retrospect, I saw these banners as cousins to the banners used to such great effect by the Nazis at their rallies. When, many years later, I was asked if I could devise an updated version of the tall banners, I had qualms, and the idea went no further.

I continued doing regular graphic work for CND until 1966, after which I thought it was time for someone else to take over. I was happy to contribute to the movement again in 1988, when it commemorated 30 years of 'peaceful protest . . . in opposition to the nuclear threat'. I designed an exhibition in the Lethaby Hall of the Central School of Art and Design, London. Though it was well received, I had a slightly odd feeling about the whole thing: surely we weren't celebrating, were we?

PROFILE

There were still enough nuclear weapons in the world to wipe out its entire population several times over. There still are. This, and similar reservations, should always be at the back of one's mind when commenting on the 'effectiveness' of graphic design in sociopolitical contexts. I do not wish to disparage or dissuade my fellow designers from involving themselves in such activities – far from it – only to ask that they go into them with a clear vision of the limitations as well as the undoubted benefits.

FIRST THINGS FIRST, 1964

A manifesto

We, the undersigned, are graphic designers, photographers and students who have been brought up in a world in which the techniques and apparatus of advertising have persistently been presented to us as the most lucrative, effective and desirable means of using our talents. We have been bombarded with publications devoted to this belief, applauding the work of those who have flogged their skill and imagination to sell such things as: cat food, stomach powders, detergent, hair restorer, striped toothpaste, aftershave lotion, beforeshave lotion, slimming diets, fattening diets, deodorants, fizzy water, cigarettes, roll-ons, pull-ons and slip-ons.
By far the greatest efforts of those working in the advertising industry are wasted on these trivial purposes, which contribute little or nothing to our national prosperity.

In common with an increasing number of the general public, we have reached a saturation point at which the high-pitched scream of consumer selling is no more than sheer noise. We think that there are other things more worth using our skill and experience on. There are signs for streets and buildings, books and periodicals, catalogues, instructional manuals, industrial photography, educational aids, films, television features, scientific and industrial publications and all the other media through which we promote our trade, our education, our culture and our greater awareness of the world.

We do not advocate the abolition of high-pressure consumer advertising: this is not feasible. Nor do we want to take any of the fun out of life. But we are proposing a reversal of priorities in favour of the more useful and more lasting forms of communication. We hope

PROFILE

PROFILE

that our society will tire of gimmick merchants, status salesmen and hidden persuaders, and that the prior call on our skills will be for worthwhile purposes. With this in mind we propose to share our experience and opinions, and to make them available to colleagues, students and others who may be interested.

Signed:

Edward Wright	*Bernard Highton*	*Harriet Crowder*
Geoffrey White	*Brian Grimbly*	*Anthony Clift*
William Slack	*John Garner*	*Gerry Cinamon*
Caroline Rawlence	*Ken Garland*	*Robert Chapman*
Ian McLaren	*Anthony Froshaug*	*Ray Carpenter*
Sam Lambert	*Robin Fior*	*Ken Briggs*
Ivor Kamlish	*Germano Facetti*	
Gerald Jones	*Ivan Dodd*	

CHAPTER 7

Roughing
The thumbnail stage

Once, I had a student who, in an assessment, was complimented on her drawing ability. She was confused by the compliment, and I suspect she thought I was making fun of her. We talked, and it became clear that she believed good drawing had to be both realistic and representational. This was the confusion. Her drawing wasn't bad as a piece of representation, but it wasn't really very good.

By contrast, I don't believe that drawing is for recording the world: that's only one of the many jobs it can do. Drawing is a way of using marks as a whole toolbox to do a job: sometimes that job is making pictures that look like stuff, sometimes the job is about capturing ideas. In the student's case, she was clearly rather good at the idea-capturing bit. She made lovely thumbnail roughs: they were clever and clear and funny.[1] The thumbnails were poor at capturing images, but brilliant at capturing ideas.

Put simply, roughs are preparatory drawings. They enable us to solve a whole group of different problems before we spend time and money on manifesting our designs in the world. The theory here is that paper and pens are cheap, but producing a graphic job is expensive: and so you sort the ideas first and make the ideas second.

A rough drawing (when it is doing its job) is a simple thing: a small drawing that captures a single idea. That is all it should ever do. It is in itself a shallow and unlovely thing, but it does not need to be anything more finished. It does not need to communicate with a broad audience, nor act as an investigation of a material process; it does not even explain itself to others; all it does is store a single idea, from your head, on paper.

WHAT DRAWING DOES

There are lots of different types of visual culture that come under the title of drawing. Engineers draw plans, scientists draw diagrams, even fine artists draw (sometimes). Each is perfectly suitable for its purpose, each does a different job, and so each looks different. So, we must be very careful when someone says a drawing is either good or bad. We must think of the job needing to be done and see if the type of drawing is the very best type of drawing for the job.

Imagine a solid block, a four-sided pyramid called a tetrahedron; with the corners representing conceptual drawings (ideas made visible through drawings, e.g. a heart being symbolic of love), schematic drawings (complex things made simple to understand through drawing, e.g. the electronics inside your TV being organised so that you can understand how they connect), representational drawings (drawings that look like things, e.g. a portrait) and expressive drawing (drawing that is aimed at transmitting an emotional charge, e.g. the drawings of Saul Steinberg, where the media represent the emotional state of the subject); all possible drawings could sit within the space defined by the solid.[2]

A graphics job would move between thumbnails, right up in the conceptual pole, to development roughs, which rest between schematic, expressive and conceptual poles, because they deal with laying out and developing ideas and testing the representational tools that express them, and finally end up as presentation roughs that are between expressive and representational poles, because they deal with the communication of a concept.

However, humble as they are, roughs have a value above any other type of drawing for a graphic designer. The roughs are the seeds of the job. If they are too few or too weak, the job will be a frail and empty thing; but cultivate a good, personal way of roughing out ideas and you will never be stuck staring at a blank screen.

There are different types of rough, lots of them with lots of local names. In this and the chapters that follow, I will be talking about three classes of rough. I'm not claiming that these are official terms or that your tutors will use them; I'm not claiming that the same terms will be used in other countries or even other firms; I'm not even claiming my terms are right; I'm simply saying that they are descriptive and clear. So these are the terms I'm going to use.

We have 'thumbnail' roughs, also called *scamps* or *idea roughs*; they are butterfly nets for your ideas. They are traditionally called *thumbnail drawings* because they are small, the size of your thumbnail. The term *rough* here means 'unfinished', not scrappy, and indicates a contrast with the finished piece.

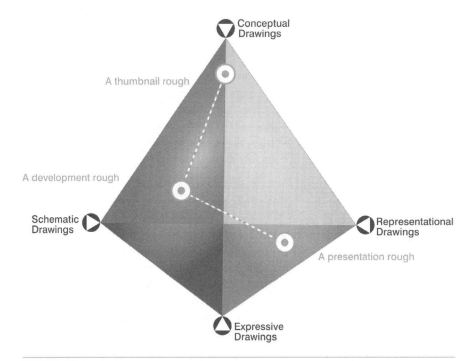

FIGURE 7.1
Drawing is a small word for a lot of different things

We have *development roughs*, including: brainstorms, draught storyboards, paper prototypes, maquettes, shared drawing, etc., which allow you to select from among your ideas, test them, experiment on them and refine them, until you develop a single workable solution.

We have *presentation roughs* that explain your ideas to a client or working partner in the design community (a print specifier, web coder, video crew, etc.) in ways that make sense to them and allow them to contribute to making your ideas real. These could be as screen tests, animatics, finished images, package prototypes and many other tools for explaining yourself.

Looking at the first two types of drawing raises the question in many students as to why they would even bother spending the time putting pen to paper when we can boot up our Mac and just let the creation *happen*. Many very talented student designers clearly feel that thinking about design is a poor companion to doing it.

There are many things I could say here. I could mention that the *OED* defines design as thinking about future action, and however true this is, and it is, I would sound old. I could recite the old saying, 'measure twice, cut once'. But, in truth, the answer is very simple. If you don't put the time in developing and polishing your ideas, you will totally deserve the weak, flat, dull ideas you get.

Let's list some of the ways graphic designers and communicators use drawing:

- We draw to get the ideas out of our head into the world.
- We use them to make decisions about our ideas and then to evaluate these decisions.
- We use them to test alternative versions of an idea.
- We use them to test the reactions of others.
- We use them to explain a concept sometimes, even in this digital age.

Sometimes, we use drawing actually to create (materialise) the finished piece. (Yes, shock! horror! some graphics can be drawn!)

The material products of each of these functions will look massively different; each of them will be carried out in a different way; and each will be judged by different criteria. So, a perfect rough drawing (the subject of this chapter) will make a thoroughly weak communication in itself. It will say everything to you and nothing to the designer at the next desk. Then again, it is not really meant to. It is unlikely to communicate to the videographer, illustrator or 3D visualiser on your project team what they need to know to materialise your work. That is the job of one of the last in the family of roughs, the presentation rough. There are rare exceptions to this rule: if you are ever lucky enough to see the thumbnail roughs of Saul Bass, you would swear that you are looking at the real thing. But, even with Bass's heavenly roughs, his intention was simply to record a single idea, so that he could move on to the next. Other types of drawing will allow exploration or evaluation (development roughs), or communication of ideas and technical process values (presentation roughs); but the thumbnail rough is a net: it catches ideas as they float past, that's it.

Hold on a moment! Why shouldn't designers make themselves three times as productive and do all the jobs in one?

As far as researchers can tell, the reason is the same as asking why your Mac crashes when you're running fifteen applications at the same time as you have a hundred windows open and you're backing up your hard drive.[3] Quite simply, you don't have the processing power to do it all at once. When you're making, for example working on some meaty HTML code or doing video edits, your brainpower is heavily invested in controlling processes. When you're being creative, your brainpower should be devoted to thinking, and so we need the most minimally costly method of recording your ideas for future development. A pencil and a piece of paper are pretty minimal in brainpower terms.

To make a job look really good takes 100 per cent concentration. Technical *mastery* (in contrast to 'just good enough' working) requires that you be exclusively focused on the technical process. If you are distracted by trying to think up clever ideas at the same time as you are working, you can't be exclusively focused on the technical. You are cheating yourself by trying to do both jobs at the same time.

So, my advice is to take time thinking, then take time doing and, at every stage, do the job right.

TECHNIQUES

Why spend time drawing out roughs? Is the act of sitting down and dragging a pencil across a page actually going to make you a better designer, artistically, socially, creatively? Well yes, it does, and let me explain some of the ways.

The process of drawing – getting out your tools, some paper, clearing a space and sitting down – has a ritual quality to it, and as such it calms the brain. It puts you in the right frame of mind, in exactly the same way getting ready for a party or putting on the right gear for a sporting event does. You go through the process and the act of acting like a designer brings you a little bit closer to being the design star we all long to be. This is what I was told at art school, and, strangely enough, it seems to be true. Let me explain.

Now that you are prepared, you can begin. You move your pencil (or crayon, marker, brush, lolly stick, whatever) across the page and you change the paper, but, surprisingly, the drawing is changing you. Physically, it seems to change the way you will think. And when I say 'change', I don't mean in a misty 'meditation making us all better humans' sort of changing the way you think; a change actually happens. Drawing will measurably change the way your brain is ticking along, at that very minute you draw and after you stop, altering its patterns of processing. These alterations are exactly the sorts of change that are beneficial to a designer. Drawing promotes a reduction in delta and theta brain waves (which are associated with sleepiness and sleep) and an increase in alpha and beta brain waves (symptomatic of relaxation in alpha waves, and alertness in beta). An alert and relaxed graphic designer sounds like a productive one to me. The study I am quoting, by Belkofer and Konopka (2008), also shows an increase in activity in the temporal lobes, which 'are concerned with language, emotion, memory, sense of time, and mystical states of consciousness' and are 'the part of the brain where images and meanings are associated'.

The drawing is setting you up to think better. The combination of you, the paper and the pen will slow the world down for you, while speeding your mind and narrowing your focus to nothing but the page. The world will shrink to you and the page: real life and all of its distractions will fade away. You are actively putting yourself in a place where deep thinking can be done.

Let's review the things that the rough drawing will do for you: it will put you in the place where you can clear your mind to think of ideas and it will then catch those ideas.

I've worked with people who have very definite ideas about how we should rough – 'definite' in very specific, very narrow and very predetermined ways. One lecturer I knew insisted on layout paper (it had to be layout paper): this layout paper would be subdivided into square cells (twenty to an A4 sheet), and the cells would be filled in order until three sheets had been filled. This work then had to be pinned up by pegs on clothes hangers, which would be hung on the students'boards. This was declared to be 'good' for the students. No counter-argument could be sustained.

The view I take is that completing a specific technical process is much less important than getting the ideas out. The suggestions that follow are just that, suggestions; not orders – never orders. They are simply ways of working that I have seen students find helpful in the past.

To start off, let's look at the roughing protocol suggested above:

Layout pads/paper

Why you should use it: Layout paper is lovely stuff, and it hardly bleeds if you use markers. If Idea 1 is good but not quite right, you can lay another sheet over the top and try out Idea 2. It takes graphite pencil really well. You can draw a grid of boxes on one sheet and use blank sheets on top. You will feel like a 'real graphic designer'. It is great for drawing layouts (unsurprisingly).

Why you shouldn't use it: Layout paper is kind of expensive (compared with some of the stuff I use for roughs: photocopy paper or wallpaper lining paper). Coloured pencils don't work well on it. It shows up everything underneath (which is distracting). It gets mucky very fast. It crinkles and rips.

Neither good nor bad, layout paper is an inessential treat. It won't make you work any better, but it might make you feel better about your roughs. So what about all the little boxes?

Small boxes

- **Pro**: As mentioned below, you can compose your rough idea against a framing device. So, if the object of your rough is in the distance, we can draw it proportionally small against the frame; if it needs to be big, it can fill the frame; if our object is huge, we can 'break' the frame. The frames impose a size limit on our ideas, which seems bad until you consider the alternative: a huge rough may seem stronger than a small one, not because of its quality, but merely because one is big and the other small. It makes a sequential design easy to visualise, e.g. animation or interaction. It allows you to see how many ideas you have generated and instantly judge them side by side.

- **Con**: Some ideas are just not square. It can be dispiriting for some people seeing three pages of empty boxes in front of them (not me, I must say).

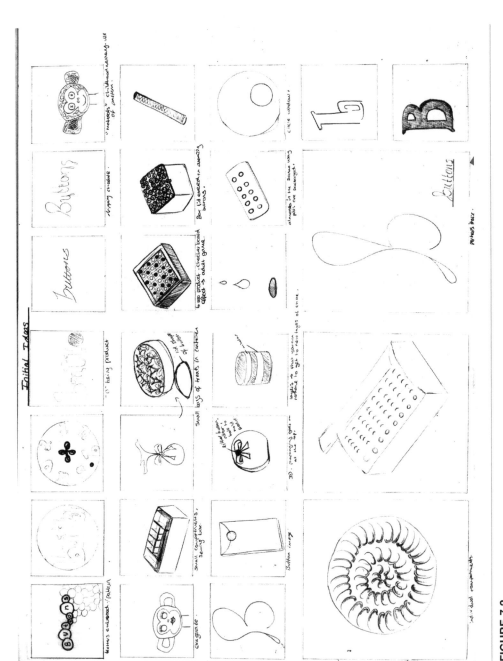

FIGURE 7.2
Caroline Green's roughs

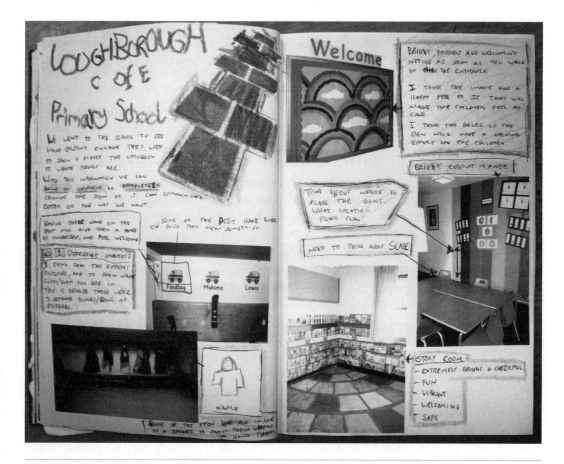

FIGURE 7.3
Matt Hopkinson's research roughs

It takes time to draw the boxes (see below). I quite like the 'little boxes', except when doing web design or layout, in which case they become a problem, not a solution.

Once again we have a way of proceeding that is partly good, partly bad.

Filling of the sheets

- **Pro**: Setting yourself a target is a positive thing.
- **Con**: It is depressing to see a room full of students who hate themselves because they have only managed to fill two out of three pages of roughs, when they should be applauding themselves for producing two pages of loveliness.

Do whatever feels right for you and can be shown to be effective in allowing you to pour those lovely ideas out of your head on to paper. However, there are some principles that I would like to add, principles that have proved themselves useful to me in the past.

- **Draw first**. Explain later. This one is interesting. A fresh idea in our head is like our dreams and memories. Once we start telling the idea to someone else, we start to confabulate, which is to say make up stories around the idea. This might end up well, but might end up erasing the value of the original idea in our head. However, if we draw the idea first, then talk about it afterwards, we have preserved the original and can potentially add our confabulations as ideas 2, 3 and 4. Do it the other way round and you have lost the pure original forever.

- **Colour**. Colour is a great help if used sparingly, but try to use it only when the coloured parts make a difference, clearly marking out a point out as special. Think of Frank Miller's *Sin City* (either the original comic or the film), where a splash of colour says more in a monochrome world than it would in our conventionally coloured one. For designers, drawing a rough with a splash of colour can say everything: it can indicate a canary in a coal mine, a blue moon, someone red with anger or green with jealousy. If we rendered every frame with colour, not only would it take ages to fill our sheet (making us miss all the other lovely ideas we would have had during that same time), but it would also reduce the impact of the individual idea. Only use colour as a form of shorthand, to help you record what you need to record, quickly and accurately.

- **Be prepared**. Always carry something to draw with and something to draw on. You never know when an idea will surface: be ready to catch it. Note: Once again, the important issue is catching the idea before it goes or mutates into something else in your head.[4] To this end, it does not matter at all what you are drawing on. You can always stick it into your 'proper sketchbook' if you need to.

- **Never censor your ideas before you put them down**. Never ever decide whether they are good or bad before you draw; never decide whether they are wrong, rude or offensive; never try to get tricky with the colour, style or composition if it is not an essential part of the idea as it appears in your head. By stopping to judge the quality of the idea in your head before putting it on paper, you will diffuse, mutate or lose it. Just put the idea down. Later, if you hate the idea as it sits on the page after you have drawn it, you can always scalpel it out and throw it away.

- **Do try and keep a variety of drawing materials close to hand**. This is not the same as 'be prepared'. Where that is about capturing ideas while out and about in the world, this is about being able to express visual difference from an idea on paper. Different marks and strokes, some fat, some thin, some broken or smooth, will turn a roughed out house into a palace or a slum. Having a variety of tools, close to hand, is useful.

- If roughing out is just not working for you today (and sometimes it doesn't), **do something relaxing**, but not mentally stimulating, instead. Don't watch TV or surf the net.[5] Take a walk, have a cup of tea or talk to friends; do the washing up, go to the gym or take a shower. All of these activities will disrupt your current blocked mental state and allow your mind to wander. It will act like a reset button. The human brain is naturally inclined to make connections, to link things together and look for patterns, when it is in a relaxed state. The time between waking and sleep has been shown to be particularly powerful at stimulating the imagination to make connections. If you try and 'work the idea', to force it into submission, all that will happen is that you will think yourself round in circles, chasing the same stale strand of ideas and imagery. Sometimes, it's helpful to just take a break. (Employment safety note: Some of this advice may be tricky to enact in a studio. Bosses might not like you going to the gym or showering in the middle of the day. They should, but they don't.)

How many roughs is enough? The principle is that you set yourself something achievable, twenty or thirty ideas, and just go for it, which, on a good day, is a workable scheme, but, on a bad day, often seems impossible. So here are some tips that work.

1   **Don't think (too much), just draw**. This will work for the first five or six ideas. If you stop to consider the worth of one rough, you may never get to the next.

2   **Have plenty of material related to the brief lying about**. See where the work you did in the previous chapter on research comes in? The association of images, comments and ideas you have uncovered through research will often spark associations, especially in connection with your first rough ideas. This should be good for another five ideas at least. Don't assess the ideas at this stage, just slap them down on the page.

3   **Be widely read and generally informed**. If the inside of your head is a knowledge vacuum, how do you expect to be able to make connections between the world and your work: you have nothing to connect with. So, when the ideas drop off, take a break and read a newspaper, listen to the radio or take a walk. The core subject matter will still be swimming around the back of your head, and your brain, lovely graphics tool that it is, will start making connections. Get the ideas down; don't stop to assess them. Another five ideas appear on your page.

4   **Look at your roughs**. Now take elements from one rough and apply them to parts of another rough. This should be good for another five roughs. That's twenty down.

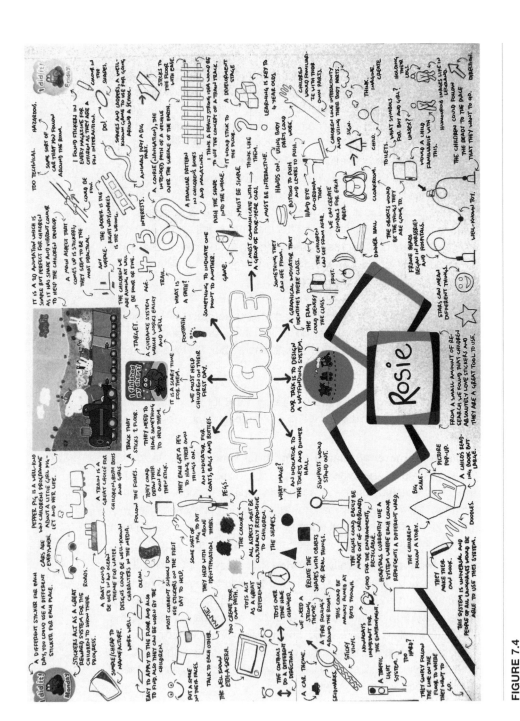

FIGURE 7.4

Nick Reid, one of my students, shows lovely roughs with no sign of boxes

5   **Look up the key words that frame the subject brief** in a thesaurus or dictionary. For example, I could look up 'handbook' in my handy electronic *Concise Oxford thesaurus* (on my phone) and find; 'manual, instructions, ABC, A to Z, almanac, companion, guide, guidebook, etc.'. All of which spark some sort of response. On its own, this might spark another few ideas by bringing you face to face with a raft of ready-built cultural concepts that have been tested for fitness by being common concepts connected with that word.

If we then tried the thesaurus game again with the word 'graphic', we get words such as 'visual, symbolic, diagrammatic, lurid, shocking and uninhibited'. So, rather than combining the words 'graphic' and 'handbook', let's try: 'shocking companion', 'uninhibited instructions', 'diagrammatic ABC', 'visual A to Z' and 'lurid guide'. Aren't those lovely combinations? Don't you just want to get in there and play with them? So that's another five ideas in the bag.

6   Now, the next idea is a little dangerous, because it allows you directly to mine a seam of existing visual culture, but by this time our brains are getting tired, so we'll take the chance. We can **enter the search term in a web search engine and then mine the results**. This is dangerous, because we'll often end up eating another creative's leftovers, but it can be fruitful, again because our results are indicators of the popularity of these images, in relation to the search criteria. They show us what others in the world think your search term means. The reason we are doing it now is because this is far enough into the research and development process that it is unlikely to hurt, and might actually help.

So, in the case of the search term 'graphic handbook', we get some old favourites, such as Ken Garland's 1966 *Graphics handbook*, which is kind of helpful in a limited way – because it is a pre-processed solution, fit for a certain time and place, which is not now – but we get some much more lateral suggestions, which can spark some interesting responses. There is *How to shoot the U.S. Army rifle: A graphic handbook on correct shooting*, which features a striking, modernist Second World War cover, which has got to provide some inspiration. There are some lovely Polish biological diagrams,[6] a purely typographic library card,[7] an e-handbook for a fracture analysis,[8] images of a 1967 Swiss Modern handbook from the Basel School of Design,[9] and a book on plastering walls and ceilings.[10] A wealth of strange connections to be made with what we already have.

Five more ideas brings us to thirty. We could stop there, but these thirty ideas are only the beginning, not the end. Speaking personally (as a designer), but also from my observations (as an educator), most of these thirty, hard-won ideas will stink. Let me qualify that: there will be strong ideas, weak ideas and really weak ideas: we only want the strong ones. The rest can be discarded (because they stink).

Which is easy to say, but quite difficult to do. How do we measure the quality of the individual idea?

To measure the quality of our ideas, we need a reference point. Fortunately, we have one ready built: a full set of cultural rulers, thematic maps, conceptual tape measures and material GPS coordinates supplied by our briefing process. The brief sets the boundaries for our work: are we selling, preserving, informing, charming or provoking? A campaign for a Christian church will have different values from one for a casino; a package for Eid biscuits will use different imagery from one for a hen-night kit. Addressing the wrong cultural values will see our work being rejected as meaningless by the user. So, we assess the value of our roughs against the values provided by our brief and research.

Beyond these values, we should consider the following technical considerations.

1   **Is the job doable?** In the 1950s, the Coca-Cola company considered firing rockets at the moon, with warheads designed to spread dark powder on impact. The idea was that they could use the dark aftermath of the explosions to write 'Coca-Cola' on the face of the moon. Beyond the ethics of such a move, the technology and cost of the idea, in the 1950s, placed the concept in the realms of pure fantasy. If your idea can't reasonably be expected to be made on time and on budget, drop it and move on.

2   **Is the job legally viable?** Many good ideas are so strong because they tap into existing cultural streams. Some of these cultural streams will be hedged around with copyright restrictions. It might become very expensive, very fast, if you trespass on someone's existing copyright. If you're not sure, consider losing these ideas too.

3   **Does the form of the job, the media it is made of, speak the right graphic language?** It is entirely possible to have a job that in isolation works beautifully but that, in contact with the visual culture of the user, speaks entirely the wrong language, e.g. Playboy logos on clothes worn by children. The associations are incompatible.

4   **Is your idea exciting?** This should be your key consideration; never develop an idea that doesn't excite you. There are too many merely workmanlike designs. 'Exciting' is in the position it is (the final one) because, if an idea is 'doable', 'legal', 'speaking the right graphic language' *and* 'exciting', then it's a winner, and you have to develop it. If it is exciting, but not doable, legal and speaking the right graphic language, then we can't use it.

So, we have thirty odd ideas and a set of guides we can apply to select the best ones; what more do we need? What more could we have done?

Let's think about the structure of our roughs, the actual layout and material processes that we use to create them. Are all of the thumbnails the same scale? If not, then we might end up selecting an idea based on its size and prominence on the page, rather than its comparative worth.

FIGURE 7.5
A fairground fun house that seems rather keen on some existing cultural images

Fairground graphics frequently play fast and loose with the concept of character copyright in their decorations. Make no mistake, this is illegal, whether the owners of the intellectual property wish to go to law or not. Dare you follow suit?

We can solve this problem, and in doing so gain some real advantages – showing scale, composition, framing and inclination – if we draw a set of empty frames of equal size on our page before we begin (Figure 7.6). The frames stand in for the boundaries of the graphic (the edge of the paper, the screen, etc.) and allow us to scale and align our thumbnails to make our ideas clearer and more communicative.

Look at the images in Figure 7.6. There are four views of the same serifed upper-case 'T'.

1. We have a 'T' that is tiny compared with the frame. We will read this as small, insignificant or far away.

2. We have a 'T' drawn as if we are seeing it from below, foreshortened by perspective. We will read this as monumental.

3. We have a tight close-up on the barb of the serif. This could be read as either very large or very close.

4. We have a 'T' roughed in at an angle, and from on top. The viewer is either flying over it, or looking down at it. In all these cases, the spatial relationship to the frame adds value to the 'T'. In combination with more complex elements, the compositional treatments become more powerful.

5. We have a couple in a tight embrace, lit by a searchlight. We, the viewer, are slightly above them and at a distance. We could be observing a romantic dance or a couple kissing. The composition is quite static and pretty calm. Now, imagine if you will that we can zoom right in to the next image . . .

6. We see, in tight close-up, a vampire about to bite its prey. The intimacy of the rough and the way the image elements are framed by the edge of the image make us uncomfortably close observers of a supernatural attack: the turn from one emotional atmosphere to another through composition is a technique as old as they come.

This transition will be clear in the head of the designer planning a scene. To capture it takes a couple of thumbnails. Each is a quick drawing, lacking in finesse, and simply records an idea. The addition of a compositional element turns them from notes without context to subject specific records of an idea.

HOW TO DRAW ROUGHS

The roughs in Figure 7.6 are drawn in the same medium. We might want the consistency that using the same media for all of our thumbnails gives, but perhaps colour is a vital element, in which case the question becomes 'should we use colour?'.

This brings up the question of the 'right' medium for doing thumbnails in. As a student, I was told the answer was always pencil. But then again, I trained as an

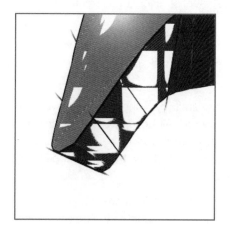
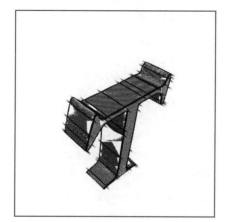

FIGURE 7.6
Using frames to impose meaning

illustrator. People I know who trained as graphic designers were assured that magic markers were the only way to develop. Once again, we are seeing a cultural phenomenon naturalised as the truth.

Pencils do have advantages: a 2B pencil can provide sharp black lines and soft tones, but pens give really high contrast and make punchy little thumbnails. Markers can whack in solid blocks of strong colour. Magic markers (which are so expensive that I can only afford them now) are fantastic, but are only limited in the aesthetics that they can address. Pastels are vivid.

In truth, there is no *correct* medium for roughing in. There is no hidden 'eleventh commandment' that only applies to graphics. The rule for choosing a medium for roughing in is simply: 'choose something that you are comfortable with'. Why? Put simply, when you are roughing, you should not be having to concentrate on using a difficult or unfamiliar medium. Your entire attention should be directed towards thinking of ideas.[11]

Use a medium you are comfortable with and only vary that medium for a good reason. If your favourite medium is cumbersome for a task, if it gets in the way, then use something easy.

When all is said and done, however, rules are arbitrary;[12] the ones I've given you and those that I'm about to give you certainly are. All I can say in their (and my) defence is that they have shown their value as a basic working set of principles for me: you are free to warp, bend, break or experiment with them when your personal experience shows you a better way. I insist.

Your thumbnails might need notations to work. Some things are complex – time-based media for example, or interaction design – a little note at the side to remind you what happens next can be a great help. For speed, and thumbnails are all about speed, textual notes can be very useful. In composition with your drawing, the text can imply a large amount of data. If the idea a designer is capturing has to happen in a blizzard, putting the word 'blizzard' is much easier and faster than fitting dots representing flakes of snow into your rough. You can also use text and graphic devices such as arrows to indicate movement, or the passing of time, or transformations.

Many, many, well-intentioned people, including a good many art and design lecturers, swear that spider diagrams are a viable method of recording your ideas (I teach many good young designers who have been told just this at high school): I must disagree. Spider diagrams are a highly effective method of seeing associations between ideas, but this is simply not the same thing. The spider diagram's strength in communicating associations to a broad audience is, at the same time, its weakness in dealing with the task of getting ideas from your head and on to the page. The rough drawing process is all about using a distinctive, *personally relevant*, system of coding. Frankly, we should not care if anyone else understands our roughs, as long as we do.

For example, if your lecturer says 'antipathy' and you feel like dealing in a little visual humour, go right ahead: draw that angry ant. The word 'antipathy' is itself simply a culturally defined indicator of a given meaning (technically, it is what is called an arbitrary sign).[13] Its meaning is, at one and the same time, both sharply defined (you can look it up in the dictionary, which is socially sanctioned) and wholly defined by the context it sits in (it may be in a limerick or a court record, and will mean different things in each setting). As such, words are wholly insufficient to record the complexity of a thought in your head; they are a code, a culturally defined code that you learned through contact with your family, society and education. They are not you; they are not your thoughts; they are an exterior system for coding your ideas that allows others to get an approximate handle on what you are saying to them at any given time. To give you an analogy, it is the difference between a TV picture of a person and the person themselves. They may look similar, but one is a simplified coding, a shallow, culturally predefined version of the original. The original is complex, unexpected and rich; the code is simple and easy to understand. You can hug the real person, talk to them, argue with them, kiss them or simply walk around them; in the same way, an idea drawn straight from your head has a richness of association (for you) that words never can. An (argumentative) philosopher would point out that a rough drawing is also a coded idea, and I would agree.

However, it is an idea coded by you, for you. It represents a small and perfect cyclic system: you draw the rough, and the rough signifies something back to you. Let's perform a little experiment to demonstrate the point. If I were to ask you to draw a sign to mark an exit from the building you are currently sitting in (no words – that's cheating), I can guarantee that your rough drawings would be different from mine. Why? Because setting cultural codings and shared life experiences to one side, and even with a graphic as mundane and oft repeated as an exit sign, we are different designers in a different place and will display different responses.

All that matters about the thumbnail rough is that it captures your idea in a way that you can later release. The process of release is examined in the next chapter: 'The development rough'.

NOTES

1   Unsurprisingly, she became a rather good designer and works in London.

2   Some fine arts theorists would add purely abstracted drawings such as Robert Weibel's gunpowder drawings, André Masson's automatic drawings, Dadaist cut-ups or drawing-based performance art. There are so many local notions about these forms that I don't really feel free to comment.

3   Back-ups are good. No matter how paranoid you think you are, you aren't paranoid enough.

4   My wife got me my own bath crayons, after I used my kids' ones for drawing ideas on our bathroom tiles.

5   These will pollute your head with someone else's visions.

6   See: www.google.com/imgres?imgurl=http://www.marekkultys.com/img/i9_ bachelor_s2_4.gif&imgrefurl=http://www.marekkultys.com/podrecznik.html &usg=__CFgaA-3dA8PFsLr6HmD1iR3PexY=&h=437&w=300&sz=18&hl=en &start=10&itbs=1&tbnid=V0k9_gATjsvlbM:&tbnh=126&tbnw=86&prev=/images %3Fq%3Dgraphic%2Bhandbook%26hl%3Den%26gbv%3D2%26tbs %3Disch:1.

7   See: www.ebookcomputer.com/screen/coverpdf/12–15575.jpg.

8   See: http://rci.rutgers.edu/~denda/e-Handbook/.

9   See: www.flickr.com/photos/yearofthesheep/4182694230/.

10 See: www.infibeam.com/Books/info/Tom-Lemmer/The-Complete-Guide-to-Finishing-Walls-Ceilings/1589232836.html.

11 I have a huge tool chest of drawing and making tools. It must weigh in at 10 kg and has everything from dip pens to French curves to those neat little scalpel compass combinations that let you cut out circles. Some of the tools date back to my student days; some are very new. Most are cheap (bought from second-hand shops); some are expensive. Despite using computers for something like twenty years, I still use drawing tools.

12 To be decided by one's liking; dependent upon will or pleasure; at the discretion or option of any one. 3. Derived from mere opinion or preference; not based on the nature of things; hence, capricious, uncertain, varying.

13 The Swiss linguist Ferdinand de Saussure demonstrated that words (and by analogy images) are signs: a cultural composite of the signifier (the outward representation of the sign) and the signified (the meaning being transmitted). He pointed out that signs tend to be arbitrary (subject to an individual's choice, not an outside law or principle). For example, in English-speaking languages, the sign for a dog's bark is 'woof'. A dog does not actually pronounce the word 'woof'. The word is a sign composed of signifier: 'W-O-O-F' and the signified: the sound a dog makes. German dogs say 'Wau!', Arab dogs go 'Haw!', and Korean ones make the sound 'Mung!' These words have been assigned to the noise a dog makes by the combined choice of a culture.

THINKING THROUGH DRAWING

Steve Garner

There's a lot of talk in drawing education about the dexterity of the hand, the significance of gesture and the acuity of the eye, but more important than all these put together is the ability of our brains to scrutinise the images we make and to be creatively inspired to remake, redraw and reinterpret. Sometimes, we need to think before we draw, but there are other times when our creativity only manifests itself if we draw at the same time as we think. At these times, it's like having a conversation with yourself – we draw to see what we're drawing (Figure 7.7).

Sometimes, we are pleasantly surprised by the way a line captures intention, and sometimes we can be frustrated that an image we create on paper or screen doesn't match our cognitive vision. Being creative with drawing is not a two-stage process. Humans rarely develop concepts in the mind's eye, only committing to paper once an idea is fully formed. The creative process is one where the mental constructions and the drawn representation leap frog over each other, in a process moving between the external, the internal and the external again.

So, why should this process be of interest to those seeking a career in the creative professions? Well, if you accept that your brain is your most significant creative asset, then you need to nurture and develop its abilities. First, you need to train it to control your eyes: that is, they must scrutinise the visual world you inhabit. Simply looking is not sufficient; they need to linger, so that the mind can drink in the detail of the built and natural environment. Only through this will you acquire the building blocks required for imagination. Second, you need to train your brain to question the visual information it is receiving. You might subconsciously ask yourself whether a scene is symmetrical, or whether one detail is bigger than another and by how much (Figure 7.8). You might prefer to analyse distortion, colour, perspective, texture or a host of other possibilities. You need to develop the capacity to be dissatisfied, so as to provoke more questioning. And, third, you need to train your brain to do something with this dissatisfaction. You need to be able to make responses that change situations. You need to move from a process of scrutinising, understanding and criticising, to a more constructive one, where you offer conjecture regarding what might be. Of course, all this will be hard work. Just like our arm muscles, our brain gets tired if we work it hard. It complains and seeks an easier life. But, resist its nagging, because with training come agility and an ability to tackle jobs that once seemed too complex or too difficult.

C@SE STUDY

C@SE STUDY

For over 35,000 years, drawing has proven to be a most sophisticated human tool. It has clear value as a means of communication. But it is its value as a support to creative thinking that really distinguishes it. Drawing helps us scrutinise the world. Through drawing, we come to understand. It helps us question and, vitally, it helps us respond. No matter what creative profession you might be aiming for, drawing can help your brain give form to partly imagined ideas; it can capture your thinking, enabling you, and others, to offer comment and development. Drawing and thinking are inextricably entwined. Drawing both assists in the training of the brain and relies on the brain's innate and developed capabilities to make drawing meaningful. If we subject our drawn outputs to the same scrutiny with which we might view the world, then a powerful synergy exists between drawing and thinking. We might deliberately introduce ambiguity into our drawings so that our minds are presented with multiple alternative directions, or we might juxtapose elements to see what we might see. The real value of drawing in art and design is its ability to support us in holding a conversation with ourselves. Go on, talk to yourself.

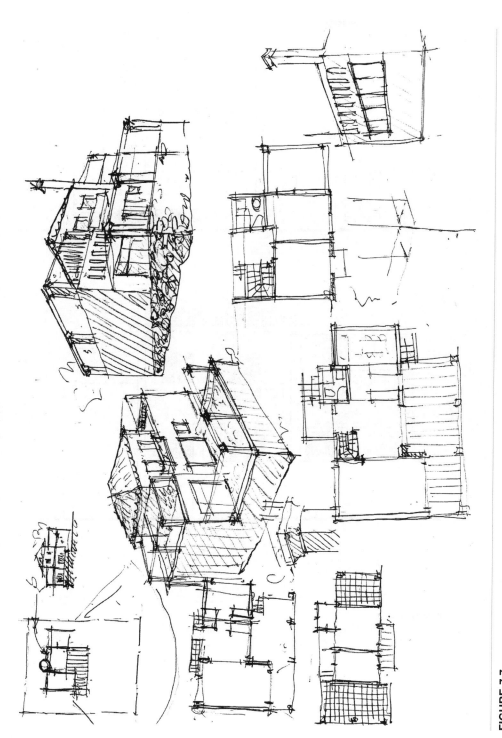

FIGURE 7.7
'We draw to see what we're drawing'

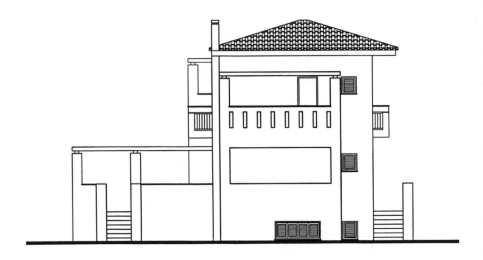

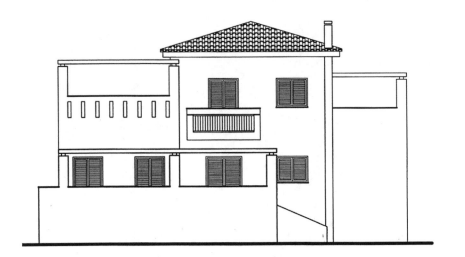

FIGURE 7.8
Is this symmetrical? Is one detail bigger than another?

CHAPTER 8

Roughing
The development stage

The designer's need to resolve a visual idea in more detail in order to make decisions about its appropriateness prompts a change in the pace and style of drawing activity and, during the course of synthesis and development, a shift of attention from concept to format can be seen to take place.

(Pamela Schenk, 1991, p. 173)

So, here we are, sheets full of roughs lie before us, with two or three excellent ideas standing out as winners; what are we going to do with them? A common approach is to leap to the making, feeling that there is no time to waste. When time is money, it would seem foolish to waste it by rehashing an idea we already have, right?

Well, no! Once again, the reason for taking more time now is to waste less later and, more importantly, to waste fewer production resources later.[1]

The truth is that all we have achieved in roughing out thumbnails is to capture some ideas and crudely sort them for value to our job. But this is not the way our minds will experience this process. In our head, those ideas seem strong and vibrant and right. They will seem complete and beautiful; they will sparkle in the sun and dance in the moonlight. When we drag them into the world, we find they are ill defined, unresolved and a bit sad.

The ideas in your head seemed so wonderful because your brain is filling in the detail on a second-by-second basis. You wonder if the text needs to be in a serifed font, and, magically, it is. You wonder if the dog (which is the key to the concept) is better as a Great Dane or a chihuahua, and the idea of a dog in your head instantly morphs from one to the other. This is the wonder of the creative brain playing with an idea: its product is powerfully plastic.

In terms of production, this plasticity of thought is a disaster waiting to happen. A hazy scheme in design can have its details filled in in a hundred ways, most of which will be weak; some of which will be disasters. Psychologists have a term for this human ability to fill in details that aren't there: it's called *confabulation*. We all do it. Most of the time, it's not a problem – we add detail to make the story funnier; we add events to make explanations more convincing – it's human nature. The designer needs to be *sure* of his or her design intentions and to be able to articulate them clearly, without room for misinterpretation by work partners. The alternative is a hazy instruction to the printer such as 'serifed font please', from which we get 10-point Caslon (the printer playing safe) when we wanted 6-point Baskerville. We say 'dog' to our runner, and our vagueness doesn't get us the Saint Bernard of our dreams but a man in a dog suit, ruining hours of potential shooting time.

If we don't sort these problems out before we start making, others *will* do it for us, we will lose control, and the job will be compromised.

DEVELOPING IDEAS FOR FUN AND PROFIT

'Braha and Reich mention the important trap of "poor quality knowledge" that can lead to "potentially exploring only inferior parts of the closure, leaving out the more promising solutions"' (Hatchuel and Weil, 2009). The 'closure' that Hatchuel and Weil are talking about is a working design idea. The 'inferior parts of the closure' are those weak, ill-thought-out solutions that are a feature of the development process. Development drawings are knowledge out in the world where we can play with it. They are ideas, explored and tested to the point that we can have confidence that we have a meaningful conclusion that might just work.

If we have hopes of seeing our ideas successfully materialised in the world, we must be exact. We must take that butterfly of imagination and pin it down, so that everyone working on the job can study it and agree what they see. We must take our ideas and refine them, eliminating the rubbish bits (and every idea has them), strengthening the good bits and defining the qualities of the job as exactly as we can.

By getting the idea 'out of our head and into the world', we can see it exposed. Then we can take three courses of action:

- we can approve it as a whole and refine it for production;
- we can reject it in its entirety and try something new; or
- we can examine it as a flawed but still useful plan and work on correcting the flaws.

These operations can only take place when we have something in front of us to evaluate. Trying to hold it all in your head will not work.

'Design is a reasoning activity which starts with a concept (an undecidable proposition regarding existing knowledge) about a partially unknown object *x* and attempts to expand it into other concepts and/or new knowledge' (Hatchuel and Weil, 2009, *C-K design theory: an advanced formulation*). This quote is a wordy, but canny, summation of what development roughs are intended to do. They are an exploration into making new knowledge; a way of exploring the territory of possibilities available within the limits defined by the job. The function of the development rough is essentially to open up new territory, a space for the idea to grow in, and then to reduce these possible options down to a manageable job.

These are the functions opened up to us by the development rough:

- **Examination and refinement of our thumbnails to extract the important qualities**. The thumbnail has caught an idea; through the development rough we can exploit it. Consider the development of a typographic form, an upper-case letter 'O', for example. The thumbnail roughs might tell us that it needs to be a serif character. As a serif, our 'O' will have *stresses* on the stroke (parts will be thin, and parts will be fat), with the amount of stresses depending on their historical association. The stresses could be aligned vertically or be angled from the vertical, also depending on the historical period they are associated with. These fine details are unlikely to be fully formed in your imagination. A combination of social and historical knowledge, experimentally combined through drawing the character and its fellows, will give your letter the perfect form. The thumbnail idea becomes a working plan.

- **Development of the working details of the job** (what materials, what form, what characteristics). Drawings can capture any object you can imagine; drawing is a cheap and direct medium for exploring ideas. What CGI can visualise slowly and expensively in exquisite detail, a development rough can do, quickly and cheaply, in just enough detail for everyone involved with a project to be able to understand. Drawings can simulate diverse materials. Smoke typography, marshmallow packaging, animated rats: drawings can do them all. Development drawings (as in sequential storyboards) can map out a video in low detail and do character design in great detail. If you can imagine it, you can draw it. If you can draw it, you can share it.

- *Having it all*. We can try multiple versions of an idea quickly and easily on paper. A designer can use layout pads to trial twenty layouts in an afternoon, or, by working one layer over another, organise multiple versions of the same pack. Typography can change colour, font or size by the simple act of taping different overlays over a master drawing. Trialling work becomes quick and convenient. We can afford to experiment, we can afford to be free with our ideas, because there is no expensive downside.

- **Avoiding disappointment**. As designers work on a job, they often fall in love with it. The more time they put in, the more reluctant they become to abandon it if it goes wrong. They will put in extra time to try and correct the job, avoiding the knowledge that the time is a waste, and the job cannot be saved. The very cheapness of a development rough means that it is easier to walk away from when it all goes wrong.[2]

- **Testing the details of the job**. For example, does the idea work as well when it is a billboard-sized video wall as it does as a thumbnail rough? Figure 8.1 is an image I took in Times Square in New York (March 2010). A perfectly reasonable fashion shot of some lingerie becomes something entirely different when it is on a video wall the size of a house. A designer somewhere thought that a pair of flower-patterned knickers 10 m high were just fine and wouldn't look at all strange on the street. Wrong! A job can quickly get out of control in our head. Once again, this is a matter of available brainpower versus the number of tasks it is being asked to control. By bringing all the elements together on paper, where we can see them, we can synthesise them in ways that allow us to make sense of all of them as a group, not as a bunch of isolated elements. In the Times Square example, I suspect that a few more drawings would have clearly demonstrated the potential flaws in the job. The designer could have tested scale, location, sequential design and environmental factors (day, night, visibility), quickly and economically. Visit the website of the videographer and graphic communicator Johnny Hardstaff and see the number of preparatory and development drawings he does of character design, prop and scene development, storyboarding, etc.,[3] drawings to prepare for digitally intense video. As a complete professional, Johnny knows how important it is to get the details right.

- **Coordination**. Design is a tricky business. It works more easily when the team are all pulling in the same direction. Drawing helps to dissolve misunderstandings about design intentions. Simply by drawing and sharing these drawings, we can avoid costly misunderstandings, especially when dealing with colleagues in adjunct areas of design (e.g. photographers can be shown how the photographs should be structured; model-makers can be given information about the form of prototypes, etc.). Because we must never forget that . . .

Graphics is a game we play in teams!

Drawing is an activity that can be done in private, with the results shown to others, but it can also work publicly as a tool for integrating a group's thoughts. This in itself serves several useful functions, including sharing the burden of development. Other people will see things differently from us. We may think that our ideas are works of genius, perfect in their clarity and in need of protection from those in the world who might sneer at them. Not so: our ideas need to be seen in the world and tested against the world.

FIGURE 8.1
Giant knickers in Times Square

FIGURE 8.2
Cars carrying meaning

Only by trying them out on our colleagues can we know. In doing so, we will uncover potential issues before they become problems. You never know – your colleague might improve on your work, leading to a better job.

- **Being playful**. Drawing is so quick and so cheap that we can take a chance on a wild idea or experiment, without losing a thing. Drawn development is essentially free of any limits imposed by time, scale or materials. Get strange, get exciting; it's only a piece of paper – what have you got to lose?

- **Drawing associations**. Design, especially graphics, is all about association. A car is never just a car: it's an outward display of ambition and status (see Figure 8.2). A flag represents a nation for sure: but what does it represent and to whom? The images in Figure 8.3 all show different uses of the flag of the United States of America, from officially sanctioned flags flying over government buildings and hanging in schools, to unofficial but sanctioned patriotic associations, to tolerated but unsupported uses, finally moving to the culturally unacceptable uses such as burning flags as a protest against US foreign policy. The associations that make meaning come from a complex web of cultural interconnections between the receiver, the maker and the cultures they inhabit, but this is never a one-way process: through development drawings, we can design our own interconnections. We can take our research and our thumbnail roughs and combine them in all sorts of wonderful new ways to invent new concepts. Sometimes, simply taking a few minutes to try out some associations from the research we have gathered can spark some exciting developments.

FIGURE 8.3
Stars and Stripes

- **Solving complex production problems on paper before they come up in reality**. Only by taking the job apart (on paper) can we see how the job will need to be constructed in production. In most graphics jobs, there will be a mess of interconnecting tasks that rely on some preceding task being completed first. In management, these are called *dependencies*. A dependency must be satisfied before the next phase of the job can be undertaken. Through working things out on paper, designers can organise the stages of the job in a way that is efficient and workable.

- **Dealing with changes**. Changes are a living feature of design jobs: the client asks for additions, the producer's feedback imposes changes on the job to fit a workflow, or your colleagues have bright ideas; whatever the reason, development drawings make it possible to accommodate these changes in ways that a fifteen-layer Photoshop file can't (e.g. quickly and economically). Reorganising the wrapping of type and image round a net that was originally a one-piece, but has now become a three-piece for production reasons positively requires a drawing on which to work through the permutations of elements.

- **Having a dialogue (with yourself)**. The development drawing can act as a placeholder for your design ideas, a kind of imaginary third hand holding the idea down while you manipulate it. It can be very difficult to assess the value of your own ideas in your head, let alone try variations on a theme. By contrast, it becomes frighteningly easy to judge your own work when it's on paper: the weak points will leap off the page in contrast to the strong. This kind of working swiftly becomes a way of checking up on yourself, before you make an error and show someone else.

When we do the development-rough process right, we will be actively searching for flaws in our design process. Development drawings are for exploring areas of weakness in search of improvement; we will be looking for better compositions, better typography, more exciting concepts, more beautiful imagery and more effective media. Through uncovering the flaws in our plan before we produce our pieces, we will be making our ideas bulletproof. That has to be worth the time.

The doing part of the development rough is quite simple. You draw, and keep drawing, changing the elements as you go. As you finish each change cycle, pin it up on the wall next to the last sheet, so that you can assess its quality against the previous pieces. Through this constant cycle of change and assessment, we can see which elements of our design are working and which are unnecessary and thus must be removed. And, because drawings are so quick to change and so flexible as a medium of representation, if we find we have taken out the wrong element, we can just try again.

THEORY

Many people regard choice as rational. In fact, the governments of the world invested all their collective faith in financial markets governed by rational choice. And we've all seen how that worked out.

So, as a designer talking to designers, let me tell you that the only rationality of choice we will ever encounter comes from those who will use our designs, from our background knowledge and from our working process. This is the measure by which we can judge the rationality of our design.

We all like to think that we make calm, reasonable choices in our lives. The evidence from the cognitive sciences would tend to indicate that we tend to *do* things first, and then create an internal narrative to explain the action.

This 'do then think' approach is entirely natural, like picking your nose, but, like picking your nose, it is not a desirable attribute. In a graphic communicator, it is a positively counter-productive one. This is not to say that you should think before drawing, quite the opposite: you *must* draw your ideas out of your head; but, at some point, you must judge them, not fall in love with them. All of which is made simpler by having them there in front of you.

> Design, like all problem solving activities, involves reasoning – making decisions, expressing ideas, verifying and evaluating proposals, and ultimately, taking action. For designers, drawing is a vehicle for design reasoning, and therefore the spontaneous marks made on paper during sketching form a partial record of the designer's thinking.
>
> (Yi-Luen Do and Gross, 1996, p. 1)

The design researcher Bryan Lawson has defined a number 'traps for the unwary' that trick designers into wasteful errors of thought, errors that can be avoided by spending some time developing your ideas on paper.

The category trap

This is Lawson's name for believing that a previous solution to a similar design problem will work for this problem. In the real world, we all do this a bit. We know a client, we know what they like and we skimp on the development. Bad idea!

More worrying is what happens when a designer sees something beautiful in another designer's work, and seeing it work well for that category of client, decides to apply it in his or her work. The worry here (and I'm as guilty as the next designer) is falling in love with work in magazines and on design blogs.

Let's think about this for a bit. If a designer, having some experience in magazine design, has found a workable set of specifications for type, layout grids and page format, which has previously worked well for a weekend supplement for a British *red-top* (a tabloid newspaper), and has then decided it will still work well for a computer magazine or, even worse, a high-end fashion magazine, they will be in for a severe disappointment. Each set of designs works or doesn't work based on the relevance of the cultural construction the designer makes. Each design is a one-shot solution (remember the *wicked problems*). This is not to say that you couldn't use the design above, but you should only use it is a viable solution, not because the original looked cool.

The solution: every job is a different job. While experience should guide us to towards good choices, reworking old successes doesn't guarantee new ones.

The puzzle trap

If you are reading this book, you are probably interested in graphic design, and so you will be aware of the idea that graphics is 'about problem-solving'. This is certainly an important (and fun) feature of the subject, but not the whole thing. There is a massive satisfaction to be drawn from problems; humans even have a socialised form of the activity in puzzles. Lawson, however, points out the dangers in confusing the activity of solving puzzles and the activity of finding solutions. One form of thinking does not naturally fit in with another. Puzzles are problems with artificial constraints; the constraints are restrictions on your normal range of actions; the constraints make the puzzle fun. Adding extra boxes to a crossword would spoil the fun. Using cheat codes on a video game quickly becomes a bore, but finding the right combination of buttons to do a new move is rewarding; these are the elements that are designed to give players the mental reward of having solved the puzzle.

Design is not a puzzle to be solved. There are no automatic constraints to be overcome. The constraints come from the job; the constraints are manufactured by the job. If we make assumptions about what we can and can't do, we are locking off a range of potential solutions.

One of the best examples of this I ever came across came, not from a graphic designer, but from a social scientist. Professor Steven Gilson, of the University of Maine, was working on a project to make the web more accessible to disabled users. Now, there are about a million graphics solutions: changing fonts, resolution, colour and contrast, iconography, photography, moving images, etc.; and a million more from industrial design: surface materials, Braille displays, haptic devices and many more, but Gilson had not allowed himself to be constrained in his thinking and found another way. He built a web portal.

On a user's first visit to a portal, he or she answers a quick series of one-off questions about the nature of their physical impairment. The user can then view the whole of the web with the portal dynamically reformatting the pages called up, so that they become visually accessible to the user. A brilliant solution, because it has escaped the puzzle trap.

The solution. In your development, allow yourself to be led by the research and idea-generation process that led you here. If the job leads you in a direction that moves the solution beyond the initial requirements of the client, but otherwise offers an excellent prospect for success, then talk with the client about the definitions of the job. Remember what Rittel says about wicked problems: 'In solving wicked problems there is no exhaustive list of admissible operations.' We are allowed to do anything that works.

The number trap

Lawson is by origin an architect. His formulation of the number trap has a high relevance to architects and industrial designers who work within the constraints of regulation. The problem is one of good designs being turned bad by central regulation.

Although it seems that this is of less relevance to graphic communicators, the number trap is, in many ways, a reformulation of Rittel's 'Every wicked problem is a symptom of another, "higher level," problem'. Let me explain. The regulator's constraint will be a considered response to another, higher-level problem. If we take the constraint as a given, we are walking back into the puzzle trap by not designing freely, and so may miss out on effective solutions.

For example, the UK Department of Transport provides an excellent document covering the use and application of graphical marker systems for road safety. It gives, to the millimetre, specific guidance on how and where to place your signs and road markings for best graphic effect. It is an intelligent and well-formed system but, for all its care, it cannot adequately cover every possible problem. The real world is always messy, fails to conform to the neatness of rules and is often in flux (moving from one state to another). A designer working on a road-signage scheme may well come up with local solutions that are improvements on the generic rules. Unfortunately, the rules will not bend, and this is the graphics number trap.

The solution. If we have developed a strong, effective solution, which we can demonstrate works well, we have an obligation to talk to the agency that forbids the deployment in its current form. We should work up a visualisation that clearly demonstrates the strength of our solution. We will almost certainly fail in our attempt to raise a challenge (the powers that be have their own belief systems that they will defend too), but we have to try.

The icon trap

Lawson points out that one of the dangers in development drawings is that we get trapped in the beautiful and sensuous nature of the activity and forget that it is a tool, nothing more. A good designer draws until he or she has developed a solution, at which time they move on to manifest the idea in a way that allows the job to be tested for the next level of challenges, making it technically fit for purpose (which is the development rough itself).

The solution. Never forget to review your work. We draw to discover and challenge, not for fun. Stick it all up on the wall, sheet by sheet, book by book, mock-up by mock-up, and evaluate your work. If, in your opinion, the work is good to go, stop drawing.

The image trap

The image trap is the one that all designers will fall into. The image in question is not the one in the hands, but the one in our head. As I've mentioned before, designers fall in love with their ideas. We love the image in our head. As with any love, we defend it from attack as vigorously as we can. I see this happening all the time when working with my students, and questions are raised about their work. The normal, first response is to invent reasons on the spot why the design works, rather than checking whether it does.

Falling into the image trap is something we are all prone to doing; it's not about intelligence. Students and designers both will spend so much time refining their

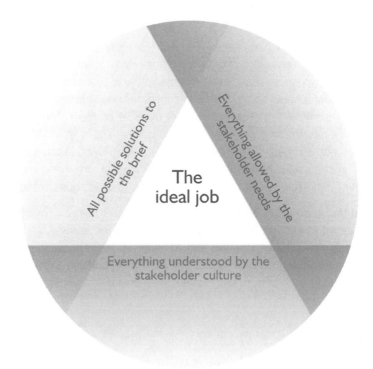

FIGURE 8.4
Avoiding the image trap

relationship with a problem (a natural function of complexity reduction) that they will have mentally rejected, not just all other solutions, but the possibility of all other solutions, and they will defend these choices to the death.

The solution. Keep in mind that the boundary, values and nature of the job are defined by the triad of brief, stakeholder need and stakeholder culture. If our designs take us off the edge of this map, we are wrong. There is no viable excuse of, 'we just need to educate the user, and then they'll understand how the design works'. If education of users is not part of the brief, if the stakeholders need to be educated to use our design, and if the design makes no sense within the existing cultural framework, it makes no difference how much we love the design: it's a bad design. It must be cast out, and we need to move on.

It is this tension between 'spontaneous marks' and 'designer's thinking' that makes drawing so valuable. We do, we see, we evaluate, we do again, and so on, until we've established a working plan.

The problem with development roughs, as a concept, is the sheer volume of ideas that it potentially opens. The term 'open ended' doesn't really cover it. We can see that, in any cultural system of interrelated potential design elements, the chances of any given designer just 'happening' to arrive at a working (let alone good) design solution are close to zero.

As Dennet (2006) notes:

> All design work is ultimately a matter of trial and error, but a lot of it takes place 'off line,' in representations of decisions in the minds of people who consider them carefully before deciding for real on what they think will work best, given the limited information about the cruel world in which the designs must ultimately be tested.
>
> (Dennet, 2006, p. 187)

Let me offer a brief example. If we imagine a very simple design job with the following potential elements:

- 1 page x paper size (say a choice of 2) ×
- background colours (4) ×
- choice of type colour (4) ×
- choice of shade (10) ×
- choice of font (rather than allowing access to all the fonts in the world, let's keep it to the OS agnostic 6 of Arial, Courier, Georgia, etc.) ×
- a choice of type size (say 10–16 point = 10, 11, 12, 13, 14, 15, 16), i.e. 7
- = 13,440 potential combinations.

At a rate of one choice per second – and not allowing for sleep, food, trips to bathroom (and we've all had those kinds of job) – we have three and three-quarters hours of continuous work, just to evaluate which elements we might use. Not to actually put them together in the first place you understand: if we designed these at a rate of one every ten minutes, that would take an additional ninety-three days.[4]

This calculation only looks at one page and does not even allow for the subtleties such as small caps, differential shades for different letters, composition or artworking the job. Design carried out in this way would never happen. A successfully completed design job is way beyond the possibility of chance. So, we can essentially discard chance (or luck) from consideration as a source of successful design solutions. However, on a daily basis, the graphic communication design process clearly does work, played out against a multitude of cultures all across the globe. Somehow, we are beating the odds, and doing so in a way that is so unlikely as to be almost unbelievable. This 'unlikeliness' is one of the classic hallmarks of an emergent system at play.

The social scientist Luhmann coined a term for this dramatic (almost implausible) movement from a sea of possibilities to a functional and distinct system: he called it the *Komplexitätsgefälle* or complexity differential.

> Luhmann defines complexity in terms of a threshold that marks the difference between two types of systems: those in which each element can be related to every other element and those in which this is no longer the case. In information-theoretical terms, complexity designates a lack of information that prevents a system from completely observing itself or its environment. Complexity enforces selectivity, which in turn leads to a reduction of complexity via the formation of systems that are less complex than their environment. This reduction of complexity – Luhmann speaks of a complexity differential (*Komplexitäts-gefälle*) between system and environment – is essential. Without it, there would be nothing, no world consisting of discrete entities, but only undifferentiated chaos.
>
> (Eva M. Knodt's Foreword to Luhmann, 1996)

This, for me, is the key. Design must operate on some level that is more than 'inspiration', 'craft', or 'referencing culture'. If we ran through all of the combinations of elements available, 'those in which each element can be related to every other element', we would have a near infinite sea of junk – conjugations and syntheses of elements that would make no sense (even if we accept the linguistic theorists' idea that visual communication has some sort of internal grammar and syntax) and tiny islands of meaningful design. On one hand, we have cultural chaos and, on the other, cultural systems, and the description of the pathway from one to the other is *complexity reduction* through design.

Luhmann speaks about how the recipient of a communication makes an act of selection from the available meanings:

> If one begins with the concept of meaning, it is clear from the start that communication is always a selective occurrence. Meaning allows no other choice than to choose, Communication grasps something out of the actual referential horizon that in itself constitutes and leaves other things aside.
>
> (Luhmann, 1984, p. 140)

However, he also talks clearly of the act(s) of selection that must be made by the person forming the communication:

> As far as information is concerned, *alter* [Luhmann's term for the originator of a communication] must view himself as part of the meaning world in which information is true or false, is relevant, repays utterance, and can be understood . . . In one respect he must interpret himself as part of what can be known about the world, for the information refers back to him (otherwise he could not apply it).
>
> (Luhmann, 1984, p. 141)

In Figure 8.5, we see a diagram of the process, where every possible appropriate choice is squeezed down and filtered by the design process to leave a splendid finished idea.

In short, we, the designers, take all of the possible choices and, with a knowledge of the user's culture, select a very small subset of the possible design elements, through which we make effective communications seemingly in defiance of all the laws of probability. The engine for this process is the development rough.

Considerations of the production process in design are also a matter of taste. There are many viable technical routes to our chosen destination. Many are rendered unsuitable for social and cultural reasons. Medical advice from a gossip magazine carries different social values from that from a broadsheet Sunday supplement, which is, in turn, considered less reliable than that from a formal medical website or from a doctor. We would be happy to receive free legal advice from a top international lawyer, less thrilled to take it from the back of a cereal packet. Personally, I've never taken romantic advice from an anime.

The social uses we make of production and communications technologies are very specific. The technologies carry specific meanings for certain social groups. Pensioners are unlikely to be effectively communicated with by use of rich media delivered through mobile phones; the young are. Viral media will self-target specific communities: for example, the buzz generated around *The Watchman* movie was masterfully orchestrated, targeting those web-literate comic-book fans most likely to form the opinions of other fans, while entirely bypassing those who were the wrong demographic (movie critics).

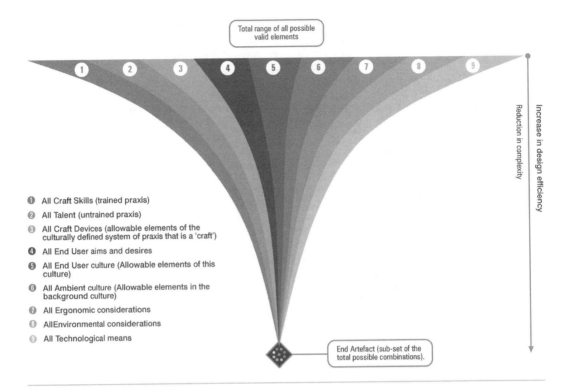

FIGURE 8.5
Complexity reduction in graphics

If we use technologies in a blunt, unresponsive way or, worse, use specific technologies simply because we enjoy them, we will produce weak designs that fail to reach those we need to touch.

This matching of the technical means of deploying your idea and the social values that a technology embodies is a tricky business. There are always media that we like working with, things we feel comfortable with; a good designer will alter his or her technical responses to fit in with the needs of the client. I once heard the designer Bob Gill state that a designer should never start a job knowing how the job would finish; that the form of the job should be the result of the brief, not the designer's skill set.[5]

For example, the designer Chip (Charles) Kidd designs book covers; he is arguably the finest designer of book jackets in the world today.[6] Each cover is a distinct gem; each cover gains its individuality from a meaningful technical approach based on the subject of the book, combined with a knowledge of the reader the book is aimed at. So, while the covers tend to be based on some variation of text and image, the sheer variety is quite dazzling. Each is an appropriate and meaningful whole. For example, the 2004 cover for Philip Galanes' book *Father's day* features a simple photograph of a yellow wool jumper, with the type stitched onto the jumper's label.

Referencing the story, while still working as a design, the cover is graphically effective and completely defined by the job. If Chip Kid's work was merely a matter of personal taste, his hallmark diversity would be notable by its absence.

Don't forget, design is not necessarily about painting, printing, drawing, carving, cutting or gluing; it is about devising a plan for future execution.

By working through the job, we avoid falling into these pitfalls and are ready to work it up to a point where we can show it to a client, a production house, a friendly technician, or anybody who has a stake in our job. This is the presentation rough stage.

NOTES

1   The truth being that, in economic terms, design time is cheaper than production time.
2   Fiction is full of heroes who 'just don't know when they're beaten'. This is a fine attribute in a hero but a lousy one in a designer. If a design isn't working, walk away and get a better design.
3   See: www.johnnyhardstaff.com.
4   With no sleep or breaks.
5   During his talk at the *2010 New York Design Experience* at Parson's School of Art, NYC, 18 March 2010.
6   The author James Ellroy is quoted by Jeet Heer, in the Canadian newspaper *National Post*, as saying that Kidd is: 'the world's greatest book-jacket designer' (Heer, 2003).

     John Updike (the grand old man of American literature) says of Kidd: 'In a field, book-jacket design, where edge, zip, and instant impact are sine qua non, Kidd is second to none' (Updike, 2005, p. 26).

CHAPTER 9

Roughing
The presentation stage

The basic work in the development of our ideas has been done. We are in a position where we know what must be done, we know how we should do it and we can be reasonably sure that the job will conceptually fit with client and user. All we have left to do is prepare the job in a way that explains itself to the people who need to understand it. This explanation will be the presentation rough. We'll also be looking at what to do when you just haven't been able to reduce down your ideas to a single gem, but still have to show the client, or when you know you have the answer your client wants, but also have ideas that would work better.

Once again, the way we go forward is defined by the people we have to work with. The simple truth is that what we show clients is, in large part, determined from a close analysis of them. In previous chapters, we have looked at the ways in which we can separate clients' wishes from the actual demands of the job, as defined by the combination of client and user: now, we are looking directly at the clients and only the clients, because right now they are the only people we have to convince. We will be looking at the ways that the material form of the actual design is determined by the clients and the job, but also how the form of the work we are presenting is defined by the clients: their culture, the organisation they represent and their personalities. A presentation rough for an animation will be different from that for an interactive presentation, which will be different from that for an editorial job: this is obvious. What is less obvious is that a presentation rough for one company in a particular business will often be different from one for another company in the same business. The form of the presentation is defined by the prevailing culture of the clients and the production professionals who will materialise the job.

Historically, the work presented to the client and the final job were often the same piece of work. It was something called camera-ready artwork, a piece of finished artwork that could be photographically transferred to printing plates or scanned to a press. You would show the work to the client in as finished a form as you could manage, and, if it was approved, it would go from there to the printer, who would perform all kinds of magic and put it together.[1] A modern designer will typically 'Mac up' a job on screen in a form that is pretty close to the final product, and is certainly close enough to give clients all the information they need to make an assessment about completing the job on an industrial scale. If the designer is smart, the presentation work will also be giving the clients subliminal pointers about where their money has gone and where more of it is about to go and provide a conceptual frame for the job. Call it a proof and you wouldn't be far wrong. If the material qualities of the job are not right, we should not be surprised if the client gets cold feet.

So far, I am conscious of emphasising the mental, internal, idea-driven parts of the job. Well, not now. If your work doesn't wow the client, all the work we have done so far is worthless. If the presentation rough does not explain what happens next in a way that seduces the client, we might not get the chance to make anything happen. This bit is about making, and making things beautifully. This is where you get to shine by seducing the client through your work.

Let's look at some of the ways that different designers will approach presenting different design jobs:

EDITORIAL

Editorial design is a fascinating process in that it is two processes masquerading as one. As such, there are two different ways of presenting editorial presentation roughs. Let's break this down: first, a periodical magazine will not be designed from scratch every issue. No one has the time, and, even if they did, it would produce a visually inconsistent mess that would make it difficult for the reader to know, from page to page and issue to issue, where to look and how to 'read' the design.[2] So, editorial designers design a master design from scratch, which collects page and style templates, and, together with dummy text and images, put together a full working model of the end journal. The whole thing may not have a word of readable text, but, to the client's eye, will give an accurate impression of the end publication.

Because the touch and feel of the papers used in a magazine are so evocative of qualities of class (go out and stroke the paper on *Grazia* and *Vogue*: they are quite distinct; now go and find one of your local free papers and repeat the experiment), sample issues are quite likely to be run out on press. There will be an interesting tug-of-war between the designers on one hand (who want their work to be beautiful) and the publishers (who want economy in everything), and so you might actually end up seeing several copies made up, on different grades of paper, as a way of finding the perfect balance of quality and cost. This will typically happen once every few years.

However, there are also issue-by-issue presentations of the editorial design. Every issue, the editor will want to have as accurate a picture of what she is putting her name to as is possible (don't forget, editors are down the chain of command from publishers and have to answer to them). For this purpose, a combination of digital proofs and printed proofs will probably be used. Digital-proof (almost certainly Adobe Acrobat) files have several huge advantages when one is preparing an issue. If Acrobat files are set up properly, they are essentially as accurate a representation of a printable job as can be produced without actually running the job out. They can simulate all sorts of operation that happen on the press, while having a complete suite of mark-up tools that allow the job to be checked over and commented on by all the people involved in the job. So, it is common practice for designers to ready the issue and pass it out as an Acrobat file for checking and commentary.

ANIMATION

Animators would traditionally produce a simple line-art version of the job, called an animatic, which served the function of allowing all the stakeholders in the job to assess the progress of the animation. Colour was absent, and sound would often be absent too, but the animatic would give enough detail about framing, composition, movement, edits and flow of the animation for a client and its team to judge it, without the costly process of rendering. In the process, mistakes become less costly to correct, and changes and additions can be accomplished (relatively) swiftly, without a fuss.

Nowadays, something similar happens. Rendering has changed as an activity; theoretically, it is done automatically by the rendering process.[3] This sounds easy, until you consider the contributions made by the artists *skinning*[4] the sets and background, the work put in by the lighting artists, the post-production guys, the special effects teams – the list goes on. There are several chains of professionals behind the completion of a digital graphical animation. So, once again, there is a strong financial imperative for us to be sure of what we are doing before we assign all these costly professionals a round of costly and time-consuming jobs.

As a result, where an animatic was once (and may well still need to be) done, you will also find all kinds of preliminary render being used instead: a class of presentation rough that give the kind of useful information that professionals and clients need to see. They are quick renders of the movie (e.g. wire frames) that, as they don't use any form of intensive rendering (e.g. HDRI and ray tracing), can be run out really quickly as a test of the same project. In addition, there will be other teams working on preparing still renders of the animation, checking textures, refining character poses, assessing backgrounds, etc., and checking that the finished piece will look as it is intended to.

The clients will expect to see both of these elements together – the moving and the still – as a presentation of progress. This combination is pretty effective as a method of informing the clients about what they can expect to see at the end of the job. When the go ahead is given, the two elements – animated but low-res and still but high-res – will start to be brought together.

WEB AND INTERACTIVE MEDIA

It would seem to be obvious that a screen-based medium would require a screen-based, interactive presentation rough. Most of the time, this is a logical assumption. Some of the time, the costs of developing the full screen-based site, including the interaction and any custom multimedia are prohibitive. Clients will want to assess the job before committing to the full expenditure. At times like these, there is a range of options to be considered, where some or all of the choices can be combined in whatever combination serves the job best.

Interface designers have a method of testing interfaces called a *paper prototype*, which uses the full-screen design (complete with its look and feel) printed on sheets of paper, one sheet per page. Interface designers use the pages to test whether a user can navigate his or her way to specified targets, before they commit to costly coding and construction. We can use the same method as a way of communicating with clients, users and coders. So, although we won't be recording their interaction, the printed pages can act as a prop to support our explanation of the whole job before it is actually built.

We can do something similar, for on-screen use, using Adobe Acrobat files. Most graphics programs can produce Acrobat files, but some (Quark XPress or Adobe InDesign, for example) can actually build in navigation links that are supported in Acrobat Reader. In this way, you can rough out your site in a way that you can mail to clients, and they can navigate and comment on it with the built-in mark-up tools.

Last, you can build a subset of the whole site, showing some interaction and a meaningful sample of the different page types and layouts and containing some of the multimedia content.

If you are going to be presenting for web and interactive media, it is always very sensible to include a visualisation of the full page structure, a diagram showing the possible links, internal and external. While this serves a design purpose, more importantly, it also serves as an illustration to the client of how much they are likely to end up paying you, as web pages are traditionally costed by the page.

PACKAGING

There was a time when packaging was presented to clients as a package (possibly with some support visualisations). Much packaging is still presented in this way, but some interesting digital tools have emerged. Tools such as EskoArtwork or RealPro

3D-Packager allow designers to take their artwork direct from the program they are creating it in and transfer it to a package, from where they can rotate it, illuminate it and animate it for display to the client. If the client asks for it, they can quickly make changes and update the whole project.

Even if you need to present a client with a material artefact – a maquette or prototype – technology has made the process much smoother. Some packaging design houses have combined printer/routers that print then cut into the materials that a package would be produced in, allowing completely convincing, one-off packages to be made. These can be very convincing arguments for a client.

Once again, it is very useful also to present a client with a visualisation of the product in context: on a shelf, in a home, etc.

ILLUSTRATION AND PHOTOGRAPHY

Illustration and photography presentations are essentially very direct, because the visualisation is generally the actual product. It is uncommon for an illustrator or photographer to have to do a presentation visualisation for a final piece; it simply makes no sense. However, this is not the whole story. It is entirely possible for an illustrator, commissioned to do a whole series of illustrations, to have to complete one or more to a fully rendered state as a proof of concept (and skill and timekeeping). In such cases, it is typical to have one fully completed piece and potentially all the other images (depending on the size of the commission) available in a planned form.[5] In the same way, a photographer who is doing a complex shoot – with lots of lights, models, costume, location, etc. – will need to produce a visualisation that answers all sorts of question raised by the clients about where the money is about to go. For example, David La Chapelle's preparatory drawings (which combine collage and drawn material) are a necessary preparation for his beautiful images.

In the case of illustration and photography, it is probably wisest to take advice from your commissioning client, as, in contrast to other forms of design, they are almost certainly designers and familiar with the process.[6] Ask the commissioner what stages of preparation, rough, client approval and production they want.

VIDEO/MOTION GRAPHICS

These are probably the most expensive types of graphic communication, and so they represent a job that absolutely will not be allowed to proceed to go to full production without very complete presentation roughs. I am told that two days of shooting a commercial is likely to cost £300,000.[7] As such, no client will allow you to 'do it on a wing and a prayer'.[8]

Therefore, in designing for this area, the designer will have to provide answers for a number of stakeholders. The clients will have to be convinced, and drawings, renders and visualisations do this job admirably. However, there are technical colleagues who will have to be briefed by the designer using various kinds of presentation rough: storyboards, renders of scenes to capture lighting, moodboards of materials, technical schematics of props and sets and character designs. The list is formidable, which is why looking at the visualisations of a professional videographer or director is always a humbling experience.

The trick here is to commit entirely to the project. Don't skimp on the preparatory and presentation work: as the task of making the video or motion graphic is so expensive and time consuming, and the process of editing and post-production is so hurried,[9] a designer who mucks up is likely to find that he or she is never offered the chance of trying again. So, consider everything that you can think of and ask fellow professionals (camera crew, lighting artists, etc.) for advice on what they need to see.

The most common question that students ask me about storyboards (for video, motion graphics or animation) is about how many frames need to be drawn for a storyboard: the answer is very simple. Every time something changes on the screen, draw a frame. The important thing to consider is the element of change. If I were storyboarding the dacha scene from Tarkovsky's film *Solaris*, it would make a pretty sparse storyboard.[10] The scene takes several minutes to make a very slow pan round the Kelvin dacha. Nothing much happens. If I were to take the construction-site chase scene from Martin Campbell's *Casino Royale*, I would have a real job on my hands, as so much happens. Cut chases cut, angles change, we move from close-ups to panoramic shots at dizzying speed; all of which would, of course, mean lots of frames.

TYPOGRAPHY

The typographic world has developed its own testing schemes that give meaningful feedback. Novice typographers often see the art in the design of the individual characters, but miss the real craft, which is making the whole mass of glyphs work together.[11] You see, once you have your twenty-six upper case, twenty-six lower case, twenty or thirty punctuation marks and a handful of ligatures, there is enough material to put together a functional type file. None of these characters and glyphs, however, will have anything of how they combine with each other, and, if this isn't handled carefully, you have laboured over making a textual mess that will look ugly on the page and make other typographers cry.

When you load a type file onto your computer, along with the visible components (a set of new type characters), you get a set of rules defining how the characters work together. For example, the *kerning tables* tell each character how it relates to each other character. So, the 'O' in Arial will know how to relate to the 'o' and the 'l' and the 'r'. The number of possible relationships is mind numbing. To cope with this, typographers use two forms of presentation rough to help them make sense of what they are doing and to share their conclusions with peers and colleagues.

There are typographic test phrases that use all the letters in the English alphabet. The oldest is probably:

> The quick brown fox jumps over the lazy dog.

Picturesque as the phrase is, it doesn't actually show many combinations of characters, and so it is difficult to judge their form and colour in combination. Stephen Moyle (as quoted in Karen Cheng's book, *Designing type*) designed the phrase:

> NUN EVADE MADAM MIRROR EMANATE
>
> NINE MINIMUM HANNAH IODINE

The rationale here is that the combination tests some of the more commonly problematic pairings and triplets of type. For example, the 'ROR' triplet is problematic, because you have the variable curve of the left-hand 'R' playing off against the curve of the 'O', which in turn plays against the straight upright of the right-hand 'R' (which handily simulates other upright + 'O' combinations).

There are whole sequences of tests; Cheng's book is an excellent grounding in the subject. For our purposes, however, we should avoid the minutia and move on to setting a beautiful *type specimen* page. These have been the staple of typographic exhibition since typography was conceived. To make a specimen page, you need to have some phrases that demonstrate the ability of the type to function as a body text: an example as a headline; some examples showing different weights; italics and bold versions of the text; possibly the ornament; all composed to show the client that it addresses the context they need served.

CORPORATE IDENTITY

ID projects need to be framed within the context of the company and the field within which the company operates. There are common features in the presentation that make sense, but other features that will be incredibly specific.

Traditionally, you would need to show the individual elements of the logo in isolation, as a set of logos or logotypes or type samples against a white page; you might need to add a black box or two if the element is going to be sent through a fax (does anyone actually fax any more?). These would be printed on high-quality stock to show the clarity, colour and detail of your beautiful design. A more contemporary set of applications might have a screen-based content to demonstrate that your corporate identity is functional on-screen, both on the web and in emails. (So many people neglect email, which is odd, considering it is often the front line of contact with a company, and I don't just mean a logo at the top of the page: we need to see type, colour, images, etc.)

Beyond these obvious 'corporate' uses, we need to consider the ways in which the company's identity faces the public. Does the company have uniformed employees? If it does, you need to visualise an employee wearing the uniform. If the company has vehicles, you need to explain how the ID is applied as colour, logo, type, etc. on the company vehicles. Every contact point between the client company and its customers should be considered (if not actually visualised). Then, the designer must rank these in importance and schedule as many of these as they can usefully do, within the length of time that they have.

GENERAL RULES DERIVED FROM SPECIFIC CASES

The specific cases given above are limited in their reach; every presentation rough will be slightly different. So, here are some general principles that you can use in adapting and modifying your work to show a client:[12]

1   **Remember that each job is individual**. There are no general *rules*, just useful principles.

2   **Choose a medium that promotes your work**. For example, when I give a lecture to my students, I use a piece of free software called Skim. Skim is a .pdf reader that accesses Apple's *Core Image*, *Core Animation* and *Core Video* technologies, which are sophisticated graphics and animation engines built into the Mac OS X. The reason I use it is that Core Animation has some very beautiful transitions built in to it, and any application that uses the Core suite gains access to the transitions. The upshot is that, every time I flick from slide to slide, I get that fantastic rotating cube effect that Apple computers use. Because of the choice of presentation medium, my job looks much lovelier than it otherwise would.

    A poster might be printed, and you might well show the client a print, but you could also matt it on to a video of a poster site to simulate a drive by of the finished piece, which is a stronger sell.

3   **Choose a medium that explains the application of your work**, a medium that is not just sympathetic, but actively supportive of the job. If the work is better shown off on T-shirts by models, then do it. If you need to show it on a smartphone, then show it on a smartphone, or at least mock up an animation of the correct scale and resolution. Clients are not stupid; if they see something that makes them doubt the viability of the job, they will pounce on it.

This will also include different versions of the job for different stakeholders in the job. While the client will want to see the finished piece, you might well supply versions that carry extra details about the typography, layout, timings, materials, etc., for the production technicians. Be considerate and don't make the stakeholders in a job work for a living: that's your job.

4   **Don't just show one thing – use support materials**. Demonstrate the application of your job in as many ways as you can. For example, a classic presentation of a logo design would have different *colourways* of the logo presented on the sheet for the client, and perhaps some indications of scale. It is so much better if, in addition, you can show the logo photoshopped on to a client vehicle, give them a mock-up of the company uniform in the new colour with the new logo sewn on, show them the logo on a product pack, etc. I'm sure that you get the idea. Make it easy for the client to love your work.

5   **Don't introduce confusion into your presentation roughs**. Never, ever, present your work in a way that is more spectacular than the work itself: the work will look disappointing by comparison. Never present your work in a way that distracts from the work. Contrast this with point 2: my use of Skim supports the work. It frames it without distracting from it. If I presented my lectures in a clown costume, the costume would become the star and distract from the lecture. Remember that the human brain, fantastic as it is, has limited processing power and tends to wander.

6   **If possible, give the client the real thing to hold**. If that isn't possible, give them the best mock-up you can; failing that, give them a really good simulation. Never ask the client to imagine or take a job on faith (they can't).

People, clients included, put up barriers to the world because, on some level, they know that they can be seduced by ideas, stories and physical phenomena. We're just built that way – open to the world and as curious as a troop of monkeys. Salesmen use this insight to their advantage all the time: 'Just feel the cloth sir', they say, 'Take it to the window and look how it sparkles in the sun.' Well, we can play this game too. By giving a client something to hold in the hand, as long as it is lovely, we are giving them a chance to make a personal, and subconscious, connection with the job.

But, if possible, make it robust. Whatever method you use to display your work, make sure that it is strong enough for a decent level of handling. There is nothing quite so embarrassing as your work falling to bits in front of a client. So, if your job is too fragile to show in substance, take a series of photos. Once again, a fragile piece of work will impute subconscious connotations of weakness to the job itself.

7   **Bring backup**. Be prepared for a client who wants to see more or ask questions that go deeper. For example, if you are designing the look and feel of a website, it would be sensible to include material explaining the structure of the site, some examples of other sites in the sector (to show

that your work is better) and some samples of your work on an optical medium that you can leave with the client. This is in addition to the material directly supporting the job (point 4); this is an opportunity for the client to get to know your take on the job better.

It helps to think of a presentation rough as being a metadesign. The prefix 'meta' means 'beyond' or something at a higher level. Here, we are talking about a design above the design. The design we have created to solve the problem is here framed within a higher level of design, which provides a client (or your tutor) with a way of understanding how clever you have been and how effectively you have solved the problem.

I commonly advise students to produce secondary designs that frame their work for other tutors (before assessment). This metadesign work will obviously include thumbnails and development work (not that clients will need to see this, but your lecturers will, because they are, in part, assessing your development processes), but should also be presented through material processes that create a 'wow factor' because they enhance and frame the design, and with supporting material giving depth to the context, allowing the client to dig deeper in a rewarding way, giving them an enhanced sense of ownership and expertise about the job.

Once again, this metadesign is, in reality, just being a graphic communicator, by which I mean, considering the clients and their cultural framework, and then designing for them.

NOTES

1   The last time I did this, I gave the printer a camera-ready background with images attached, and a marked-up sheet of type that was specified on a *type-fitting table* to fit as 10-point Times in the space I had allowed. The printer laughed and took me off to see the Mac in the back room.
2   See Beatrice Warde's essay, *The crystal goblet* in Chapter 2 for more on this subject.
3   It's not; it still requires an expert tweaking it.
4   Skinning is the application of *texture maps* (graphics files that simulate textures in digital models). Each is combined with the (complex) geometry to make a model look right. It is one of those theoretically automatic but actually highly skilled jobs that abound in animation.
5   Note: if the job gets cancelled at this stage, it is customary for the illustrator to get some of the commission for the time they have put in. This is generally 30 per cent of the full fee.
6   Which might be the case in other fields, but is not always the case, with more design companies and groups being small companies. Now more than ever designers often deal directly with the client.

7   Thank you, Johnny.

8   If for no other reason than the contract may well make you liable for the costs of the job if it fails to materialise.

9   It will invariably be done on rented facilities, which tend to be booked out to make the maximum money. If you overrun, you will be surcharged (or thrown out), because other professionals will be waiting.

10 A dacha is a Russian country-cottage home.

11 I have a, mostly finished, typeface on my computer where it has sat for the five years. It's called *Aphid* and, while it has a complete character set and looks lovely on-screen, it is useless for real uses, because I have never had the time to fix the kerning and side-bearings to the point where it is finished.

12 Remember: no hard and fast rules. A good designer treats every job as different; we judge each situation and respond appropriately.

ROUGHING/DEVELOPING IDEAS

Johnny Hardstaff

Increasingly, I am approached (as a director/designer) not just to realise a script or idea (as was the custom in advertising) but largely now to initiate the core idea, develop it and then execute and deliver the finished article. This is where the graphic designer comes into his/her own in contemporary moving image, and, given that almost every image moves in this digital age, moving image is increasingly where we will all be working.

The Philips Parallel Lines 21:9 Cinema Project offered a loose conceptual framework (five lines of dialogue to be interpreted by filmmakers in any way they chose) within which I developed the idea of *DarkRoom*. For the film to be commissioned, it had to reference 'cinema' (in this case *Rear Window* and *Blade Runner*) in a way that society would understand and find appealing, and then become its own unique entity.

I'm most comfortable using commercial opportunities for self-expression (self-expression has forcibly carved itself a chasm in graphic design of late), and this project provided me with exactly that opportunity. So, I simply took elements from my sketchbooks, fragments of my ideas that I have liked and wanted to explore, things that I have seen in Hong Kong and Japan, things that I have done, childhood obsessions, my exhibitionist swinging neighbours, and carefully fused them together to construct a story that, though referential, would also hopefully be in some way original. Of course, I had to test this idea to a great extent, tweaking and fine-tuning until it became what you see on the screen. I storyboarded over and over. I made animatics. I agonised over elements of it, not least its look and atmosphere, and then I drew it all again and again.

Most importantly, I constantly tested the logic of the story and the strength of the idea itself. A bad idea can never be made good. A lame idea can never be made strong enough. I'm a real believer in 'gut feeling'. If something feels instinctively promising and exciting, only then is it worth pursuing.

I never accept commissions that I am not excited by. If I'm not itching to have a project on my showreel, then I won't do it. And it is exactly that which informed my developmental process, and always does. A project must please my own peculiar tastes and standards, and exceed my expectations for it, and the responsibility for this rests solely with me. Every decision we make throughout the process of realising a project is vital, and

C@SE STUDY

C@SE STUDY

so, to avoid tangents and disasters, I constantly measure the idea against my aspirations for it.

In short, when developing a project, I look to create a masterpiece that, were it to go nightclubbing on its own, would pull and sheepishly come home some two days later minus its shoes. In truth, I never quite get there (at least, I always tell myself that I have not), which is what drives me through the protracted developmental process of the next project ad infinitum. In truth, it's the process and the anticipation that I love.

I am my own harshest critic, but, interestingly, when developing the film in my sketchbook, I knew almost immediately that I would rather like *DarkRoom*, if only because it worked so well on paper.

If I was afforded only one opportunity to irresponsibly impart some advice to a student, I would say this:

Attention to detail is everything. Test your ideas on people you don't know, as your friends and family will lie. Constantly aspire to individuality. Work furiously hard. Work your way, not in the way expected of you. Don't replicate, initiate. Making something that doesn't thrill you will always result in a disaster, so, above all, only ever make the work that you want to make. You have to utterly love doing it.

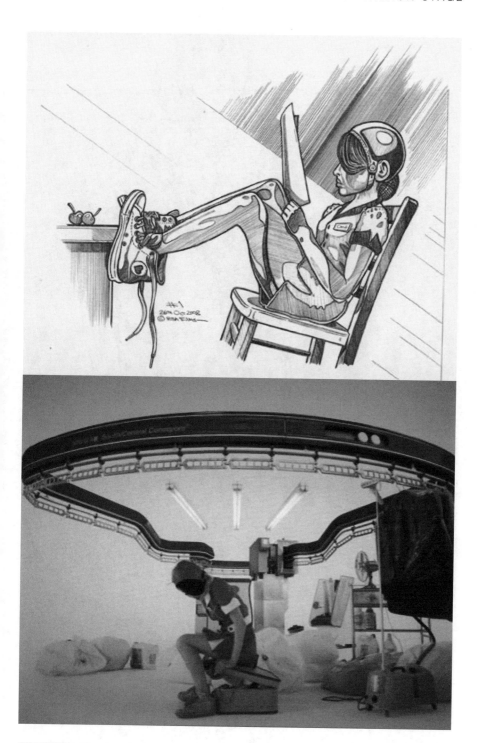

FIGURE 9.1
Hardstaff was commissioned by MTV to direct and design the 60-second advert
'Cherry Girl'

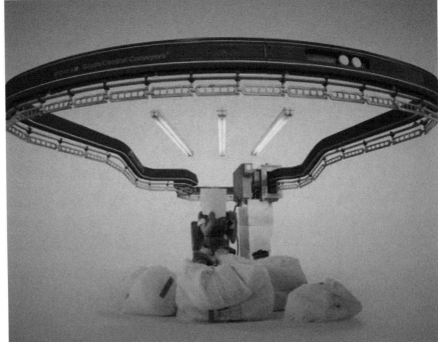

FIGURE 9.2
Cherry Girl was part of MTV Switch, the channel's climate change initiative in 2009

FIGURE 9.3
Cherry Girl

CHAPTER 10

Presenting to the client

WHY IS THERE A CHAPTER ABOUT PRESENTATION?

Presenting to your class and your lecturers is one thing; presenting to a client is a completely different emotional roller coaster. If you get nervous and make a mess of a presentation in class, your cohort might giggle a bit (hopefully not, but they might), and then they'll tell you where it all went wrong: you've lost nothing. Essentially, you know that you'll be presenting to people with whom you share a common life experience, and that substantially eases the strain.

A client is a different proposition. Presenting to a real live client quickly becomes a more emotionally charged situation for even the coolest student; the clients have ownership of things designers want and can only get by making the right impression. While money is the most obvious of these things, and is often the assumed reason for designers making presentations, secondary considerations such as access to work and the opportunity to get other more exciting jobs in the future are often more important. Implicitly, clients also offer us, through the jobs they have to give, a kind of social purpose that all designers crave: a designer without a job to work on is a sad kind of creature.

The pressure is on, because presentations call for a set of skills and attitudes that are not always the same ones that naturally make for excellent designers. A group of people who are self-selected for imagination and good hand skills are not necessarily the right people to shine in front of a crowd. Presentations make designers stand up and perform, and, in this chapter, we'll take a brief look at some of the things we should consider in presenting to clients.

WHAT WILL HAPPEN IN A CLIENT PRESENTATION?

In theory, presenting to clients is about making a considered case to the client about why your design solution is the best one available. In reality, it is often something of a popularity contest. Clients and designers sometimes just click, and, in clicking, the client may select a job on the basis of personal preference, gut instinct about the person if you like, and not according to the quality of the idea at all. The client often buys into the person, not the work.[1]

Take the theory at face value: that a presentation is an opportunity for a designer to give context and verbal and conceptual support to the work he or she intends to produce in response to the client's expressed needs; it would be lovely if this played out in the real world. The reality is somewhat more nuanced.

Real-world presentations are a kind of cross between a graphics job and date. The graphics-job part comes from making an informed design assessment of the cultural framework, the world-view if you like, of the client. This is a design problem and needs to be treated as such, with research and planning. In the same way that we research the background to the job and design accordingly, with a presentation we find out what we can about the client (possibly also the client's client and the end-user) and demonstrate to them that our work represents the most intelligent, appropriate and meaningful way of addressing their needs.

The date bit comes from showing clients that both they and the designer have aligned values, that, in the designer's person, they represent the kind of individual that the client wants to spend time with. Design is a very personal affair. This alignment calls for an assessment of what clients are looking for in a design partner, and, although it might seem superficial, this might mean turning up in the right clothes, arriving by the right means, dropping the right names, in fact, acting like someone on a date; in short: carefully constructing the right persona.

WHAT WOULD YOU BE EXPECTED TO DO IN A PRESENTATION?

Not make the client feel stupid by speaking down to them would be a great place to start. That would seem to be an obvious sort of thing to say, but you would be surprised. Flattery is too crude a term to use for the task of presenting, but, in honesty, it captures something of the nature of the operation a designer undertakes. Flattery is a communications task: for it to work, the flatterer has to have a functional understanding of the person being flattered. In much the same way, a designer needs to know the client to be able properly to pitch to the client.

We have to explain ourselves and our work favourably, in a way that doesn't leave our clients feeling unclear and out of their depth,[2] but that subtly suggests that agreeing to your design solution represents the smart choice, and God forbid that our work has uncovered a weakness in the clients' understanding of the problem.

Bear in mind that a designer will generally be speaking for between twenty minutes and three-quarters of an hour when presenting work to a client. This time represents a small window of opportunity in which the designer has to make his or her case. This, in turn, means having to structure his or her thoughts in a way that makes best use of the time to explain this structure to the client, leaving no possible doubt in the client's mind that this design solution is the only possible solution.

In practical terms, the designer has to redefine the client's problem so that the designer's solution becomes the only logical way forward in the client's mind.[3] The designer will not simply be sticking work up on a wall and letting the client gasp in wonder at his or her manifest genius: for a start, they cannot work on the assumption that there will be a wall handy. What the designer will be doing is using any appropriate means to make their point as clearly as they can to the specific audience. This might involve paper-based presentations, models and maquettes, or something entirely digital.[4]

The designer presenting will be expected to answer the client's questions, to put their mind at ease. They will help the client decide on the means of manifesting the work and secure funds for this production. They will be confirming who owns the end work and making sure that they will be paid in a timely manner.

HOW SHOULD WE DRESS?

There are no simple rules to give here, except that our clothes should be sensitive to the clients' culture and not challenge their preconceptions. This might manifest itself as a sober business suit or suit dress – I certainly had one for corporate clients – but not necessarily. A suit really won't cut it for a music industry client and would look strange in most London design studios. Your task is to do some research about the company and, from this, make an educated guess about what would look right on the day.[5] Remember that, although you are a designer, when inside the presentation you are an actor and salesman, and your clothes are props that help you play the right role.

Make sure that your clothes are clean and don't have obvious holes; make sure that they support the role you are playing on the day. Don't wear clothes that contradict the role and don't wear clothing that distracts the client from the work. This could be read as dressing in a dull manner, but that's not the case at all. A smart designer might well dress in an outwardly weird way that supports the work and presentation, perhaps echoing themes in the work or in the client's public presentation. Advertising giants Weiden + Kennedy once made a presentation at D&AD dressed as clowns.[6] To be honest, this seemed gimmicky and pointless at first glance, only later making sense when we realised that the costumes expressed W+K's belief that the company represents the fun and crazy side of the global advertising industry (in opposition to the dull and sensible). They were manifesting this corporate belief in a way that supported the rest of their presentation.

WHAT SHOULD WE PREPARE?

I've done a lot of presentations in my career and, although I hardly ever use notes any more, I still like the reassurance of having a set to hand. Most people are not at all comfortable presenting to an unfamiliar audience, and this discomfort shows through in their presentation. Having a prop they can lean on when it all goes wrong is a massive help. If you start to stumble, go for the notes.

In your notes, you should use a bit of good graphic design craft to structure the note text with an 'at-a-glance' hierarchy. Break the notes down as: things to say, things to show, things to do and things to know. This structured text can be printed on cards or sheets of paper, the trick being to discard the notes as and when you've finished with them. It helps to keep count and give the audience a clue how far into the talk you are.

- **Things to say**: This is self-explanatory. These are the topics that will accompany the different parts (slides, hand-outs, etc.) of your presentation. Try to not just read them out; this is boring to watch.

- **Things to show**: This is a visual or textual note of the material you will be displaying to the viewers. Place this material close to the 'things to say', giving you a textual and visual reference for what to say when. For example, because I tend to leap ahead when I present, I like to put the 'things to show' at the top of a paragraph of 'things to say', which provides a nice visual punctuation that prevents me accidentally jumping to another topic before I've finished the one I'm on.

- **Things to do**: This is a set of notes that tell you what physical attitude you should be adopting as you speak. I have seen some ferociously dull presentations in my time, with the presenter standing dead still and speaking to the clients. This is a classic way to kill a presentation and no way of convincing them of the brilliance of your job. So, put information in your notes telling you if you need to be handing out a sample or making a joke at a specific stage of the presentation.

- **Things to know**: This is a little piece of stage magic that can work wonders, making you look more expert than you are. All of these four 'things' will be informed by an understanding of the clients and their organisation (research that you should have on hand from the design process). So, while there will be core issues around the presentation that will be addressed by the 'things to say', there may also be peripheral issues that come up: facts and figures, opinions and history. If you have these facts at your fingertips (or in your notes), you can appear spookily well informed about the important things in the clients' world. For instance, if you suspect that a client might reasonably ask for the figures for the number of journeys made daily on the London Underground, then have that material in your notes.

If you need a ritual (a lucky charm in your pocket, a breath mint to put your mind at ease), that's fine. Do anything that you reasonably believe will put you at your ease as you present. Drinking alcohol before a presentation is an exception. Drinking does not help. It's bad in presenting terms for a couple of reasons. First, you need to be sharp when you present, and alcohol dulls your wits. Second, alcohol is a diuretic (it will make you need to visit the bathroom), which is not helpful when standing up in front of clients for any time.

If possible, have an alternative solution to the job in your bag, not as fully worked up as the main piece, just in case.

Sort your work into things the client must see and things it would be nice for the client to see. The 'must see' things are the mandatory elements of the job: those things the client has asked you to do. The 'nice to see' elements are extras that might make the job more compelling, if there is time, for example development materials that give context and depth to the job.

Last, arrive early. Travelling is one of the most unpredictable parts of modern life. Give yourself masses of time for things to go wrong. If you arrive early, find the place where you have to be, make sure you know where your final destination is, and then kill some time in a cafe.

WHAT SHOULD WE BRING?

The material you bring breaks down into two parts; things you show the client and things you leave with the client. They are not the same. As discussed below, not all clients are uniformly honest (the majority are, but there are always exceptions). Where we will be showing the client high-resolution, most expensively printed and lovingly rendered motion graphics, what we leave behind will be low-resolution, watermarked prints and nicely rendered (but screen-resolution) stills. We should never leave work behind that is of such a high quality that the client could possibly cut us out of the job, taking our work straight to the production house. Unfortunately, there are always some rather naughty clients who want quality design without having to pay the price.

What do we show the client?

A smart designer shows the client the very best, most persuasive work that they can. The actual material form this presentation takes will vary according to the job, with the nature of the job defining what we can bring to the presentation, what we can expect to be able to access and, finally, what will have the best chance of communicating our intentions to the client. I'll use a website as an example.

In presentation terms, a website is probably best displayed as a website, this much is clear; reality is generally a pretty convincing argument. However, presenting a sample site to clients raises a host of secondary problems. For a start, clients are not normally well informed about the technical nature of the jobs we do. They won't understand that the 'look and feel' of a site (the graphics bit of the job) is completely separate from the functionality of the job (the coder's and developers' contributions) and are likely to be disturbed by a site in which the links, multimedia and server-side functionality aren't working. In this case, the designer doing the presentation would have to explain to the listening audience that some of the material will be missing and that it will be developed at a later stage. Putting up an apparently 'broken' site won't get the message across.

Second, and more prosaically, we need to consider how we get our site into the client's hands. An ideal solution would be giving them all an iPad preloaded with the site (wouldn't that be lovely?). But putting my designer fantasy to one side, who on earth has a bundle of iPads lying around waiting to be used? And even if they were available, dragging them into a presentation would be a task in itself.

Working from online material is no better. If a designer is showing a site that she has left online, can she be sure that web access is available? I've seen good designers trying to present online media they couldn't access. If a designer brings a copy of their work in on optical media (DVD or CD-ROM), will the client have a player capable of playing the right format? If a designer has a USB pen drive, can they reach the socket to plug it in? Will the client even have the right software to work the site? Perhaps the designer should bring their own laptop? If so, will they be able to plug in the video and drive the right video device?[7] My advice is to phone up beforehand and ask what kit they have to display on, and then bring along a couple of backups just in case. From this example, we can see that there is no substitute for keeping in touch with the client and applying a bit of common sense in preparing for your presentation.

Show your work to its best advantage, and, if that means spending a bit of cash, then spend the cash: get good-quality prints on good-quality media (not necessarily high-end photo paper from an inkjet printer, which has become a stereotypical mark of a lazy designer); show something that has seductive material qualities, even if it costs a bit more. The old proverb 'spoiling a ship for a ha'porth of tar' applies here.

If your product is a drawing or other image-based material, then work to a scale that flatters it; in the old days, illustrators would work to twice the scale the job would be printed at, with the work being reduced down later for production, a practice that hides all sorts of weaknesses.

A designer working on-screen should produce the best quality renders that they can produce in the time they have, and, if that means that they don't have time to render the entire piece, then they should simply do enough full-size renders to explain what the work will look like, leaving the rest as a low-level *animatic* or animation that shows the connecting motion and flow of the whole piece.

If your work is 2D, then mount it on to sets of boards. Boards allow the work to be handled by the clients and propped up on all kinds of available surface. The board also protects the work from handling damage. Do try to avoid mounting on to weird colours and surfaces of board, unless there is an excellent reason for doing it. Mirrored hologram board is lovely – pre-schoolers love it – but mounting work on it raises all sorts of questions that are distractions from the work. Unless you have a strong reason to do otherwise, mount on black or white. Similar considerations apply to screen-based work. Think very carefully about the way you introduce your work: effects should only be applied if they make the work stronger.

What do we leave the client?

We are likely to need to leave the client a copy of the work, something for them to assess and discuss with other stakeholders in the project. A smart designer will never leave work that can be taken to production. This means that, although we will have produced excellent-quality prints and renders, and shown them to the client, what we actually let out of our sight will be sub-production-quality material. For example, we might place the work on an optical media disk with the work formatted as a .pdf, with editing disabled. This is easy enough to do from most .pdf distillers (see Chapter 12), where you can disable the ability to print/cut/paste/copy, etc. A file formatted in this way enables the client to examine and comment on the piece, without being able to cut you out of the process. If you're feeling really paranoid, set the .pdf distiller to down-sample the images to screen resolution (which will make them unsuitable for commercial print).[8]

For interaction work, save samples of the work as publishing files (Flash .swf, for example) rather than authoring files (Flash .fla or .xlf), if possible lock them from editing, and include some sort of watermarking (carrying your contact details and a copyright notice) for the screens. This should increase the effort it takes to steal a designer's work to the point where it becomes easier and cheaper to pay them than cheat them.

For other screen-based work (e.g. video and animation), simply save the files in a lossy file format such as MPEG-4, at a lower screen size (e.g. 768 x 576 SD, as opposed to 1080 HD) and at a lowered frame rate (e.g. less than 24 fps). This will give the client a perfectly acceptable video to view and make decisions about; it simply won't be good enough to work from.

We must leave a CV with the client. This might seem superfluous, considering we're already in the running for the job, but it never hurts to leave contact and other details with the client, to remind them why you are worth dealing with. For the same reason, it is also advisable to leave some older (and published) work samples; hopefully they will show your breadth as a designer and encourage them to use you on different projects.

MAKING AN ENTRANCE

Your entrance to the presentation should be an example of positivity. Don't skulk in the doorway, don't hide in a corner – this is likely to be read as shiftiness. Walk into the presentation with all the confidence you can muster, identify any people you know, nod, smile and wave at them. Even if you are faking like mad, try and look like you belong. If you don't know anyone in the room (it can happen), smile and meet people's eyes (don't fixate on a single individual, that might come across as creepy).

Take the initiative by asking questions that establish your role, such as, 'Where would you like me to set up?' or 'Do you have a socket for my laptop?'. The questions are largely unimportant in themselves; what is important is that you are seen as active and eager to get on with the presentation.

Set up your presentation, take a moment to make it look its best, then turn and ask the room if you can begin.

WHAT SHOULD WE KNOW?

By this stage, and with some designer research behind them, a designer should be a mini-expert on the job and the peculiarities of the field. As I noted above, it might be a good idea to formalise this knowledge in notes, but a designer should be able to engage with the clients, if not on equal terms, at the very least in an informed way.

Specifically, the designer should be capable of explaining why the approach they have taken is a valid approach. This explanation could take many forms, but, if the designer finds that they couldn't sum up their rationale in a single sentence, then they should consider writing the rationale down. This may seem to be a fatuous statement, asking a designer to sum up a complex chain of design decisions in a sentence, but we're only considering a rationale, not the way that the rationale is satisfied.

You see, as designers work through the development process, they make a stack of considered choices, each one defining an element of the job, and each one a conversation worthy in its own right, but only if you are talking to another designer. For the clients, this designerly detail may well come across as gibberish. This is why a designer might find it worthwhile to consider how to reframe their approach in a way that the client will understand.

At this stage, the designer should also be able to answer some or all of the following questions:

- How will it be made?
- How much will it cost per unit or per run?
- Who could make it?
- When can it be made?
- When can it be deployed?

These are all completely reasonable questions that will come naturally to the business mind, and they will need answering. More difficult issues may arise around the issue of ownership of the design and are addressed in Chapter 16.

WHAT SHOULD WE SAY?

From the start, let the clients know that you're happy to be there and excited about the job, even if you're not. As a rule, try and be positive; even if you have difficult news for them, don't start on a low note.

Don't rush to the climax of the presentation; let it emerge in its own time. Try and arrange your presentation in a series of small peaks that lead up to the really good stuff. This is fairly standard salesmanship. You show the crowd something fun and get them wound up about it, then you pull something even juicier out of the bag and rouse the crowd to a fever about that, and so on, until you get to the actual object of the presentation. In this way, you should be able to encourage a level of engagement with the watching clients that will get them emotionally committed to your job. We want them committed to the job.

That said, don't over-promise what the job can do; if anything, promise less than you believe the job can achieve and let the clients be pleasantly surprised.

Have a prepared statement (see above), but don't try and stick relentlessly to your agenda if the clients have questions and observations. Your research should have prepared you for a conversation that roams a little.

HOW SHOULD WE ACT?

I have a colleague, an academic of many years' experience, who swears that she learned everything she knows about presenting from a youth spent doing amateur dramatics. If you think about it, this makes perfect sense: presenting is a kind of stagecraft. As such, the advice to 'just be yourself' is possibly the worst advice a presenter can ever be given. Many people who are brilliant and charming presenters are in truth grumpy, rude, flippant, nervous, mean-spirited and sarcastic; however, when presenting, they've learned to fake it in a way that allows them to get their message across. This is not something that happens naturally; it's something that has to be worked on and practised hard. This is one of the reasons design lecturers like to get students talking about their work; talking in public is a skill that has to be practised if it is to look natural.

These are some basic bits of advice:

- **Give a *thin briefing*,** by which I mean, don't give too much unnecessary detail. Have the information to hand if the client asks, but don't volunteer it. Let the client lead. If they want to unpack extra issues, that's fine.

- **Don't say 'um' or 'er'**. Technically known as 'placeholder words', we all use them as a way of buying some time while we think about what we say next. Despite the fact that using placeholders is pretty much universal, it is still often read as hesitation or lack of confidence. The advice is to take a moment of silence and think fast; the silence will be read more positively than the placeholder will.

- **Never, ever, bad-mouth yourself or your work!** Boasting is bad, a fact that is drummed into us from early childhood, but we never seem to be taught the other half of the equation, which is: don't underplay our gifts, don't speak badly of ourselves. With every group of design students I teach, I see smart, decent people who, when asked to speak about their work, start with, 'I'm not very good at . . .' Don't do it! Clients are very rarely design-literate. If you say bad things about yourself or your work, they will believe it. Your work will grow smaller and duller in their mind as you talk. So don't boast, but don't show false modesty either.

- **Maintain eye contact**, not with a specific watcher, but move your gaze from person to person as you speak, visually including all the watchers in a series of successive dialogues.

- **Smile as you speak** (unless you are delivering bad news) and, if you can, make the watchers chuckle a bit. Laughter is a relief of emotional tension and can also act as a bonding mechanism for a group.

- **Try not to rush your speech**. It will only cause your audience to ask you to repeat things that they missed in the rush. Pace yourself and pause if you need to.

- **Don't talk in a monotone**. If the watchers look like they are losing interest, don't raise your volume, drop it and speak quietly. This has the effect of forcing the watchers to pay attention. Listening to quiet speech takes more brainpower than listening to loud speech, requiring more effort to discriminate your speech against background noise.

- **Don't stand still**. It's boring to watch. Move around occasionally, point out important features of your work as they come up, think about 'working the room' by stopping and talking to individual watchers. Watch a good stand-up comedian working a crowd: they never stop moving, and this dynamism is read as possessing energy. What you are doing is sending the object of focus (you) across the visual field, causing the viewer to have to pay attention to keep up.

- **Self-disclosure**. Self-disclosure is a psychological term describing the act of telling others about oneself. It is one of the building blocks for forming an intimate relationship with someone. For our purposes, a small disclosure of an appropriate fact about ourselves can really help establish our credentials as someone with interests aligned with the client's.

WHAT SHOULD WE ASK THE CLIENT?

There are various bits of information we need from the clients before we finish the presentation.

- First, ask the clients if they are happy with the overall tone of the work. Note that we're not asking if they like the job, a question that forces them into an all or nothing position about the work we've done, leading to a decision that might not go our way. We are asking them to commit to the job in a series of small steps, steps that allow them to express specific dissatisfaction with elements of the job without rejecting the whole.

- If they have reservations about the work, ask them to explain and specify those bits they have concerns about; this mentally isolates troublesome parts of the job from the whole job. The explanation ties the negatives down to a series of elements that can be addressed and corrected in turn by the designer. This keeps the job viable and allows work to continue. Take any reservations the clients have extremely seriously; listen to the client and fix the problem.

- Ask the clients about the parts of the job they particularly like; this puts the clients in the position where they are are mentally committed to the whole job through the proxy of the parts they like. It is entirely possible for a client to like a job and dislike specific parts of it. We can always fix the problematic parts later if, and only if, the client is willing for the bulk of the job to go ahead.

- Now we need a specific permission involving the client agreeing the budget for the production. In itself, this can be a tricky proposition. A client might love the idea of the job but baulk at spending a small fortune on the material that the designer feels is essential for the job to work. Many clients will feel that graphics has the characteristics of a kind of cultural wallpaper that can be spread over cracks in their corporate image, or a shopping centre or a failing brand; as such, they may believe that the material isn't as important as the imagery and type applied. Be prepared carefully to explain why the material choices are important for the functioning of the job and the benefits they will bring.

- Establish who will produce the work, and whether this choice of production is your job or whether it has to go through some sort of competitive bidding process supervised by the client organisation. Many government institutions are legally obliged to undergo a bidding process; if this is so, be prepared to suggest the names of production houses that can manage the job.

- Establish a firm production schedule that you can both agree on for the work actually to be produced and delivered.

- Although the schedule of payments to the designer should have been fixed at the pitching stage, it is always worth bringing up the question of when you can expect to receive any remaining payments. At this stage, if you haven't received payments that you have been promised, make it clear that the job cannot go on until the client has met their obligation to you, the designer.

WHAT SHOULD WE DO IF THE CLIENT HATES THE JOB?

If the client really hates the job, make efforts quickly to establish if their negative feelings are so strong that the job is essentially dead. If you find that it is, then you have to disengage yourself from the approach you've been presenting so far as fast as you possibly can. This is where the suggestion of having a nicely rendered alternative hidden in your bag might just pay dividends. (I'm not really suggesting that you always work up two plans, just suggesting that, if you're not confident of the reception of your principal plan, it makes sense to spend a little time on a paper-based alternative.) Offer an alternative; see if you can persuade the clients to let you try a different approach.

Ask the clients if there are any parts of the job they like, which bits they can live with, and which bits are so objectionable that they've killed the project. If the clients can identify some positives, you might be able to talk to them about making changes.

If the client has completely taken against the job, then all we can do is bow out gracefully, having made sure that the client understands that they are financially liable for the development work you have done up until this point.

WHAT SHOULD WE DO IF THE CLIENT LOVES THE JOB?

This is a simpler case altogether. Briefly and modestly accept the praise and then capitalise on it. Tell the clients how much you've enjoyed working with them; ask if it is OK to use the job in your promotional material and if you can quote them as expressing pleasure with the outcome. Gently hint that you've enjoyed working with them so much that you'd like to work with them in the future. (This works: a single good job can net you years of happy employment.)

TROUBLESHOOTING! WHAT TO DO IF THE PRESENTATION TAKES A NOSEDIVE

If there are technical problems that are the presenting designer's fault, all you can really do is apologise and offer to deliver the presentation at a time of the client's choosing. Frankly, this should never happen; even if it's a case of the clients crowding around a single laptop, a designer should always have a backup plan.

However, disasters do sometimes happen: client equipment can malfunction; websites can crash; cars can break down, stranding the designer in the wrong part of town. Be gracious and keep in touch with the clients.

Some presentations are beyond saving from the beginning, but these are not generally about the designer at all. It is extremely rare for a design to get this far without the designer getting some hint of trouble and being able to suggest a remedy. More typical is the presentation that runs foul of local organisational politics. Projects can get stalled for years because of committees and factions within the client organisation insisting that their individual needs are satisfied before the job can go ahead.[9]

A variation on this theme is the inter-organisational vendetta that is played out via external contractors (in this case, the designer). If a designer feels that individuals in the watching audience are attempting to use the presentation to attack other watchers, they should not respond in any way at all. They should avoid joining in the sniping, not take up any offered opening for criticism and refuse to participate in the nasty little game. Don't play with politics you don't understand.

CLIENT HONESTY AND BEHAVIOUR

Now, this should be a non-starter of an issue. The stock in trade of the designer is their intellectual property (IP), and clients should understand this. Unfortunately, some clients seem to be confused about this relationship, and, where the client would never consider driving into a petrol station and leaving without paying (that would clearly be theft), they might well consider allowing a designer to solve a problem for them and not paying up. Even worse, they may still use the designer's IP at a later date, without permission. It has happened to me at least once in my career. Some clients may even attempt to involve you in deliberately stealing another designer's intellectual property, producing 'looky likey' copies of someone else's work.

As far as the law is concerned, this is a crime. But, where petrol stations are protected by cameras that provide evidence of the crime, it can be incredibly difficult to prove wrongdoing in the case of intellectual theft. Clients may deny that they ever worked with you; they may claim that the work was weak, and what they eventually used is a wholly redesigned solution to the same design problem; they may claim that they arrived at the solution independently; most commonly, they will simply go silent and not respond at all (trusting that the designer will give up before they do). However, there are a few things that you can do to make this intellectual theft a little less likely.

1   If you have concerns about a job, post a hard copy of your designs to yourself by special or registered delivery and (this is very important) don't open the letter when it arrives. You now have a dated piece of evidence that can be opened in court, showing when you did the design (as evidenced by a government agency).

2   Keep backups of your correspondence, not just on your home computer though; save copies to remote servers (such as GMail or MobileMe). Once again, these third parties will independently date the receipt of the backup, providing you with date evidence of your communications with the client.

3   Use a third-party service (either email or an FTP service such as YouSendIt) to carry any of your work samples to the client. This is another independent way of dating authorship of your design.

4   Belong to a trade association or union (see Chapter 16, 'Getting paid and more'). They have resources that they might be able to make available to you in fighting a dispute. It's not guaranteed, but most trade bodies will see the value in defending an individual member's interests if, in doing so, they are defending all members' interests.

5   Join a cooperative. By working cooperatively with others, you can mobilise the resources to take legal action (even a humble legal letter can be expensive).

6   Buy some legal insurance. It's an expensive luxury until you need it. Talk to a specialist business insurance broker.

7   Lastly, if you are caught out, and the client refuses to do the right thing, talk privately to other designers you know.[10] Find out from them if they know of any other cases where the client has acted in bad faith. Tell them your concerns about the client's behaviour. The design world is a tight enough network that word will quickly get around, and the client will find it hard to get good design work in the future. This is no real help to you, but will start to cultivate an environment where it is harder to cheat designers.

WHAT SHOULD WE KNOW AT THE END?

At the end of the presentation process, we should know if the job is going ahead; if it is going ahead, we should know who is producing the job; we should be sure that the money to pay for the production has been agreed; we should have an agreed schedule of work; and we should know that we have the support of the clients. Most importantly, we should know that we have achieved a meaningful design solution.

NOTES

1   It is worth noting that, in my experience, clients will often sustain a longstanding working relationship based on a personal preference for working with an individual. If a client can work with a designer they like, and who also does excellent work, they will. If a client has to work with a designer who is difficult but who is talented, they will, but only until the moment they can drop them for a good designer they like working with.

2   Which is where the not talking down to the client comes in.

3   This does not mean lying to the client. But it does mean directing their attention to the values our designs bring to solving the solution.

4   One of the best presentations I ever saw was given by the Catalan Photographer Siqui Sánchez at the University of Zaragoza. Siqui was demonstrating how a photographer can light a scene. He brought some equipment with him, but used the geography of the classroom, which had west-facing windows, through which the sun was slowly setting; he used the cabinets in the room as stands and props, and he even pulled students out of the audience to act as models. It was wonderful, because Siqui used the total environment as his stage.

5   Remember there are no set rules. I once turned up to present at the London offices of a big French bank. My suit was sharp, my shirt was pressed, and my shoes very shiny. Unfortunately for me, it was *dress down Friday*. I looked like a fool when speaking to a boardroom full of people in sweatshirts.

6   I still have a T-shirt from the day. It's blue, with nasty typography that reads 'Crazy'.

7   Considerations such as this are the reason that many designers travel with a bag stuffed full of adaptors and cables, just in case. I always carry a Mac Mini to VGA adaptors, a USB extension cable with about eight different swappable USB plug types, memory sticks, audio jacks, an extra bluetooth adaptor. If I'm presenting, I add my iPod Shuffle (it works on Mac, Windows and Linux as a pen drive), a DVD-ROM with the presentation (in .pdf format for maximum compatibility) and an app on my mobile that allows it to act as a remote for my Mac.

8   I'm sure this seems overblown and crazy. In truth, you wouldn't believe the effort that I've seen some clients put in to avoid paying for design work.

9   I know of at least one website that took two years to meet the client organisation's expectation. I pity the designers involved.

10 The 'private' is important here: if you go public about your concerns (on a blog for example), you may well find yourself accused of libel by the person who has stolen your design. After all, you have just made a public statement that might damage the client's reputation and cause them financial loss. Legally, they have the right to seek redress.

CHAPTER 11

Semantics and graphic languages

Malcolm Barnard

INTRODUCTION

You are quite likely to have encountered the word 'semantics' in a phrase going something like, 'Oh, that's just semantics . . .', where the speaker indicates that some matter is of trifling importance, that hairs are being split or that the real issue is being avoided. If so, you have encountered an idiot, as well as the word 'semantics'. Semantics has to do with meaning and signification and, as meaning and signification are the most important things human beings or graphic designers ever involve themselves with, semantics is neither trifling nor hair-splitting nor issue-avoiding. The word semantics comes to us from an ancient Greek word that meant 'to show' or 'to signify'. The alignment of the visual (in 'show') and the meaningful (in 'signify') is not merely a happy accident; it illustrates the centrality of graphic design to the production and reproduction of meanings in human life.

These thoughts lead us to other thoughts, and they start raising questions: what sort of thing is meaning? Are there different sorts of meaning? Where does meaning come from? Is graphic design a language or a collection of languages? If graphic design is the production and reproduction of meaning, can it also be the challenging and contestation of meaning? The following brief chapter will try to explain how central meaning (semantics, if you must) is to culture and graphic design.

IS GRAPHIC DESIGN A LANGUAGE?

Simply, graphic design is not a language. To call graphic design a language is to make two mistakes. The first is to assume that, even if graphic design were a language, then there would be only one. If graphic design could be a language, then it would be many, many languages. The second is to assume that graphic design is the same kind of thing as English or Spanish. It is not: graphic design does not possess words, grammar or syntax in the ways that natural languages do, and it cannot be translated into any other natural language. The relation between linguistic signs and signifiers is arbitrary, but the relation between graphic signifiers and signifieds is not. To call graphic design a language is to use a metaphor, and the one thing you do not want to do with a metaphor is let it get out of control. To this extent, then, graphic design is not a language, and there are not different graphic languages.

What we have, and what probably misleads people into thinking that graphic design may be, or may be like, a language, are different cultures holding different values and beliefs. Those different cultures are identified as different cultures by the different values and beliefs that they hold. And those different values and beliefs are what produce different meanings within and between different cultures. Meaning and cultural identity are therefore both products of difference: differences between cultures are produced by different values and beliefs held by people and the different meanings that they give to things, including items of graphic design – colours, typefaces and websites for example. The different meanings, like the different identities, are the products of the different values and beliefs the people hold. It may be this series of complex relations that confuses people into thinking that graphic design is a language, because it is the interplay of these differences that produces and reproduces cultural meanings and also allows groups and meanings to be challenged. The following sections will explain in more detail the relations between cultural identity, cultural values and meaning.

WHAT IS MEANING?

Meaning is a product of representation: representation is using one thing to stand for (represent) something else. When you describe a typeface as 'boring', you are using the word 'boring' to stand for, or represent, that typeface: the typeface is now meaningful, if boring. You might now ask where the meaning of boring comes from. The trouble is that any answer you receive will only be another representation. One answer might take the form of other words, other representations, such as 'dull' or 'uninteresting', for example. The trouble is that these words themselves may need explaining, and that can only be done with other words, other representations. Another answer might be to give an example of a boring experience. The trouble is that any experience is only meaningful, and to that extent possible, once you have used something to represent it. Consequently, a good way of defining a culture is to suggest that it is a group of people who all agree on what things can stand for what other things, what sorts of thing count as possible representations for other things. That is to say, cultures are groups of people who agree what meaning things have.

Meaning, therefore, is not a property of objects, events or typefaces, images and layouts. These things are not available to us until we have used ideas and words (representations) to describe them and thereby make them meaningful. Meaning does not naturally occur 'in' or as a part of graphic design. Centre/margin layouts are not naturally 'cheesy' or 'childish' or 'charming': they are, or mean, these things because groups of people decide and agree that they are, or mean, these things. They agree that these representations (words) can be applied to them and be used to describe them. Similarly, meaning is not decided by individual designers or groups of designers. You can try to persuade your tutors that the script typeface you have chosen or created for your young men's aftershave product is hard and urban all you like, but, if the culture thinks it is feminine and gentle, you will not change the meaning. This is tricky, and the role of the individual in the cultural production of meaning is not easy to describe. However, insofar as an individual is a member of a culture, that individual plays a role in the production of meaning, but meaning is not simply the product of individual intention.

Meaning is the product of the relation between a culture's values (the beliefs and ideas its members hold) and objects of experience. Strictly, there is no experience until it has been made meaningful in that relation. Therefore, meaning in graphic design is the product of the relation between a culture's values and graphic design. Insofar as individuals are members of a culture and share that culture's beliefs and values, then the individual's take on the general culture's values is what produces meaning and is what explains how meanings differ between individuals, within cultures as well as between cultures.

There are various elements of graphic design. At the most fundamental level, there are colours, shapes and textures. Those colours, shapes and textures are used to make the elements of the next level: images, typefaces and layouts, for example. And those images, typefaces and layouts go to make up the elements of the next level: advertisements, interpretation panels, websites and corporate identities, for example. Different cultures will give different meanings to those colours, shapes and textures, just as they will give different meanings to layouts and then to advertise- ments and websites. Gunther Kress and Theo van Leeuwen (1996: 186 ff.) analyse and explain many layouts by relating them to the cultural values held by different groups of people. Left/right, top/bottom and centre/margin layouts all mean different things according to which culture is viewing them. For example, left/right layouts indicate the presence of old/new material in those cultures that read from left to right, and centre/margin layouts are used more in Eastern cultures than in Western ones, because of the influence of Confucianism. One of the most famous essays on advertising ever written, 'Rhetoric of the image' by Roland Barthes, analyses and explains in great detail the various levels of meaning in an advertisement for Panzani pasta. Barthes provides the basis for the model of meaning proposed here by linking signifier (image) and signified (meaning) to some very specific cultural values and beliefs (Barthes, 1977). He says that, in order to understand the signified of 'total culinary service', for example, one of the connotational meanings that he identifies in the ad, one must live in, or have experience of, a culture that is familiar with supermarkets. This may sound trivial, but it is not: it is tying meaning and representation to culture and demonstrating that shared values are necessary in order to produce and understand meaning. The next section will explain these matters in more detail.

HOW IS MEANING PRODUCED/REPRODUCED?

Meaning is culturally constructed by individual members of different cultures. Different cultures will have different values, they will hold different beliefs and they may, therefore, give the same elements of graphic design different meanings. This is where meaning comes from, and cultures will be interested in reproducing themselves and their values through the use of graphic design. They will be interested in ensuring their own survival and persistence: this is what is meant by social and cultural reproduction, and graphics has a major role to play here. However, given that it is about the construction and reproduction of cultural identity through the graphic communication of meaning, it is also where challenge and contestation come in. Graphics is also where meanings and the positions of cultural groups holding those meanings can be challenged, and their legitimacy can be contested. This section will consider three examples of the production and reproduction of meaning and three ways in which this production and reproduction produces and reproduces cultural groups.

In Muslim cultures, some shades of green signify Islamic beliefs and values; in some Irish cultures, a shade of green signifies nationalism; and, in other cultures, green indicates a concern for the environment. Among the ideas, beliefs and values held by Muslims are 'paradise' and 'heaven' and 'believers in God'; it hardly needs saying that these beliefs and values are not held by all people, and that holding them is one of the things that makes one a Muslim and differentiates members from people who are members of different cultures. These are the values and beliefs that give meaning to the colour. The colour means something specific within a belief/value system, and it is the relation to the belief/value system that makes the colour mean what it does within that culture. So, green means 'paradise', because paradise in the Muslim belief system is full of greenery, lush vegetation and so on. Green also refers to the believers in God in heaven, who wear green silk, according to the Quran.

Irish nationalism is a different belief/value system, and green accordingly means something different in relation to that different culture. A green flag featuring a harp has been associated with Ireland since the mid seventeenth century; it has been associated with St Francis and is the colour of the shamrock, both closely linked with Ireland. So, it is the relation to the belief in an ancient, united and identifiable Irish nation that generates the meaning of this colour for Irish-nationalist cultures. When environmental groups use the colour green, it means the establishing of a caring and responsible relationship with the environment. The values and beliefs of the environmentalists involve caring for, preserving and using the earth's resources responsibly. The beliefs and values of the group generate the meaning of the colour.

In the European culture of the 1950s, Helvetica was 'functional'; in America in the 1970s it was 'classy'; and in 1980s Britain it was 'trendy' (Mills, 1994, p. 129). These are slightly different kinds or types of example from the ones above. Helvetica is still not naturally meaningful, and it is still not up to individual designers to decide the meaning of the face, but the cultures seem less different, and the values and beliefs in relation to which Helvetica is differently meaningful are slightly less diverse. Europe in the 1950s was rebuilding itself; many countries still had rationing, and the effects of the Second World War were still clear to see. One can imagine that the values (desires, in this case) held by such a culture would involve efficiency, new beginnings and clean starts. Consequently, Helvetica would be seen as functional: with its lack of clutter, absence of serifs and consistent thicks and thins, it is clean, it is efficient and it is modern and forward-looking. In 1970s America, different values prevailed, and Helvetica meant something different. Mills suggests that it was 'classy'. American corporate culture would also have valued efficiency, but it also looked towards Europe, and Italy in particular, as providing something that was different from mainstream American values and design. Consequently, the Helvetica that the Vignellis produced for Knoll, American Airlines and the New York subway in the late 1960s had the meaning of 'classy'. The 1980s in Britain was known as the designer decade, and designers were the heroes of both popular and high culture and fashion. The values of being fashionable (or trendy, as it was often called) and of wearing, drinking and living in 'designer' clothes, 'designer' water and 'designer' furniture were paramount. Consequently, in relation to such a dominant culture, Helvetica would be constructed as 'trendy'. Its meaning is produced by relation to the dominant cultural values.

For those holding conservative values, the meaning of Benetton's 'United Colors' advertising campaigns of the 1980s and 1990s was degeneracy and miscegenation. For liberals, the same graphic designs meant ethnic cooperation and racial harmony. Clearly, if you believe in and value racial and ethnic purity and separation, then you will not be well disposed towards images of members of different racial and ethnic groups kissing and having fun together. The meaning constructed by the relationship between your values and the image will be one of unhealthy miscegenation. However, if you have more liberal beliefs and values, then the meaning those values will construct for the ads is one of optimism and cooperation. In both cases, the values and beliefs that involve racial/ethnic identity and appropriate relations between those identities generate the meaning of the adverts.

These are all examples of meaning being produced in the relationship between cultural values and beliefs and the visual material. We can see that the visual material, the graphic designs, is the same, but the meanings that are produced are different, because the values and beliefs of the cultural groups doing the interpreting are different. The reproduction of meaning is simply the continued production of these meanings by a dominant group. The dominant cultural group is dominant partly because they are its values and its meanings that are being produced. The dominant cultural group ensures its dominant position by continuing to ensure that they are its values and beliefs that are used to generate the meanings of events and phenomena.

HOW MAY MEANING BE CHALLENGED AND CONTESTED?

The positions of dominant cultural groups can be challenged by the meanings that they produce being contested. This is achieved by using alternative values and beliefs to produce alternative meanings, and it is usually an alternative (subordinate) group that is doing the challenging. Another way of saying this would be to say that a challenge is mounted by it being suggested that images, events or phenomena are given different representations from those the dominant group would want to give them.

Capitalism, the environment, US foreign policy and the English royal family are all areas or topics where graphic protest has effectively provided a challenge to dominant economic, political and cultural orders and the meanings they would like to (re)produce. XTC, Hard-Fi and PIL are all bands that have used the graphic design on their CD and record sleeves to challenge and contest the positions of dominant ideas and beliefs and the cultures that hold them. The graphic design for PIL's 1986 CD, cassette and vinyl output consisted simply of the words 'Album' and 'Compact Disc' printed on them. The design for XTC's 1987 *Go 2* took the form of a manifesto, in white typeface on a black ground, in which the nature and function of the graphics usually adorning CD and album covers was thoroughly critiqued and described as a 'con', a trick played on consumers in order to sell product. And Hard-Fi's 2007 *Once upon a time in the west* declared 'No Cover Art' and 'Expensive black and white photo of band. Not available' on the various releases. All are trying to challenge the position of either a dominant economic system (capitalism) or those in control of that dominant system (the record-company owners, for example). And all are trying to contest the dominant positions of that system and those people by providing alternative meanings for their CD and record covers. The cover usually means a sophisticated and visually persuasive marketing tool, but the alternative (anti-capitalist, and anti-consumption, up to a point) values of the bands have subverted it to mean a critique of capitalist values and beliefs.

Micah Ian Wright's graphic interventions into, or remixes of, pro-war posters and recruitment posters provide an example of a related collection of groups being challenged. In 'Oh, don't get up . . .', we are presented with an FBI agent in someone's bedroom, telling a sleepy US citizen that he doesn't need a warrant. The implication and challenge is that the Patriot Act permits the FBI to enter and search one's house or investigate any other private places, including one's library record, if necessary (see below). The beliefs and values of the Bush government and its supporters (that 'homeland security' is threatened, and that genuinely patriotic citizens will not mind a few infringed liberties) are being contested by a group who hold different beliefs and values. This other group, whom Wright is supporting here, would consist of opponents of the Bush government and its friends in the military and oil industries: liberals, pacifists and other left-of-centre groups. Their beliefs and values, that liberties are indeed being infringed on behalf of an illegitimate war that is being fought for private gain, are used to construct the challenge in this remixed poster. In 'Books . . .', Wright is spoofing a First World War poster that encouraged people in England to send their spare books to the front, where bored and distracted soldiers could read them. His point is that the Bush government is not interested in intellectual activities such as reading books, because it believes that books contain all manner of critical and seditious thoughts. Wright and the groups he is supporting believe that Section 215 of the Patriot Act enables the FBI to seize a citizen's library records to see what s/he has been reading. They are using their beliefs and values to change the meaning of the poster and challenge the position of the dominant groups in the United States.

CONCLUSION

Thus, semantics is not 'mere semantics', and graphic design is neither 'a language' nor a single 'semantic system'. Rather, graphic design, and illustration, come to that, is the name for a collection of processes in which cultural power is negotiated through meaning. Semantics is to do with meaning, and meaning is to do with representation, the use of one thing to stand for another thing. In these processes of signification, by means of graphic design and illustration, meanings are produced, reproduced and contested, and cultural identities and positions are similarly produced, reproduced and contested. It is not by accident that cultural studies uses the word 'negotiation' to describe these processes: it means 'no rest', and there is indeed no rest in the production and challenging of meaning.

CHAPTER 12

Doing the job

The designer and director Johnny Hardstaff once made a rather effective advert for Orange Telecom by dribbling paint, very slowly and luxuriously, over various surfaces and filming the whole lot very beautifully.[1] I mention this because there are many ideas inherent in the concept of graphics, and dribbling paint isn't generally one of them: as it stands, the advert was an effective piece of visual communication, without ever relying on traditional graphic design processes. It defied the logic of tradition, but succeeded by understanding the culture it was aimed at.

This is the distinction this chapter aims to make. It's about the creation of effective and beautiful work, but not about its manufacture or broadcast (which is in the next chapter); it's about the moment of your personal input – after the client has said yes, but before it has gone to your partners in production.

PROCESSING YOUR CONCEPT

We have a realised idea (the presentation rough), which the clients have said 'yes' to, the users seem to understand the work, and your production partners seem to think it can be made without blowing a hole in the budget. The final obstacle on the road to production is us: we have to be able to make our idea real.

Many readers will be thinking that, in this case, the chapter could be summed up as, 'Boot up my machine, fire up Photoshop and go for it'. This will *probably* work, if by work you mean the production of yet another identikit piece of graphical fluff, suitable for filling space but not much else.[2]

So, if graphic communication practice isn't, by necessity, about using the otherwise awesome Adobe Creative Studio family, what is it actually about? What guides and principles are there for producing wonderful work? If you want to do work that people will remember, there are a number of things we must consider.

Medium

The man who taught me Photoshop made the (ever so blasphemous) comment that many users of the software called it 'God', because it could 'do anything'. For many tasks, this has some truth. I'm not sure I would go as far as awarding the program spiritual qualities, but the number of things that you can't simulate with a mature graphics application such as Photoshop is quite small. Simply put, if you can conceive of it, you can probably do it on-screen. You can simulate letterpress type on varied stocks, add a suntan on a pasty-faced rock star or recompose *The Birth of Venus* on the Hudson River.

However, just because you can, should you? The famous media commentator Marshal McLuhan commented that, 'The medium is the message' (1964), by which he meant that the designer's choice of the pipeline that feeds us visual culture is in itself full of meaning for the people receiving it. I *can* simulate a piece of letter-press typography in Photoshop (and so can you), but the material qualities of a letterpress document – the way that the paper has been indented by the type, the texture of the paper, the way the inked line breaks within the fibre of the paper – give a quality to the end product that communicates 'handmade' and 'quality' which the simulation won't. Sometimes, this 'authenticity will matter sometimes it won't'. We can see this effect in the direct-mail documents that are sent out with 'fake' handwriting, postmarks, stamps, paper grain, etc., in an attempt to indicate a degree of personal care that is, in fact, completely absent. The end effect is of one big fake.

If you don't believe in the significance of materials, finding the argument about materials unimportant or fanciful, and not buying the way that viewers read meaning into the material qualities of an artefact, just ask yourself why very few of our lecturers wear rubber clothing to work. The thought of an academic taking to the lectern in a rubber one-piece is too comic to be taken seriously. Certain materials are just *wrong* in certain contexts; as we discuss later in the chapter, the semantics of material just don't allow it.

The human eye is very good at recognising the *real* (semantically appropriate) *thing* from the fake (semantically inappropriate) in the world. Culturally, we see the imperfection inherent in handcrafted items and natural materials as a signature of a certain kind of authenticity that carries secondary sets of social meaning.[3] This is only an example: I am not saying that graphics is only real if it is handmade (that would be foolish) or even that it is more real in some way; it is simply the case that every production method comes with its own attached meanings, and we can't escape this truth, so we have to work with it.

This is not even something that is restricted to material processes. Screen-based media carry similar sets of material choices that either strengthen or undermine the concepts we play with. Parker and Stone's TV show *Southpark* has very specific styles that look handmade, anarchic and impromptu (as if the viewer is seeing a piece of bedroom rebellion): the truth is that, although the pilot was shot with paper cut-outs and stop-frame animation, all the rest is the result of carefully planned work, constructed using high-end CGI software (originally *Alias PowerAnimator* and now *Alias Maya*), software normally applied to create photo-realistic 3D animation and graphics. The show's producers have taken an informed and inventive look at achieving the required semantic connection with the audience in a way that allows a fast response to world events, at an acceptable cost.

A good designer should be considering the medium as a distinct set of choices that will add authenticity and value to the job.

What workflow?

Thinking about graphic-communication workflows should start with an understanding of the end aims of the job and work backwards from that point. Graphic designers and communicators, by this point in the game, should have considered how the message will be encountered by the end-user. Is it through a poster or mobile phone, a package or a computer game? This knowledge of the final encounter will drive the choices made in material construction. A graphic operation aimed at improving driver behaviour at a dangerous intersection makes specific physical and material choices that demand specific production workflows. (Remember *wicked problems* from Chapter 2: 'there is no exhaustive list of admissible operations' (Rittel).) Each workflow is different, because each job serves a different end.

What can be said is that the production professionals we work with will be very aware of the pitfalls lurking in the workflows they run. If designers take the time to speak to the production technicians, seeking advice from them, not on the concept, which the designer owns, but on the ways the concept might be realised, then we can avoid a plethora of pitfalls in the process. Telling the producers what we want to do, and with whom we want to connect, can produce very positive results, with the production experts coming up with unexpected insights that can produce cost savings, time savings or possibly creative advantage.

This is precisely the reason that working designers spend so much time in developing strong and clear presentation roughs. Spending the time on the roughs directly equates to an easier time explaining our design intentions to the production professional, which in turn may well save us time and money later.

What output?

Once again, the message is very clear: if you want a job done right, speak to the technical team that will make it happen. Many graphics writers talk about 'industry standards'. The trouble with industry standards, when working in an industry as technically dependent as graphics, is that the industry continually leaps ahead of the standards writers. New equipment and applications continually diminish the pool of knowledge that informs the standards. Played against this trend is another that, with the cost of constant upgrading, sees some very old kit being kept in production simply because it still does the job. This pair of competing trends means that a particular production house may have some very specific demands in terms of the files it needs for its workflow.

Check your ideas on output against your research, against your understanding of the user and against your plans. Armed with this knowledge, it should be a simple task to explain your intentions to the producers.

Assuming that we have established a good rapport with our producers, the choice of output should be clear, with many of the small errors or unconsidered issues that might have cropped up being caught by the technical professionals.

That said, I'd like to offer a warning: treat the production people as people first and producers second. They have some serious knowledge that they can place at your disposal, if, and only if, they feel inclined. This doesn't mean that they should be allowed to control the design process, that is the designer's job, but it does mean they should be consulted. The law says nothing about them having to correct a designer's mistakes if they don't want to; they are only obliged to do the job you ask them to. They *will* normally tell you if something is about to go wrong, but, if you are rude and arrogant, they just might not. By simply standing by and letting a technically flawed job go through, the production technicians can make a rude designer look like a fool.

PLANNING FOR CREATION

You might reasonably ask if planning wasn't what the whole roughing and development stage was about, and it was, but that was planning for a different purpose. This is planning to inform the production technicians about what we want them to do for us and, in doing so, avoiding wasteful production runs. These are some of the things we can do to help producers:

- **Produce strong visuals** to explain your intentions and then make sure that the technical people have seen them.

- **Try and place the visuals in the right context**. So, if the artefact is a package, don't just show a drawing, or even just a maquette. Give them both and, if possible, a nice 3D render that shows the different specials – foils, embosses, etc. – that will be used on the job. Make sure that everyone involved in the production understands the nature of the game being played. If the job requires a specific location, then render the job onto a picture of the location to give scale and orientation, showing how it integrates into the environment.

- **Mark up your pieces and your files in a clear and intelligible way**. Only use private codes if the people on the receiving end are likely to be able to understand. Send a list of the elements and artefacts you are sending, so that the person at the other end knows what's there and what isn't. This care with naming should extend down to the elements in a file: if you have a layer in a Photoshop file that is to be used as a mask in an After Effects motion graphic, don't just leave its name as 'Layer 1'; name it something like 'Motion Graphics mask'. Make life easy for the people producing the job.

- **Now organise your files in named folders**. This is *absolutely essential* if you are working with a form of medium that is dependent on properly named links: e.g. desktop publishing or web files. Not organising your work will not just make the task of production more difficult; it can actively destroy your hard work.

- **Flight-check the job** (or test it using an online code validator tool if you're working on the web).[4] If you're not sure about 'flight-checking',[5] then talk to your producers and ask them about how they want the job structured and delivered.

- **Make sure the production professionals have a phone number or email address** where they can contact you for advice on how you want the job handled.

- **Write down what you want the production technicians to do for you**. Send a paper copy to the producers and put an electronic copy as a Read Me file on your disk or in with your file transfer archive.

- **Ask to see proofs or trials** (this may be outside the budget for your job or inconvenient for other reasons, but it is pretty important); failing that, ask to see a *soft proof*.

Traditionally, there was a whole range of photomechanical technologies (e.g. bromides) or laminate systems (DuPont's *Cromalin* or Kodak's *MatchPrint*) that allowed for an accurate (more or less) one-off copy of a print job. This would be used to confirm the viability of a print job before time and money were spent on a full print run, but was slow and expensive. These have been replaced today with units that are effectively super-sized laser (electrophotography) printers. These printers will also do daily service as short-run print units, but are built to be colour accurate and to use special media and toner that allow transparencies, tints, gloss and watermarks, etc. The Canon C1 is an example of this type of proofer. There are also large-format inkjets that are used for bigger colour proofs, such as the Epson Spectroproofers. These can print up to B0 sizes (1,000 × 1,414 mm), printing up to twelve colours (C, M, Y, K, light C, light M, light Y, light K, matt black, light light black, orange and green) from a substantial roll of paper.

Although these lovely machines are cheaper, faster and more adaptable than the older photomechanicals, they can sometimes be inconvenient (your client may be in a different region or country from your printer), or perhaps the designer and client just want some reassurance before paying for a conventional proof; this is the point at which a soft proof shows its value.

It helps to understand that all digital files that are about to be printed go through a process called a raster image processor (RIP), where the native graphics output is converted into a form the printer can read. Adobe Acrobat or other .pdf *distillers*[6] are in fact RIPs; we can then see that a .pdf file is effectively graphics, frozen in time a moment before they are printed. This means that a .pdf is a powerful representation of our output: the text will look as it does on paper, the colours are pretty accurate, and the transparencies and gradients look much as they would in print. In short, the .pdf has the potential to stand in for a proof as a way of checking the validity of a print run. In addition, the .pdf can be used to mark up the job; this means that the designer, client or producer can make notes, suggestions or corrections and send them between the stakeholders on the job.[7] This is the essence of a soft proof.

Not every .pdf is a soft proof. For it to be a soft proof, you need to do the following:

- Make sure that the job is sent in the correct colour model: e.g. CMYK, RGB, etc. (see next chapter). Check with your production technicians.

- Make sure that your own colour settings are consistent across all your software.

- When outputting the file, set the device (printer) to the one specified by your producer. This means the .pdf software will attempt to reproduce the known characteristics of the device and thus produce an accurate reproduction.

- Set the file to 'preserve the CMYK or RGB numbers' of the colour model you are using. This will simulate the colour values in the display of the output file, but won't actually change the colour data on the file. You can see the way it will output on different machines without changing a thing.

- Make sure that you are using 'black point compensation'.[8] This will allow the .pdf to display the darker portions of the image properly by adjusting the dynamic range to match the intended output device.

- Use the 'simulate paper colour' option. Paper is never truly white, certainly nowhere near as white as the computer monitor, and so this option will dim the whites to give an accurate impression of the printed image (the paper will be the whitest part of any print image).

- 'Simulate black ink' does the opposite of the 'simulate paper colour' option. The combined effect of ink on certain media will produce a very dark grey, not a black. If this option is ticked, the .pdf generator will use the device profile to calculate if the black needs to be lightened to display accurately.

If you do these few simple things, you should end up with a pretty good rendition of the final job, one that, while not being as good as a fully calibrated print proof, is often good enough to answer most questions that the stakeholders are likely to have.

- Multimedia work will involve renderings of the screens to show the clients and producers the work to be done. These could be the actual screens that will be used in the final piece, but might lack the underpinning code and rich media; as such, they are good enough for everybody to see what needs to be done, but substantially cheaper to change if there are problems. Strangely enough, a very good way of sharing these files among the stakeholders is to use Acrobat files. Although a print format by origin, Adobe has integrated all sorts of multimedia capabilities (Flash, video, 3D, etc.) into the format that allow it to be used as an effective prototype for multimedia, ebooks, etc.

- CGI work can be prototyped quite simply by setting up your job and turning off as many bells and whistles as you can. For instance, radiosity, caustics, HDMI, sub-surface scattering and a host of other CGI technologies, which make the product of a CGI render look so cool and lifelike, will also slow any machine to a crawl and, in turn, force the designer to use specially built render farms if they want to hit the client's deadline. This is a problem if changes need to be applied. Simply turning all of the unnecessary rendering options off and setting your job to render at a smaller size and lower resolution will allow the production of a good-enough output on which to make intelligent decisions, and this is what you need to convince a client to spend the cash on a full render, in the knowledge that they will get an excellent result.

SEMANTICS

Well-read readers might have wondered why, while Malcolm Barnard talked about *semiotics* (and the *semantic*) in the previous chapter, I haven't yet. This late arrival was a carefully considered choice, and I would like to explain why. Semiotics – the study of symbols and the symbols' ability to carry meaning – owes its origins to linguistics (the study of language). As such, it finds much of its expression in research and theory around spoken and written language. More than this, it often encourages researchers and writers to believe that meaning and symbols grow out of words and then to play written and spoken *language games* with things that are essentially visual, things that don't require any textual (text-based) interpretation.

That said, an understanding of semiotics is pretty much essential if we are to make the best graphic communication choices when making our work. To avoid this possible confusion – thinking like a linguist, when you should be concentrating on thinking like a visual communicator – I've decided to change the way the game is normally played and look, not at the visual through the written, but at the theory through the visual and material.

Peirce and Saussure

Like all good stories, we begin with a couple who shared a single idea, an idea that would change our understanding of the world. However, this couple never met, and

FIGURE 12.1
Arbitrary language

they both died without knowing the other even existed. What makes them a couple at all is the fact that they had a common realisation about the way language happens. Both Charles Sanders Peirce (pronounced *'purse'*) and Ferdinand de Saussure worked (without any great fame) as academics in the nineteenth and early twentieth centuries: one in America and the other in Switzerland. Neither one of them was much good at publishing, and both of them were mainly regarded as influential by their students: in de Saussure's case, his known works are mostly compilations of lectures he gave, compiled and edited by his followers.

Both Peirce and Saussure recognised that the words we use to describe things, to capture concepts and even to evoke emotion are *arbitrary* (*OED*: 'To be decided by one's liking; dependent upon will or pleasure; at the discretion or option of any one'). There is no natural connection between the word and the thing. This means that, when a dog says 'Woof, woof!' in the English-speaking world and 'Mung, Mung!' in Korea, the dog is not actually speaking in English or Korean, but making a doggy sound that culture has arbitrarily decided will be represented by a particular combination of letters and sounds.

For designers, this was a massively important revelation, because it places designers in a position where they can see that the symbols we use are socially and culturally meaningful, but not natural. This, in turn, leads us to the realisation that we can look at these culturally meaningful and completely unnatural symbols as a way to learn something about a specific culture.

Saussure believed there was a simple pairing between the thing and the idea the thing stood for: this pairing is called a *dyadic sign*.[9] It is the circular pairing in Figure 12.2, 'Semantic dyads and triads'. Unknowingly, on the other side of the Atlantic,

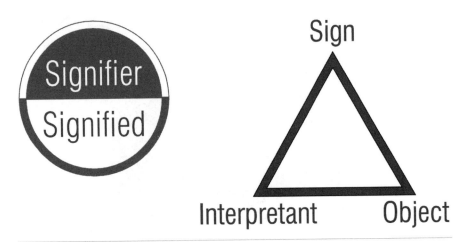

FIGURE 12.2
Semantic dyads and triads

Peirce came up with a similar, but rather more useful, way of thinking about the problem: he gave us the *triadic sign*. In a triadic sign, Peirce divided the sign into three distinct parts: the signified (here called the *interpretant*), which is the idea being communicated, and the signfier (here called the *object*), which is the thing carrying the burden of the meaning. So, in our dog example, the sound 'woof!' is the signified, and it is signified by the word (or the typography) *w-o-o-f-!*. This far and you would be right in thinking that this is much the same as De Saussure's dyadic signs, but what Peirce realised was that there was a third element, *the sign itself*. This is a massively important point to consider. When we see the sun, we don't think, 'large hot thing in the sky signified by the letters s-u-n'; we see the idea and the object as a unified thing: the sign. It is important for graphic communicators to understand this unification, because the viewer will not be seeing the difference between the signifier and the signified; they will not see an alternating signifier and signified (as in de Saussure's model); they will only see the unified sign, and people make signs.

Let me offer an example. Typographers talk about certain 'good design features' that aid readability of type, in large bodies of text, on the page. One of these has always been the use of serif faces, on the theoretical principle that the serifs (the little flicks at the end of the strokes in a type character) add extra visual distinctiveness to the shape of the typeset word, distinctiveness that allows the brain (which reads words on the basis of the whole word shape, not individual letter shapes) to read faster and with less stress.

However, later research, after the advent of the web, mobile phones and the associated time spent in screen-based reading, shows that the *digital-native* generation reads sans serif type better than serif.[10] This was perplexing to some typographers, but not to semioticians (people who study semiotics). They point out that, when the benefits of serifed type were measured, what was actually being measured was the cultural familiarity with that shape of letter (not an innate quality of serif typeface being easier to read): magazines, newspapers and books were set in these forms in the past, and so these were the forms readers grew up with. A later, screen-based generation of readers grew up with sans-serif forms on games, mobile phones, TV and computer monitors that became more semantically familiar to them and so easier for them to read.

Designers can use the ideas and objects to which people give semantic significance to carry out a kind of reverse engineering, a way of investigating the sign and the way the **users** *apply* the sign. 'Users' is emphasised here because it should be remembered that the meaning always comes from the user, not from some external place. This is a debate that has been played out in the semantics community as the 'structuralist' vs 'post-structuralist' argument.

There are some common terms that I should explain about now. These are terms that are common across the study of semiotics. First, we have the key term in the subject, *the sign*. A 'sign' in this context is not referring to a 2D piece of type or even a logo on a building. It refers to anything that stands in for an idea, a cultural object that is commonly understood to mean something specific for that culture. So, although the object might be natural – for example 'the white cliffs of Dover' are natural – the meanings that the cliffs are used to communicate are dependent on the culture. For the ancient world of the Greeks and Romans, they were symbolic of the whole country, because they represented the first part of the country the civilised world would encounter (they called the country *Albion*, which means 'the white country'). For the British Empire of the Second World War, it was symbolic of 'fortress Britain', a literal wall against the hostile forces on the other side of the channel. A sign does not have to be a physical object; it can be an idea, a spoken word, a hairstyle or anything else that people use to give meaning to their world.

If we take the sign of the white cliffs as an example, the thing carrying the meaning is called *the signifier*, and the meaning being carried is *the signified*. The two are not naturally connected; their relationship is arbitrary: the signifier can be anything that the culture believes is reasonable to be used as a vehicle to carry the meaning.

Structuralist semioticians believe that there are global structures, general grammars, universal ideas that are separate from, but inform, the ways in which we can understand and work with reality and the imagination. Structuralists believe that, although there will be a mass of different expressions of stories and ideas, there will be certain common *metanarratives*[11] that are universal, such as *the hero*, *the villain*, *love*, *resolution of difference though conflict*, *the father*, etc. These metanarratives are said to be, in some form, universal, and it is said that studying the differences from the universal narratives tells us something about the culture that owns the narrative.

For the structuralist Roland Barthes (who is great, and you really should read his book *Mythologies*), there were two main 'orders' of signification.[12] There is the 'first order of signification', which is the order of simple, literal relationships between a thing being named and the symbol used to denote it. We call our feet 'feet' as a common way of talking about those things on the ends of our legs. There aren't any value judgements implied by the use of that specific *signifier*. This is characteristic of the first order. They are neutral signs (or more or less neutral, compared with words such as: plates of meat, stump or flat-foot). In graphic terms, we might think of a visual communication existing at the level of the sticky price tag on a packet of sweets: a tiny piece of gummed paper with a simple monospaced text of the price on it, stripped of any tricky design values and having almost no cultural significance beyond the ability to tell me how much my pack of mints costs.[13]

By contrast, if we were looking at the second order of signification, Barthes tells us that we are entering the realm of myths: not so much the classical Greek myths, or indeed any national or religious systems of stories, though these are all definitely in Barthes' category of myths. No, Barthes was thinking about all the complex systems of symbols that we use to tag the world, so that it becomes easier to understand and more meaningful. If, linguistically, we replaced the word 'woof' with 'yelp', we might imagine the noise a small dog makes when we trip over it. A graphic equivalent might either be jazzing up our price tag (foil it, print it in a stylish script, add some letterpress) to suggest something of high worth, or perhaps sticking the original, simple and cheap price tag on a high-value item (a Rolls Royce, perhaps) to imply the item is of low value. In both cases, we are tapping into pre-existing concepts, ideas in the air, so to speak, that carry pre-existing connotations that we are borrowing to apply to our item, so that the meaning changes.

These second-order significations are the flow of ideas and symbols that make up culture. When my kids hear a catchphrase on a US television show and, thinking it's kind of catchy, repeat it at school, they are manipulating second-order signs: borrowing a sign that carries existing meaning and dressing themselves in the sign to borrow some of the meaning for themselves. When a graphic student repurposes an existing graphic – something like the ubiquitous 'Stay calm and carry on' poster – making a witty, ironic statement about a contemporary issue by contrasting the existing meaning's historic symbolism with a new twist, they are working with second-order signs.

This system of ideas (connotations) being in the air, existing as a cultural atmosphere that we must breathe in to make meaning, is what Barthes calls myth. In *Mythologies*, he talks about such diverse things as holidays and food, striptease and religion. Each short essay shows us that objects have a life beyond their physical nature, a life as carriers of ideas. Barthes' *Mythologies* is so massively useful for anyone involved in working with culture because it teaches us not to take the things around us for granted, showing us that steak and chips, for example, can be a symbol of a return to nature for intellectuals, a representation of bourgeois life and 'the alimentary sign of Frenchness'.

The third order of signification moves us beyond Barthes' myths and into the place where the myths are formed. In third-order significations, we are dealing with the common ideologies that form the environment within which the myths and the first-order namings exist. These third-order signs can be things such as gender models, religious world-views, national identities, political beliefs or even the ways in which we express ourselves sexually. They are the framework against which we daily measure our acts, ideas and emotions. Brave is brave against our culture's ideologies, hot is hot, and cold is cold. Third-order significations are the 'laws of nature' for our culture. To be a man or a woman is to inhabit different frameworks of reality, different third-order significations. For the sake of argument, we might talk about ideas such as democracy and capitalism as third-order significations: concepts that have no tangible existence (you cannot buy a dollar's worth of democracy or weigh out a kilo of capital). They are entire worlds, with laws and moralities, geographies and histories all of their own. That said, designers must take care: just by saying that these ideologies are intangible, doesn't mean that they aren't ideas that people take so seriously that they would die for them.

The manipulation of second-order signs happens within frameworks defined by the third-order signs. There will be myths (second-order signs) that simply make no sense

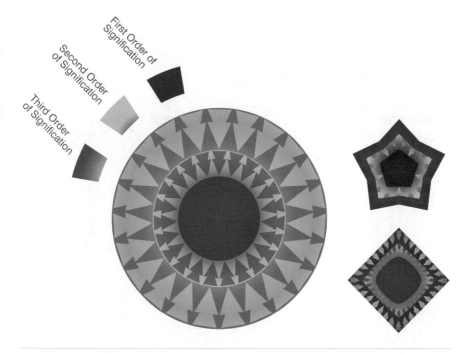

FIGURE 12.3
Semantic orders. In the figure, we can see the third order of signification (the outer ring) shaping the second order (the middle ring), which in turn shapes the first order (the centre). The small diagrams show how differently formed third orders will create differently formed second and first orders, in the same way that different cultures create different concepts and words

outside the third-order world they come from. Think for a moment about the application of Western typographic rules about line length, leading or letter spacing and consider how none of them can be unthinkingly applied to Arabic typography. The 'rules' are only rules within the framework proved by Western ideologies.

So, while the first (denotation) and second orders (connotation/myth) of signification can have a slight upward effect on the third order (ideology), e.g. symbols can have an effect on the ideology, the downward pressure from the ideology to the symbols and names is generally stronger. (Look at the novel *1984* by George Orwell, where the ideology renames and redefines the symbols, so that Orwell's 'Newspeak' redefines all sorts of common concepts in ways that favour the needs of the ideology.)

This might seem like the death of opportunity for designers and communicators, blocking their hope of creating excellent work. If these structuralist arguments (that there are wide-ranging grammars of ideologies that stack the rules of the game) are correct, then there is little we can do except recycle existing concepts. However, the nature of signs and symbols is more complex than this.

The post-structuralists would point out that meaning, while often conforming to the three orders above, is often far more local than it is global. The ideologies that frame people's myths are often frighteningly local. Going from street to street in a global city such as London or New York makes this abundantly clear: one street over, and the language spoken will change (even if it is apparently English, the way it is used will change), the graphics used will be different, the paint on the window frames and

Individuals

Society

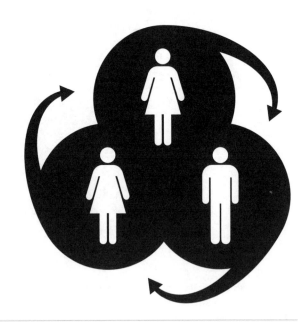

FIGURE 12.4
Individuals make society; society makes individuals

the goods sold in the shops will change. In so many ways, ideology is local. This links with the earlier chapters on research, where we saw that the context of the user's culture is the driver for the design choices we make.

Post-structuralism often locates the creation of meaning with the individual, which is problematic for graphic communicators, because we very rarely deal with individuals. There are ways round this problem, if we accept that the three orders of signification are created by the action of individuals (but affect the group culture), and that the group culture acts on the individual. In Figure 12.4 – culture feedback – we can see that each individual contributes to the culture, which in turn effects them. In this way, designers can have their cake – graphic languages *do* work in the real world – and eat it – they don't force communication on everyone, only aiding communication with those select people the message is aimed at.

MATERIAL SEMANTICS

You hold a book, and, as I'm writing this on my Mac, I can only assume that the publishers will print it on some sort of nice coated stock that takes the ink well and handles nicely. The fact that it is a book represents a specific set of semantic material choices. It didn't need to be a paper book at all: it could have been released on the web (as Lev Manovich did with his book *Cultural analytics* on YouTube), which was a distinctly meaningful choice of publishing medium); it could be printed on *bible paper*, so that it felt like a dictionary or some other book of scholarship (which personally I love); it could be printed on waterproof plastic *Tyvek™*, so that you could leave the book in the messiest studio with no ill effects. Even the choice of printing as a medium is a semantically meaningful choice: the book could have been produced by a team of calligraphers writing on virgin parchment, with illuminated drop-caps, and bound in calfskin: some kind of medieval/design fusion fantasy.

Each of these choices would carry meanings. Each of them would speak to some sort of cultural meaning held by a specific audience, and each choice might potentially alienate another audience by making it feel that the book just wasn't for them, before they even have a chance to read it.

Material choices, through associations with previous events, conjure whole narratives, narratives that cannot be conjured through other materials. I took the photo in Figure 12.5 at the first protest against the UK government's reforms of higher education (HE) and HE funding.[14] It shows a University and College Union flag flying in front of Parliament in Westminster. The fluttering fabric evokes other flags waved in other protests, visually recalling an entire history of campaigning and dissent; at least, it does for me, and this is one of the big distinctions between structuralists and post-structuralists: the post-structuralists understand that meaning rests with, and is created from the floor upwards by, individuals and communities; it does not come from the top down, from encyclopaedias, experts and style gurus.

FIGURE 12.5
UCU banner

THE SHOCK OF DETACHMENT

There is a lovely quote from Barthes' book *The semiotic challenge* (chapter 'The semantics of the object', p. 185) that demonstrates the point:

> I am thinking, for example, of an ad sometimes seen on French highways. This is an ad for a brand of trucks; it is a rather interesting example, because the ad writer who devised this poster has produced a poor ad, precisely because he has not thought the problem through in terms of signs; seeking to indicate that the trucks last a very long time, he has represented the palm of the hand with a sort of cross over it; for the adman, it was a matter of indicating the truck's lifeline; but I am convinced that according to the rules of symbolics, a cross over the hand is perceived as a symbol of death; even in the prosaic order of advertising, the organisation of this very ancient symbolics must be explored.

This quote shows a writer who assumes that everyone understands the world in one way, and that this way is his way.

Now, although the main thrust of semiotics was originally in linguistics, it makes a lot of sense to think in terms of material qualities as semiotics. Barthes considers this relationship between objects and meaning explicitly in the book *The semiotic challenge*. He asks us to think of objects not as words in a sentence, contributing to the final meaning without having an independent meaning in themselves, but as sentences made up of elements of meaning and containing whole meanings.

Barthes uses the example of a revolver (a kind of pistol) to explain that it carries multiple elements of meaning within it that contribute to a final end meaning. He calls this a *syntagm*, an assemblage of fragments of signs that make the meaning. In many ways this is an excellent metaphor: we can imagine revolver 'A', the sort of chromed toy pistol with red plastic handles, stamped with pictures of rearing horses on them, that I played with as a kid and that carries associations of childhood cowboy games; we can think of a heavy, 'Dirty Harry' .44 Magnum Smith & Wesson pistol, symbolic of a certain machismo attitude to law enforcement in films; we could be looking at the Charter Arms *Pink Lady*, a hot-pink revolver for women (I'm not making this up) – a mash-up of signs that must make sense for someone, but is bewildering for me (I'm not the right demographic). Each of them, in Barthes' terms, is a kit of fragments of signs composed to speak to a specific audience.

As graphic communicators, we can play this game too. Let's think about the most humble and direct form of graphic communication: the poster.

The function of the poster is simple: a direct graphical shout to the crowds as they go past, a call to action. The semantics (the things we expect a poster to do and talk about) are much more complex. Posters are public exposure of ideas; they are for public expression of opinion. There are ideas in books, comics, direct mailing, films and TV that would be semantically wrong when put on a poster: a person asking their partner to marry through a ninety-six-sheet poster[15] would be pushing the boundaries of what a poster might be expected to do (they might equally be read as highly romantic or deeply insensitive). Anything more private exposed in a poster will disturb people through the disjoint between the concept of public expression and the exposure of uncomfortable, private information. The Barnardo's shock campaign (in 2003) scored 330 complaints (the *Guardian*, Monday 24 November 2003) for addressing child cruelty in ways that challenged public notions of what should be shown on a wall.

Made from paper and ink, the basic form of the poster has changed little in the last 200 years (longer, if we look at the Chinese dàzìbào form of big slogan poster). The materials and reproductive techniques semantically speak of certain qualities:

- universality of message (the same message goes everywhere);
- an impersonal public quality of statement, not a private means of address (the message is impersonal, speaking to 'the public');
- constancy: posters are also expected not to change (which undoubtedly contributes to the joy the makers of the *Harry Potter* films show in magical moving posters).

It is the combination of these three qualities – universality, public address and un-changingness – that makes posters such a potent tool (and symbol) for political work. They represent a one-way traffic in ideas, from the empowered to the disempowered. Posters very rarely act as a dialogue: by their nature they are monologues. This, in turn, is what makes hacks, modifications and graffiti on posters so powerful: it's the intended target for the communication saying, 'NO! I disagree!'

At some level, designers have become aware of this 'playing against semantic type' and now set up dialogues between pairs or groups of posters as a substitute for the normal unbending monologue of the poster. More sophisticated still is the Amnesty International poster designed by Jung von Matt (2009): the poster shows a man about to strike his wife, but, through the application of facial-recognition software, the poster knows if you're looking at it. If you do look, the poster shows a happy couple: the image is changed through the user's gaze. The tagline for the poster is 'It happens when nobody is looking'. The addition of the technology turns the whole unchanging and universal semantic aspect of the poster on its head, by playing against the public nature of the poster to talk about the public/private nature of domestic violence. A very clever piece of graphic communication, which succeeds through playing semantic games with the materials of a graphic object.

This kind of game-playing is perhaps most obvious in packaging, both in food and cosmetics, a pair of fields where the differences between products can easily be swamped by issues around price. Companies respond to this by using the semantic characteristics of materials to give the products connotations such as: class, sexuality, fun, quality, cheap and cheerful, serious, caring or ecologically neutral. The actual produce may be none of these things; it doesn't matter, as the combination of these semantic fragments is likely to still be read in the way intended by the designer.

For many reasons (not least, my interest in the product), the semantics of chocolate packaging is a good place to see this in action. For example, Cadbury's Bournville brand underwent something of a makeover in recent years: out went the old red and gold packaging (playing a very old semantic game of red and gold being significant of royalty and thus quality), and in came a new livery of dark, almost black, brown, with splashes of colour – colour applied in an apparently slapdash way, creating a vibrant contrast with the dark background and suggesting the experience of sweet notes in your mouth against the dark background of the cocoa. This might seem fanciful, but it is almost a direct transcription, and illustration if you like, of the phenomenon of eating the chocolate. In contrast to the old packaging (which was like an elderly relative in their Christmas clothes), the new packaging is empty enough of connotations of class or age or gender not to offend anyone, yet specific enough to speak to those who prefer cocoa to sugar in their chocolate.

In the mock-ups in Figures 12.6 and 12.7, we have two fictional chocolate bars: Logo Sweet Chilli and Space Rocks. Each has been designed as an amalgam of existing products that semantically address different audiences. Just by looking at

FIGURE 12.6
Space Rocks bar

FIGURE 12.7
Logo Sweet Chilli bar

the two images, we could tell which one might be a special indulgence for a serious chocoholic, and which is aimed at a hyperactive eight-year-old. I'm not even going to say which is which, because I believe it to be obvious within the context of a modern Western culture.

In material terms, this difference is created by a combination of these semantic fragments making a distinctive sentence. The Space Rocks bar is clearly packaged in a plastic sleeve, and a low-quality one at that: the plastic wrinkles in the light. The colours are high, a trick known in packaging as giving a product shelf presence, which is the quality of a package visually popping out against the competition in a shop. Shelf presence is vitally important for sweets and other cheap foods that compete on the basis of cost: bright print colours are a cost-effective way of adding shelf presence. The black background increases the visual 'punch' of the other colour, and the overly busy background of stars makes the small type less legible, but it adds a vibrancy to the design, while echoing the phenomenon of the 'pop-rocks' bursting in your mouth, presenting a feeling of childish delight. The main type is blocky and exceedingly bright; the scale of the type is the visual equivalent of a salesman shouting the name of their product; and the colour of the type carries high contrast and is in the orange–red range of 'hungry colours'. Together, the semantic statement is one of 'fun', probably with a capital 'F' and possibly set in bold. Not of class, not of sophistication, but definitely fun.

By contrast the Logo brand chocolate plays several semantic tricks with materials all at once. The pack is a slim cardboard box, and the box is sharply creased, which can be done because it is smooth, stiff and bright card specially made for food packaging. Get some quality chocolate from the supermarket, tear the card and look at its composition; now try that again with a cereal box. You'll see the cereal box is bendier (less stiff) and of a much coarser fibre. As soon as we pick the pack up, it feels precise and rigid, both of which give it semantic connotations of being well constructed. To the eye, the pack carries a soft sheen (the result of the right inks on the right board), and is not shiny or matt, which would carry connotations of either industrially cheap or eco-simple.

There are subtler effects at play here too. The plastic wrap of the Space Rocks bar is pretty much airtight, which gives it a long shelf life, but at the expense of the sense of smell. By contrast, the high-status Logo brand is wrapped in crisp foil that allows a tiny hint of the smell of the product out, a powerful stimulus for emotional recollection and an incentive to consume. The surface of the pack not only is organised in a harmonious way, but uses several 'specials', extra production processes that can be quite costly to set up but that add a lot of appeal; these include foils (metallic plastics that are heat-bonded to the board to produce the effect of metal set into the surface) and embossing (using a metal form to press a pattern into paper or board); both of these will catch the light in interesting ways on the shelf as a consumer walks past. When the foil wrap is peeled back, the tearing makes a very specific sound that is culturally characteristic of high-quality chocolate.

In semantic terms, the combination of all of these fragments will spell out quality, in contrast to the 'fun' of the Space Rocks bar. But, here is the point: neither of these bars is real, and the journey we have just taken is entirely built on existing semantic elements that are present in the culture, just like real packaging is.

Semantics is often painted as a game played with words; I hope this chapter has shown you that it is a game played daily, knowingly or unknowingly, by every person who does anything remotely creative in their lives: not just designers, but cake makers, gardeners, amateur photographers, hairdressers and people getting dressed for work in the morning; every one of them is composing meaning into new semantic constructions.

NOTES

1   See the advert on Johnny's site at: www.johnnyhardstaff.com/index.php ?menu=yes&section=showreel&job=X&v=13935195.
2   Personally, I love Photoshop: I've been using it since 1992, and learning it earned me the money that paid for my wedding, but it's by no means the only graphics tool, it's not even the only image-manipulation one.
3   A fake Louis Vuitton bag made in smooth plastics would lack the qualities of even the cheapest knock-off. The imperfections in leather are part of the material qualities we expect in the product. To emphasise this point, Apple Computers has launched a line of letterpress Christmas cards (www.apple.com/ilife/iphoto/#create-letterpress-cards) complete with a lovely

promotional video of old-fashioned letterpress printing, extolling the virtues of hand-finished products.

4   The World Wide Web consortium's *Markup Validation Service* for example. Find it at: http://validator.w3.org/.

5   See Chapter 13 for more information on flight-checking.

6   The software that codes the content as a .pdf file.

7   This functionality is supported by Adobe Acrobat Pro (Mac and Win) and Reader (Mac, Linux and Win), the free Skim reader (on Mac), Apple Preview, PDF Mod (Linux) or pdftk (Win). All of these, except Acrobat Pro, are free.

8   The black point is the point of absolute blackness in the picture.

9   A dyad is a pairing or a group of two things.

10 A term coined by Marc Prensky to indicate those born after the digital dawn of the late 1980s (Digital Natives Digital Immigrants, 2001, available at: www.marcprensky.com/writing/Prensky%20-%20Digital%20Natives, %20Digital%20Immigrants%20-%20Part1.pdf, accessed October 2010).

11 A term that means a story that is over and above and that frames the story.

12 Signification is the term semiologists use to talk about action of an object having a meaning.

13 The book makes technical sense as a hybrid book, online or for e-book reading. A choice that might well fit in with the lifestyles of young designers better than a traditional book.

14 10 November 2010, London.

15 Excessively large at over 12 m long.

CHAPTER 13

Deploying the job

INTRODUCTION TO PRODUCTION: THE IMPOSSIBILITY OF UNDERSTANDING THE WORLD OF PRODUCTION

There are certain truths in our working life that we all have to get our heads around – to understand and assimilate as part of our world-view – before we can go forward to design glory, and the one you are likely to run into first is that *you will never be able to master every single graphics production and broadcast technology in the world*. This is no reflection on you as an individual: it's just the way it is. Let me explain.

You may be an excellent web designer with a brain full of obscure CSS and PHP code, but you will be working with image technicians, server-side coders, database developers and other experts in their field with vastly superior levels of skill in this small and special place. Your work may take the form of beautiful *autographic* print design, but the materials you use are subtly formulated by print chemists who know which formulas will last and which will fade; knowledge that you don't need to have to do your job as a designer, because they do.

As a designer, there is always knowledge you need beyond that you already have. No designer operates in a vacuum, no designer carries the entire burden of the job: we are part of a team, with each individual operating to his or her strengths. Your strengths as a designer will be in understanding visual culture, in having beautiful ideas and in making powerful visual statements. This truth is partly founded on commerce (your time is too expensive to have you operating a press; the press is too expensive to have you misusing it), but mainly exists because there are simply too many technical processes: processes that are continually updated, refined and discarded. An individual has no chance to master more than a small handful.[1]

Take note: this *does not* mean that you, as a designer full of talent and ambition, cannot design for any number of diverse fields: give it a try. But, you *should* know the production basics of any field you intend to work for. You have to develop skills that will allow you to explain your intentions to those who will actually make them real.[2] The production experts will, in turn, advise you how to make your ideas fly.

Understand the general principles of a process, its strengths and weaknesses as a communication medium, and then articulate your ideas on paper so clearly that the person who understands the subtleties of the production process (the production designer or technician running it) can manifest your work, efficiently, appropriately and above all without making any mistakes that you have to pay for.

This chapter will look at the things you have to do to make sure that your job has the very best chance of turning out right.

As a lecturer in graphics, I attend print and production trade-shows to try and keep up to date with the changes in the graphic production landscape, and every time I attend a show I am amazed by the changes, and excited by the opportunities, that have opened up for brave and witty design in the near future. I am also frankly terrified, because there is simply so much to know and so little time to learn it. This is why the chapter is called 'Deploying the job' not 'Making the job'.

The *OED* defines the original meaning of *deploy* as:

1. (in Caxton) *trans.* To unfold, display. *Obs.*

with a secondary meaning of arranging troops and resources.

It is this dual aspect of *unfolding* an idea, of *displaying* a means of expressing the idea, taken with the organisational aspect of 'arranging troops and resources', that is so close to the truth of a modern designer's life.

WHAT CAN I MAKE?

Visiting *Sign and Digital 2010* at the National Exhibition Centre, I talked to a Mimake[3] representative who showed me one of their current flatbed ultraviolet (UV) printers. It can print to the height of a man by the width of two and it can print on media that are 5 cm thick. The rep assured me that the next model could print on media 10 cm thick: this means that we're talking about being able to feed a king-sized mattress through a printing press. How mad is that? What was once a print-to-paper-only process is a print-to-anything-less-than-10-cm-deep process. The possibilities are crazy! The company demonstrated a BlackBerry phone that they had fed directly through the press and claimed to have printed on a laptop: my colleague wanted to see if you could print directly on to a door. Other technologies on display at the show could print and cut out a job in one pass.

With technologies like these, the problem becomes 'how do I explain my design to a producer?', not 'could I make it?'. Communicating your intentions to the production technicians should be thought of as another graphics job in itself. This time, however, we must understand the needs of the producer – his or her working culture and economic and technical landscape – and then use our skills as a visual communicator to explain the job to them. When working within an ultimately facile production environment, we have to narrow the choices to make it easy for the production technicians to make it work.

The very variety of tools that we can throw at a job can be a problem in itself. I once sent a job to a printer in a compressed digital archive. The printer tried to open the archive file in QuarkXPress. Quark told the printer the file was corrupt. The printer told me the file was a dud. I asked the printer if he had read the 'Read me' file I had included with the job, which explained how to open the archive and extract the Quark file. He said 'No, he hadn't'. So who was at fault?

The answer is that I was.

My failure was in not understanding the time pressure the printer was under, nor that he was unlikely to be a technical geek like me, knowing what an .SEA[4] file was, and I hadn't made the existence of the 'Read me' file so obvious that the printer couldn't miss it. I hadn't understood the printer's workflow. Next time, I knew. Next time, I sent a printed list of contents, including a printout of the 'Read me' file addressed to the printer. I made sure my wishes were heard.

This is what this chapter is really about, making sure that you make yourself heard in getting your job produced, making sure that you can manage a complex production process that others will complete.

Here are some of the things we can do to make everybody's lives easier and our jobs run more smoothly:

1. **Ask the production professional how the process works in their company**. What kinds of file format they take, what they don't and why. When the print design world went from being a QuarkXPress-only shop to one that used InDesign too, the phrases 'We don't have a copy of InDesign in our works' or, even worse, 'We're not sure we can print from a .pdf file' took on a special horror. It is absolutely no use creating a masterpiece in Microsoft Publisher and expecting a commercial printworks to be able to print it from a native file. But, if you were an Open Source software freak using *Scribus* to produce a book, the application's commercial grade .pdf engine would provide you with perfectly serviceable prints.[5]

2 **Ask the production professional how they typically take in jobs** and don't accept answers that evade the issue such as 'We're industry standard'. There is no such thing.[6] Each company will have its own minor variations (preferred paper suppliers and stock, specific inks and printers they favour) and its own quirks.

3 On the basis of this information, **draw up a production schedule for your own use**. You need to know if it's all slipping behind.

4 **Ask for formal confirmations of your production schedule**. If you need to have a job in at an editing suite in a week, the job needs to be ready in a week; it is no use being late and expecting your slot to be held. In the same way, if you turn up with your job to a print company and they aren't ready for you, they are in the wrong.

5 **Pre-flight, pre-flight, pre-flight**.[7] Make sure that the files are all present and correct at your end (so that, if something goes wrong, you can prove it wasn't you). Use professional software, with as much detail about the production process entered in as you can. You need to know that your job is fit for production. In screen–based media terms, make sure that your files are *exactly* the specification asked for.[8]

6 **Give the digital files in the form the production house asked for**, but also give them **proofs, material samples, renders, written instructions, maquettes** or anything else that you can that will clarify your intentions.

7 **If you can, visit and make a personal contact**. You cannot overestimate the importance of knowing the people who will be working on your job.

8 **If you can't visit, make sure that the producers have a phone number and an email address**; then make sure that you are available to them when you said you would be. You need to shepherd the process through to completion.

9 **Set a deadline for proofs** that allows for a complete catastrophe not to throw you off course. Try to get it done early. If things are overrunning, reschedule as early as you can.

10 **Ask for proofs before you pass over any money**. If the job is not right (I'm tempted to say perfect), don't pay for it until you are satisfied. If you are satisfied, tell the producer, and tell your colleagues. Good service deserves recognition.

That said, you *do* need to understand the nature of the path your design will travel along to the waiting hands of the user. This path is known as *the workflow*. Workflows come in all sorts of shapes and sizes. Some workflows are gloriously short (shorter is better: fewer things to get right, fewer things to go wrong); for example, an editorial illustration, Flash banner, or your self-promotional website represents a pretty direct pipeline from your head to your potential clients. By contrast, a richly illustrated book, animation or a large multimedia project is a nightmare workflow of subcontractors, time-lines and production schedules.

Interestingly the start of the workflow, the combination of designer and computer, often seems so ubiquitous that commentators write of *convergence* in design. Their assumption seems to be that, as most graphic communications originate on a Mac (still) or a PC (occasionally), using a very small set of applications (mostly produced by Adobe), a worker from one sector can be a worker for another.[9]

The truth is that, although we have the ability to take a little side trip into one another's territory every once in a while, we really are at the twin mercies of our knowledge of what happens next after the design leaves our desk and of the design professionals who will run the workflow.

For the sake of simplicity, Figure 13.1 (see pp. 216–17) is an abstracted model of the real processes. For example, web design and multimedia are separated. In reality, web and multimedia design have many commonalities, but, in industrial terms, have enough differences to make treating them as distinct a helpful thing to do. For example, a video delivered from a local media source to a kiosk will be a substantially different beast from one delivered over the web to a PC client: one being a great deal larger, having a higher frame rate and giving a much better-quality experience, because the technical constraints affect the design process and so are treated differently.

In Figure 13.1, designers are in the centre; this is a piece of self-flattery because, in reality, we are partners with clients, producers and users, but, as this is a book for designers, we leave ourselves there. As mentioned above, whatever our interests and personal expertise, our practice will currently tend to be computer-based at some point (the blue cluster); this is not necessarily true, but the number of designers producing work autographically on a mass scale is very small.[10] From this cluster of aligned digital processes, the work radiates away from us to other clusters of production and, you would assume, feeds directly to the users. However, much of the output of the graphics industry feeds directly back into the industry, serving other workflows. So, an illustrator or photographer might send work to a publishing house, which might then feed it to a multimedia house. Eventually, our product moves into the public sphere and adds to the visual culture of the world, from where, of course, it feeds both into the heads of our clients and our own.

Figure 13.1 may seem dense and confused, but, as its designer, I'm worried about the stuff I've been forced to leave out. The diagram is a simplification of the reality, which is that no two designers will share the same experience of design, where small companies become more and more common and form *ad hoc* relationships with each other to snag big clients. All of this makes it even more important for you as a designer to know your own technical processes intimately, to be familiar with the production processes of your core business, and to know a little about everything else.

There are some general principles that are pretty universal in dealing with graphic production files. They are universal, because they are the result of technical constraints, not cultural factors.

TASTE

Technical considerations in design are also a matter of taste. There are many technically viable choices we might potentially opt for in a graphics job, but many are unsuitable for social and cultural reasons. Medical advice from a magazine carries different social values from that from a medical website or from a doctor. We would be happy to receive free legal advice from a top international lawyer, but less thrilled to take it from the back of a cereal packet. Personally, I've never taken romantic advice from an anime.

The social uses we make of production and communications technologies are very specific. The technologies carry specific meanings for certain social groups. Pensioners are unlikely to be effectively communicated with by use of rich media delivered through mobile phones; the young are. Viral media will self-target specific communities; for example, the buzz generated around *The Watchman* movie was masterfully orchestrated, targeting those web-literate comic-book fans most likely to spread the word to other fans, while entirely bypassing those who were the wrong demographic.

If we use technologies in a blunt, unresponsive way or, worse, use specific technologies simply because we enjoy them, we will produce weak designs that fail to reach those we need to touch.

This matching of the technical means of deploying your idea and the social values that a technology embodies is a tricky business. There are always media that we like working with, things we feel comfortable with, but a good designer will alter his or her technical responses to fit in with the needs of the client. I once heard the designer Bob Gill state that a designer should never start a job knowing how the job would finish; that the form of the job should be the result of the brief, not the designer's skill set.

For example, the designer Chip (Charles) Kidd designs book covers; he is arguably the finest designer of book jackets in the world today. Each cover is a distinct gem; each cover gains its individuality from a meaningful technical approach based on the subject of the book, combined with a knowledge of the reader the book is aimed at. So, while the covers tend to be based on some variation of text and image, the sheer variety is quite dazzling. Each is an appropriate and meaningful whole. For example, the 2004 cover for Philip Galanes' book *Father's day* features a simple photograph of a yellow wool jumper, with the type stitched onto the jumper's label. Referencing the story, while still working as a design, the cover is graphically effective and completely defined by the job. If Chip Kid's work was merely a matter of personal taste, his hallmark diversity would be notable by its absence.

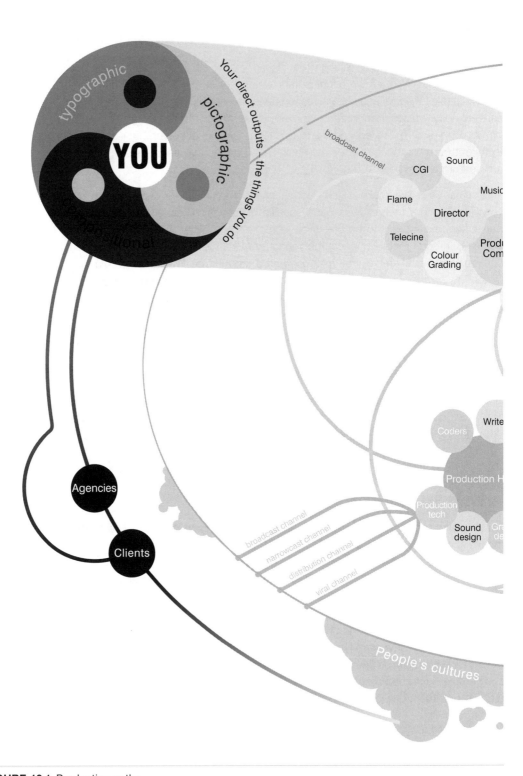

typographic

pictographic

compositional

YOU

Your direct outputs – the things you do

broadcast channel

CGI

Sound

Flame

Music

Director

Telecine

Produ
Com

Colour
Grading

Write

Coders

Production H

Production
tech

Sound
design

Gr
de

Agencies

Clients

broadcast channel

narrowcast channel

distribution channel

viral channel

People's cultures

FIGURE 13.1 Production paths

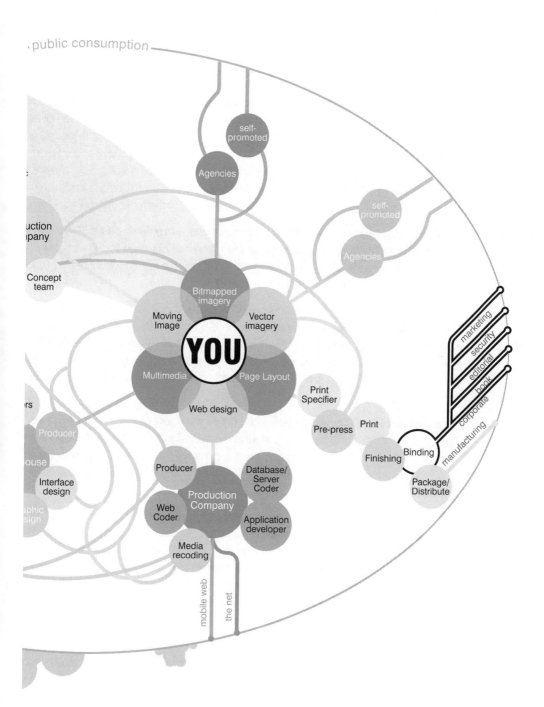

.public consumption

With thanks to Johhny Hardstaff for his kind advice about the Moving Image production workflow.

THEORY

There was a time when any talk of *deploying* a graphics job meant printing it; more than that, the word 'deploy' would not have been used at all, and the word used would have been 'production'. So, in a spirit of honesty and clarity, I hope you will forgive me a little detour into some of the unspoken assumptions around production for graphics and the philosophy of technologies used to communicate. There will be explanations of why the following chapters talk about deploying a graphic job rather than printing or producing it. I will argue that, whatever the method you end up using to communicate your idea, it will gain its validity, strength and meaning from the brief and from the user's need, not from an unthinking devotion to historic crafts. And this combination of media and presentation makes *deploy* the most appropriate word.

Print has historically been believed to be synonymous with graphic design. Unpacking this belief is foundational in representing the difference between those who regard themselves as graphic designers ('We print!') and graphic communicators ('We'll do whatever it takes to get the message across!').

Print design represents a continuous strand of material crafts stretching back to the great pioneers of the field: Gutenberg – who everybody knows as a print pioneer, but who was in truth a business brain, a kind of Bill Gates for the print revolution – and Peter Schoeffer (Schöffer), who was the first print master and arguably the first art director. Many would argue that the world of graphics was born on the same bed as print.[11]

Over 400 years of historic continuity, with print as the agent of mass communication, has bred an understandable feeling among those designers who work through print that (a) the way in which they do graphic design is sanctified by history, being both normal and natural, and (b) print design *is* graphic design; the only *true* way to do graphics.

I've listened to graphic designers, who should know better, tell students that the word 'graphic' means 'print' and therefore 'graphic design means print design'. Not true. The *OED* gives us a base-line of meaning for graphics as: 'relating to visual art, especially involving drawing, engraving or lettering'. Its Greek origin is in the word *graphikos*, which is derived from *graphe*, meaning either to draw or write. The second-ary meaning is given by the OED as 'giving vividly explicit detail'. Thus, the literal meaning of graphic design is a visual or a visualised plan.

So, we have a basic meaning so broad as to cover absolutely any traditional means of forming a visual communication – drawn, calligraphic, typographic, photographic or print – and still accommodate any conceivable modern form of communication – information graphics, HCI, web design, animation, film, etc.

This distinction would be of purely academic interest if it weren't for the fact that so many of the rules that we have for graphic communication (doing *anything* to get the message across) stem from graphic design (producing a 2D print job).

Even before the computer arrived to shake up all of our lives as designers, this insistence on tradition being the rule was challenged.

- Between the two world wars, we see Tschichold, El Lizzitski, etc. tackling the issue thrown up by communications that moved across national boundaries, challenging purely local ways of doing graphics.
- The work of Saul Bass shows us a supremely talented designer moving from traditional printed imagery to work that moves.
- The typography of Herman Zapf or Matthew Carter spans an era when typography was transformed from being dead chunks of lead locked into a chase to pulses of light carved into photographic film,[12] to sets of digital code dancing on a screen.

This change was brought home to me (a student of painting and photomechanical technologies), in a very personal way, when the computer challenged everything I had been taught by letting me animate, typeset and build interaction into my graphic images. The rules had changed. Society had changed. What choice did I have but to follow?

Today, when designers click the button that says 'print', the job may well go to a 2D printing press, but equally the artefact carrying your communication could be printed in 3D, may be automatically repurposed through .XML into parallel print and web-based streams, or be destined to be used on an e-book reader; and these are just 'print' media.

If we look to less traditional means of graphic communication, the range of possible design responses becomes dazzling in its variety. We have interactive video media that track the passer-by and roll them into the image on display, books that can link to rich media, performance art, viral media, locative media and so many other ways to connect with our audiences.

In short, we should remember that a designer is a planner, a deviser of schemes. We are the mad thinkers; we conceive plans to change the world; we do not have to be the people who actually print every document, paste up every poster or edit every frame of film. We *must* be able to transmit these ideas in a clear and lucid way that communicates how we intend for our ideas to be deployed in the world.

So remember, when you make beautiful and brave work, to talk to those people who need to hear your message. The medium you use to produce your work should not be chosen because of historical habit or because it matches your personal skill set; rather, it should be the natural end result of the specific combination of the message you need to communicate and the people you need to talk to.

COLOUR

How humans see colour

Colour is a sensuous thing, literally. It evokes all kinds of emotional response by hooking directly into our sensations, and many designers use it in a clumsy, unthinking way, which is a waste. Controlling your colour, both creatively as a designer and across the production process, is a fairly essential skill for any designer.

Humans see colour as combinations of red, green and blue hues, blended to make all other colours. The cones, the cells in the eye that see colour, are sensitised to pick up one of the three primary colours.

The colour we see is produced through:

- **emission** (light radiates from something, it glows and we see the emitted light);
- **reflection** (light is mostly absorbed by an object, with a portion being reflected, e.g. a tomato is red, because the green and blue components are absorbed, but the red part is reflected);
- **refraction** (where light is scattered in a way that separates the different frequencies of colour, which are re-emitted, e.g. a butterfly's wing has no actual colour, but has microscopic scales on its wings that scatter light in a way that makes it look as though it does).

Colour through emission is how we see images on screen, or through film, or through projection. It produces what is called *additive colour*, which is colour that gets lighter and brighter, the more light is added to it. For example, red light + green light makes the colour yellow, which is lighter than either (more light is being emitted).

Colour that works through reflection includes print processes, dyes and pigments in plastics and, in recent years, e-paper displays: both black and white, or colour displays. There are also some exotic display technologies, such as Qualcomm's *Mirasol* displays, that produce coloured video images from reflected light. These are *subtractive colours*. The more subtractive colours that you add to a mix, the darker the colour you get (you are absorbing more types of colour, so that there is less left to reflect as colour). For instance, red and green inks mixed together will make a darker brown than either of the components.

There was a time when mentioning refracted light would have been an abstract nonsense in a graphics book, but a liquid crystal display (LCD) functions, in part at least, through the refractive properties of the crystals that give it its name.

HUE, SATURATION AND LUMINOSITY

We measure colour quality through reference to three factors:

- **Hue**: The range of colour being represented. Is it a red, an orange or a yellow? This is the hue. Hue says nothing about the strength or lightness of the colour.

- **Saturation**: The strength of the hue being represented. A strong red has a higher saturation than a pale pink, but might be the same hue.

- **Luminosity**: The brightness or darkness of the colour. A luminous red will, if the luminosity is reduced, become a dark red, then brown and, eventually, when the luminosity is reduced to 0 per cent, black (see Figure 13.2).

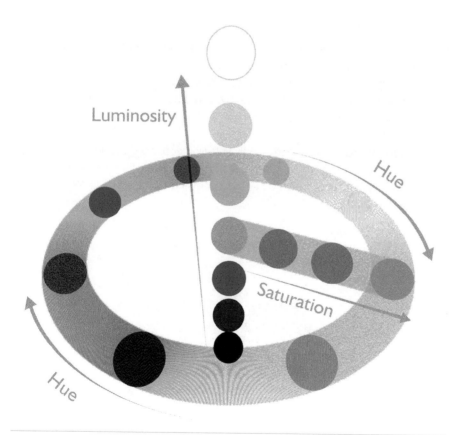

FIGURE 13.2 Hue, saturation, luminosity

Analogous, primary, secondary, tertiary and other colour schemes

Colours work together to create various effects, some harmonious, some clashing and some that just seem to work. These are called *colour schemes*, and variations of the same design using different colour schemes are called *colour ways*.

It helps to visualise colour relationships by visualising the primary, secondary and tertiary colours arrayed along the rim of a circle in what is called a colour wheel.

- **Primary colours** – red, green and blue – directly relate to the cones in our eyes.
- **Secondary colours** are direct mixes of the colours: red + green = yellow; green + blue = cyan/green–blue; blue + red = violet.
- **Tertiary colours** are the six colours that are mixes of the primary and secondary colours.

A list of colour schemes

This is a list of some commonly used, formally recognised colour schemes and, while they carry some weight, they should also be read as a cultural shorthand. So, for example, complementary colours would be a no-no for most uses. However, we still see them being used: in Hindu iconography, some soft-drink packaging and some music industry design – in these environments they excel.

- **Monochrome**: These are simply tints (lighter or darker shades) of the same basic hue. As such, for a graphic communicator, they are a very simple way of imposing design coherence across a job (see Figure 13.3).

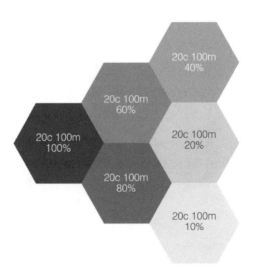

FIGURE 13.3 Monochrome

- **Analogous**: These are colour schemes where the main colour is matched with colours on either side of it on the colour wheel. Because the colours are similar hues, they work to produce sympathetic, harmonious schemes. So, if orange was your main colour, the analogous colours would be red and yellow (see Figure 13.4).

FIGURE 13.4 Analogous colours

- **Complementary**: Complementary colours are the colours from the opposing sides of the colour wheel, e.g. yellow and purple. Many books on colour theory amusingly say things such as, 'complementary colours have a vibrant quality', which I can only assume means that they believe the word vibrant means headache. Complementary colours do have a value. They emotionally communicate tension (look at some of the lovely work

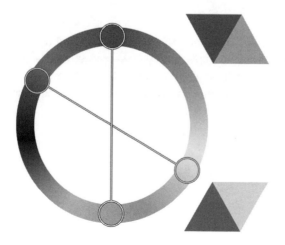

FIGURE 13.5 Complementary colours

produced for the rock venue the Avalon Ballroom, in the late 1960s and early 1970s). They have high levels of contrast, which means that they are excellent for uses that require people to see them, especially yellow and purple, which have both hue contrast and tonal contrast going for them (see Figure 13.5).

- **Triadic**: These are three colours forming an equilateral triangle around the colour wheel. So, red, green and blue are a triad. This does not need to be the only working triad; any combination of triadic colours is viable, for example, orange, blue–green and violet work too. Triadic colours keep many of the energetic qualities of complementary colour schemes, but tend both to be subtler and to lack their clashing qualities (see Figure 13.6).

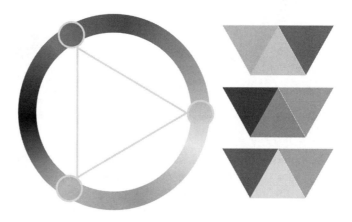

FIGURE 13.6 Triadic colours

- **Tetradic**: These are four colours spaced in a square around the colour wheel. For example, red, yellow–orange, blue and purple form a tetrad. Because tetrads contain pairs of complementaries, they have a natural vibrancy, but, they also incorporate some of the qualities of the analogous schemes (e.g. red complements green, but is in an analogous relationship to both purple and yellow–orange). This balance of relationships can be tweaked by making a *skewed tetrad*, where, although there are pairs of complementaries, the pairs don't form a square and are closer to each other (see Figure 13.8).

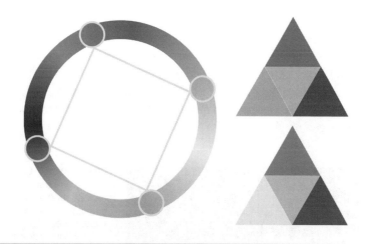

FIGURE 13.7 Tetradic colour

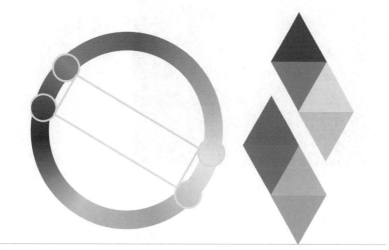

FIGURE 13.8 Skewed tetrad

Because the basics of colour are cultural in construction, its schemes and combinations are more or less the same across media, independent of the means of production we use. However, the colours we *can actually use* are distinctly affected by the means of production. Simply put, there are colours that you might design for, which the clients may love and the users might squirm with excitement over, that you absolutely can't use in your chosen medium.[13] As a designer, you not only need to understand how colour is put together, but also how you can make it happen.

Gamut

Different production media have different colour qualities. They have different ranges of colours that they can display and, more importantly, that they cannot display. The total range of colours that any process can display is called a gamut (sometimes a *colour space*). Some colour models have huge gamuts, approaching the total range the human eye can see, and some have terribly restricted gamuts that restrict what designers can do with them (see Figure 13.9).

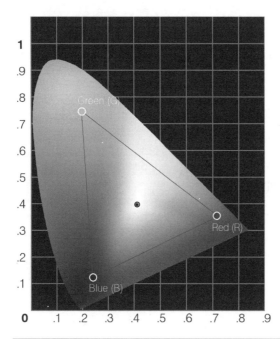

RGB Colour Gamut
The curved mass of colours represents the toal range of colours that an average human eye can see.
The triangle inside is formed by pure Red, pure Green and pure Blue and contains all the colours that could be displayed on an RGB display. This triangle represents Adobe RGB 98.
Other RGB gamuts may show a smaller range of colours (e.g. sRGB).

FIGURE 13.9
The RGB colour gamut

I'm not keen on rules, but this is rule that you must understand:

> **Always keep a parent image in a big gamut, and work with a child image in a smaller gamut.**

Following this rule means that you will be able to do any colour corrections in an image with a larger gamut (with a bigger range of colours) and then control the downsampling of colours, yourself, into a new image with a smaller gamut. The alternative is relying on automatic processing, which will give inferior results.

The main gamuts are listed below, in descending order of the number of colours they can display.

L*a*b* colour

As mentioned above, different devices (and processes, such as CMYK printing) have varying abilities to display colour. In 1976, the international body that defines colours[14] decided that there needed to be a definition of colour that was independent of the device or process. The basis of the new colour model is that of the human visual system and the colours that system can perceive. The human eye can (on average) distinguish about ten million colours through sense impressions made by light falling on the cones in the eye, which are sensitised to respond to red, green or blue light. Specifically, through the triad of red, green and blue, the human eye perceives three combinations of difference: light to dark, blue to yellow and red to green.

In the same way, the L*a*b* model is defined by three components. The 'L*' is the lightness component; the 'a*' is a red–green value; and the 'b*' is a blue–yellow value.

This would only be of abstract interest if it weren't for the fact that, when graphics applications do a conversion of an image from one colour space to another – RGB to Pantone ink for example – the image's colour values are first converted into L*a*b* colour space (because it has all perceivable colours in it), and then the equivalent colours in the target (Pantone) colour space will be selected as being the best match (see Figure 13.10).

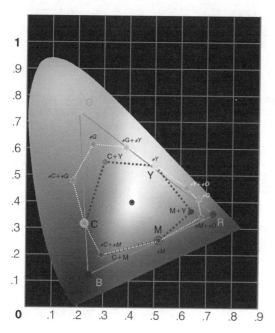

Print Colour Gamuts
Because of the subtractive nature of printed materials a printed gamut is likely to be substantially smaller than an additive one. We can add more colours (thus more print passes), but more colours mean darker results.
CMYK (black dotted line) has a very small gamut compared with RGB. Notice how weak it is in greens, oranges and purples.
To compensate there are alternative print systems called HiFi systems. The one demonstrated, is the Pantone Hexachrome (dotted white line) system, which adds Orange and Green inks. As you can see it has a much wider gamut.

FIGURE 13.10
Print colour gamuts

RGB colour

RGB is an additive colour system, which means the more colours added to the mix, the more luminous the colour. In Figure 13.11, the red, green and blue channels have been separated out, and we can see that, individually, they are substantially dimmer than the combined channels.

The human eye can, apparently, distinguish around ten million distinct colours, a claim that is over fifty years old but still seems to stand.[15] RGB is a subset of L*a*b* colour, but 24-bit RGB can still display more than half again as many colours as the human eye can see (around 16.7 million colours).

Somewhat confusingly, 24-bit RGB isn't the only type of RGB colour in use. There are also 30-, 32- and 48-bit versions. All of these colour spaces can record colours that exist outside the colour space humans can see. In either 30- or 48-bit colour spaces, the extra colours are used to minimise distortions in colours when performing image corrections or colour conversions. Don't think of the extra colours in terms of extra colours that somehow exist outside the range of visible colours (such as infrared or UV); they are simply finer distinctions than a human can see. As such, their value is that, when a computer is doing a transform, rather than making some sort of artificial choice between two tones of a colour that are both slightly wrong, it can make an exact choice.

In 32-bit colour spaces, the extra 8 bits (24-bit + 8-bit) are not used to store extra colour data but to store masking data (this is technically known as an *alpha channel*).

24 bit colour = 16,777,216 colours

R - 8 bit 0 - 255	G - 8 bit 0 - 255	B - 8 bit 0 - 255

32 bit colour = 16,777,216 colours + 256 levels of masking

R - 8 bit 0 - 255	G - 8 bit 0 - 255	B - 8 bit 0 - 255	a - 8 bit 0 - 255

30 bit colour = 1,073,741,824 colours

R - 10 bit 0 - 1023	G - 10 bit 0 - 1023	B - 10 bit 0 - 1023

48 bit colour = 281,474,976,710,656 colours

R - 16 bit 0 - 65,536	G - 16 bit 0 - 65,536	B - 16 bit 0 - 65,536

FIGURE 13.11
Colour bit values

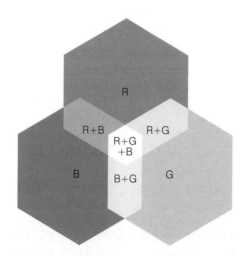

Additive Colours

In an additive colours system the colour is the result of direct emission of a particular wavelength of light (they glow in a colour).
So red is red because it is a light at a wavelength of 650 nanometers.
Combinations of two or more colours make a third, lighter colour, because the new colour has the combined energy of the two component colours.
There is a total increase in the energy as one colour is added to another.

FIGURE 13.12
Additive colour

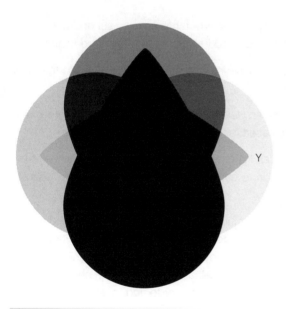

Subtractive Colours

In a subtractive colour system the colour is created through the reflection of a single colour and the absorbtion of all other colours. e.g. yellow ink is yellow because it absorbs all colours except yellow. The colours in the diagram are *overprinted* (where one colour is printed over another to create a third); as the colours are combined the overprinted colours will be darker than the component colours as each colour contributing to the new combination will be absorbing some of the wavelengths of light previously reflected by the other colours.

FIGURE 13.13
Subtractive colour

As said previously, the RGB colour space can display any colour that a human can see, which is not the same as saying that every RGB device (monitor, smartphone, etc.) can. Some devices that claim to be RGB have lesser versions of the colour space (16-bit RGB has only 5 bits per channel); all devices will have built-in shortfalls in the colours they can display, to some degree or other. The general rule of thumb is that, the more insanely expensive a display device is, the better it will do its job.

However, even the limited versions of RGB will display some colours that cannot be reproduced by conventional CMYK printing: vivid greens, purples and oranges. This is where HiFi colour systems come in.

HiFi colour

HiFi colour is the term for specialist prints done, not with conventional four-colour processes, but with an extended range of ink colours formulated to fill in some of the gaps left by CMYK printing to give a wider gamut.

Hewlett Packard, for example, produces printers that, in addition to CMYK, have light cyan and light magenta, which allow for production of paler tones without half-tone problems.

Du Pont has a HiFi system called *Hypercolor*, which has an extra set of CMYK plates that print more inks in selected places to add sensitivity in tonal reproduction.

Küppers/*Opaltone* add red, green or blue ink plates to CMYK to increase the tonal range.

Pantone has a specialist system called *Hexachrome*, which has additional green and orange inks that allow for an increased range of colours to be produced.

There are even companies, such as Hallmark Cards, who are reputed to use their own specially developed ink blends to enhance existing inks' 'punch' for specific technical reasons.[16]

All of these processes, for graphic communicators at least, are quite straightforward to prep images for. This is what that mysterious extra *colour mode* in Photoshop, the *Multichannel* mode, is for. This, simply speaking, allows you to manipulate your existing graphics (RGB, CMYK, etc.) as normal, and then add extra channels either to produce tonally richer images, to include 'spots' or to add 'specials'.

This would be excellent news if it weren't for the fact that there aren't many printers out there who have such a thing as a six-colour + perfecting printer[17] out there. Such things do exist, but you will have to pay extra to buy time on them. So, as always, the message should be that designers must go and speak to their printers to find out how far they can push the technology for their clients.

CMYK

CMYK is a bit of a historical accident, by which I mean its adoption as the standard full-colour system for print was not the result of careful planning by the print industry, but one of those cases where something is adopted for the lack of any competition. The combination of cyan, magenta, yellow and key (black) has more to do with the fact that these inks could be found in most print shops. However, the combination has some real problems as a choice of inks. Cyan is a distinctly green kind of blue, magenta is a blue-range red, the yellow is just on the green side of a spectral yellow, and the black, in darkening the other inks, makes them look mucky.

There were earlier four-colour print systems; some, such as Le Blon's red–yellow–blue–key (RYBK) make more sense because they can produce decent oranges, greens and purples, which CMYK fails to do. The issues with CMYK can be addressed by using a HiFi system or by adding a fifth spot plate. The current generation of digital printers often has a fifth printing station built in, allowing for exactly this kind of printing.

CMYK has disappointing characteristics compared with RGB. As you can see from Figure 13.10, there are whole areas of the spectrum that it just cannot reproduce, areas that, when converted from RGB, will at best lose all of their punch, but that will often change beyond recognition. For example, most purples will instantly become grey as soon as you convert them. Sadly, there are no magic solutions to this problem. You can:

- make sure that there are no *out-of-gamut* colours in your job, which is a pain;
- ask your clients if they can spring for the additional cost of an extra spot plate;
- possibly go to a full HiFi print, if you have a printer who can handle the job, and if the funds are available; or
- experiment in Photoshop and your DTP package with substituting one of the existing ink colours with another ink, e.g. rubine red for magenta.

One of the unspoken problems with CMYK arises from the problem with *half-toned* prints attempting to reproduce skin tones. Colours and colour blends are made by placing patterns of tiny dots on the paper – densely where the colours need to be strong, sparsely where the colours are pale. For example, while the richer red and orange parts of a peach would print nicely with a tightly packed combination of magenta and yellow inks, with a smattering of cyan and black to neutralise and add punch to the deeper tones, the lighter parts of the peach skin will be made by printing more widely spaced dots, showing more of the white paper beneath.

SPOTS AND SPECIALS

If you were designing for a company that used a lovely fresh green for its branding, it would be difficult to match the colour in a conventional four-colour process, because the colour will be outside the printable range. However, your printer could quite easily mix up a bucket full of the right colour ink and feed it into the press. This is *spot colour* at its simplest.

In production terms, this one-colour print is simply a case of setting up a monochrome image in your favourite graphics package and giving the printer a sample of the colour or a colour breakdown (its RGB colour values). The printer will mix up your specified ink colour, produce its monochrome plate and, instead of printing it in black, will print it with the green ink. The end result will be a single-spot-colour print.

Even if a job required a single colour of the range that *could* be printed through a conventional CMYK process, why would you? For example, olive green can be made with the CMYK formula C-48, M-12, Y-100, K-0. As the black (K) plate is not needed, we don't need to touch that, but there are still three plates to make. It would make no economic sense to do so – you would have to make three impressions on the paper to produce a single colour – and so we don't. In this circumstance, we print a single spot formulated to be the correct colour and save the cost of three wasted impressions per sheet.

In addition to this kind of single-colour printing, we can use spot colours to enhance, extend or replace conventional inks. For example, we could replace magenta with warm red to change the range of colours we can make: suddenly a whole range of oranges becomes available to you.

Extra spot inks can also be defined to complement the existing four-colour process, as in a HiFi process. However, designers might want to add other effects to the job. Roland, for example, has developed new microfine *metallic inks* that print like *metallic foils*, but, as they are printed through a press, can be overprinted in combination with conventional inks to make some quite lovely metallic and pearlescent effects. These extra effects are called specials. Through adding extra channels that become extra plates – which could become special inks (metallic, dayglo, UV reactive, thermographic, etc.) or sport varnishes, embossing plates, cutting dies – we can add a richness and beauty to our jobs.

In Figure 13.14, the centre image is an original CMYK image, the left-hand one has the cyan ink replaced with a reflex blue ink, and the right-hand image has had warm red substituted for magenta.

FIGURE 13.14
Colour on a replacement plate

In printing particularly pale, large areas of an image – pale skin for example – the patterns of the print will be perceptible to the viewer. This is particularly true in older printing schemes, where the screens had regular patterns that would reinforce one screen's pattern in spots where it intersects with another colour. Stoachistic/frequency modulation screens help, but generally speaking a better solution is to talk to your printer about getting an extra *pale-magenta* plate made. Pale magenta is exactly what it sounds like, a pale version of regular magenta ink, the theory being that you can print the pale-magenta dots at a much greater density than the regular magenta, giving a pale pink with no noticeable half-tone pattern. The same would be true if you were looking at printing large pale-blue areas, a sky or an ice field, where you could ask your printer for an extra *pale-cyan* plate to be made and printed.

Index colour/web-safe colours

It is possible to make a fairly good approximation of a full RGB image with about 256 colours – not great, you understand, but acceptable. This approximation is an *index colour*, an early technique to simulate full-colour images on screen when working with older processors, limited memory and archaic telecoms. Where an RGB colour image is made from a long 'data word', 24 to 42 bits of data, an index-colour image is stored as 8 bits (or fewer) of data.

Indexed colours aren't truly a colour system, but, as they are dealt with in this way in software, I will follow suit; they are in fact a way of recording a specific palette, a palette of 256 colours (8-bit), 16 colours (4-bit) or 4 colours (2-bit).[18] The palette could theoretically be any colour or tone you like. For example, you could get great monochrome reproduction of an image with an 8-bit index-colour image, because 256 tones of grey, ranging from black to white, are a lot of tones from which to make an image.

Problems arise from the inability to simulate 16.7 million colours with 256. Index colour simulates the tones between members of the palette through a process called *dithering*, which is the close cousin of half-tone, in that a gradated scattering of dots is used to simulate a bigger tonal range. Dithering almost works, but doesn't. The problem is that dithering happens at the level of individual pixels, rather than the kinds of minute dot produced in print, which means that gradients are often coarse and visible against the image. This is why index colour has gone the way of the dinosaurs, except for a kind of reincarnation on the web through .GIF and 8-bit .PNG files.

What index-colour images (such as .GIF and .PNG) do very well, and is one of the reasons that people still use them, is reproduce typography and logotypes across the web. Even compared with highly compressed image formats such as .JPG, an index-colour image will produce high-quality type at very small file sizes. The 256 colours carry enough variation to allow very sensitive type rendering, where a .JPG of a similar size will have introduced damaging artefacts into the type (particularly in small type or with complex typographic forms).

Web-safe colour is, strictly speaking, part of the index-colour family. It has a very specific palette of 256 colours that are said to reproduce faithfully across Windows, Macintosh, Linux and mobile operating systems.[19] The actual palette is somewhat fewer than 256, with six monochrome tones (from black to white) and six Windows system colours, leaving 244 actual colours. It must be said that all current desktop systems and most smartphones should be able to display a full-colour image with little or no problem and only a small degree of colour shift from machine to machine.

Duotone

It is possible to create coloured, but not full-colour, images and spreads with two or three plates, and very beautiful and effective they are too. These are monotones (one plate), duotones (two plates) and tritones (three plates). Although you cannot simulate true full colour, it is possible to get sensitive and attractive effects.

Greyscale

Greyscale is a term used to define both monochrome black and white screen images and printed black monochrome inks on a white ground. On-screen, the term typically refers to 8-bit monochrome images, with a single channel producing 256 shades of grey, from 0 (black) to 255 (white). It can also refer to 16-bit images, with a single channel containing 65,536 shades of grey.

Care should be taken in translating colour images to greyscale ones. Simply discarding the colour can lead to washed-out images. Programs such as Photoshop can control the process through control panels, or the designer can manually control the process through working with layer to create deep blacks, bright whites and even mid-tones.

Bitmap

A bitmap is a confusing piece of naming in that it can both refer to *raster images* (below) and to a 1-bit image. A 1-bit image can only have its pixels in two states: on (white) or off (black). Bitmap images produce a very crude form of tone through dithering, but it doesn't look good. Just about the only time you are likely to find, and work on, bitmap images nowadays is when designing icons for screen, where there are often 1-bit masks for the colour icons.

IMAGE CONSTRUCTION

How do all of these gorgeous colours get pulled together on-screen and in print, transforming into clear, crisp images?

Raster images

The term 'raster' is one of those archaic terms that doesn't die but comes to mean different things over the years. It is directly derived from the Latin term for a rake (*rastrum*). The term was applied to a five-nibbed dip pen that was designed to be used for drawing stave lines for music. Equally, it could be used for drawing grids, and this is how the secondary meaning of a raster, meaning a grid, emerged. Occasionally, these images are called bitmap images (which can be confusing: see above), because they are bits of data mapped to record an image.

A *raster graphic* is a graphic image that is defined by a grid of *pixels* that will have colour values defined by one of the colour systems mentioned above. Each pixel has a set of coordinates defining its position,[20] a resolution defining the number of pixels there are in every given portion of the image[21] and data defining its colour.[22] Together, they make an image.

There are obviously quite a lot of data, and, as a result, raster files get very big, very fast. A graphic for a 32-sheet poster will create a 6.44 gigabyte graphic file, which will need some very specialist hardware to run. Remember that, every time you double the size of an image, you quadruple the size of the file. So, a 1-megabyte file will only be half the size of a 4-megabyte file.

Raster images, video or still, can also store alpha channel data that can apparently produce images that aren't rectangular. They are; it is simply a case that the extra channel data selectively hide portions of the images, or, in the case of prints, mark parts of the image as non-printing.

Broadly acceptable (i.e. lots of people can read them) raster-image file formats for general graphics uses are shown in Table 13.1.

TABLE 13.1 Production bitmap/raster files

Name (full name)/ *Pronounced*	Does well	Does badly
.JPG, .JPEG (Joint Photographic Experts Group)/*jay peg*	Produces tiny, high-quality, full-colour images if used correctly and conservatively.	Can wreck images if used carelessly. Don't re-save .jpg images as .jpg files; if you do, you will apply one set of .jpg compression over another, producing blocky, jaggy, images.
.TIF, .TIFF (tagged image file format)/*tiff*	Produces substantially smaller graphic files without damaging drops in quality (as long as you use LZW or ZIP compression). Compatible with almost all production applications. .TIF files can also support layers, a very wide range of colour systems and print specific features.	Because it can't squeeze a file as tightly as a format like .JPG, .TIF files aren't suitable for use on the web or in interactive media (or in any application where size is an issue).
.EPS (encapsulated Postscript)	This format is very widely accepted by a wide range of applications, not just graphical, but also word-processing ones: except when it's not (see 'Does badly'.) Even more than the .TIFF files it supports all sorts of print-related goodies, like half-toning, dot gain and ink transfer information etc. Some people think that .EPS is a vector file format, others that it is a bitmap format. In truth it is neither (and both): the .EPS format is a container for other data and a set of frozen printer commands (PostScript is a printer language) that allow review and manipulation of both contained raster and vector information.	The problem is that there are multiple forms of .EPS and not all are compatible with all applications that claim to be .EPS compatible. The file format is bulky (it contains both the actual graphic data, a preview file and extra data about the file). There are all sorts of boxes to check and buttons to click which *you should never do* unless you actually have been asked to apply specific settings by your printer.

TABLE 13.1 *continued*

Name (full name)/ *Pronounced*	Does well	Does badly
.DCS (digital colour separations)	This is a special sub-class of .EPS that divides your job into four separate colour files (one each for CMYK) and an extra file that contains the information about how it all fits together. In the DCS 2 format spot colours can be contained and still produce a single file.	The files need to be stored together, it can be wasteful of disk space.
.PSD (PhotoShop document)	There once was a time where you would be very unlikely to use a .PSD to transfer work from one designer to another. But InDesign, QuarkXpress, Fireworks and Dreamweaver can all be viably addressed with a Photoshop file. .PSD files can support pretty much any combination of colour systems, spot colours, transparencies, layers and vector information you can imagine.	The very versatility of a .PSD is part of the problem. .PSD files can be huge (running into gigabytes), can contain incompatible elements and can create problems that can choke a press. .PSD files are really only for working and transfer, not really for production processes.

TABLE 13.2 Vector production files

Name (full name) /Pronounced	Does well	Does badly
.EPS (encapsulated PostScript)	This format is very widely accepted by a wide range of applications, not just graphical, but also word-processing ones, except when it's not (see 'Does badly'). Some people think that .EPS is a vector file format, others that it is a bitmap format. In truth it is neither (and both), the .EPS format is a container for other data and a set of frozen printer commands (PostScript is a printer language) that allow review and manipulation of both contained raster and vector information. The vector information contained in an .EPS is the full array of information needed to display and edit a graphic. It will contain information about work area size, fonts, colours, embedded or linked bitmapped images.	The problem is that there are multiple forms of .EPS and not all are compatible with all applications that claim to be .EPS compatible. The file format is bulky (it contains both the actual graphic data, a preview file and extra data about the file). There are all sorts of boxes to check and buttons to click which *you should never do* unless you actually have been asked to apply specific settings by your printer.
.AI (Adobe Illustrator)	The .AI file is a wholly Adobe-owned format and as such would seem to be an odd production file. But the file format has been around for so long that it has become accepted as a means of transferring vector image data across a large number of applications outside the Adobe stable. So while it is obvious that Photoshop and InDesign will read the files, so will QuarkXpress, CorelDRAW, and many 3D programs. The .AI format can contain information about masking and transparency layers and fonts.	The .AI file has the potential to cause problems in all sorts of ways. Starting with the fact that users can only work with a single page at a time and including some sophisticated transparency settings which don't transfer to non-Adobe products, and including some non-standard treatment of fonts. In short there are some useful guides when working with or sending out .AI files: 1 Save a copy of your file and only work with the copy. 2 Flatten transparency. 3 Turn text into outlines. 4 Potentially saving your copy into an older (possibly) much older version of the format to make sure the next person in the workflow can use the file.

TABLE 13.2 *continued*

Name (full name) /*Pronounced*	Does well	Does badly
.PDF (portable document format)	Most industry workers would swear that a .PDF file was a vector format; it's not. Nor is it a bitmap. It is in fact a final frozen form of the document, captured before it goes to the press, not to the RIP,[26] because technically speaking generating a .PDF means that it has been RIPed and the .PDF is the end result, a fully processed print file. As such a .PDF can contain both raster and vector information. This is not to say that .PDF files cannot be edited, they can be edited by pretty much any vector graphic application.	.PDFs do some interestingly bizarre things to text blocks. Because the .PDF is a print file that has not actually been printed the text is fully set, and cannot be selected, and copied as a block of text. What actually happens is that text will paste as lines of text, with hard-returns at the ends (which means that the designer working from a .PDF has to edit all the returns out and reset the text).
.SWF (ShockWave Flash)	Adobe Flash files not only function as a nifty way to export rich media across the web, they also serve as an effective way to share vector graphic information. In addition the files can act as containers carrying multimedia data. More importantly the files can contain sequential vector data, which is useful because Adobe has positioned the format as one that can be created and edited by a number of commercial and Open Source applications.	Flash files share some characteristics with .PDF files in that they are a final authored file, ready to be used. So while the file does carry useable graphic data it has already been processed in ways that make the data footprint smaller for transmission, but which also will have thrown away some of the useful data.
.SVG (scaleable vector graphic)	.SVG is an interesting format that has been around for a while, and supported in a half-hearted way by Adobe (Illustrator yes; Photoshop no), but shows some real promise. .SVG is a fully functional vector graphic format. It works well with other languages (as a flavour of .XML it is cousin to HTML 5) and can contain vector, raster and can also handle time-based information. There is even a print-capable version. More importantly, there are a multitude of editors, and it is supported by every browser except Internet Explorer 9 and below.	The disadvantage is that not all versions of the file format are completely compatible with all editors (though the free and Open Source *Inkscape* seems in practice to be able to open, edit and export any type of .SVG).

ICC colour profiles

The *International Color Consortium* (ICC) is a computer-industry group that has set up a means of accurately passing colour information across different operating systems. ICC colour profiles are coded descriptions of the characteristics of specific monitors, printers, scanners, etc. They are saved with image files to tell one machine about the colour characteristics of the machine the image originated on. Receiving machines can be set up to adjust their own internal display settings to simulate the originating machine or to adjust the image to display accurately on the receiving machine.

On Apple computers, ICC profiles are called *ColorSync* files and can be manually created (with a fair degree of accuracy) from within the 'display' control panel.

Colour matching

Colour matching is an extremely complex operation, worthy of a book on its own, and all I am going to say here is that it is possible by following the instructions in the Mac OS 'display' control panel, the Windows 'display colour calibration' or a Linux alternative (there are a number that work with ICC profiles); you can ensure that your monitors are displaying your images properly and, in the process, generate an .ICC profile that can be used to set up your graphic applications so that they display both accurately and consistently.[23] Having established a system-wide monitor calibration, you can go to each individual application you use and adjust the colour policies to bring them all into line with one another.

Vector images

The other dominant way of creating and displaying graphics (both for screen and print) is a vector image file, where every pixel in a bitmap image is a fixed quantity, having position, size and resolution that are defined and inflexible; a vector file is all about flexibility. The same vector file can be produced at the size of a stamp or at the size of a building, with no lack of quality.

This sounds like everything a designer could ever ask for. The downside of vector images is that they are incapable of producing photo-real images. Quite simply, the kind of fine detail that fools the human brain into perceiving a flat print or screen as a window into another world is absent in a vector image. It is the nature of the technology.

Vectors are created by sets of mathematical formulas that connect points with lines of controlled curvature (vertices) to make shapes. The shapes – which can be font forms, illustrations or parts of a page layout – can be filled with colours or bitmap images, be left empty or be made transparent.

Each of the points can be selectively adjusted at any time to be edited; each object can be transformed,[24] and the parameters of the image itself can be adjusted, added to and reshaped without the look of its contents being affected.[25]

In a bitmap, every pixel, whether it is printable or unprintable, has a value that is recorded as data, and so this makes a bigger file. In a vector image, only the actual printable (or viewable) data are recorded. So, an A4-sized square has data on: four points (the corners), the four lines connecting the points, the line and its fill. An A0 version of the same image will produce the same-sized file, because the only changes will be in the numbers defining the object. The file may have data on the thickness of the connecting lines, but increasing the thickness of the lines makes no difference to the file size, because all that is changing is the number telling the file how thick to be.

Although, as a designer, you might specify a size for a vector image, the elements themselves are actually independent, having no innate scale. This means they can be zoomed in on during editing and scaled massively in production, with no loss of quality.

Vector files don't lose quality by being edited (every bitmap operation changes, and sometimes degrades, the image), because all that happens is that the parameters of the element are being changed, and the elements are effectively re-rendered with every new viewing. They can be transformed without degradation and, as such, are effective production files.

This flexibility makes vector files massively useful in all sorts of application where clarity is important but fine detail isn't. Fonts are stored in specialist vector formats; architects and industrial designers use modified vector files (the nature of a vector file means that all the physical dimensions that are used to control a computer-aided manufacturing process are already present in the file); the same vector graphics logo can generate the smallest letterhead or drive a vinyl cutter.

Halftones

In the same way that screen-based images are composed of arrays of coloured dots, so are printed images (there are some exceptions below, but they are rare). The dots are called half-tones, and they form images by clustering together to increase density in dark areas of the image and, through interaction with other inks printed in half-tone arrays, create subtle blends of colour. Lighter areas of the image have fewer dots; darker areas have more. Richer colours are created by interactions of lots of dots. Paler colours are created by sparse interactions of dots. At a normal reading distance for the job, the eye and brain smooth out the image, allowing it to be read by the viewer as an image rather than a combination of dots.

Historically, half-tones would be created by exposing chemically sensitive plates through a screen (a literal, not figurative, screen or mesh), made of lines etched on glass plates. Some screens were coarse, having an open structure, and these would produce large half-tone dots. Some screens were fine and would produce fine dots. Later, mechanical and digital processes reproduced the same sort of screen for newer print processes. For example, digital processes impose a screen on an image for production.

Ideally, when inked and printed, the screens work with each other to produce a clean, coloured picture. Colours are created by a combination of dots in various proportions and various positions, fooling the eye into seeing the composite colour, not the individual dots. However, this effect is often exposed: try walking up to a big poster hoarding (a billboard) and see the structure of the dots appear.

Unfortunately, these screens produced a very definite grain with a direction, which could be very distracting to the viewer and damaging to the image. To counteract this, the screens would be rotated at angles that would cause *destructive interference*. Interference is a process where two or more waves (or patterns) reinforce each other at certain points to create a new pattern, called a *moiré pattern*. This manifests itself in a print as clusters, waves or beads of half-tone dots imposed on the print. By causing destructive interference, these patterns won't arise, and the print will print true.

PIXEL VS VECTOR

In Figure 13.15, we see a small target image I designed to be a testing challenge for bitmapping. The large number of circles is a particular challenge, because pixels, being square, do not naturally form smooth circles. The size ratio between the squares (pixels) and the circle they form must have lots of very small squares to fool the eye that it is looking at a convincing circle. If the ratio between one and the other is wrong, the circle stops looking like a circle and starts to look like a pile of building blocks.

This isn't a problem for vectors, because, having no resolution, they have no surface granularity, no grain, no texture. You can zoom in and never see any difference.

In the figure, A is the whole text pattern. Produced in a vector drawing application, it is shown here at its native size and resolution. B is a section of the same graphic blown up to 400 per cent and shows no sign of degradation. C is a section of the enlarged image, now blown up to 800 per cent, and is still as smooth as ever. D is an outline view of B, showing the *control handles* of the selected letter 'e'.

If we look at the bitmap version of the file (Figure 13.16) (from the same source, I promise), we start to see the problems. At 400 per cent (F), the image is grainy and lumpy. At 800 per cent (G), it has developed a severe case of what designers call 'the jaggies'. At 3,200 per cent, it looks like a cross between Lego and a retro 8-bit game.

FIGURE 13.15
Vector graphics

FIGURE 13.16
Raster graphics

The currently favoured alternative solution is a process called (somewhat confusingly) a contone image[27] or frequency modulation (an *FM screen*), where digital processes arrange the half-tone dots, not in a regular pattern but by *stochastic* form, where the dots are randomly displaced to prevent the sort of structured patterns that would both cause moiré patterns, but that also allow the viewer to see any sort of screen pattern at all.

In the sample in Figure 13.17, I've created a deliberately coarse half-tone screen of a white-to-red gradient. The left-hand side has been made as a conventional half-tone; the right-hand side is a contone/FM screen. The structure present in the conventional half-tone is absent in the FM screen area.

In Figure 13.17, the left-hand side of the image is a contone four-colour image (with a deliberately coarsened screen), and the structure of the screen is invisible in the image. The right-hand side of the image is a very coarse conventional screen, in which the structure is *very* visible, including some interesting moiré patterning developing in the blue areas.

FIGURE 13.17
Half-tone screens

Contone

The word 'contone' is a contraction of the two words 'continuous tone', and continuous-tone printing has long been a dream of printers. Imagine being able to use a magnifying glass to zoom in on an image and to be unable to see the structure that supports the image.

There is a moment when children work out that the TV or monitor image is actually made of coloured dots, and they can be found with their eyes pressed as close to the screen as they can. By contrast, a child viewing a true contone TV would never be able to play this game. No matter how close they got to the screen, they would never see anything other than smooth gradients.

Unfortunately, the dream of true continuous prints is not currently something that designers can really expect to achieve, in mass production at least. Many manufacturers

FIGURE 13.18
Half-tones making a four-colour image

try and fool us into believing it can be done, for example by having printer software varying the dot size in various parts of the picture to achieve a smoother effect, but the dots are still there.

The only process that does produce (anything like) a true continuous tone image is a very expensive art printing process called a *collotype*. A glass plate is treated with a specially treated photosensitised gelatin. The grains of gelatin react to light and dark in the image by clustering in some places and not in others. The clusters of grains are genuinely microscopic and, when treated appropriately, behave like a lithographic plate, attracting ink in certain areas and repelling it in others, thus forming a printable image. Collotypes produce very smooth contone images for two reasons: the grains are tiny, and the shape and distribution are non-uniform. Just don't forget that collotypes are expensive; but, if money is no object, they are beautiful.

PRINTING

When printers talk about individual passes through a press, they talk of 'impressions', and, until very recently, the act of 'im*pressing*' an image was what printing did, pressing ink on to a surface. In fact, as far back as the ancient world, 5,000 years ago, people had a system of image reproduction through impression called a *cylinder scroll*. This was a cylinder made of stone, glass or ceramic, with a three-dimensional relief on it telling a story. When the scroll was rolled on to wet clay, it reproduced the image, possibly many times over. In common with modern graphics, the stories were a mixture of text and image. It is likely that, at some time, a bright proto-designer tried printing an image with paint or ink. I say designer, not artist, because the nature of the cylinder suggests a thorough planning process. Not only are the images and text arranged formally, according to a socially meaningful plan, but the materials needed to make the cylinders are refined, carefully selected materials, worked by specialist tools. This was a designed product.

So, we can say that the idea of printing/image-making by impacting an image on to a surface is over 5,000 years old, but, more than this, we are privileged to be designing in a time when a second, wholly new form of printing technology, which doesn't depend on impacts, has emerged.[28]

Conventional print technologies

The word 'conventional' is a bit of a misnomer. We're not talking about a single, lone printer powering a press with his own body any more. As I write, I've been notified that Fuji have a wide-format press that will print around two-thirds of a kilometre square of CMYK material in an hour.[29] Imagine that: 600–700 m^2 of print – that's a football pitch. The title of conventional print covers some decidedly unconventional processes.

But, for the sake of simplicity, I'll ignore the exotic variations and will talk about some of the basic technologies and how they work: letterpress, screen printing, gravure and lithography.[30]

Even within a seemingly simple process such as pressing an inked surface, there are variations. Along with artists' autographic processes such as linocuts, or the kind of hand-inked woodblock prints authored by Hiroshige, there are a couple of very old ways of impressing an image on to a surface.

Intaglio printers

This was a process where the pattern to be printed was carved into the surface, ink was applied so that it filled the carved areas, and any surface ink was wiped off, leaving the plate clean except for the flooded, depressed areas. Paper would be pressed against the plate so firmly that it would deform into the depressed area of the plate and pick up the ink. This may sound like a clumsy process, but it was capable of producing beautifully fine work: this was one of the ways that banknotes would be printed. This is the top part of Figure 13.19.

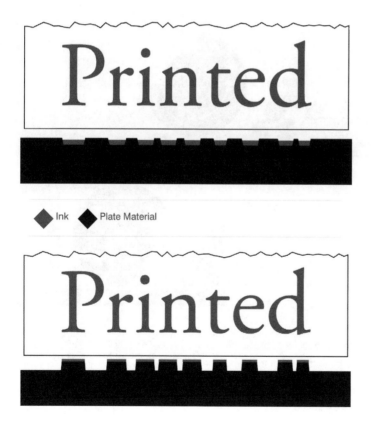

FIGURE 13.19
Print diagram 1

Relief/letterpress

This is the direct descendant of the cylinder scroll: a raised surface that repeatedly transmits an image to the medium. In the case of the letterpress, which includes traditional, set metal type, it is a process where a patterned surface (typically metal or wood) is inked so that there is ink on all of the raised areas, but not on the depressed areas. The *substratum* (we can't say paper, because it could equally be textiles or plastics) is pressed against the inked surface, which transfers the image. This is the lower section of Figure 13.19.

The printing plate in both letterpress and intaglio processes means that the plate will have to be made in the reverse of the end image for it to be printed the right way round. There was a real skill in setting type in such circumstances: a traditional typesetter had to manually set the text back to front.[31]

Letterpress

In its traditional form, letterpress was what Gutenberg used to print his books. In modern times, light-sensitised plastic plates with a metallic back are used for this

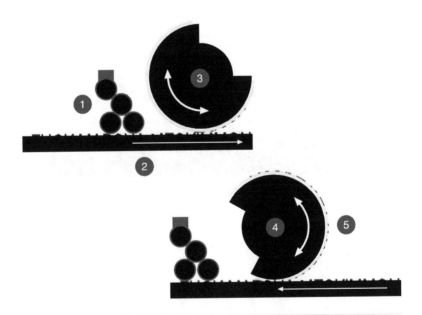

1. A series of rollers transfer ink from the resevoir to the letterpress/relief plate.

2. The plate moves as the Impression Cylinder with the attached substrate (read as paper, plastic, etc.) '3.' rotates bringing the paper into contact with the inked plate.

4. The rotation of the Impression Cylinder will bring the whole of the substrate into contact with every part of the printing plate.

5. The image is transferred to the substrate.

FIGURE 13.20
Letterpress

purpose. The plate is exposed to a transmissive image, and the non-printing areas are washed away. The plate is then attached to a press. The plate is inked, and the substratum (the medium to be printed) will be moved across the plate. There are many variations: in Figure 13.20, we have a flatbed letterpress printer.

Growing in popularity as another modern variant on the letterpress is *flexography*, where a rubber or plastic plate is produced and is bonded to a metal cylinder (see Figure 13.21). The printing plate is inked by a secondary *anilox* plate, which carries the screened cells that contain the ink. Flexography isn't always great at producing high-detail images: the rubber plates are capable of producing clunky line art and blocky prints, but little else. However, more sophisticated photopolymer (plastic) plates are now capable of printing at 150 lines per inch (60 per centimetre), which translates to about 300 dpi. As such, flexography is commonly used to print huge runs – packaging, for example (your crisps packets and bags of peas).

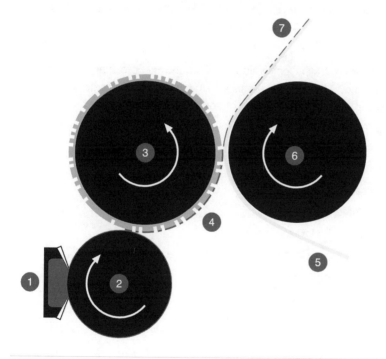

1. Chambered doctor blade system ink reservoir.

2. The *Anilox* roller transfers a consistent supply of ink...

3. ... to the *plate cylinder* which supports a soft printing plate '4'.

5. The substrate (paper, mylar, etc.) is fed in a constant process between the plate cylinder and the *impression cylinder* '6' causing a transfer of ink making the print impression '7'.

FIGURE 13.21
Flexography

Screen printing

Screen printing (sometimes called silkscreen or serigraphy) is an old technology, with some specialist applications for graphics and a very bright future in high technology.

The origin of screen or silkscreen printing is so old that no one is sure when it was. It seems that the first complete system was from Japan (some say China).[32] It seems that, by 500 BC, there was something that was more or less akin to the autographic screen-print and stencil processes taught in many art schools today. The technique arrived in the West in the nineteenth century; once again, no one seems terribly sure where the technique landed and who used it. Commercial secrecy in print was such that techniques were frequently applied and modified, with the only people knowing what was being done being the select crew who were actually in the print shop.

What is known is that experimental work was done on the Continent in the 1870s with silk fabric screens and that, in 1907, Samuel Simon was granted a patent on a silkscreen process in Manchester. The full screen plus stencil plus multicolour plus squeegee process had to wait for the American printer John Pilsworth, in 1914.

Now, we have ultrafine polyamide screens and stencils that are made by photo exposure, and, although the process has some craft associations, it still provides valuable service in a large number of specialised fields.

Kripphan (p. 58) lists:

- textiles/materials;
- printed T-shirts;
- printed toys;
- fronts of televisions, radios, etc.;
- automobile dashboards, measuring equipment, etc.;
- packaging (plastic bags);
- printed circuit boards;
- large-format advertising posters.

There are also a number of very specialist screen-printing rigs that are designed to print on to curved surfaces, including balls and cans.

The screen-printing technology in Figure 13.22 looks very primitive but is valid for current automatic processes, the differences being the machine-controlled squeegee and ink flow and the huge size of the screens involved. The fundamental technology is very familiar.

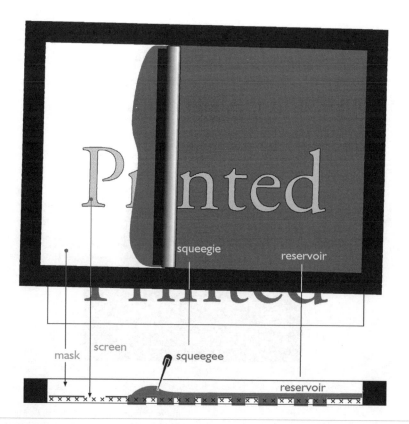

FIGURE 13.22
Screen print

Gravure

Gravure is an intaglio print process often used for very long print runs; the set-up and handling of *rotogravure* plates keep it that way. Kripphan notes that, realistically, only runs of 500,000 or more are economic with gravure. That said, the high quality of the finished product makes gravure the ideal process for design work that is going to be widely distributed and that needs to convince people, with a high-quality finish, e.g. magazines, catalogues, security printing (banknotes, passports, etc.), plastic films and metal foils.

The highest-class plates are made through a mechanical engraving or etching process, with a computer-controlled cutting machine carving evenly spaced, but variable-depth pits into the surface, to make up the image.

The image quality is high, particularly with the modern, computer-controlled processes. Kripphan notes: 'a gravure-printed image comes very close to the continuous tone tonal gradations of an original. The image effect is improved even more by the fact that, after the ink has been transferred, the liquid ink flows somewhat.'

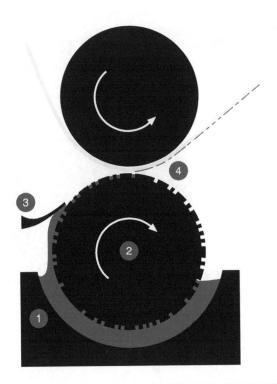

1. An ink reservoir called the *ink fountain* holds the printing ink.

2. The ink is scooped out by the rotation of the *gravure cylinder.*

3. Surface ink is scraped off by a flexible *blade* and the ink is forced into the pattern on the surface of the cylinder.

4. Ink is transfered by the media being passed between the gravure cylinder and the impression cylinder, forcing the media into contact with the ink.

FIGURE 13.23
Gravure

Designers should make no mistake: this is a heavy industrial process and needs expert handling. Take advice before committing a client to the combination of cost and difficulties represented by gravure.

Lithography

The word *lithography* literally means drawing on (or image made on) stone, and this is historically what the process was. A limestone block would be drawn on directly with a special waxy pencil and then treated with a chemical solution that made the un-drawn-on areas (the negative) attract water. The wax was removed with turps, but would leave a molecularly thin layer of oily residue that would attract the ink.

The term lithography is used to apply to a vast family of linked processes, each with their special characteristics, and each with drawbacks. Although there are too many

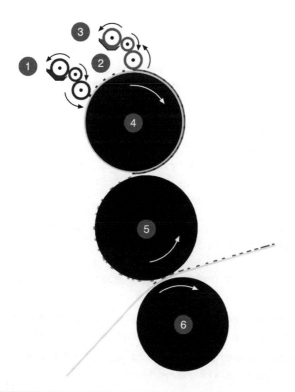

1. A set of rollers prepare the plate cylinders' *lithographic plate*.
2. The damp surface sets up the pattern of oil-repulsive and oil-loving elements of the print.
3. Oily ink is added, it sticks to the oil-loving parts of the pattern.
4. The lithographic plate rotates to bring the oil and water patterned surface into contact with the *blanket cylinder* where a reverse of the image is transfered.
5. This reversed image is transfered to the media (now the right way round) by being squeezed between the blanket and impression cylinders.

FIGURE 13.24
Lithography

variations to discuss here,[33] the collotype method mentioned above, for example, is counted as a lithographic form, because, even though it has completely different qualities, there are some common features.

The process still works by dividing the surface of the printing plate into two areas, one that is water-loving (hydrophilic), which will not be printed but exists in opposition to a second area, which is water-hating (hydrophobic) and oil-loving and which attracts the ink. However, printers no longer use wax pencils and stone, but lasers, plastics and engraving machines.

You will commonly hear printers talking about *offset* lithography. This means that there is a second roller, called a *blanket roller*, that stands between the print plate and the printed medium as the means of transmission: as such, in offset litho, the plate never touches the medium.

Non-impact print technologies

After several centuries of printing comprising images impressed on to a surface, in the space of fifty years, new technologies have appeared that are not only rivalling the industrial power of existing forms in printing beautiful 2D material, but are applying the same technology in creating 3D objects.

The technologies that underlie non-impact printers are diverse and are only clustered together for two reasons: the first, as mentioned above, is because they don't transfer images through impressions (they have no master, no plate or stencil), and the second is because they all only work as the end of the line of a digital workflow: all of them need computer control to form the image.

So, as a means of projecting an image from a device to a surface, you are likely to encounter three technologies:

- **Inkjet**: a group of miniature nozzles spray minute drops of ink on to a substratum.

- **Laser printing** (technically, *electrophotography* or *xerography*): electrically charged pigmented dust liquid is fused on to a substratum.

- **Dye sublimation**: dye is heated to gas in carefully controlled conditions and then solidifies on the substratum.

Inkjet

There are three basic technologies that generate the microscopic dots of ink that form the image in inkjet printing:

- There are so-called *continuous inkjet* printers, which pump the ink in a continuous stream, with the ink being given an electrostatic charge. If the stream is meant to hit the paper – to form the image – it is allowed to pass through without interference. If the stream is to be 'turned off', so that it won't impact the medium, a second static charge is applied to deflect the stream into a gutter. This form of switching is done extremely fast, with the 'waste' being fed back into the system.

- There are thermal inkjets, where a small electrical heating element heats the ink, causing a bubble in the ink flow that compresses the ink and causes it to squirt out of the nozzle, on to the paper.

- There are piezo inkjets, where a tiny piston made of piezo crystal (a crystal that expands when an electrical current is passed through it) pushes the ink through a nozzle on to the substratum.

The inks are built up in sequence, with time allowed for the inks to dry. The drying slows the printing process, and so, in contrast to domestic inkjets, industrial ones often use special inks that harden on exposure to UV light. In these machines, prints

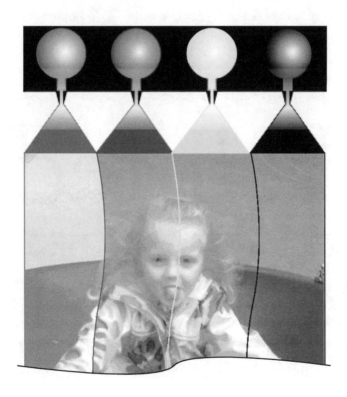

FIGURE 13.25A
Inkjet: the basic technology

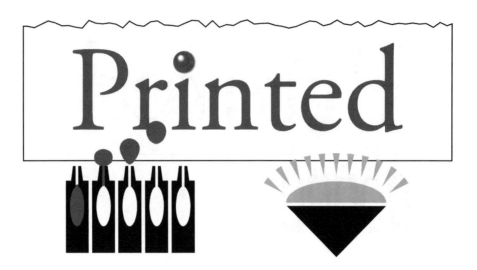

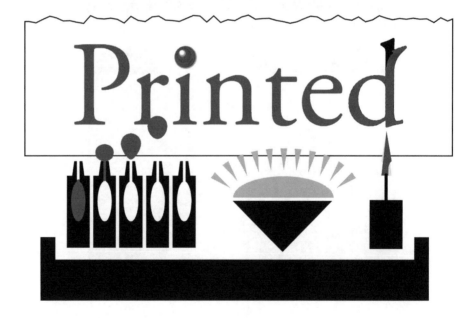

FIGURE 13.25B
Inkjet: some interesting variations

are passed under either UV lamps (hot and wasteful of electricity) or, in newer machines, arrays of UV LEDs, which instantly harden the inks, allowing for a much faster turnaround for individual prints.

Inkjets are often used for proofing, because they can overprint different drops on the same area, as defined by the image pixel, to build up subtle tones. This means that they can produce excellent and colour-accurate images. However, print speeds, although perfectly acceptable for proofing purposes, are too slow to compete with systems such as lithography or gravure in large-run printing.

Inkjet prints have many advantages, and chief among them is that the printing heads (the parts that actually do the printing) are themselves pretty small, meaning that they can be manoeuvred in all sorts of interesting ways that allow them to print things that would not normally be printable.[34]

For example, the Mimaki printer mentioned at the beginning of the chapter is an inkjet where the head travels backwards and forwards on a track, which is itself mounted on a track that can move the length of the printing bed. More than this, the head can be raised and lowered while printing. So, in effect, the head can print on to any part of a cube formed by the width of the bed, by its length, by the height it can be raised and lowered (5 cm). What this means for a designer is that prints can be accurately made on curved and irregular surfaces. Mimaki showed samples printed on golf balls (small and with an irregular surface), a vodka bottle (curved in different directions), a BlackBerry smartphone and a laptop – all printed on the same flat print bed.[35]

This kind of work simply could not be printed on a litho or laser printer, because the printing equipment is simply too big to be moved, and the paper has to be bent around the machinery. Inkjets today can print to a high degree of accuracy and, with UV hardening inks, on a wonderful variety of surface materials, not just absorbent ones. In addition, many of these speciality presses can be equipped with a *router* unit, meaning that non-square jobs can be cut out as they are printed.[36]

Laser printers

Laser printers (technically electrophotography) depend for their functioning on the ability accurately to impose fine patterns of static charges that will attract a printing medium to them. Each colour component of a laser print is served by a separate 'drum'. Each drum is statically charged, and then a light beam is played over the drum to form the pattern.[37] Toner is applied to the drum, sticking to the charged areas but not the uncharged.[38] The charged pattern is pressed into the medium and melted with a hot roller into the substrate.[39]

The downside of the process is that the equipment needed to print each colour is bulky and needs to be duplicated for each colour. This means that the medium needs to do the work of bending and conforming to the process, which in turn means that the path the printed substrate has to pass along may end up being extremely

1. The printer drum is given a static electrical charge.

2. A light source (a laser or LED array) knocks off electrons making uncharged areas on the drum. This process forms the non-printing areas of the image.

3. Toner is mechanically applied to the drum and sticks to the charged areas.

4. The toner is transferred to the paper.

5. The paper passes between heated rollers which melt the toner into the weave of the paper.

6. A brush removes excess toner. A lamp exposes the drum to remove excess charge and the process begins again.

FIGURE 13.26
Electrophotography

convoluted. This in turn restricts both the thickness and rigidity of the material being printed. If it's not thin and not bendy, it's probably not going to go through a laser printer.

Industrial electrophotography machines range in size from the big to the really big (e.g. some Indigo presses are taller than a man and almost 40 m long). However, they have a truly massive advantage: because no films or plates are used in the process, individual print runs can be very short, jobs can be reconfigured on the fly, and customisation of individual items is possible. In short, you can connect an electrophotography printer to a customer database and run out highly individualised jobs with no difficulty at all.[40]

Although the same could be said of inkjet-based jobs (and, indeed, there are circumstances where customisation *on press* is already done), the speed of the inkjet is so slow compared with that of the laser printer that large runs of customised prints are more practical on the laser press than on the inkjet; however, inkjets can customise more versatile media. Once again, it is a balance that requires good advice from your printer.

In recent years, full-colour laser printers have made leaps and bounds in terms of quality and, while they cannot match a top-quality gravure or litho print, the colour-matching is better, and the prints can now look pretty good.

Dye sublimation

Properly speaking, this is thermal sublimation printing. This technology is not commonly associated with traditional graphics activities – posters, leaflets and books – but it does all sorts of things that make it very useful for an inventive graphic communicator.

Sublimation is a term that describes a sudden transformation from a solid to a gas without a liquid stage in between. In the case of a *dye sub* printer, the dye is the material that sublimes, travelling as a gas from the film where it fuses to the surface of the substratum. It is this fusing, together with the high print quality, that makes dye-sub printing the staple of the promotion and marketing industries.[41] The surface does have to be pre-coated with polyester (or other polymer) to provide a viable base for the sublimed dye to bond with, but these materials can be applied to pretty much anything, from fabric to ceramics to metals. To put it simply, dye-sub printers can print to: sheet aluminium, clothing (as long as it's not cotton), luggage, hats, credit cards, business cards, baubles, fridge magnets, keyrings, glass, licence plates, mouse mats, signs, work vests and much more.

The main disadvantage of such systems is that they are wasteful in their use of consumables. The coloured dye is stored on sheets of material called ribbons. As the ribbon passes over the material to be printed, heating print heads or lasers selectively and variably heat the ribbon. The hotter a spot becomes, the more dye is released. The more dye, the denser the colour, and one spot can be overprinted a number of times to further increase the number of tones that can be produced. However, each heating of an area of ribbon means the ribbon has to be moved to bring fresh material into play. This means that, if the image being printed isn't very dense, the ribbon will end up with much of its printable area being wasted, and the ribbon cannot be recycled.

3D

You might ask why I have a paragraph on 3D in a section on printing. The answer is simple: in recent years, applications of inkjet-printing technologies have allowed 3D digital files to be printed, as one-offs and as short runs. Although this is never going to produce items at the sorts of cost that un-unionised workshops in the emerging world can, it will allow a designer to produce one-off models to show clients, in the same way that we currently do with print proofs, and, trust me: giving clients a proof of their new toy or character to hold in their hands is a powerful tool of persuasion.

A final note

This is not the end, nor is this short list intended to be a definitive list of print techniques. Professor Kripphan's book (2001) runs to over a thousand pages, without any excess. I hope this, in some way, explains why I made my opening comments about print and production technologies being too complex and too diverse to be understood in their entirety. In reality, you will be looking at specific workflows, paths from designer to user, and this is the domain of the production expert. Ask the technician, ask the editor, ask the printer.

SCREEN-BASED

Screen-based media have been the *next big thing* for twenty years now. The screen has been about to 'destroy the publishing world' for as long as I have been a designer. It hasn't, and the people who think it will and should have made all sorts of assumptions about the ways new technologies attain cultural relevance.[42] What the new media have done is create a novel and parallel system of publishing that has grown like crazy, bringing us media forms that have never been seen before: blogs, wikis, e-books, social media, fan films and so much more. All of these operate very well without invalidating the media of the past.

This process is what the media theorists Bolter and Grussin (2000) have called *remediation*. They say that remediation is the process wherein old stories are told in new ways, ways influenced and added to by the new media.

This is a principle worth remembering for designers: the new is not wrecking or supplanting the old, it is supplementing it, and in ways that are driven first and foremost by people's needs, not by the artist, inventor or pundit. So, once again, designers need to look first at the needs and culture of the user; how they use the technologies they use; what the technology means to them; and only then should the designer choose the appropriate medium to serve these needs. If you disbelieve me, look to an old story such as Little Red Riding Hood or Robin Hood. Look at the multiple retellings mediated by new technologies. None of these makes the other tellings of the story invalid: the old still works; the new works for new audiences.

Remember this when dealing with a glamorous type of medium that clients are likely to have read about, that they have been told about by a friend 'who knows', or have seen demonstrated on TV. They will see this new medium as having taken on a special lustre, a special magic, which makes the client feel that they must have this medium, even if it makes no sense in brand, marketing or communications terms for the client and their organisation. Remember media (of any kind) work because they carry a cultural value.

This is a message that should have been hammered home by the collapse of the first *Internet bubble*, where hundreds of businesses sprang up online with no business plan and answering no social need (only to crash and burn). And, lest we should feel smug, much the same is happening now with e-books, where everyone is jumping on the bandwagon, and no one is sure what the bandwagon does.

However, assuming that your client has told you that they want you to produce a website for them, and you have actually established that a website will do the job, we'll examine some of the things you should do when working on-screen.

Web

A word of warning about websites: if you ever get designers who have worked on websites together for a chat, one of the topics of conversation that is bound to come up is the client's tendency to wait until long after you have designed the site before they give you the material that the site is built to contain. This is extremely frustrating for the client, as the job appears to stall, but is more annoying for the designer, who now has to start stalking the client to get the materials needed. So, as a word of warning, when you are in the planning stage of the job, do take some time out to establish a clear list of what materials the client is providing you with and a timeline for when they will provide them.[43]

First, let's clarify what the role of a graphic communicator is in designing a website. The role of the designer is to design the site, not build it. This is not to say that a designer cannot build a site; it is just that this is not our primary role. The coders who build the *back-end* of the site – the .PHP or AJAX, etc. – are skilled and expert in ways that designers probably aren't; just as we are expert in the ways people use culture to communicate, and they're not. The designer and coder form a complementary pairing: either could make a website, but it would just be a stronger website if they worked together. In industrial terms, this process of graphically designing a site to communicate effectively to a specific audience is known as *look and feel* or *skinning a site*.

Let's first dismiss a couple of myths about web design:

- **Myth**: web designs are produced in HTML.
- **Fact**: there once was a time when this was true, and many sites we use today are partly or mostly constructed in HTML, but HTML is a tool designed for constructing a page at a time and, when faced with something on the scale of Amazon.com or Facebook, it is inadequate to the task. For these companies to operate an HTML-based system, they would need to pre-design every possible page that might be called on by a user. That's a page

for every product Amazon sells and a page for every person on Facebook. Clearly, this would be madness, and so we have *web applications* built of *scripting languages* (such as .PHP: Hypertext Preprocessor). PHP writes code that is only partially embedded in an HTML page;[44] the bulk of a page's potential code is absent and is generated (on the fly, every time), when triggered by a user request, from data held on a database.

As such, there is not much here for a designer to do, and, until we consider how the page gets its visual identity, there will be little for us to do, but the generation and definition of visual identity are the graphic communicator's meat and drink. A graphic communicator working on the web is unlikely to have built the .PHP code, or the SQL database, but he or she will have constructed a set of visual rules about how the page will look. These rules will commonly (but not exclusively) be constructed from combinations of images (.jpg, .gif and .png), multimedia (.mov, .mpg, .swf, .flv, etc.) and text, all told where to sit, what to look like and how to behave, by combinations of *Javascripts* and *CSS* CODE.[45]

- **Myth**: web designs must follow mechanical sets of design rules. Design craft, cultural knowledge or talent play no part.

- **Fact**: there is a whole complex school of knowledge called human–computer interaction (HCI) design, which is a close cousin of graphic communication. HCI is replete with principles derived from psychology and ergonomics, which regard human responses as universal. So, although these rules present valuable insights (and they genuinely do), a user's culture will frequently be so strong and real to them that it will override so-called universal responses. In common with any other form of visual culture, the only safe option is to research into, and talk to, our users and clients. A good designer should know the HCI rules and then test them against the worlds the users actually inhabit.

- **Myth:** web design is about expressing yourself.

- **Fact**: this is quite as dangerous as the previous myth. The myth is often phrased in terms such as: 'My site is fun, you have to spend time exploring it to understand it' or 'People often don't get my site first time out, you have to grow into it' or, my favourite, 'It's an experience. You don't use my site, it happens to you.'

If a site is a pain to use people will just walk away. This has been demonstrated by research. However, there are exceptions to this. If a user has no choice, they will use it: e.g. if a bad bus timetable website is what you have, you have to use it;[46] a government website that you have to use to register for benefits will be used, no matter how weak it is;[47] and your university e-Learning platform will be your means of access to learning even if it stinks.

However, most websites have to be *sticky*:[48] they need the user to return again and again to function.

If you, as a designer, design a site that a user cannot simply access, both because it functions in HCI terms but also because it communicates well as a graphic artefact, then they will just go somewhere else. Web design is a communication design task: as such, it's not about the designer (and their ego), it's about how well it serves the user.

- **Myth:** you have to be a code geek/code monkey to be able to design websites.

- **Fact:** this is a partial truth. To design a web presence along the lines of the massive interlocking array of sites that the BBC fields is a massive technical undertaking, with some graphic communications tacked on. To even get the sites to function individually, then work together, is a real problem: a problem that has to be handled before you get to the semantically sensitive task of designing an effective look and feel.

  However, a simple website (for example promoting your work) should not be beyond the wit of any designers to make themselves. There are WYSIWYG[49] tools that allow designers to work as if they were using a desktop-publishing tool, such as those found in InDesign or Quark,[50] for example: NetObjects Fusion (Windows), Softpress Freeway (Macintosh) or KompoZer (Linux). These sorts of tool allow a user to generate a working site, with linked multimedia, email, etc., without getting bogged down in code.

  However, that said, it is always useful to have a code buddy on hand to help out.

CSS stands for cascading style sheets. Concentrate on the 'style sheet' portion for the moment. CSS tells HTML and some other elements how to behave. For example, it can tell text to be styled in a specified font and to be a certain point size and colour. More than this, it can define the size, location and layering of the container holding the text. In fact, CSS can (and, in the case of dynamic websites, probably will) define the structure of the page. It is not just a style tool; it is a pixel-perfect layout tool too.

More than being able to style layout and other graphical content, CSS can work with Javascript to do this in a dynamic way. Through CSS and Javascript, users can vary the style (and layout) of a page to suit themselves,[51] or create cross-fades between content, or even do something as simple as create boxes with rounded corners that can expand and contract.

Colour on the web has been discussed above, but images on the web present their own problems, beyond those created by colour shifts between operating systems. Theoretically, image formats are platform independent, and we can use any type of image in a website, but only in theory. In practice, there are a limited number of supported image formats that work across all operating systems and environments.[52] Even with these few 'safe' image formats, there are quirks.[53] For example, before Internet Explorer 7, transparency in .PNG files wasn't properly supported (and ICC colour profiles in .PNG still aren't), and .SVG files can provide excellent cross-platform vector images but are not properly supported by Internet Explorer (apparently IE 9 will support them). This is another example of why, as graphic communicators, we must be very sure of the client we are designing for before we decide on a particular technology of delivery.

All of these file formats and codes are lovely technologies, and they are as rewarding for the right graphic communicator as typography or illustration or packaging, but, in common with these fields of design, web design must be driven by considerations of clients and users and culture. We are not code monkeys; we are designers.

Interactive/rich media

A whole range of media tools have emerged in the last decade that allow the moderately technological to produce fully functional interactive media, and, as such, much of the *conceptual stuff* is covered by the section on web design and coding. More distinctive for a discussion of rich media is the way that interaction has begun to leak into 'regular publishing' workflows. Adobe Acrobat files can carry motion graphics (including video), 3D objects that can be manipulated in real time and web links. Theoretically, you can embed interactive .SWF files within an Acrobat one; you can certainly embed .FLV (Flash Video). And all of this can be authored from within InDesign (or you could do similar things from within QuarkXpress).

What this means for designers is that we can see a natural tendency for the act of authoring interaction moving from being an activity that is technically beyond a designer, held hidden behind a curtain of code. Instead, it has become an activity that is accessible to authorship by the designer and for consumption by the user.

The main difficulty for the designer is changing the mindset needed to author a document that is responsive to client interaction, that moves and changes over time. Designers working in these interactive and enriched media forms have to think in terms of a total experience: not aiming for a first impact, but for a coherence of design that leads the user and offers them an engaging, meaningful and beautiful experience – a kind of cross between the coherence of book design and the visual scene setting of a movie.[54]

You might notice that this area is light on specific technical detail, and the reason is simply this. I could talk about modern interactive development environments such as *Unity* or *Flash*, which can author individual environments, but I suspect that these are transitional forms, representing a halfway stage between the code-driven tools of the past (I remember with horror learning Lingo for Director 3) and proper designer tools that will function in a way that doesn't impose a barrier between the act of design and the act of deployment.

This has happened in the area of 3D modelling, where older modelling packages were entirely or mainly based on entering text-based parameters for 3D objects, without any direct form of visual feedback (in *POVray*, you had to specify the type of object – sphere, cube, plane, etc. – through numeric values, as a kind of coding exercise): you punched in numbers, with no clear idea of how things would turn out, and then hit the render command with your fingers crossed. Now we have beautiful 3D tools that allow constructing 3D worlds to be like playing with toys: Poser is like the best dolls' game in the world; Modo is clay on steroids; and 3D modellers such as Cinema 4D or Maya are like Lego crossed with the world's coolest modelling kit. All use analogues of real-world processes to do computationally complex things: you rotate, you drag, you bend, you twist, you squeeze and gouge. All hide ferociously complex number crunching. You can dig down and play with the numbers, but you rarely will. One day, interaction will happen this way, and programs such as Acrobat show the way.[55] Designers should have tools that bend to them; the designers shouldn't have to bend to the tool.

Until that day, the advice must be:

1 **Work with the client and the user** to develop a thorough understanding of the problem.

2 **Organise your ideas**, make a thorough plan and test your ideas on paper before you deploy them on-screen. Now, this might seem like a weird thing to say: paper is antique; screen is not. But, there is a design process called *paper prototyping*, which allows a designer to nail down fine detail without expensive coding and development.

Paper prototyping is a process where screen *models* of the finished design are made (often in Photoshop) and presented to the client or user. The person being tested is asked to attempt a specific task – navigating to a particular page, finding some specific data – and is presented with a printout of the first page. Their attempts to navigate, using the paper proxies, are recorded for later analysis. The user *clicks* on the printed buttons, and the designer gives them the paper page that the click would take them to in reality. By watching a number of people attempting to use our paper prototype, we can learn how people will actually use our design, without a line of code being written.

3 **Use the information** you have uncovered to produce a 'bible' for the project, a guide that lays out the rules that the project will conform to: the layout, the type, the placement and styling of the graphics, the acceptable use of images.

4 **Keep a close eye on where your media resources are stored**. Make folders and sub-folders. Keep your images in *Images*. Keep your audio in *Audio*. Rich-media projects generate so much data that, if you don't, you will never be able to keep track of it all. Make sure that you give your files meaningful names.

5 **Test**, at every stage.

6 **When the test shows that something is wrong, fix it**. Don't pretend that everything is fine, on the principle that it will all work out in the end. It won't, and the problems will multiply.

Working in rich media/interactive media is massively rewarding work if you are organised.

Reality: mixed, augmented and virtual

This is really a notion, a provocation if you like, because the technology is immature but shows massive potential.[56]

Imagine being able to tag anything in the world that has a geographical position. Not just the real and tangible, but the gone and fantastic. Imagine graphically tagging the Hanging Gardens of Babylon (gone but not forgotten) or the Sleeping City of R'lyeh (never existed).

All of this is possible within the realm of **augmented**, **mixed** and **virtual realities** (AR, MR, VR):

Augmented realities are effectively magic lenses where the viewer sees both the world and the virtual tagging and annotation. So, for example, in the PSP game *Invizimals*, a camera is attached to the PSP that feeds a real-time image to the screen. The software adds virtual monsters into the field of view (which you can catch, play with, train, etc.). The interesting part is that the virtual monsters are aligned to the world in such a way that they look (more or less) as though they fit in.

In effect, the technology adds designed objects to the world. Theoretically, these objects can be any size or scale, and of any medium. Jelly castles and smoke whales, protest banners and marketing opportunities can be imposed on pretty much any part of the real world, but in a way that breaks no laws, because the AR makes no permanent physical changes to the target. So, although my annoyance at the banking system would be met with a prison stay if I painted something on a city bank building, if I created a giant leech in AR that was attached to the self-same building, I would be breaking no laws (not even breach of the peace, because my AR modification is invisible unless you download the specific channel to view it on your smartphone). More than this, the same location can have different tagging, depending on the user's interests.

Mixed reality is a halfway house between AR and VR. Rather than imposing small modifications on the world, it merges two worlds to create a whole new space. As such, you're not likely to find a guerilla-marketing approach to MR: too much of the real world needs to be modified. A successful example of an MR system is the BBC/gameware-development children's show *Bamzooki*. The show demonstrates both the strengths and the weaknesses of MR. Shadows, lighting and focus are consistent across both the virtual and the real, creating a convincing illusion. However, because of the high processing cost of calculating every possible field of view in real time for the MR, the shots have to be fairly static. It's too difficult to make the virtual and the real mesh convincingly.

Full **virtual reality** is what is called an immersive environment. You are totally enveloped by the environment, theoretically with all of your senses being fed information in a coordinated way, with no access to anything from the *real world*. This has been a popular cultural theme for years: from the novel *Neuromancer*, to *Star Trek*'s holodecks, to *Tron*; unfortunately, the reality (to pun) is much less real. VR is very difficult to do in a convincing way. Once again, the problem is calculating the visuals in a way that fools the brain, because, in the world, the viewer has a field of view that changes all the time: as we glance about, the view changes, but the changes are consistent. In a VR, a casual glance to the side means the scene needs to be redrawn to maintain the illusion. This takes time. The trick is to *cache* the possible views, just in case they are needed. To do this fast enough, in high enough detail that the viewer doesn't see the changes, is not currently practical.

This is why those VR roller coaster rides you see at fairs and seaside resorts require that you sit in a specific place and not move. Go too far to the side, and the illusion is ruined.

Motion

Once again, we see that motion graphics is a technically demanding area of graphic communication that benefits from both very careful planning and good co-workers who can actually make the processes work.

At this point, I know there will be people who say that modern motion graphics applications, such as Adobe After Effects or Apple Motion, make motion graphics a game that anyone can play, on their own, with no help. This has an element of truth to it (but only a small one). Apple Motion, for example, has a beautifully direct and comprehensible interface that offers a nice shallow learning curve. This ease of software manipulation can fool the uninformed into thinking that the software is doing the design. This is not true; at best, it is making the production workflow shorter and less labour intensive. The design is still a complex and demanding task, but now it is one spread across hundreds of images, not one.

The 'good co-worker' will handle the production and distribution end of the job, making sure that colour grading is appropriate for the broadcast media, that the file formats and compression are right, processing the media and packaging the files in ways that make sense for the broadcast and distribution end of the job; without their expertise, the job will be slow and may well stumble on technical obstacles.

The designers' role is to plan the job thoroughly, so that the technical co-workers know what to do. They organise the structure of the show in detail, so that the clients know what they are about to see, and so that the appropriate material can be gathered and shot. Look at some of the drawings Johnny Hardstaff made to help his colleagues understand how he wanted his ideas to be realised (see Johnny's piece on pp. 163–7).

The success of the job depends on both. Your task as the motion designer is to plan, to supervise others, to direct and to assess the work. This is not to say you won't get hands-on with the making – graphic communicators who work in motion/video graphics are a very technical bunch; it is just that the processes are expensive and need to be run by a team.

Here is a list of things that you need to do to make a motion job work; the entries are in the order in which they need to be done:

1   **Plan the job thoroughly**, as images, images that you will develop to a point (on paper or on screen) where others can see what needs to be done. This includes character and scene development (what stuff looks like, in detail), storyboards, possibly *animatics*, and quite possibly *location shots*.

    At this stage, your preparatory work should be able to answer any question that the client could ask about the proposed design.

2   **Make a list**, based on the prep work, of everything that needs to be in the movie. Think carefully about this. If your storyboard calls for an actor standing by a road as a car drives by, we clearly need an actor and a car, but we will also need someone to drive the car, otherwise the shoot breaks down. If you need a lot of lights, or a rabbit dyed red, this needs to be done.

3   **You need to have booked your production facility access**: be it university or the commercial world, you will need to have established your right to be on a piece of kit for the time it takes to do the work. Every year, in every university that I know, the second semester becomes a whirl of upset student designers who can't get access to equipment they need because they haven't booked it out. Industry is much the same, except more expensive. Organise access to your equipment upfront.

4   **You need access to property and locations**. Get the permissions in the planning, not the shooting, stage.

5   **You need permission to use other media resources** (music, image, video, code, etc.) before you use it. This requires time and negotiation.

6   **You need to select your human resources** – actors, technicians, make-up, scenic artists, etc. – and check their availability.

In conclusion, screen-based media form a glamorous field of graphic communication; at least part of the glamour comes from the fact that you have to be a very thorough and organised designer to make it all work. In fact, all design requires more care in the planning than in the doing; and the doing needs a mountain of care.

NOTES

1 Please feel free to try and prove me wrong. It would be a fun way to spend a life.

2 What I have been calling *manifestation* because we're no longer talking about print vs screen or 2D vs 3D. But we are talking about taking something imaginary (an idea) and making it real in the world.

3 A major Japanese industrial printer manufacturer.

4 A .SEA file was a Self-Extracting Archive file, a compressed set of documents that needs no special software to open itself up.

5 If you are short of cash, and don't feel like breaking the law by using cracked software, you could usefully look at Open Source software such as the DTP application *Scribus*, which is free and works pretty well on a Mac.

6 Ask them about .jdf files for their process. A .jdf is a digital file that describes a set of print production technologies (what Adobe calls, 'the intent of a printed piece, as well as each process step required to achieve that intent'). In effect, the .jdf is a set of templates generated by the production house that defines how their particular presses will function with specific inks and media. In combination with flight-checking software such as Adobe Acrobat Pro, it will check your job and alert you to problems with your job.

   A good printer will let you have the .jdf for their press, effectively meaning you can run the jobs digitally to iron out bugs before you blow a load of money doing it for real.

7 Pre-flight (pre-flighting) is a process where the job is effectively tested for fitness as if it were going through a real RIP on to a press. Sophisticated ones can have profiles loaded that give precise information about the nature of the press, materials and inks, so that the files going to press can be assessed for suitability on specific jobs.

8 Don't argue with the client's specification and substitute file types, codecs or compression schemes. The wrong file types can muck up a screen-based workflow very effectively.

9 Once, when working as a multimedia designer, my art director gave me the job of designing a video-cassette case on the basis that I knew Quark XPress. I gave it a go, but I don't kid myself I'm a packaging designer.

10 Literally produced by a person's own hand.

11 Personally, I would argue that communicating visually, as opposed to any other function of visual culture, has always been an option for humans. Print isn't even the first *mediated* way humans visually communicated; that would be cave and other palaeolithic art.

12 Photo typesetting.

13 Or more likely could use, but it will cost you more, be more difficult, etc.

14 Yes there is one. It is called the *Commission Internationale d'Eclairage (CIE)* or, in English, the International Commission for Lighting.

15 See Judd (1953).

16 Apparently, they overprinted fluorescent pink as a duotone over magenta to improve skin-tone reproduction.

17 Two full print systems placed end to end with a special feeder in between that flips the sheets over to print the other side. In effect, it means that sheets can be printed on both sides in one pass.

18   In case you're curious, it works out as: 8 bit = 2^8 (2 x 2 x 2 x 2 x 2 x 2 x 2 x 2); 4 bit = 2^4 (2 x 2 x 2 x 2); 2 bit (2 x 2).

19   There is some debate about this. Differing machines within the same family of operating systems will have different components and different display characteristics. So, anyone hoping to get exact colour fidelity will have to manage the process in detail.

20   Horizontally and vertically, measured from the top-left corner of the image.

21   The more pixels there are packed within a given area of the image, the finer the detail it will carry. This is known as the *resolution* of the image, because it defines the finest detail that can be resolved in the image.

22   As defined by one of the colour models above.

23   The consistency is more important than the accuracy. Your job may not be accurate in industrial terms, but a good printer will give you proofs and help you make adjustments; but, if the colour is not consistent between the applications on your machine, you will make time-wasting errors that will add up until you have no idea which on-screen colours you can trust.

24   'Transformed' is emphasised here because it is a specific term. Technically, a whole series of manipulations – scaling, flipping, rotating, skewing, etc. – are mathematical transformations and are common across all vector-based images.

25   Many of the illustrations and diagrams in this book have been produced in a now discontinued application called Freehand, which supported multiple pages, of different sizes, and rotations. Something similar can be done in the latest version of InDesign.

26   A *raster image processor* is a special computer that takes graphical information and drives a printing press.

27   It's not a contone image (see below); at best, it's a 'kind of contone image, but not'.

28   I'm aware that some might argue that screen printing isn't an impression method. I would argue that a printer still presses the ink through the screen on to the paper; in this, I'm using Helmut Kipphan's naming scheme for print, as the Kipphan book, the *Handbook of print media*, is simply the most complete book on print production that I know of.

29   Fuji Onset S70, 700 m² per hour.

30   If you have time, and are interested for your dissertation or something else, see if you can get Kipphan's book. It really is pretty impressive: it covers everything.

31   I'm told upside-down too. But I suspect that this may have been a tall story.

32   According to Jacob Israel Biegeleisen, the author of *The complete book of silk screen printing production*, although the Chinese and ancient Egyptians both used stencils to transfer images, the Japanese were the first to actually combine the stencils with a support network to keep the design intact. Not a screen, but a web of human hair.

33   Once again, look up Kripphan if you really need to know.

34   The ink is fed by pipes from a reservoir, meaning that the print heads can be remote from the ink.

35   Mimaki is not the only company that produces printers that can do this, only the one that designed a mesmerising stand at IPEX 2010 to demonstrate its machines.

36 A router is a computer-controlled high-speed drill bit that can carve out material with high accuracy, without slowing down the print process.

37 The photons (an individual quantum of light) displace the electrons (an individual quantum of electricity), knocking out the charge.

38 Toners are microscopic beads of resin with coloured pigments embedded in them. Dry toners appear as dust; liquid toners consist of a carrier liquid, with the toner suspended in it.

39 Which is why my friend and colleague Matthew Fray gets so upset when students put acetate through his laser printers. Yes, the toner will stick to the acetate, but, in doing so, the acetate melts into a lovely gluey mess that sticks all over the inside of the printer. Take pity on your technicians and don't do it.

40 Having seen some of the custom printing software, I must report that, although it works, it really needs good designers to make sure it works well.

41 Kipphan quotes 1,800–2,400 dpi resolution for dye sublimation printers; however, the way images are built up by dye subs is fundamentally different from those of other printers. As such, resolution figures don't tell us a lot about the actual quality. Just take it as read that the prints will be good enough that they are often marketed as 'continuous-tone' prints. Ask your printer for samples and details.

42 The assumption often seems to be as simplistic as, 'new is better, people want new'. The reality is more complex. People want meaningful.

43 I'm using the term *material* here to talk about all the stuff that clients will want the site to contain: the images, the text, the links, the multimedia, the video.

44 The HTML page is a shell, containing the common page elements – logos, buttons, etc. – but no actual content.

45 Javascript is a programming language that tells elements on a web page how to behave. It is behind such popular features as the 'Lightbox' function, but, more interestingly, it can tell CSS objects how to behave; for example, how to look one way in the morning and how to look different after lunch.

46 My local bus company's site is weak, but I had no choice except to use it. Now I have a handy Android app that gives me the same information that I once had to surf the web for, but in a form I can use. I'm not using the site again.

47 There is an HCI principle called the *power law of practice*, which says that people will get better at using a bad interface pretty fast, but only to a degree; after the initial improvement, they will find the site no easier to use. A bad site will never get better through repeated use.

48 'Sticky' is a term to indicate both the attractiveness of a site and people's desire to return to it time and time again.

49 What You See Is What You Get, a term that indicates a computer-driven process that uses analogues of real-world manipulation processes – cutting, pasting, dragging and dropping, drawing directly, etc. – rather than entering code or instructions, as in writing HTML code directly.

50 You *could* export forms of web pages from both InDesign and Quark. You'll still need to refine them in another web-design application.

51 Which is a pretty sophisticated way to work with disability standards that can disadvantage other users. For example, styling your page to suit users with

dyslexia will disadvantage those with visual impairments. By allowing the user to modify the page, everyone can use the site.

52   Operating systems are the basic code that underpins the operation of other applications. Android, Mac OS, Ubuntu or Windows are all operating systems. Environments are the combination of an operating system and the device it runs on. For example, Android runs on phones, tablets and embedded devices.

53   By *safe*, I mean both common and platform independent: .jpg, .gif, .png.

54   As such, I would strongly suggest that you read Jeff Raskin's *The humane interface*. He was brilliant and clear in his understanding of the human dimension in screen design.

55   This is not a new concept: Jeff Raskin wrote, in *The humane interface*, of the need for software to bend to the human and not the other way round. The 1990s application *Kai's Power Show* made equivalent presentation software of the time look clumsy and slow-witted by hiding the power of the tool beneath an intelligently designed interface. Everything was about direct manipulation by the designer: complex sorting and ordering of media was made obvious and simple.

More remarkable was a piece of software that Adobe purchased from Macromedia and then allowed to disappear called Authorware. Authorware was probably the most remarkable interactive environment I ever used: you simply dragged a branching timeline of multimedia elements on to the working area and told the components how they interacted with tick-boxes, buttons and very occasional bits of code. I suspect that the reason for its disappearance is that developing such friendly applications is tough on the developer, in contrast to applications that make the user sweat more.

56   Read more in Chapter 18, 'The future'.

NOTES FROM A PRINTER TO GRAPHIC COMMUNICATORS

Matthew Fray

Once the concept of a job has been agreed, a designer needs to think about where will it will be produced; but, before this production stage, it is a good idea to start off by contacting the printer, if the job is to go into print, as he/she will be able to advise on a number of issues that will arise when going to print. These issues will include:

- transport costs;
- language translations for further publications (style sheets);
- colour profiles for the printer being used in that firm (these can affect monitor calibration, scanning and printing);
- the choice of materials that are available for each individual piece of work, and how best to achieve a good result at a reasonable cost to the client. For example, if the client wants a foil stock, special inks will have to be used for the ink to dry properly. The printer may even decide to put the job through a drying machine to cure the ink by UV light. Recently, digital printers have been developed that print metallic inks so well that they look like foil. *Large format printers* are now getting larger and able to print on to a wide range of materials and thicknesses; technology changes, and your printer will understand these changes. See www.rolanddg.co.uk, www.mimaki.co.jp, www.uk.heidelberg.com and www.komori.com for a wide range of printer manufacturers.
- print finishing;
- special folds and perforations for cutting and creasing;
- binding: perfect binding, saddle-stitched, side wire-stitched, case-bound, deckle-edged, embossed, de-bossed, punching, drilling (swing tickets);
- the types of glue to be used on the product, for strength and applications (e.g. food);
- costs and estimates for the job: these are important parts of the job, as going back and asking for more money is not very professional.

In this way, you can use the combined years of experience your printer or print-finishing company has to get the information correct for your specific workflow and understand the types of file they expect for their production workflow.

C@SE STUDY

C@SE STUDY

Pre-press tasks will need to be taken into consideration for the job. Most of these can be done, commonly, by the designer. But, by talking to the producer, you can get accurate information on: scanning, colour correction, size of images and resolution for output, which are all important factors to be considered, as are: RGB or CMYK, duo tone, half-tone Lpi; which of these is used will change with the stock being used, which is important to stop the image filling in or looking too coarse. Whether dot dither or inkjet/UV printers are used will vary if the image could be used at large scale. Dye inks, UV inks, etc. fade, and longevity of the product will also need to be considered, and the printer can help you with these choices.

Ink spreads as it sinks into the surface it's printed on; this is called *dot gain*, and the printer will also be able to advise on the amount of dot gain for the press the print is to be outputted to.

In fact, if you want your job to come out right, take time to speak to the people who will make it happen.

CHAPTER 14

Situating
the job

Getting your design made is only half the job. There was a time when it might well have been the whole deal. In the past, much of the stock in trade of graphic design was what we call *site independent*, meaning it didn't gain or lose very much by its physical relationship to the world around it. Perhaps another way of looking at the issue was that we, the designers, had so little influence on the way in which our products were sited that we had to design as if the location of the work didn't matter.

Today, things are somewhat different: designers have opportunities to weave the design into the environment in ways that enhance the message; sometimes, designers have the luxury to design the whole environment to be the message.

Even if the designer won't be involved in any formal level of decisions about siting, it is useful to design as if they were. There are very good reasons for the designer to consider the way their work will be sited.

The visual environment in the average developed-world town or city is chaotic today in a way that I doubt was true in the past.[1] I'm not going to get involved in the argument about whether this visual chaos is beyond control and driving the young mad (as far as I can see, people have a tremendous capacity not to see things that they don't consider important). But, I would point out that our man-made environment is dense with image, text, lighting, video, 3D display and official signage: it's a mess. A mess in which designers have to place their work, in the hope that it will, in some way, be seen as different and meaningful.

The image in Figure 14.1 is from the small, British seaside resort of Walton-on-the-Naze. This is not central London, nor Times Square in New York, nor the Ginza in Tokyo: it's a tiny town on the edge of the North Sea, but look at the visual confusion.

FIGURE 14.1
Visual clutter

Count the number of individual graphic interventions crammed into this one small space: I dare you! How would a designer effectively design for this space? There is layer upon layer of textual and pictorial communication screaming to be heard.

Location is a tricky game and one that we need to play well; otherwise, our work contributes to the visual chaos without reducing it. Worse, it contributes without being seen at all. So, what can we do in practice to make our work stand out in the world?

SITE SPECIFICITY

When designers used to talk about a site for their work, they would have been talking about a poster site, or perhaps point-of-sale resting on a counter, but certainly an insert cordoned off from the world. There were some outstanding exceptions to this rule, such as Times Square in New York, but these tended to be: first and foremost, advertising sites and, second, places where the character and status of the site came from the advertising. So, the giant, steaming pot-noodle advert (twenty storeys up and steaming twenty-four hours a day) gained its specific meaning as a crazy, over-the-top piece of advertising because it was situated in the world capital of crazy and over-the-top advertising: Times Square, New York.[2]

Designers cannot always design for a specific location, but we should always have a location in mind and, if we're smart, suggest locations through our presentation roughs. At the very least, designers must make the case through their visuals that certain locations and situations are preferable. In an ideal scenario, we should be designing work that naturally combines with its location to enhance the communication.

However, the argument can be made that design can be site-specific in some diverse and interesting ways. In the south of England, there are chalk hills that have had images carved into them for millennia: our ancestors found that, by simply cutting away the lush green grass to expose the white underneath, a strong image could be produced. The most famous is the Cerne Abbas man – a figure (some say Hercules) who has been visible in his 55 m-high glory for well over a millennium. The giant stands as a living symbol of ancient England.

That is why the Lynx remediation of the Cerne Abbas man is such an effective piece of graphics (see Figure 14.2). It wittily complements the existing meaning of the hyperphallic original by connecting it with the current Lynx ad campaign (he's not just a giant, but he's a giant to whom the girl giants flock through the power of Lynx). Put the giant in another place, and the meaning is diffused or lost forever.

FIGURE 14.2
Lynx at Cerne Abbas. With kind permission of Lynx.

Combinations of design and location like this add massively to the value of the communication. It is easy to imagine other location-specific combinations that carry stinging messages formed of the combination of place and visual.[3] There is even a global trade society specifically dealing with the promotion of environmental graphic design – the Society for Environmental Graphic Design (their site, including the archive of award-winning design can be found at: www.segd.org/).

TIME SPECIFICITY

Design can be made responsive to time in the same way it responds to location. A design might be intended to catch the eye of a specific urban audience. If we take a big city junction (in my head, I'm thinking of the junction of Oxford Street and Soho Street in London's West End) and look at the people using it at different times of the day, we find that there are distinct tidal flows in the passing population. In the early morning, there are the street cleaners and delivery people; they are followed by the office staff and messengers, but only for a short time; by about 10 a.m. they'll all be in work. About this time, the tourists take over. Come lunchtime, the office workers flood out and head down to Soho Square for lunch. They disappear back into their offices for the afternoon, and the tourists come out again. Then, the rush hour builds, peaks and dies in the middle of the evening, and a mix of tourists and clubbing locals comes out.

If we wanted graphically to engage the tourists but not the locals, or the clubbers but not the rush-hour commuters, we could design an intervention that was only active at the time when our target audience was there to be engaged with. I'm not talking about the guys with the billboards advertising a golf sale that appears to have been going on for the last forty years.

The intervention itself could take a number of forms: it could be mechanical, only activating at certain times of the day; it could be a flash mob convened at a specific time and place to act as the nucleus of the design; it could be a display system that modifies the environment at specific times: it doesn't really matter, as long as the intervention is sited in such a way that it is only 'there' when the users need to see it, and gone when they are.

AUDIENCE SPECIFICITY

We are all used to large, online marketplaces such as Amazon springing the opportunity for targeted impulse purchases on us, based on a seemingly miraculous knowledge of our interests. Of course, the website and the applications that drive it have no real understanding of you or me, but do have access to our buying trends, others who purchase in a similar way and others who have different preferences but have looked at some similar items, all of which make it worth the site flicking up an item at you on the off-chance that it will actually persuade you to buy. All of this is underpinned by masses of data on previous purchases and sets of probabilistic algorithms that say this item is likely to intrigue you and this one will repel you.

This is accomplished on a site-by-site basis, but what would happen if, for example, your mobile-phone location could be tied to your web traffic, time of day and mobile usage? What would happen is that Apple, Google and Microsoft would spend millions of dollars on developing smartphone operating systems that could capture these data and, in the process, generate very specific information about individual trends that would allow for very audience-specific communication. Google has been quite explicit in citing this kind of huge aggregation of data as the reason for their Android operating system.

In a few years, expect to start receiving time-aware, location-savvy and very personal communications through your handset. Although this is a technically mediated way of bringing audience specificity to your communication with users (and using the kind of template-based customisable techniques discussed in the previous chapter) that is capable of producing shockingly personal communications to us,[4] there are other methods that, while entirely low-tech, can target the correct people.

One such is the marketeers' technique of identifying the *alpha consumer* for a particular group, that person who everyone in the group wishes they were, and getting them publicly to endorse, identify themselves with, or simply be seen talking about, the product the marketeers want engaged with. By adopting this essentially viral idea, by using a group's own *memes* to create an environment where the users self-target themselves into position to receive the message, we can speak to exactly the right people.

SCALE

Humans carry a rather complete image of their universe around in their heads. They are accustomed to certain things being certain sizes. So, although if we change the shape of something the immediate identification is lost,[5] if we change the scale we place our brains in a dilemma: we know it is a clothes peg; we just don't understand how it is 5 m tall. The end result is a cognitive displacement that emerges as wonder and amusement.

Put simply, make the small big and the big giant, and your work will instantly stand out in the field of view. Because of the way the visual system works, it is likely that people will not be able to stop themselves looking.

MOTION

In the same way that size makes things *pop-out* in the field of view, motion triggers some of the oldest parts of the human visual system (called the preattentive system) by instantly grabbing our attention. We catch a motion in our peripheral vision and we instantly swivel our heads to see what it is.

I suspect that, if we installed a motor to make a poster hoarding tilt backwards and forwards (it would have to be promoting something like a car's road-holding capabilities; perhaps the car would stay still), we would have people stopping in the street just trying to understand what they were looking at. Once the viewers' attention has been captured, they are ours to work with.

INTERACTION

Interaction does not necessarily mean *computer interaction*; rather, it means understanding how systems of people, the cultures they make and the symbols they use work together. Then, using that knowledge to guide a message through to the people you need to get it. Let me offer an example.

How do you publicly express disagreement with a government that has made it clear that it will tap your phone, censor your tweets, pull down your websites, shoot at demonstrations and torture those it captures? Last year, in answer to these problems, the people of Iran invented a new way of beating repression through the adoption of a form of graphic intervention using the monetary system. At first, protestors wrote slogans on the banknotes, then went on to print pictures (including those of kidnapped friends), slipping the banknotes into circulation. Once in circulation, it would be assumed, *good citizens* would hand in the notes and end the cycle. Instead, and here comes the interaction, the authors of the scheme knew their work would provoke one of three responses: the notes could be handed over by loyalists, but they weren't the targets of the communication; the notes could be passed on, as quickly as possible, by the undecided, who will have had to read the message to notice it was there; last, the notes could reach those in opposition or who might potentially be in opposition, and here the message has met the person it was designed for.

The doctored banknotes were so successful that the central Bank of Iran and the government made it illegal to spend or accept the notes, thus turning every shopkeeper in the country into an agent of the state. It was the only way to stop the message.

LIGHTING

Applying lighting to highlight a graphic is a necessity, but, beyond the simply functional, we can play games with light that can drag attention to our work among the mass of other work. As mentioned below (see Alexanderplatz Station), by darkening a normally well-lit environment, we immediately summon up a certain spooky atmosphere, but, beyond this, we could combine this imposed darkness with point sources of light to define focus. These sorts of effect can be seen in museum design: for example, the fashion exhibit at the Musée des Arts Décoratifs in Paris has the fashion hall in darkness, with the dress exhibits in cones of light.

Working with the pre-attentive nature of vision (see below), we can also use flashes of light. It has been shown that a flash of light will capture people's attention, causing them to look for the source.[6] While you wouldn't want to do this on a street (you'd cause drivers to crash), you might find it has value in confined environments, such as an underground access tunnel, where it would cause people to miss other posters or information graphics and focus on yours.

As a final thought on light-based applications, use mirrors. There are so many fun games that can be played with mirrors.

ENVIRONMENTAL MODIFICATION

Environmental modifications can range from the massively visible, such as Vince Frost's Abundant Australia pavilion at the 11th International Architecture Exhibition of the 2008 Venice Biennale, where the entire environment was treated to Cristo-style wrappings, to smaller and less visible, such as the Garment District plaques embedded on Manhattan streets.

Texture, colour, material qualities, can all subtly communicate with the right audience, without impeding access for the passer-by. I will never forget the innocent joy of coming across Josep M. Subirachs' typographic doors on Gaudi's Sagrida Familia in Barcelona. They carry the Lord's Prayer in fifty languages and are visually arresting and movingly communicative for a Christian audience.

GO GUERILLA

In Prenzlauer Berg, a district of Berlin, the roads are lined with Communist-era blocks of flats. The blocks are seven or eight storeys high and have peaked roofs and chimneys on top of that. Prenzlauer Berg is a conscientiously trendy place, and there are elaborate graffiti and tagging everywhere. At the top of one of the chimney-stacks, 30 m off the ground, is a single tag standing proud above all the others. This tagger has realised that, to be noticed, you must stand out.

So, perhaps the guerilla approach is a way to go. Not anything as clumsy as fly-posting (which, apart from being illegal, is pretty ineffective), but things that have no right to rest in the viewers' visual environment but are there nonetheless and, in being there, can do some good work. Whatever my personal opinions are, as a designer, I recognize the effectiveness of the murals (of both sides) from the Northern Ireland conflict.

Take a look at work by the Lebanese designer Rana Saad. She designed a set of interventions intended to help summon up a spirit of national belonging, without evoking the divisive intercommunity violence of the past. To this end, she designed projected graffiti that, in combination with sound systems, modified urban areas in the Lebanon.

The equipment that Rana used was portable and left no lasting trace. The work was guerilla graphics. It often says more to do something without permission, as a provocation, than it does to obey the rules.

LOCATIVE MEDIA

Locative media are digital media that know where you are and change the content and the display of that content in response to your geographical location. They are currently the 'hot new thing in advertising if we can ever make any money from it'. (This echoes the early days of the web, in that everybody knew it would be big and make money, but no one actually knew how.) That said, it is potentially one of the most important developments in the field of graphic communication.

Prior to locative media, the design intervention would be largely unaffected by the location: a flyer for pizza in New York was the same as a flyer in Sydney. By contrast, if we were using locative media to serve a global pizza business, it would be simple to create a digital flyer that would know where you were, make our special offer in the local language, in the local currency, and give details of the local restaurant. Now, this is clearly a fairly one-dimensional piece of marketing, but let's consider some of the things we could achieve with a location-aware piece of graphic design.

An example of the power of such locative media is the *Transborder Immigrant Tool* developed by the Electronic Disturbance Theater (a North American group of artists/ agitators). The tool takes real-time data – about geographic conditions, information on private and governmental border patrols and about food and other aid stations set up by migrant support groups – calculates the user's current position, plans a safe route and then feeds it to mobile phones, where it gives live data to migrants making the hazardous border crossing (several hundred people have died making the crossing).

AUGMENTED REALITY

Lastly, and it is a bit of a cheat, we have AR systems. The cheat is that they do nothing, in reality, to the environment and have by themselves no situation in the world. However, they represent one of the most exciting possibilities in graphic communication. There is quite a bit more in Chapter 18 on the subject, but, to be brief, it is now possible for designers to apply virtual markers – textual, pictorial or interactive – to real places, markers that pop up on your smartphone with the right software. If you own an iPhone or an Android smartphone, I urge you to download the Dutch AR application *Layar* right now. It is a window into a wonderful world.

HOW WE SEE AND LOCATE

Researchers into perception are agreed that we experience the world as an active process, not as a passive one. Old models of perception were rather like the old *Beano* strip *The Numbskulls*, where little folk live in our heads and navigate our bodies through the world according to information that is piped into our heads as a TV picture.

Researchers such as Alva Nöe and Colin Ward point out that we see the world through an active process, with our senses constantly being tuned and retuned in response to mood, environment, biology and culture. We will miss things in the world because we're angry that we would notice when we're in love. In a visually crowded space, designs will be hard to see; in a physically crowded space, we might be too distracted to even look. Our biology makes us blind to things outside our cone of vision, and, importantly, events that happen rapidly enough are effectively invisible. Our culture makes us blind to beggars on the street and casual prejudices in our friends.

Users will not passively consume our work, nor will they see the world in homogenous ways: cultural and environmental factors will make each choice of location for our work more or less suitable.

The following thoughts on location are adapted from the work of Dr Colin Ward (1999), a psychologist and computer scientist who studies the role of perception in HCI design. You might ask what relevance HCI has for graphic communicators, and the answer is very simple: HCI designers have spent at lot of time working out how the human brain interprets what the eye sees, for the purpose of visual-communication design. Much of their research is directly applicable to graphics as an occupation.

Ward tells us that vision is like a searchlight – it sweeps back and forth, bringing things into view, and things outside the cone of our vision are invisible – so, without wanting to state the blindingly obvious, make sure that you site things where they can be seen. In common with many obvious things, this might be obvious, but obvious things are frequently not considered. For example, I'm thinking of a poster in my neighbourhood designed to alert drivers to the presence of motorcyclists. I pass the poster every morning, but can't read it, because it has been positioned behind a set of traffic lights, in a way that obscures the text from one lane and hides it completely from the other. To see it in full, I have to park, walk back to the junction and use the zebra crossing. Not smart placement at all!

THE STRANGE PLACEMENTS CHALLENGE

There are so many examples in the world, it would be impossible for me to name them all.

As a challenge, why not find the **dumbest siting** of a graphic you can find? There are enough of them out there. Of course, the worst ones will be functionally invisible, and you won't be able to see them at all.

Send them in to me.

Ward gives designers three useful points that we can measure the location of our designs against (1999, p. 156, 'Visual monitoring systems'):

- **Channels**: The method through which we receive visual information. These can be exotic – a viral ad on a mobile phone – or prosaic – such as the window in your room.
- **Events**: The important visual data on the channel. These are noteworthy things happening on our channel. So, on the mobile phone, it could be your viral ad starting up or delivering the advertising sting; looking out of your window, it could be you noticing that it is starting to rain on your washing on the line. This is where some of the ideas I mention above get their power from: motion, lights, scale all work because they are events in our visual field.
- **Expected cost**: The cost of missing an event. This is the subtle one, the part that needs consideration by us as designers. The expected cost of you missing the punchline on the mobile-phone viral is very small – you can simply replay the ad. The cost of missing the rain out of your window is more severe – your washing gets soaked. The cost of missing a stop sign on the road is potentially lethal.

The combination of these three events forms impediments on the user being able to see the designer's work. For example, a driver will alternately be concentrating on: the road (channel = the window), the car controls (channel = the dials/VDU) and driving instructions (channel = road signs, road markings, satnav, etc.). These examples are placed in order (from highest to lowest) of the *expected cost* of missing them: ignoring the road is extremely risky, not seeing the controls is moderately risky, and missing signs is annoying. If we then add your graphic communication into the mix, there is simply no competition. In a choice between looking at your graphic in passing and getting lost, or not looking and getting to a destination, your graphic will be functionally invisible. The driver will not see the graphic. Competing for a user's attention in any of these cases is tricky. We need to site our communications in places

DINNER AND A MOVIE

Let's run a little thought experiment. We all know the sorts of advert that get shown before films at the cinema. They fall into two broad categories: versions of TV adverts and those cringeworthy local adverts, neither of which is necessarily appropriate for the social time and place in which the audience find themselves. Which of the adverts in the table would be most successful for the listed audiences? Some of the films are semantically located for a specific after-film event; others will just not present the right influence.

Showing	Film and rating	Advert for
11:00	*Big Saturday Morning Kids Cartoon Movie III*, UU	Fast-food restaurant
13:00	*Superhero*, PG	A local late-night bar
15:00	*Big Dumb Action*, 12A	Local comic-book shop
18:30	*Bride Dresses in the City*, 15	Cinema sweet counter
20:40	*Mean Spirited Sadistic Horror Fest VI*, 18	Wine bar/restaurant

where the viewer will be able to be in the right mental state to understand that our design is there. A good designer will be considering semantically meaningful image, text, media *and location* as integral parts of their design.

Anyone who knows me will know this is an obsession of mine. I hate those 3-metre-long painted arrows in car parks that no one pays attention to. They are an exercise in futility. Every time a driver goes the wrong way round a supermarket car park, a graphic designer dies a little bit inside. We must never confuse making a symbol with controlling people. Let's make our designs clear, functional and meaningful, and then put them where people can see them.

This kind of searchlight focus is technically known as *tunnel vision*. Tunnel vision has been associated with air disasters, where pilots have been so distracted with keeping a plane in the air that they've missed the eventual cause of the crash. Psychologists tell us that tunnel vision is more severe when the viewer is under stress (both emotional stress and the stress of trying to absorb too much detail at once), which is fair enough. However, the level of stress needed to impair the viewer is frighteningly low. In Ward's excellent book (*Information visualization*) he talks about a *high-load* (high-stress) situation being picking out a letter drawn from six alternatives, compared with a *low-load* test being picking out a letter from a pair of choices. The difference was a drop in performance from 75 to 35 per cent in the task. If we carelessly site our work in areas with a competing high visual load, we are making life harder for ourselves.

Short of tying our users to a chair in a field directly in front of our work, what can we do? The smart designer incorporates his or her design into the environment in ways that use the environment to frame and highlight the design. Thus, we have the chimney-stack in Prenzlauer Berg, or the inventive advert for a 'vampire experience', which was sited in a darkened passage in the Berlin U-Bahn station at Alexanderplatz. To move from the U-Bahn to the S-Bahn or the street, you had to pass through the passage, which was covered in wall-to-wall graphics that converted it into a cobbled dungeon. Although the imagery was mundane, the location – a dimly lit and cramped passage – forced the viewers into a claustrophobic space where they were forced to engage with the design message: this makes it a successful design.

There are more direct things we can do. Ward highlights an element of human perception called *pre-attentive processing*. This kind of processing happens before we are aware of the thing we are seeing. Scientists speculate the system has evolved to help us survive encounters with the unexpected: a tiger hiding in the bushes, a mosquito buzzing round your head, changes in the environment that are significant. The pre-attentive processing sets us up for action by grabbing hold of our attention and forcing us to look.

Graphic designers have (through learned *folk wisdom*) learned a lot of the pre-attentive tricks over the centuries. With regard to the sixteen types of pre-attentive trigger that Ward lists (all the results of careful testing), graphics historically utilises all of them in some way. Over the centuries, we have developed a pretty good set of working tools for grabbing people's attention. Ward also explains that, if we use too many of these pre-attentive triggers at the same time, their ability to grab our attention is destroyed. Designers instinctively know this, and a good design is an exercise in editing, reducing the elements until only the working elements are left.

ATTENTION GRABBERS!

Ward lists the following pre-attentive cues (things the brain is primed to react to without thinking about it), but remember: treat them like salt in cooking, and use them sparingly to add to your design (see Figure 14.3). We have changes in:

- line orientation
- line width
- line length
- line collinearity (how parallel the lines are)
- size
- curvature

- spatial grouping
- added elements
- numerosity (changes in number)
- hue
- intensity
- flicker
- direction of motion

- 2D positioning (how something moves across our field of view)
- stereoscopic depth (things moving closer or retreating in our field of view)
- convex/concave shading

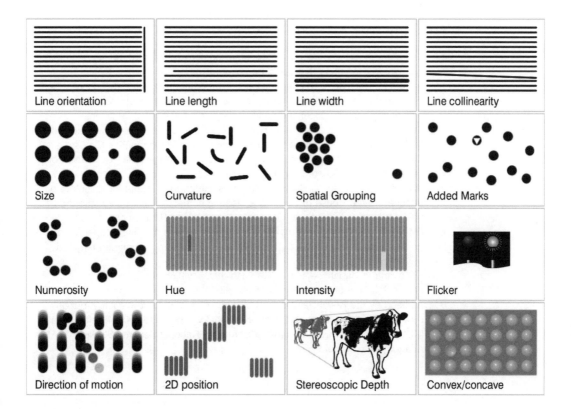

FIGURE 14.3
Pre-attentive cues

Clearly, the kind of purity of visual environment that is found in the laboratory is not found in the world. Imagine trying to design a piece of graphics that worked back on the seafront at Walton (Figure 14.1). There are so many competing pieces of visual design, both professional and amateur, that we are pretty much doomed to failure. This is so because of the limitations of the brain to see a new design among the rest of the graphic designs that have all been designed to pre-attentively grab our attention. This brings us back to the issue of location.

To sum up:

- If we place our designs in spaces where people are stressed by a high load of visual information, they will not see our design.
- However, if we pay attention to the intersection of people's lives and the environment they live in, we can design work that will achieve the exclusion of other distractions.
- This includes using strategies based on select pre-attentive devices.

Once again, however, if we don't know our audience, we can do no good.

NOTES

1   There are those who talk about the great poster explosion of the late Victorian era, where everything that could be covered with a poster was. This undoubtedly made for a chaotic visual environment. However, this chaos inhabited a single dimension of the scene. If you added several layers of official signage (e.g. local and national wayfinding schemes), additional unofficial signage (e.g. site entrances, car parking lots, etc.), vehicle graphics, projected imagery at night and kinetic adverts during the day, it's a mess.

2   Times Square is magnificent. It should be considered the truest expression of the American soul there is. Visit it.

3   One of my favourites is Claes Oldenburg's sketch for a gigantic ballcock to be attached to the House of Commons, floating in the Thames. Every time the tide went out, it looked like the country was flushing Parliament.

4   I'm thinking of Glue London's 2006 ''Ave a word' viral for Mini Cooper. It used questions to get to know you and produced an insultingly funny ad targeted at you by name.

5   For example, Japanese sushi USB flash drives, which are unnervingly convincing right up to the moment you plug them into your Mac.

6   As used by the Royal Navy in the Falklands War, with its low-energy 'dazzle' systems (Robert J. Bunker, Editor, 'Nonlethal weapons: terms and references', INSS Occasional Paper 15, USAF Institute for National Security Studies, USAF Academy, Colorado).

CHAPTER 15

Testing the job

A rationale for why testing the completed job is worth it

> In the evaluation phase, testing is not 'user testing' in a laboratory, but the careful study of what happens after the installation of the prototype into a setting where the real users of the system (not researcher colleagues) can use it.
>
> (Nardi, 1993)

Much of the writing on the subject of graphics tends to go rather silent about what happens when the job is done, produced, materialised in the world. This is fair enough when you consider the actual doing part is done, and that, traditionally, the doing of graphics has been considered to be the thing.

However, let me make a counter-argument. The designer might well find it useful to know what went right in the job, what went wrong, and if there are any lessons to learn for the future. As, in wicked-problem terms,[1] the job is never the same twice, a sharp reader might ask what the point of checking on the values produced in the previous job is, arguing that, as the job will always be essentially unique, nothing can be learned from one job that applies to the next. While acknowledging the truth of this point, there will be elements of the job – good things we've done, good people we've met, production tools we've applied – that will apply in future jobs. The repetition will never be exact, but lessons learned from the past will often offer useful clues for future working.

More than this, designers can never be truly sure that people will understand, appreciate and use their work in quite the way we intended, and we owe it to ourselves (not to mention the clients and users) to learn something from the difference between our intentions and users' acts.

Technically, we need to refine our processes in the face of an ever-changing production environment, which takes an active process of reflection. I've seen designers who never seem to get the colour reproduction from their printers that they deserve, but seem reluctant to sit down and consider what went wrong with this print; good results are not a given: they are the end result of a continual process of review. This chapter is intended to offer the reader some hints towards a review process of research into their own design process, after the job.

CRITS: THE BEST THING ABOUT AN ART SCHOOL

Crits are not a universally popular part of the art and design education experience. Many students look on them with a certain level of understandable fear, and it might surprise the reader to learn that the crit is not always loved by university administrators (crits tie up staff resources in ways that, compared with a lecture, seem very inefficient); so why do design lecturers love them so much (and keep fighting for the time to be allowed to run them)?

First, let's look at the term 'crit': it doesn't mean 'criticism' in the sense of someone being bad-mouthed or put down; but it certainly does conform to the secondary meaning of criticism, which is 'exercising careful judgement or observation; nice, exact, accurate, precise, punctual' (OED).[2] The term crit carries meanings of both 'critique' and implications of 'criticality'. Of 'critique', the OED says: '1. An essay or article in criticism of a literary (or more rarely, an artistic) work; a review'.[3] For designers and design educators, the 'review' is the important thing. In the crit, the design staff want to see if students can 'review' their work, exercising a 'critical' set of judgements on the value of the work they have produced.

We can see from both of these meanings that the crit is intended to be a process of observation, judgement and review; it is supposed to offer the student a chance to generate 'exact, accurate, precise' information about their work; not expose them to personal, spiteful and mean commentary.[4]

All of this judgement and observation are not ends unto themselves: the critical assessment being promoted by the design lecturer is a piece of specific training being knowingly conducted by the staff to make sure the students are, at some level, involved in a conscious review of the actions that led to creation of the work on the walls in front of them. This consciousness, in a designer's mind, of the nuts and bolts of their creative processes – of a self-knowledge of their actions – is what educators call reflective learning. In the crit, design educators attempt to form reflective processes that will stay with designers throughout their life.

Successful designers will be professionally involved in reviewing every aspect of their design and performance, with a view to making better designs in the future.[5] This constant review allows them to stay fresh (and, more importantly, to avoid repeated and expensive mistakes).

HOW WE GO ABOUT TESTING THE JOB

In an ideal world, every graphics job would carry the extra budget to allow the designer to take his or her time and luxuriously run a secondary stage of research, aimed at uncovering the impact of the job on the user. In truth, I've never seen this happen, but it would be nice. It's not realistic to hope the clients will carry out this kind of review for us or even pay for it.[6] For one thing, the clients' attention is invariably so intently focused on the final material product – a poster, package, website or video – that they will have committed all their time and attention to this end. The clients may well have convinced themselves that the completed job is nothing more than a viable method for achieving their desired solution, and this focus means that the typical client is fixated on the job's end and blind to anything that happens beyond this point. This focus is fair enough: if the designer can possibly achieve a 10 per cent increase in sales or a 10 per cent reduction in dogs fouling the pavement through good communication design, then, from the client's point of view, the job is, indeed, an end in itself.

This focus on the end of the individual job is just as true for designers. At this point, designers' aims will be radically different from clients'. Designers should be thinking in the long term. They should be considering how their work is received, not just by the current clients, but by future clients (the next chapter), and, more importantly, evaluating the difference between what they intended to do and what they actually got; what they wanted to achieve and what they actually did. This is where tools that help you conduct an analysis of the job – not an in-depth probe, but a swift and rough review that will allow you to do better in the future – come in.

Let me offer an example. I used to do a lot of work in Photoshop. I would carefully work on the job, tweaking and fiddling, flattening and editing layers, as the job demanded. Then, invariably, the client would ask for some seemingly trivial change: a change that, although trivial from the client's point of view, would cost me time and the client money, because, in reality, it meant reconstructing large parts of the image from scratch. Reviewing the process showed me that, by using layers, adjustment layers, and saving many, many copies of the file as I worked, I could jump back to earlier stages without any fuss.[7] Running a quick review process saved me time, made my workflow more efficient and built me a good reputation with the clients as a designer who could make major changes at a moment's notice.[8]

So, although I don't expect any designer to run a formal critical incident review (but more about this later), there are some useful tools to consider. As Wild (1994, pp. 55–61) notes:

> The prospect of graphic designers starting to think about meaning as a result of situation of use is a challenging one. Graphic designers have not had to live with marketing the way industrial designers have, and market testing or legibility testing are often seen as pernicious activities that only reinforce the obvious.

So how do you build alternative understandings of use of performance in graphic design? I doubt that the practice will ever be quantifiable in any way, but I'm sure that any understanding that evolves will be particular and local.

For myself, I think it is worth the effort to develop some systems that allow us to appreciate the 'particular and local' in ways that allow us to operate more effectively as designers.

A useful first step is an *internal* reflection on the designer's last job, because the internal aspect is the easiest and quickest factor to work with, and the least costly for a designer to address. You'll note I don't say it's the easiest. The second step is looking at the external factors that you can affect and, finally, examining the external factors you can do nothing about. The implicit assumption here is that any good designer will automatically make attempts to fix any internal issues that they have identified as part of their normal practice; as such, I'm not going to look at internal factors that can't be fixed (any designer who has identified a set of internal problems with their practice but has no intention of changing is beyond help).

ASSESSING INTERNAL FACTORS

One tool that has shown value in the past with both designers and design students is so-called SWOT analysis. SWOT is an old management technique that is based on the creation of a framework that allows designers to list their current situation, to consider their current situation and to generate some future actions. SWOT is traditionally intended to examine all sorts of external and internal factor; however, it is often difficult to be unbiased in assessing the external, and SWOT requires a degree of unbiased assessment to work properly. As such, it is probably, in an informal review, more useful for designers to restrict SWOT analysis to their own role in the job. You see, while it is often applied in all sort of circumstances, SWOT is not a universally accepted procedure: it has critics[9] and can bring its own sets of problems with it.[10] That said, the process has shown value as a tool for reflection for designers conducting a process of internal evaluation.

The limitations of SWOT are part and parcel of its nature: the name is an acronym that stands for strengths, weaknesses, opportunities and threats, and, put simply, not everything that has happened in a job is easily fitted into these four categories, and so the results can sometimes seem contrived. The definitions of strength, weakness, opportunity and threat are also reflective of a personal position: *my* strength, *my* weakness, an *opportunity* for me, a *threat* to me; therefore, I'd advise not pushing it as a technique into places where we can't be sure that our personal positions are reflective of the true position. More than this, the results of the test are as useful as they are allowed to be. To function properly, a SWOT analysis needs a degree of honesty, a willingness to change and clarity in defining terms (don't be vague). For a SWOT analysis to work, it should be used as a prompt for personal reflection, a way of placing thoughts in the material world where they can be considered and worked on.

It works something like this.

Strengths

The designer reviews the job that they've just done and notes down those personal elements that they have successfully brought into play to do the job well, things that they have done that worked well and that they might reasonably use again: these are the strengths. Strengths are internal attributes. Good work by colleagues is not a *strength*, though it might be an *opportunity* to try to work with them again.

Designers should try and be specific in their assessment. A designer writing down 'I rock!' in a SWOT analysis is not telling themselves anything that they don't already know and, more importantly, isn't listing something good that they can act on. By contrast, a designer writing that they 'work well with clients' is getting closer to the truth. A designer recording that the process of 'keeping in daily contact with the client worked really well' has uncovered a specific strategy that they might try again in the future. Note down as many of the strength attributes as you can. Don't be too modest here: this is a private and personal process of review and not for public consumption; if the designer believes they have done something well, something that they could do again, then they should log it.

Place the strength elements in order, ranking them from 'nice but irrelevant' to 'award-winning' (or whatever seems natural and honest to you). The higher the ranking, the more important it is for the designer to roll this behaviour into their daily practice.

Weaknesses

The weaknesses will be the negative personal elements that the designer brought to the job, elements that made the job weaker and harder to complete. These will be a compound of obvious and persistent character flaws (e.g. 'I try to do too much at once'), but also situational factors that were specific to the job (e.g. 'I dislike the print specifier at that company'). Be honest: if a designer finds that they are dangerously grumpy before their morning coffee (that's me), then they need to record the fact, making sure that they book future appointments with clients after 10 a.m., and near a coffee shop.

Many of the weaknesses will be things that are beyond immediate change; for example, a designer might be freelancing in the evening, which in turn means that their freelance work is a bit hurried. The solution would be giving up either the day job or the freelance work, something that might just not be practical. Even if an immediate resolution is impossible, having this knowledge can still offer clues towards long-term development.

Rank the weaknesses from 'irritating events' to 'job-killing incidents'. The 'job killers' are things that a designer should really make efforts to fix. The fix may cause a designer short-term stress, but it will prevent long-term damage.

The nature of the SWOT analysis is such that the S and W are seen as internal factors and the O and T as external factors.

Opportunities

The opportunities are unforeseen outcomes from the job that are beneficial but need active cultivation.[11] Opportunities are the things that emerge naturally from a job and that allow you to change, to grow and to develop as a designer. For example, getting a great print job from a printer is what a designer will be naturally aiming for; actually getting one delivered smoothly and professionally from a friendly printer is an opportunity to put more work their way in the future, safe in the knowledge that your jobs will be royally looked after.

Seeing the opportunity in a job is, in itself, an unnatural process. Young designers are frequently too inexperienced to see what is normal in business and what is noteworthy. It takes practice to see when a business contact goes beyond what they are required to do, and to then respond in the right way (gratefully and personally). For example, many design companies see Christmas as an opportunity: an opportunity to send out a card that reminds the client that they are alive and in business (which sounds kind of cynical and is often as personal as a tax bill); remembering the name of the designer's partner and children cements network relationships (which is how design works). Seeing the chance to make contact, to form alliances with other designers, to get some more training or to do a Master's degree, to learn a new language or to do *pro bono* work, is what the opportunities category is all about.

Opportunities should be ranked from 'a chance for fun' to 'life-changing'. Getting a design degree is a life-changer, as it opens up an otherwise closed world to the designer, as is taking your first freelance job; going for a drink with a client might either be a chance for fun or a life-changer, depending on the situation: be cold and clinical in your private assessment of the opportunities you are presented with. Pursue the life-changers with professional vigour.[12]

A note on opportunities

There is a field of academic study called 'game theory', which is 'About what happens when people – or genes, or nations – interact' (Camerer, 2003, 'Introduction'). Game theory has a range of very interesting things to say about these interactions, and one of the key elements studied by game theory is the notion of trust: how far one party can invest their resources (intellectual, material or emotional) on the say-so of another party. From the outside, the world of graphic design and communication looks like an entirely commercial enterprise; from within, it becomes clear that it is, in fact, a tight network of personal-trust-based relationships – what is known as a 'reputation network'.[13] The reputation, the trust one designer feels for another, is the thing that ensures that a young designer gets the chance to do interesting work.

This network of trust is the thing that should guide many of the choices a designer makes in assessing opportunity. So, if a designer colleague contacts you to ask for specific, but unpaid, technical advice, then the appropriate response is probably to help them out. The rationale here is that, in helping them out, you are establishing a level of trust that will offer you a trust benefit down the line. Equally, if a designer finds themselves with the chance to help out another designer with a work opportunity, then this is another chance to build reputation and to gain trust, which can be capitalised on later. If this kind of tactical thinking about your relationships seems deeply cynical, then you may well be correct; however, game theorists assure us that this is the way the world works.

Threats

Finally, we get to the threats. Most people, designers included, don't like to think about threats, preferring to stick their heads in the sand and hope for better days to come; this is, when you think about it, a threat in itself. Understanding the nature of the threats that face them is perhaps the most important thing young designers can know: the sheer diversity of threats that they face is so vast. The most obvious are inexperience and unfamiliarity, which can be real problems. By identifying inexperience as a threat, steps can be taken by the designer to address it, which is the point really.

Threats are negative external factors, factors that bring problems for the designer with them, but that are outside the designer. Threats are quite possibly only threats in relation to the individual designer. For example, geography can be a real threat to a young designer: if you live in the heart of a great city (such as London or New York), the opportunity is access to lots of design work, but the threat is the cost of living. It is equally true that living anywhere other than a great city is a threat to the young designer, as the access to good design opportunities is reduced (sad but true).

As with the other three categories, the import things to remember in assessing the threats to a design business are honesty, detail and clarity. It is no use generalising about threats. For example, a designer who recognises a general lack of confidence as a threat is, in the threat's generality, making a hopelessly vague assessment that there is nothing useful to be done about it. By contrast, a designer who knows that they have a specific problem in presenting to clients can take useful action: they could take lessons in public speaking or do amateur dramatics. So, be specific.

List your threats in order from low-level (it's an annoyance, but you'll live) to high-level threats (this could kill my career stone dead), and work on the high-level threats with all the urgency you can muster.

In this way, by privately running through a SWOT analysis after a job, designers can generate a kind of 'to do' list of things that need to be done immediately in order to make the next job and their working life better.

ASSESSMENT OF EXTERNAL FACTORS IN YOUR CONTROL

Now that the designer has taken the time to evaluate the internal factors that affect the job, they can start to look at the external factors. The designer might take a moment at the end of the job to run a quick review of its external elements: the people who made the job, the client relationships, the user responses, technical factors and more.

This review can be as obvious as writing a list on a word processor, itemising all the individual steps, from pitching to getting paid, and then adding a note alongside those things that went right and those that went wrong. Brief as this assessment is likely to be, such a list can act as a valuable prompt for some reflection. Conceivably, this might be a bit of a grim experience, if the job wasn't a massive success. Take heart and do it anyway: looking for improvement in the things that went wrong is an entirely appropriate response (see critical-incident theory, below). It is at the darkest moment that we need guidance to get out of trouble. The completed list should serve as a prompt for those things that a designer might avoid in future jobs, things they should avoid at all costs.

Remember, this is a review process: the designer's work is done at this stage, and what the designer is doing here is learning lessons for the future, improving their chances to make powerful design that would have once appeared to be impossible.

Running checks on some of the elements in the completed job may require a bit of effort, as you'll see. Designers might not always have the time to carry out a review, but, if they do, the process will quickly show its value.

External technical factors

Typically, designers will have checked the production values of the job (print proofs to a sample print, raw footage and colour grading of the footage, etc.) as they worked; now is the time to go and see if those values transferred successfully to the artefact as it is deployed in the world.[14]

Go into the street and see the poster you designed: Does it work sympathetically with the environment? Has it been printed well? Go into the shop stocking the pack you've created: check that it sits right on the vendors' shelving; make sure that it stands out against the competition, that it looks right under the hostile supermarket lighting. See if you can bring your print proofs with you and look for unexpected contrasts between what you designed and what you see in front of you. Take notes, and learn lessons for next time.

Theoretically, work done on-screen should be much easier to check: video editing suites carry special monitors that are calibrated accurately to give a preview of the finished video that you can rely on. Web- and screen-based media should conform to colour palettes that are optimised for the target device; the display of fonts and graphics can easily be checked in the *Adobe CS Suite* through *Device Central*. That said, all sorts of unexpected differences can become apparent when you see your screen-based media in context, in the world. That a product such as Google Maps can work so seamlessly, in so many environments and across so many platforms, is a testament to the care of the developers' review process, not the natural result of common industry standards.

If you find any unexpected features of production cropping up, try to ask the production professionals for advice about future jobs. A designer who has been polite and reasonable to the technicians can get some very useful feedback. (A designer who's been a beast should be aware that any feedback might not be completely accurate.)

Beyond the technical, and in most ways more important, are the users' reactions to the job. It would be lovely if the users of a design acted like a bunch of well-trained performing animals and did what the designer told them. The reality is that this is never likely to happen (for a longer discussion on the subject, see Chapter 18). The philosopher of technology Don Ihde noted that, while everyone accepts that different readers of a book will have different personal understandings of the story, and different viewers will take something different away from the movie they've just seen, designers often assume that people will 'play the game' and use the design in one way, and one way only, and that way is the one the designer intended.

Ihde says:

> The designer-god, working with plastic material, creates a machine or artefact which seems 'intelligent' by design – and performs in its designed way. Instead, I hold, the design process operates in very different ways, ways which imply a much more complex set of inter-relations between any designer, the materials which make the technology possible, and the uses to which any technologies may be put.
>
> (Ihde, 2008, p. 20)

As a real-world example (one that you can visit and test), London Underground's Tottenham Court Road station has an officially designed route from the ticket office down on to the two Central Line platforms. A passenger gets off the escalators, walks straight through an archway, passes along a *long* passage, goes down some stairs and then goes either left (westbound trains) or right (eastbound trains): this is all very clearly signposted and forms part of a designed circulatory system for passengers on to and off the platforms. In the rush hour, the long passage gets clogged, and it can take forever to get down to the platform; as a result, the regular London commuters (specifically those going east) know that, if you ignore the signs, turn right at the bottom of the escalator and go through an archway clearly marked 'No entry', you can get straight down to the platform and save five minutes of rush-hour pushing and shoving. This is multistable design in action. The locals have learned to ignore the designer's intentions and use the no-entry sign as a guide to a useful passage. The sign design *is* being used (as a piece of way finding, if for nothing else), just not in the way the designer intended.

For this reason, it is always useful to go and, if possible, see how your design is actually being used. This is not commonly done in graphics. Whenever I see posters that are amended – by way of stickers, notes, arrows and scrawled texts – to make sense of the embedded information for the intended end-users, the people on the ground, my heart sinks. This is the classic sign of a designer getting so caught up in their design processes that they've lost sight of the people who actually matter. I have in my possession a North American edition of *Adbusters* that has its price printed in what looks to be about 7-point italic serifed type, in white, across a pale background. It took the sales person a good five minutes, with a barcode scanner, to find out how much it cost: this is design that is not thinking about the user.

For this reason, we need to get down on the street, go into the chat rooms and join the audiences, to see what people actually do with our designs. If we find that something is happening that defeats our original expectations, then we need to talk to the users to find out why, to see if there is something useful we can do about it. You see, the user is never wrong. By definition, the user generates the meaning of an artefact, the designer utilises that meaning for a communication purpose, and, as such, whatever the user does with a design (no matter how crazy) is right, and we need to know what they're doing. This is one of the lessons that come from reception theory (see below). The German theorist Jauss applied Gadamer's *hermeneutics* to explain this. A designer (or artist, or baker, or advertiser) produces a meaning that they believe will produce a specific effect: this is called *cultural production*. However, what the user actually does with the meaning, what use they make of an artefact in their lives (called *cultural consumption*), may be quite different from the designer's intention. However, the meaning that the user has generated from their cultural consumption has changed the user's culture, and it is on this new user's culture that the next round of design is going to be based.[15]

Spend some time watching how people use your design. Do they sit at traffic lights staring at the poster instead of the lights? Do they stare, uncomprehendingly, at the direction sign? Do they turn the package over and over, looking for something they can't find? Do they curse under their breath as they go round in circles on your website? Do they hum the tune from your latest commercial, but, when asked what it's from, claim not to be able to remember the product? Depressing as it might be, all of these things could happen in response to a design. The designer needs to talk to the user and find out why they've happened.

There is a field of media studies, called reception theory, that looks at this phenomenon of people playing their own games with a creative's work. The core idea

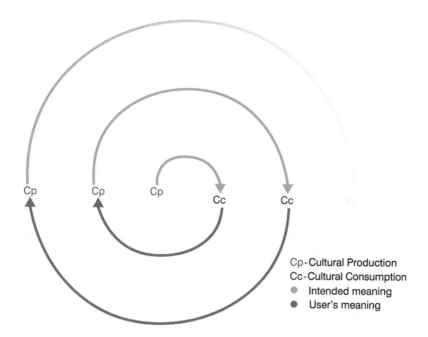

FIGURE 15.1
Cultural production

of reception theory is that communications don't arrive at a viewer who is culturally empty: viewers go and see a movie (for example) with masses of beliefs and prejudices that will form a lens through which they will receive the communication. In effect, a cinema audience watching a single film will leave the theatre having received different messages.

One of the theory's founders, Stuart Hall, encapsulated this idea as Hall's Theory (1991), which states that there will be three possible ways of reading (interpreting) a text (a communication or narrative):

1   **Dominant, or preferred, reading**: the designer makes meaning, and this is the meaning the user leaves with.

2   **Opposition reading**: the users are fully aware of the meaning but, for some political or cultural reason, choose to do something completely different with the design, often deliberately to establish a cultural opposition.

3   **Negotiated reading**: the user warps the designer's intended meaning to establish a new hybrid meaning that makes sense to them and to their community.

To see an example of this, see Figure 8.3, 'Stars and Stripes' in Chapter 8.

In this model (and it is only one model of many about communication), the designer has intentions, hopefully well founded on excellent research, that may get the design past Hall's stage 2 (opposition reading), but that are *received* by the audience in ways which aren't quite what the designer intended. You can observe this effect very easily by getting a copy of the Highway Code and a colleague who drives. Ask your colleague for the meanings of some common road signs. I guarantee that they'll be able to give you a functional explanation of the message communicated by the sign, which is good enough for getting around safely, but is not quite what's in the book, not entirely correct; in other words, their *reception* of the message is different from the designer's intention.

This inevitability of more than one way of receiving a communication is at the heart of reception theory, which is one of the reasons it has been so popular with feminist theoreticians interested in the ways in which women negotiate the messages aimed at them and the ways that they make their own meanings with them. The common methods found in reception theory are interviews and reviews of media created by the community about the design. For designers, this might usefully come down to *unstructured interviews* with users and placing questions on blogs and discussion pages that are frequented by the user group.

An unstructured interview is deliberately as far from a formal interview as you could get. The designer goes to the user and uses the design artefact as a prop to get the user talking about the design, asking questions in a staged way, ranging from the broad to the focused. So, for example, a designer might hold up the artefact and ask users if they've seen it around (nice and vague). The designer lets the users talk themselves out, recording the responses. Then they might move onto a question such as, 'Where did you see it?', only then getting into questions such as, 'What do you think it's about?', 'What do you think it does?', and trying to steer clear of questions such as, 'Is it good?', which will lead to one-word replies and possibly end the entire process.

By looking at the collected responses from all those interviewed, the designer will be able to see trends emerging in the users' understanding of the design. Those responses, intended or unintended, are what we have to work with.

Don't forget to ask permission, even if the interview is a conversation over a drink in a pub – it's only polite.

Now, not every job is going to be big enough to require this degree of review. But, I believe that, if a designer has just put up, for example, an online shop, it will be useful for them to know if it does what they think it does. If they've just made a TV commercial, then it might be a really smart idea to know if it works (the clients will really care about where their money has gone).

Other things designers can do, quickly, to review their designs are as follows:

- Talk to the producers of the design and ask them if they know of anything that could have been done to make the job cheaper, more effective, quicker to produce. I can guarantee that they will have opinions, many of which should be taken with a pinch of salt, but equally many that may give useful nuggets of wisdom that will make the job easier next time.

- It might be useful to run an informal critical incident review (as mentioned in Chapter 5). Ask the stakeholders in the job how they feel the job went, with an emphasis on the designer's role. Ask for examples of areas of good practice that they observed and would like to see again. This can be done completely informally.

- Post your design and any competing designs as a topic on design blogs (anonymously, if you feel nervous): see what your peers think of the job. Even negative comments will tell you something.

It used to be thought that the job was done when it was manifested in the world; I hope this chapter has shown you that the job keeps changing in the viewer's mind, every time it's seen. A good designer can learn a lot from these changes.

EXTERNAL FACTORS BEYOND OUR CONTROL

This, by necessity, is going to be both a brief and cautionary section of the book for the following reasons: There will, occasionally, crop up sets of events that are so far beyond our control that all we can do is cope with the effects, learn the lesson and make every effort to avoid them in the future. These factors include: companies going bust after the design work has been done but before the fee is paid; companies that prey on young designers (see Chapter 16, 'Getting paid'); unbalanced or hostile senior designers; clients with unclear or unrealistic expectations; unethical or incompetent production services;[16] trusted contacts you have come to rely on moving on or quitting (thus leaving you exposed); economic crashes wrecking the entire industrial sector; banks not lending design companies funds; and banks carelessly lending design companies funds (these are both bad things). All of these factors, and many more, are things that designers can encounter in their working life (all but one of them have happened to me; I'm not saying what the odd one out is), and there is very little to be done about them except to learn from them and move on. So, keep your portfolio of work up to date and as exciting as possible; if you are a freelance, try to work in as many sectors as you can; maintain good professional relations with a wide range of colleagues; and keep your marketing presence as fresh as you can. That said, there are no guarantees in life. Designers have to be nimble on their feet to get more work (see the next chapter).

We can see, then, that designers who do the job, get paid and walk away are short-changing everyone involved in the design process, including themselves. To work effectively, we have to check at both ends of the job.

NOTES

1   Specifically numbers 1, 7 and 8:

'(1)   *Wicked problems* have no definitive formulation, but every formulation of a *wicked problem* corresponds to the formulation of a solution.'

'(7)   No formulation and solution of a *wicked problem* has a definitive test.'

'(8)   Solving a *wicked problem* is a "one shot" operation, with no room for trial and error.'

2   See: www.oed.com/view/Entry/44592?redirectedFrom=critical#, accessed 5 January 2011.

3   See: www.oed.com/view/Entry/44607?rskey=OMJymz&result=1&isAdvanced= false#, accessed 5 January 2011.

4   If you feel that your crits take on this shape, then there are issues present that might need to be addressed. Crits are about developing mental skills in students; they shouldn't be a theatrical performance designed to make the students look small and the staff look great.

5   I believe that this is one of the defining characteristics of successful designers. All designers make mistakes; the good ones review the mistakes to see what they can learn from them for future work.

6   Reviews may well happen, but they will be for internal purposes, and are very unlikely to be built around the designer's role.

7   It also often meant 4- or 5-gigabyte folders crammed with 0.5-gigabyte Photoshop files. But it was worth it for the simplicity that I gained in the working process.

8   Which led to another round of problems, as clients who had been let down by other designers started turning up, expecting me to fix broken jobs at speed.

9   See Hill and Westbrook's meta-analysis of SWOT, 'SWOT analysis: it's time for a product recall', in *Long-range planning*, 1997, 30(1): 46–52.

10   In large organisations, SWOT is often run as a management-level activity, and as such can end up serving management ends instead of highlighting real problems.

11   For example, having a pack of mints in my pocket once led to years of employment because it allowed me an opportunity to stop and chat with another designer, which led to him giving me work and introducing me to other designers. Learning from the lesson, I carry mints whenever I'm visiting a new studio.

12   And this kind of behaviour *is* professional, not cynical.

13   A reputation network is a system where the members of the network rate the trustworthiness of the other members, with the individual ratings generating a composite score that all the members can see and base future relationships on. Amazon.com runs reputation networks to generate the scores you see attached to the vendor's profile. In a reputation network, it is unimportant how

big or small you are; what matters are results and the other members' feelings about those results.

14 I'm not suggesting that, if you've designed an ident for MTV Latino, you need to sit in a bar in Guadalajara just to see it play, though this would be nice, and every agency should be encouraged to do this as an act of policy.

15 Let me offer a real example. An eminent industrial designer (who I'm not going to name) has designed a very elegant, one-shot vaccine injector in which the needle breaks after use. This breakage is important, as medics and paramedics in developing countries have been implicated in the practice of re-using needles to give multiple patients injections with the same needle and syringe (see Simonsen, Kane *et al.*, 'Unsafe injections in the developing world and transmission of bloodborne pathogens: a review', *Bulletin of the World Health Organization*, 1999, 77(10): 789–800; available at: www.who.int/bulletin/archives/77(10)789.pdf).

The eminent designer has, then, designed a wonder needle that breaks automatically when the practitioner has used the dose in the needle. This is problematic for two reasons: first, it assumes that the practitioner is either a bad person or a stupid one – that they are exposing their patients to the risk of cross-infection negligently. Second, it assumes that every practitioner is going to have a safe way of disposing of hundreds of packages containing multiple bits of now infected needle fragments.

The first assumption may be right, in which case we are dealing with a cultural problem, not a mechanical one. The solution would seem (to me, as a graphic communicator) to be a graphic-communication campaign to educate the practitioners and so change their practice, because we know that people are smart and people are inventive and, if they can find a way of re-using the new injectors, they surely will. As such, education is the right tool for the job, the only tool that is likely to change behaviour. More than this, at least some of the injections, especially those in Sub-Saharan Africa, are done by health professionals (see Simonsen, Kane *et al.*) – professionals who presumably know the risks of cross-infection and, at some level, have made a judgement that, in those awful circumstances of poverty, failed states and warfare, it is better to inject than not inject. This makes the solution a political and economic one (possibly with some good graphic activism in the developed world to make life uncomfortable for the politicians and businessmen who could make lasting changes). Making changes in the developed world/developing world relationship is the solution, not a new needle design.

So, the needle design solution is no solution at all, because it is not engaged with the people who are supposed to use it.

16 The 'unethical' may require some explanation. There are, thankfully uncommonly, some individuals involved in the production process who attempt to skim funds from the difference between what the client pays for a production service and the price actually paid to the production house. These are bad people: try not to get involved with them.

OBSERVING PEOPLE AND TESTING DESIGN

Advice: make sure that your design really enables people

Karel van der Waarde

How do you know if your suggested solution will actually work in practice? Can you be sure that real people are attracted by your design and can interpret it in a way that supports their activities?

In the area that I work in, 'medical information design in Europe', it is legally obligatory to test how well patients can find and understand information about medicines in package leaflets. One test consists of at least twenty one-to-one interviews, and it establishes if information about a medicine is comprehensible and easy to use. The motivation for such a test is clear: if patients cannot understand the instructions, it is likely that medicines are not used effectively.

In most areas of graphic design, it is just as important that people can understand and use visual information. From a simple business card to gas bills, from posters to signage systems, and from identities to infographics, it is essential to find out how people react and act. There are two main ways of establishing this.

The first way of testing is to observe people before you start designing. Your observations will provide evidence that it is necessary to change an existing situation. Observations provide information about situations and problems from the point of view of real people. During the observations, you have to consider what they try to achieve and how visual information supports their activities. For example, do car drivers hesitate to put money in a parking meter and read the instructions over and over again? How do people look at a screen for a cash withdrawal? Do all children look at school-books in the same ways, or are there differences? How do guests look at menu cards in restaurants? For some projects, it is worthwhile to make these observations slightly more formal. This can take the form of a 'benchmark test', which establishes how well current information performs. Observations and benchmark tests might look a long way away from graphic design work, but they reveal a lot of information that inspires and motivates.

The second way of testing is an evaluation after you have designed a prototype. You show your design to people who are most likely to use it

C@SE STUDY

and ask them to perform several fundamental tasks. This can range from simply asking a few people to have a look and react, to a full-blown formal usability test. The thing that all tests have in common is that they are fairly humbling experiences. It is difficult to accept that people who are not trained to look at graphic design at all can exactly point to graphic design failures.

After a test, you have to interpret and consider the results. How you apply the suggestions is completely up to you. You don't have to accept their views, nor do you have to follow their advice. However, it would be pretty silly to ignore genuine, critical comments that show that your design needs to be modified to enable people to act.

Both *observations* and *evaluations* will provide you with convincing arguments that can help to persuade a commissioner. It gives the confidence that your design not only looks good, but actually is likely to be effective in practice. Without the results of observations and evaluations, on what basis can you provide suitable arguments?

FIGURE 15.2
Even after years of interviewing patients about their interpretation of information about medicines, every test still provides me with new and surprising insights

CHAPTER 16

Getting paid (and more)

INTRODUCTION

'Getting paid' is the title of this chapter, but that's mostly a cheap trick to grab your attention. This chapter does discuss getting paid, but also covers issues around your legal responsibilities; your moral responsibilities; your employer's responsibilities to you; joining a trades union or trade association; design advocacy; support networks; working with others and on your own; moral obligations; and, of course, getting paid. So that's quite a lot.

LEGAL (YOUR OBLIGATIONS TO OTHERS)

First, let me say, if you are in doubt about the legality of any design issue, contact a lawyer, a union rep or a trade association rep (e.g. D&AD).

The bad news about design and the law is that many sources of advice about the legal aspects of design seem to be talking about a different world from the one inhabited by working designers. Such texts are legally correct but don't reflect the nature of graphic communication as an industry, where more than 60 per cent of designers operate in companies with fewer than ten staff.

So, although it is true to say that all graphics jobs, being agreements between two parties, should have some form of contract to govern the agreement, the world is not always as it should be. On the one hand, the first magazine cover I designed was done without a contract. I gave a copy of the Association of Illustrators' (AOI) draught contract to the art director, who promised to pass it to the editor. I got paid on time, never had any problems and worked for the company again for several years; I never saw the contract again. On the other hand, a merchant bank for which I was a design consultant made me not only sign a contract but also learn the fire exits at their London headquarters (I'm not kidding) and take out £2 million of public liability insurance in case a third party slipped in my studio and sued the bank for any injury that they might suffer.

For most designers, the important thing to understand is that most of the work they will do in the course of their employment or for a commission will be governed by their working contracts, their terms of employment. For example, work for either employers or by commission is held to belong to the client as a natural consequence of the designer's being employed by that company. If a designer does self-originated work and then takes it to another party on spec, the work belongs to that designer until they assign it to the other party. Work done by an employed designer in their own time and on their own equipment is simply theirs, and their employers have no claim on it.

As such, most designers have very little to do beyond reading the contract very carefully, noting down any parts that are unclear (so that we can check on meanings and implications with the client or a lawyer) and, finally, signing on the dotted line. Caution should always be our watchword when signing paper, and there are a couple of times when designers should take extra care. Designers generally come face to face with the law in the following ways: employment law, when they enter into a job working for someone else (which is beyond the scope of this book, but a trades union or association can offer advice), and copyright law, when they are either authoring work or using work authored by others.

Although I won't comment on employment law itself, I am going to warn you about some employment situations that are at best quasi-legal – which is to say, common practice but not necessarily lawful – and that you should watch out for.

BAD HABITS

Some clients have some very naughty habits when it comes to identifying the difference between freelance and being employed. I've been both and have never found there to be a problem distinguishing between the two, but some employers seem genuinely confused. This is an important difference for you to understand. Freelance rates are substantially higher (to cover things such as National Insurance, fixed costs, etc.), but the job carries almost no legal protection. By contract, an employee is protected by the law in a number of ways, but gives up certain rights to their employer.

HM Revenue & Customs (HMRC) used to have a very clear guideline that explained the difference. A freelance designer (it was explained to me) was not in 'a master and servant relationship' with the clients. The client could not tell a designer how to dress, when to work, what equipment or processes to use or where they could work. Our agreement was simply that I would complete such and such a design task at a certain time, for a certain sum of money. Personally, I could (and did) sleep until 10 a.m., not shave and then work through to 3 a.m. fuelled by chocolate and coffee. It was my choice.

By contrast, a designer employed by someone else can be told: when to turn up and work, when to eat lunch, what the dress code is, when they can take holidays, what software to use, where they have to sit to work, etc. If a designer is employed as a 'freelance' but has to operate by the rules above, no matter what the employer thinks, they are in a 'master and servant relationship' and are employed. They can call the designer a freelance, but, as far as the law is concerned, the designer is employed and should be covered by employment law: law that gives the graphic designer employment rights.

So, beware: many companies use the titles 'freelance at . . .' or 'associate of . . .' to avoid paying sickness, maternity or holiday benefits, redundancy payments or matters of job security. Don't be fooled. Freelance is a good way to work: if you are getting paid as a freelance. An associate is a good thing to be, if you are a proper associate, but there are tax and National Insurance complications that cannot be ducked and have to be addressed. If you are concerned about your employment status and want advice, talk to a lawyer or Citizens' Advice Bureau, join a union and ask them for advice, or ask your trade association. If, as a designer, you work exclusively or mainly for a single employer, then it should treat you as a proper employee.

Another issue that particularly dogs the design industries is that of working hours, or more formally *working time limits*. Working time limits are rules in British and European law that define legal guidelines for the number of hours you can be asked to work in a week as part of your employment. The law is very clear here:

> Adult workers cannot be forced to work more than 48 hours a week on average – this is normally averaged over 17 weeks. You can work more than 48 hours in one week, as long as the average over 17 weeks is less than 48 hours per week.
>
> Your working week is not covered by the working time limits if you have a job:
>
> - where you can choose freely how long you will work (e.g. a managing executive)
> - in the armed forces, emergency services and police – in some circumstances
> - as a domestic servant in private houses
> - as a sea transport worker, a mobile worker in inland waterways or a lake transport worker on board sea-going fishing vessels.
>
> (from the DirectGov website, at: www.direct.gov.uk/en/Employment/ Employees/WorkingHoursAndTimeOff/DG_10029426; accessed on 11 October 2010)

The design industry has developed working habits that are very effective in terms of getting the job done and very destructive in terms of the health and well-being of designers. I was told, at one of my first studio jobs, that we would work as long and as late as we needed to get the job done, but that, if we finished the job early, we would all go down to the pub in working hours and on the company's account. This was true; it was just an unhealthy way to live and to design.

The law has changed. As said above, you will not be asked or ordered to work more than 48 hours a week unless you sign an opt-out. However, remember the 48 hours is calculated as an average of the hours over 17 weeks. So, an employer with an important job on can reasonably call on you to work late, or, in the general run of things, you can volunteer to work extra hours if you think it is an advantage to you: you just can't be forced to. Some sectors of the design and media industry pressure young designers to sign opt-outs (not specifically in graphics; it happens a lot in fashion, film and in other media-friendly professions, with lots of people willing to be put upon to get a job). Signing or not signing an opt-out is entirely the designer's choice; the law states:

> **Opting out of the 48 hour week**
>
> If you are 18 or over and wish to work more than 48 hours a week, you can choose to opt out of the 48 hour limit. This must be voluntary and in writing. It can't be an agreement with the whole workforce.
>
> You shouldn't be sacked or unfairly treated (for example refused promotion or overtime) for refusing to sign an opt-out.
>
> You can cancel your opt-out agreement whenever you want – even if it is part of your employment contract. However, you must give your employer at least seven days notice. This could be longer (up to three months) if you previously agreed this in writing with your employer.
>
> Your employer is not allowed to force you to cancel your opt-out agreement.
>
> (ibid.)

There is also a provision in law that grants you the right to rest. You are entitled to at least 20 minutes' break in six hours, eleven hours' break in every 24, and 24 hours of break every week, as a minimum. So, if you are working on a rush job for a big client, that's great: but, if you are told that you must work through the night, that's not so great. If you do decide to work through to 4 a.m., you are then entitled to rest until 3 p.m.

FREELANCE

Although design should always be a contracted operation, sometimes it's not. This is especially true when working freelance, where you might do work *on spec* that is then picked up by a client with an eye for new talent. The law understands that not all design work is done within formal employment and offers a degree of protection for informal designs through *UK national unregistered design right*. This right offers 15 years of protection without the design specifically being registered. Thorne and Bennett (2010) note that:

1   Unregistered design protection 'arises automatically subject to qualification'. So as long as your work qualifies (see below), it is subject to the right.

2   Your design is 'not registerable', i.e. it doesn't need registration to be awarded this right. National unregistered design right is separate and distinct from *registering a design*. Registering a design is a more complex and formal system. As such, I suggest that you talk to a lawyer or, if you are still a student, your university's *Intellectual Property Office*.

3   The design 'need not be novel but a requirement of "original" creation; must be created independently and not be "commonplace"'. The design does not need to be wholly new to the world to be covered (e.g. a completely new typeface would need to be covered by registering it as a design; a modification of the type for a specific purpose – for use in a logo for example – would not) (ibid.). In this circumstance (unlike a registered design), the law considers originality to be more important than novelty. A design cannot be original if it represents something 'commonplace in the field'. The Copyright, Designs and Patents Act 1988 states that: 'A design is not "original" for the purposes of this Part if it is commonplace in the design field in question at the time of its creation' (quoted in Thorne and Bennett, 2010, p. 26).

So, taking the famous Ché photograph as an example, colouring it in a new way and claiming that the image is yours is not going to work. The new 'design' will not be original because it is already commonplace. In the same way, most of the graphics created in the Greenpeace campaign to redesign BP's logo are not original because they used BP's logo.

4   'Infringement requires copying'. This is, or should be, obvious to any graphic communicator. Copying design work is an infringement of copyright law.

In short, you don't need to do anything special to be legally covered as an author of graphic works. The work must simply be published (not necessarily commercially; putting it on a website might do), manufactured or be present in design drawings. Remember, however, that this goes both ways. Other designers who put their work out in the world are covered too. Don't rip off the work of others.

MORAL (OBLIGATIONS TO OTHERS)

In ancient Greece, the father of medicine, Hippocrates, devised a set of moral principles advising doctors on how they should engage with their patients. They are very subtle principles and most (but not all) medical students still swear by Hippocrates' Hippocratic Oath when they become doctors today.

Things are less clear for graphic communicators. We are trained at college to 'do our best', 'make clever work' and 'serve the client', which is nice, without addressing the morality of the cause we work for. The questions raised by 'best', 'clever' and 'serve' are completely separate from those of 'right', 'appropriate' and 'beneficial', let alone answering the bigger questions about whether we should always do our best. Perhaps a designer has a serious moral conflict with the client agenda and does not want to advance it; and service might be the wrong response, because the client may not be worthy of our service. It is easy for us to say, 'I would never have designed for the Nazi party!' It is more difficult to turn down a juicy contract. How is a designer supposed to make the morally appropriate choice when they have no guidance on what 'moral' for a graphic designer looks like? If you were asked to design for a finance company promoting loans to the poorest in society, what would you do?

There have been home-grown responses to the question of the designer's moral duty from within the design community, the two most famous being Ken Garland's 1963 'First things first manifesto' and the later 'First things first 2000 a design manifesto'.

Ken Garland's original goes:

> We, the undersigned, are graphic designers, photographers and students who have been brought up in a world in which the techniques and apparatus of advertising have persistently been presented to us as the most lucrative, effective and desirable means of using our talents. We have been bombarded with publications devoted to this belief, applauding the work of those who have flogged their skill and imagination to sell such things as: cat food, stomach powders, detergent, hair restorer, striped toothpaste, aftershave lotion, beforeshave lotion, slimming diets, fattening diets, deodorants, fizzy water, cigarettes, roll-ons, pull-ons and slip-ons.
>
> By far the greatest efforts of those working in the advertising industry are wasted on these trivial purposes, which contribute little or nothing to our national prosperity.
>
> In common with an increasing number of the general public, we have reached a saturation point at which the high-pitched scream of consumer selling is no more than sheer noise. We think that there are other things more worth using our skill and experience on. There are signs for streets and buildings, books and periodicals, catalogues, instructional manuals, industrial photography,

THE HIPPOCRATIC OATH

I swear to fulfil, to the best of my ability and judgment, this covenant:

I will respect the hard-won scientific gains of those physicians in whose steps I walk, and gladly share such knowledge as is mine with those who are to follow.

I will apply, for the benefit of the sick, all measures [that] are required, avoiding those twin traps of over-treatment and therapeutic nihilism.

I will remember that there is art to medicine as well as science, and that warmth, sympathy, and understanding may outweigh the surgeon's knife or the chemist's drug.

I will not be ashamed to say 'I know not,' nor will I fail to call in my colleagues when the skills of another are needed for a patient's recovery.

I will respect the privacy of my patients, for their problems are not disclosed to me that the world may know. Most especially must I tread with care in matters of life and death. If it is given to me to save a life, all thanks. But it may also be within my power to take a life; this awesome responsibility must be faced with great humbleness and awareness of my own frailty. Above all, I must not play at God.

I will remember that I do not treat a fever chart, a cancerous growth, but a sick human being, whose illness may affect the person's family and economic stability. My responsibility includes these related problems, if I am to care adequately for the sick.

I will prevent disease whenever I can, for prevention is preferable to cure.

I will remember that I remain a member of society, with special obligations to all my fellow human beings, those sound of mind and body as well as the infirm.

If I do not violate this oath, may I enjoy life and art, respected while I live and remembered with affection thereafter. May I always act so as to preserve the finest traditions of my calling and may I long experience the joy of healing those who seek my help.

educational aids, films, television features, scientific and industrial publications and all the other media through which we promote our trade, our education, our culture and our greater awareness of the world.

   We do not advocate the abolition of high-pressure consumer advertising: this is not feasible. Nor do we want to take any of the fun out of life. But we are proposing a reversal of priorities in favour of the more useful and more lasting forms of communication. We hope that our society will tire of gimmick merchants, status salesmen and hidden persuaders, and that the prior call on our skills will be for worthwhile purposes. With this in mind we propose to share our experience and opinions, and to make them available to colleagues, students and others who may be interested.

(Garland, 1963)

The original and the 2000 follow-up have been criticised for not being terribly relevant to real designers' lives (notably by Michael Bierut, in *Looking Closer 4*). Although I, personally, agree with Garland's original in its entirety, I would note that most designers, most of the time, have to go where the work takes them, and, while that means that most of us have the luxury to say 'no' to designing for evil dictatorships and arms manufacturers, some of us don't. Many designers, especially young designers, cannot always pick and choose the projects they work on. Many projects exist within moral frameworks that are entirely self-contained. How many designers would say no to a year's security working on a high-power drinks campaign?

This brings us back to Hippocrates. He didn't attempt to define doctors as guilty or virtuous because of their practice. There is nothing in the oath to say that a doctor working in prison was under any different set of obligations to one in a maternity clinic. Where the 'First things first 2000' manifesto clearly marks any designer not intent on saving the world as lacking ambition (and possibly complicit in the end of the world), Hippocrates understood that doctors are people who need guidance not guilt. He clarified the way the doctor's knowledge should be applied as not solely of benefit to the doctor but of benefit to the patient. It's not too difficult to reframe the Hippocratic Oath as a guide to designers' relationship to their users:

I swear by Schoeffer, the first art director, by Games, Tschichold, and Bass, and I take to witness all the great designers, to keep according to my ability and my judgment, the following Oath and agreement:

- I swear to hold the values of the society of designers and communicators to my heart, and to treat my fellow designers as my brothers and sisters.

- I will design to benefit the users of my designs according to my best ability and my truest judgement and never create designs that knowingly bring harm to the world.

- I will not design work that brings harm to the world just because I am asked (with money or fame waved in my face), nor will I advise such a

We, the undersigned, are graphic designers, art directors and visual communicators who have been raised in a world in which the techniques and apparatus of advertising have persistently been presented to us as the most lucrative, effective and desirable use of our talents. Many design teachers and mentors promote this belief; the market rewards it; a tide of books and publications reinforces it.

Encouraged in this direction, designers then apply their skill and imagination to sell dog biscuits, designer coffee, diamonds, detergents, hair gel, cigarettes, credit cards, sneakers, butt toners, light beer and heavy-duty recreational vehicles. Commercial work has always paid the bills, but many graphic designers have now let it become, in large measure, what graphic designers do. This, in turn, is how the world perceives design. The profession's time and energy is used up manufacturing demand for things that are inessential at best.

Many of us have grown increasingly uncomfortable with this view of design. Designers who devote their efforts primarily to advertising, marketing and brand development are supporting, and implicitly endorsing, a mental environment so saturated with commercial messages that it is changing the very way citizen-consumers speak, think, feel, respond and interact. To some extent we are all helping draught a reductive and immeasurably harmful code of public discourse.

There are pursuits more worthy of our problem-solving skills. Unprecedented environmental, social and cultural crises demand our attention. Many cultural interventions, social marketing campaigns, books, magazines, exhibitions, educational tools, television programs, films, charitable causes and other information design projects urgently require our expertise and help.

We propose a reversal of priorities in favor of more useful, lasting and democratic forms of communication – a mindshift away from product marketing and toward the exploration and production of a new kind of meaning. The scope of debate is shrinking; it must expand. Consumerism is running uncontested; it must be challenged by other perspectives expressed, in part, through the visual languages and resources of design.

In 1964, 22 visual communicators signed the original call for our skills to be put to worthwhile use. With the explosive growth of global commercial culture, their message has only grown more urgent. Today, we renew their manifesto in expectation that no more decades will pass before it is taken to heart.

(Garland, 2000)

plan; and I will not allow harm to come to anyone through my designs, if I might prevent it.

- I will render honest and truthful service to my clients and actively promote the well-being of users through my work.
- I will not claim expertise in areas where I have none and will not pitch for jobs where peers will render a better service; I will leave this work to be performed by practitioners who are specialists in this field.
- In every place where I come, I will enter only for the good of my client and the users, keeping myself far from all intentional ill-doing and all seduction.
- All that may come to my knowledge in the exercise of my profession or in daily commerce with men, which ought not to be spread abroad, I will keep secret and will never reveal.
- If I keep this oath faithfully, may I enjoy my life and practise my art, respected by all people and in all times; but if I swerve from it or violate it, I may no longer call myself a designer.

Whether you subscribe to the oath or just try to do right, it is important that you remember that the design we make has effects on the people we design for.

HOW TO PROTECT YOURSELF

If you want to go it alone as a designer, I would recommend joining a union or trade association, finding a friendly IP lawyer, or at least reading Thorne and Bennett's book, *A user's guide to design law*. People will try and rip you off – not frequently, but it will happen. So, for your own protection, remember that design is a game played with others, and that it's both safer and more fun to play it that way. Here are some people who can help you when things get tricky.

Trades unions

I know that talk of joining a trades union isn't something you ever thought you would find in a book on graphics, but stop and think. There are many times more people who want to work in graphics than there are jobs. Many of them will work for almost nothing (see above), on the off-chance that it might turn into a real job. Although most employers will deal honestly with junior designers, there are some exploitative employers that you wouldn't want to deal with on your own; having several thousand union buddies backing you up can be a great comfort. Unions can advise on pay, they can advise on working conditions and, perhaps most importantly, they can stand with you when you need support.

In the past, there was a trades union specifically for graphic designers and those who worked with graphic products: the Graphical, Paper and Media Union; it has subsequently joined the larger Unite union, which has a 'Graphical, paper and media sector'. Now, although Unite generally deals with large, industrial sectors in print, negotiating nationally, they do deal with small companies. Unite's Graphical, paper and media sector can be found at: www.unitetheunion.org/sectors/graphical_paper __media/contact_us.aspx

For the record, I am a member of the University and College Union.

Trade associations

Parallel to trades union activity are the trade associations. Where the unions support the individual workers in an industry, the association supports an industrial sector as a whole. In graphic communication, the difference is not terribly clear: often we are both the company and the employee. There are many one-man businesses out there, with most design companies having ten employees or fewer (70 per cent, according to the 2006 BDI survey).

Because of this blurring of the roles between employer and employee, the industry associations have blurred roles in dealing with, on the one hand, many of the functions of a trades union (legal, training and trade support) and, on the other hand, functions of a typical trade association (promotion of the whole industrial sector). A good example would be the D&AD (originally British Design and Art Direction).

D&AD is known by all graphic-communication students as those nice people who host 'New Blood' and arrange for free beer on the private view night. However, their activities with students, promoting education, are only one part of their operation. They also act as advocates for design, promote good practice and get industry talking to students. The D&AD and other trade associations – the AOI, the Chartered Society of Designers, etc. – are there to support your design ambitions. Use them.

Membership of these organisations costs if you are no longer a student, but the payments are small, and many designers find that they are well worth it for the support that they get. Large organisations can help us move mountains that stand in the way of all members. In the past, I was a member of the AOI and am currently a member of the Design Research Society.

Design groups

Design groups are, to all intents and purposes, companies that are owned by all the employees. Design groups can be limited companies (where the company has a legal status equivalent to an individual, e.g. it can be sued), or they can be a partnership, where all the partners are legally liable for the others partners' debts; for example, when your friend and business partner Jo flips and runs away to Indonesia to live with the orang-utans on the company funds, you are responsible for the debts she has run up.

Design groups are not the same as design companies, though they often share similarities. Design companies often have typical corporate structures (boss > senior designers > junior designers), whereas design groups have much flatter structures, with everybody pitching in, and everybody getting benefits. Technically speaking, such companies would be partnerships or cooperatives (a company owned jointly and equally by all its members).

Design groups can be tremendous fun for the people forming them: with each person supporting the others and different people contributing different skills, problems become manageable, and tackling jobs that no one member could do becomes a breeze. If one member of the group has problems with a job, the others are there to support them. Design groups are massively useful. More than that, there is nothing to stop ex-graphics students getting jobs in the industry and working in their free time to do their own work (I'm thinking about *ShellsuitZombie* magazine here). The thing to remember is only to start a design group up with people you can be sure are as enthusiastic as you are.

Partnerships

Partnerships are simple to set up: legally, the designers are simply a collection of self-employed workers working on a joint enterprise. However, don't forget that partners have no legal identity that is separate from the partnership. What you own is at risk if the partnership goes down. If the partnership runs up debts, it is the legal responsibility of all the partners to pay them back.

There are also limited liability partnerships, which operate as partnerships but have some of the financial protection of limited companies, and partners are only liable up to the value of their investment in the business or personal guarantees that they have made to borrow money.

Limited companies

Limited companies are, in many ways, simpler, but bring administrative and legal overheads: they have to have a director or board of directors and must have a company secretary and an accountant, who must make legal declarations of the company's financial status. Taxes must be paid, and the company must pay the employees' National Insurance to the government. On the positive side, limited companies separate financial liabilities from the owners of the company (if things go wrong, you don't end up losing the shirt off your back).

Limited companies raise money to run by selling shares. For a design cooperative, this may simply be a case of dividing the set-up costs for the company by the number of designers and assigning these costs as shares to which the designers all contribute. If the company fails, the shareholders have to pay back any money remaining unpaid on the shares, not the debts the company owes.

For more information, contact Companies House at www.companieshouse.gov.uk/index.shtml.

Getting paid

For those designers in regular employment, there should be no problem: they simply work and get paid. However, things are less simple for freelance designers, those in design groups or those working on short-term contracts.

Getting paid on a short-term contract: Taking the options in reverse order, and starting with short-term contracts, things should be much the same as for designers in regular positions. Wages should have National Insurance and tax taken off at source, with the remaining money being promptly paid direct to the designer.

Where good employers will do this automatically, some might try to pass on the responsibility of sorting taxation and National Insurance to the designer, paying the designer the whole sum they have earned. If this happens to you, be aware of the following fact: HMRC does not like cash-in-hand transactions. It believes there are a very limited number of ways of being employed. It believes that you can be self-employed/a sole trader, in a partnership or in a limited-liability partnership, in which case *you* need to be paying tax through the *self-assessment* system. You could be employed, in which case you pay tax through your wages, or you can be a proprietor of a company, in which case you are receiving a wage and/or profits. (You can also be employed and self-employed at the same time, but that's a whole other can of worms.) Taking cash-in-hand is a very stupid thing to do in the long run.

In order for them to pay tax as self-employed designers, HMRC issues self-employed/ sole traders (read as 'freelances') with individual tax codes, which need to be added to invoices. This allows the employer's accountants to log and account for the money they pay out. Any company trying to pay you cash-in-hand creates multiple problems:

1   You don't have a means to pay tax until you have an individual tax number. You won't even be able to invoice until you have one (see below).

2   You may well be under-quoting for the job. If you have asked for £1,000 for a job, the government will want about 20 per cent of the money (plus National Insurance). You asked for £1,000 for the job, but you now have less than £800.

3   If you try and keep the whole £1,000, you will have avoided paying tax (which is legally bad).

4   If, by some chance, an employer successfully pays you the money under the table, there will now be a £1,000 hole in their accounts, which HMRC will want explained. When it is explained (and the company has been fined), the taxman will come looking for you.

5   Cash-in-hand will also cause problems with the social-security system. If you've earned money, claimed benefits and not declared it, you're in trouble.

6   And on, and on, and on.

There is realistically no legal way for cash-in-hand payments for design to happen. The designer must notify HMRC (including National Insurance) that they are operating as a sole trader, which affects their tax and benefit status and means that they must prepare taxes under the self-assessment framework and pay Class 2 and Class 4 National Insurance contributions. If a short-term employer doesn't do the paperwork, it is storing up problems for the designer and itself; it is better to do the job right, at the start, and work under a proper short-term contract.

If you are working for a company, getting paid should be simple. If you are in any other position – freelance, contractor, short-term worker on a project – things may get a little less simple. As I've mentioned, there are things you need to do to get paid.

1   You need to be registered with the tax authorities, otherwise your client's accounts department won't even process your forms.

2   You need to calculate how much money to charge a client. As a simple guide, you can use the following formula:

   2.1 Calculate your *fixed costs*. These are the costs of staying alive and being in a position to earn a living, not the costs of actually doing the job. So, they are the costs of: food, rent, light and heat, water rates, council charge, equipment not specifically for the job (e.g. software and hardware), phone rental (but not calls), clothes, etc.; not entertainment and not holidays.

   2.2 Calculate your *variable costs*. These are the costs of doing the job: materials, travel to the client, phone calls (but not rental), wear and tear on equipment, specialist help (hiring a printer or web coder), etc.

   2.3 Divide your fixed costs by 365; this gives you a daily cost of being alive and ready to design.

   2.4 From your variable costs, estimate what you think it will cost you to make the job. Warning: this bit will initially be a bit trial and error. Try not to under-quote. Be picky: if you are going to be spending money printing three sets of ten drawings to present to the client, calculate the cost of thirty sheets of paper, thirty sets of prints, three presentation folders, etc. Remember, you are not calculating the production costs: that comes at the end. You are just calculating what you will be spending to get the job out of your head and into the world.

   2.5 Multiply the daily fixed cost by the number of days you will be working on the job. Add the total to the estimated variable cost of the job. This should be your basic cost to do the job.

   2.6 Now double the basic cost.

   2.7 Add the cost of any production you are quoting for.

   2.8 Give the client the quote. If you feel embarrassed by the amount you are about to ask for, you can, at your discretion, vary the difference between the basic cost of the job and the doubled basic cost. Never go below the basic cost, because you will be losing money. Never offer a discount on the production cost: you will end up having to make up the difference yourself. Try not to drop below the double basic cost if you can: clients will not respect you for giving them a bargain; they will just expect another cheap job next time.

2.9 The formula is:

$$\left(\left(\frac{Fc}{365} \times Dn\right) + Vc\right) \times 2 + Pc = \text{Fee}$$

where Fc is the fixed cost, Dn is the number of days you work on the job, Vc is the total variable cost for the job, and Pc is the production cost.

3 Give the customer the fee costing and get an agreement to proceed. Do the job. Then bill them.

3.1 Note: If the client cancels the job after they have agreed it can proceed from the development to the production phase, you are entitled to some of the total fee, generally about 30 per cent.

4 You need to keep records of how much money comes in and keep some back for tax (oh yes you will!). You will also need to keep records of your costs. Talk to HMRC for advice.

5 You need to send in an invoice, which must carry: your name, the address you are operating from, your individual tax number, a phone number, an itemised breakdown of what you are charging for and why, and a serial number for the invoice.

6 Once you've been paid, and if you are working for overseas clients, you may well find that your bank gets sticky about clearing the money. All sorts of money-laundering regulations have been put in place that mean you may well have to have a business bank account in order to pay in money from an overseas source. Note: If you receive money from an overseas client, be aware that, because of currency fluctuations, the value of your fee may well go down, and you may incur bank charges for exchanging foreign currency.

7 If you are working for domestic clients, you need a bank account in any case. Shoeboxes are not acceptable.

8 You need to establish the client's protocols for receiving invoices. You need to know who needs to receive the invoice (art directors will often take the invoice in, get busy and forget to process it), how they like to receive it, and how long they will take to pay the invoice . . .

9 . . . because the invoice is incredibly unlikely to be paid immediately. Most companies pay invoices thirty, sixty or ninety days after receipt. This means they will make one cheque-run every thirty days, their accounting processes

run on a thirty-day schedule, and they want to hang on to their money for just a little bit longer. If you invoice on 1 April, you might get paid in August. Make sure you know the payment schedule, otherwise you will find the money getting a bit thin.

10 Remember that it takes five working days to clear a cheque through a bank. So, even when you have the cheque in your hand, you can't spend the money.

11 Remember that some of the money goes to tax, some to National Insurance, etc.

There are things you can do to help speed things up a bit. An ex-client of mine told me the secret of getting paid in a timely way. 'Find the Golden Person in the company', he said. 'They'll make sure that you get paid on time.' He was absolutely right. Every company has a Golden Person, the employee who knows everyone in the company and is trusted by everyone in the company. They will tend to be a middle-ranking administrator who knows who holds the levers of power. If you find the right person and make the right approach, respectful and polite, they will act as a conduit for your requests to get paid on time. If you build a good relationship, they may even be able to cut a ninety-day payment period to a sixty-day one. A smart designer will take time to understand the company culture, and the smart designer will get paid on time.

You can ask to be paid electronically through the BACS system. This will cut the bank handling period.

You can agree with the client that a longer job is to be paid in instalments, with some part of the fee paid at the various stages of the job: some paid after the development process, some paid when the job is submitted, some when the job is through production.

As a last piece of advice, assuming you can afford to, keep a little bit of the money you have made back, so that you can pay for new equipment down the road.

CHAPTER 17

Getting the next job

Self- and other publicity

Think about the ways in which you present yourself to the world on a daily basis. The clothes we wear, the way we style our hair, the accessories we exploit, all these form an outward public expression of identity. These expressions are applications of semantic signs being used to form a meaningful public face. Think about it: if you roll into a briefing in last night's clothes, with your hair in a mess, will the client place the same level of trust in you that they would if you turned up well groomed and smartly turned out? It may seem shallow, but this is literally publicity: the OED says that publicity is 'being open to public observation or knowledge.'[1]

If you are lucky enough to find yourself in the position of getting a graphics job straight after leaving college, you may feel tempted to skip this chapter. You might find yourself operating on the principle that your new job will be eternally satisfying, going on and on forever, with your bosses providing you with continual access to engaging and challenging work. Who knows? It might even happen. The current shape of the design industry would tend to make this assumption unlikely.

The graphics industry is currently in what systems scientists would call a chaotic state.[2] Although for many (myself included), the advent of Mac-based working was a blessing, it was a pretty negative time for others. Imagine the coming of the Mac as a great tropical storm: the traditional design landscape was messed up, and the mess created all kinds of new ecological niche for nimble professionals. The last twenty-five years have seen unprecedented opportunities for graphic professionals and have seen them gaining a measure of control over their creative destinies. That control is the point of this chapter. Where a graphic career was once something like a train line – predictable and ordered – it is now more like surfing – dynamic and requiring constant adjustment just to stay on course. And, whether you intend to spend twenty years in the same company or whether you mean to start your own, you need to plan your progress.

THE DIFFERENCE BETWEEN PROMOTION AND PUBLICITY

Publicity is the act of making others aware of us – of our deeds and of our capabilities. No matter how good a designer is in reality, if they are unknown to the industry, they won't work, they have no chance to make a difference in the design world and no ability to get access to the most exciting work opportunities.

Publicity is not quite the same as advertising, and promotion is different again. So, let's get some definitions that we can work with. Advertising is a communication that is paid for by the sponsor, shaped around the intention to give the sponsor a benefit. As such, it is openly representative of the sponsor's interests; for example, if we were to look at an ad for an oil company, we would expect to see something nice about the company and the company logo somewhere in the ad. Even if the ad was an *advertorial*, we would expect to see an acknowledgement along the lines of, 'This article on weight loss was brought to you by the National Liposuction Guild'. The public acknowledgement of sponsorship is important in the idea of advertising.

By contrast, publicity is a communication that is intended to offer the sponsor a benefit without being paid for (you see now why this chapter is about publicity not advertising). As such, and in contrast to advertising, the sponsor's message might be carried in a way that masks the sponsor as the author of the message. When the good folks of *ShellsuitZombies* set up their stall at D&AD's 'New Blood' and invite the Keston Cobblers Club to perform, they are creating a publicity opportunity, with those who attended going home in the sure knowledge that they have witnessed something young, funky and designerly. The combination of media and event makes this certain.

A concrete example would be that of product reviews. Have you ever wondered why magazines carry so many product reviews, and why the reviews are frequently so similar? The reviews will often be written by the company launching the product and then placed on the company's website in a *press room*, together with free copies of those beautiful, high-resolution publicity images of products that fill magazine pages. A journalist will simply take huge chunks of text and images and use them to generate the review. This is publicity, because the origins of the words, images and ideas have been masked, but, through the association of product and media outlet, a message is formed.

These definitions of advertising and promotion roughly map on to what in marketing circles is known as 'above-the-line' or 'below-the-line' promotion, above-the-line being obvious things such as advertising, and below-the-line being more subtle activities, where the game being played is subtly to build an association in the minds of users between the values of the publicity vehicle and the sponsoring company. Some examples of below-the-line promotion would be the *O2* Arena, *Orange* Wednesdays or the *V* Festival.[3] People use these resources for their entertainment value, but leave with a positive association about the company.

All of these elements – advertising, publicity, above- and below-the-line marketing and others such as personal contacts and sales offers – are elements of *promotion*, which is the communication of favourable impressions to those we need to think well of us. This sort of communication needs to give the target (for a designer: an art director, a client, fellow designers) information they can act on. For example, it is no use whatsoever producing a killer website of your work if there are no contact details. This information should be structured in a way that encourages the target in a specific course of action – giving us work, of course, but, more than that, the specific type of work that we are actively seeking – and, lastly, it needs to show the target that we are different (in a positive way), providing a justification to use us and not our competition.

In an ideal scenario, our work would do all of the talking for us. All we would need to do is sit back and watch the work flow in through the action of our beautiful gallery website. In reality, a website does nothing on its own in promotional terms, not until people know that the site is there, which is a promotional task in its own right.

Designers need to understand that their work may well be the perfect vehicle for communicating the message it was designed for, while still being a poor tool for promoting future work. Imagine if the twentieth-century guru of typography Jan Tschichold had a promotional website – one designed accurately to reflect his undoubted genius, through the work he has done, but lacking a new and distinct narrative to promote his work as a viable solution to future problems. What the visitor would find would be page after page of brilliant layouts and gorgeous type specimens, which are undoubtedly fascinating to the typographically literate, but fundamentally unsuitable as a tool for representing the enormous influence he had as a designer.

Now, imagine a site specifically designed to show this influence on the design world, using the past work he did where it was valuable, but also with testimony from those famous designers Tschichold influenced, perhaps a shot of the hundreds of Penguin editions that benefited from his design, and maybe a free font sample or two of the typefaces he designed. We start to see a site emerging that gives users reasons to return. The designer testimony is a form of below-the-line promotion that works by associating their work with Tschichold's. The Penguin link is above-the-line advertising of his product, and the font samples act as a sales promotion (a sort of 'If you liked this font, then you'll love these ones!'). Promotion is a whole other design task, in addition to, and separate from, the job of designing.

What a young designer is looking for in promotional terms is a mix of avenues that are as effective as possible while being as cheap as a wish. There are a multitude of conventional advertising opportunities out there (remember advertising equals paid), opportunities of variable value in what they give back for the money you spend: promotional pens and USB sticks, design annuals and many, many web-hosting and design companies. Each of them promises to get your work in front of potential employers and so bring you fortune and glory. Experience has given me no reason to believe that these sorts of tool are massively effective with our core target demographic: other designers. Put simply, designers are too familiar with the tricks of the trade to buy into a crude marketing pitch (which is not to say that they won't use the logo-covered USB stick you send them; they just won't give you any work because of it).[4]

More useful, in above-the-line terms, are direct promotional advertising mechanisms that reflect a designer's special take on the world in a way that will entertain and engage the potential employer's attention. In predigital times, this used to be something of a cottage industry for graphics students in their final year, with students developing *mail outs* (in the original context of the term, i.e. a paper and card artefact), with beautiful printing, intricate cut-outs, amusing design features, just jammed packed with good things that made it clear to the target designers that they had to employ this person before someone else did. It was a modern version of the apprentice's masterwork. Today, young designers have to develop a media form that is specific to their practice and engagingly meaningful to the industry sector they wish to join.

A young designer who wants to get into editorial design might find that she creates an elegant spread as a print (traditional) and a hybrid e-journal version with rich media (to show her ability in screen-based document design). Her colleague, who wants to be a videographer, would be well advised to produce an online show reel *and* to start flooding YouTube with carefully meta-tagged samples for commentators and fanboys to see.[5] The point is that the media, once again, are carrying the burden of the message to our intended audience; it's just that, in this case, the audience is another designer.

There are commercial avenues for advertising that claim to be able to do the hard work for you, which might just help if the designer is well funded and is prepared to throw a ton of money at the problem, in the hope that some will stick, and, in contrast, we have specific approaches created by the designer to pique the interest of the chosen target design company. I think you can guess in which direction my advice is going to go, can't you?

Promotion for designers was once a mass-market operation. It had to be: it was too difficult to identify the people you wanted to work with and, even if you could, it was too expensive to make individual artefacts of high enough quality to make a difference. The technical changes of the last two decades have remade the business of publicity in ways that allow some small-scale, but very focused, promotion to be done for quite reasonable costs.

BUILDING NETWORKS

Rather than jump into a list of cost-effective design publicity tools, I'd like to ask you to consider what we actually want to gain from the publicity process. A lot of the various online resources seem to assume that the reader already has a fully-fledged game plan for their path through the design industry. Personally, I'm not sure what you, the reader, want to achieve through your publicity campaign, but I'm quite confident that, in order to achieve your aims, *you* need to know. For example, getting a freelance job right now takes a different mindset from getting your lifetime dream job. The first needs a relentless progression of work presentations around every possible contact you have; the second requires a carefully planned campaign, the development of layers of specific contacts and a succession of jobs that build the right kind of reputation.[6] Consider your long-term goals and what you want to achieve with the time you're investing in your publicity.

Try this method and see if it helps.

- **Start at the end point**, by deciding what your ideal graphic job will be. Be honest with yourself and ambitious in your estimation of the job you want. You don't have to make a public confession about your ambition, so don't hold back from being bold with your future hopes. There is an excellent rationale for aiming high at the beginning of a design career; doing other-wise sets yourself a target that is so low that it won't stretch you as a designer,[7] and the achievement of a low-quality target in itself artificially restricts your future life choices.[8]

- **Think about your ideal job** and work out the necessary skills and experience you'll need to have in order to get it. If you want to end up making commercials with a top agency like RSA, you'll need (in reverse order): stunningly good films made for exciting clients; good industry contacts; technical ability; work that will be built on top of strong and exciting student projects, all put together in a kick-ass show reel; and a commitment to developing the kind of understanding of the world and the craft of film-making: this is your task for today.

  By starting at the end, with our 'pie in the sky' ambition, and working backwards to where we stand today, we can see the steps we need to take, not as a single, insurmountable task, but as an achievable series of tasks.

- **Build and maintain a communications and marketing presence** – treat graphics as a graphics job. The fundamentals of publicity are not built around the stuff we send out, but the people we send the stuff to, so take the task of making contact seriously. If you do a job, and your boss or client says, 'This is nice! You should show Sarah over at CMM, she'd love it', then, with all the politeness you can muster, you must get 'Sarah's' number or email address and, as soon as possible, get over there and show her the work. Once again, it bears saying that graphics is an industry built on networks. Play the six degrees of separation game in the graphics world and you quickly find that everyone seems to share the same acquaintances.

To help build a marketing presence, a designer should keep good records of the people they meet, logging business cards, addresses and tips electronically, to create a searchable record of people they can and should send updates to about the beautiful work they do. There are expensive business software and hardware tools to do this, but, in reality, the free OpenOffice suite has spreadsheets that work fine for the technically timid and fully functional database modules for the brave; a designer doesn't have to spend money to keep track. List the obvious things such as name and address, company and business sector, but also log the more obscure things, the nearest station, the client's interests, how formally or informally they like to be treated and their taste in sweets: list anything that might conceivably firm up that all-important business relationship. Now, the designer has a contact database that they can consult when they're visiting a client, when they're making mail-outs, or simply when they want to thank people for the work they've got through the year (saying thank you is important).

Now that you have a list of people to aim your publicity at, you can think about the specific ways of contacting them.[9] People will only employ you if they know that you are there and that you're working. A designer needs to be constantly finding relevant means of drawing the attention of potential clients and bosses to their existence. For example, when I started out, the web was a strange place that few knew anything about (most designers and design companies didn't), so there existed a blessed time for the technically informed when those who knew their way around a website could make a disproportionate impact in publicity terms, simply because they were online, and the others weren't. At that time, the web represented an excellent media choice for projecting design publicity to clients. This is not true today: while *every* designer needs to have a web presence (illustrators and videographers doubly so, because they will typically be geographically distant from their markets), a website simply isn't a comprehensive publicity tool on its own. When compared with the mass of designer websites, an individual young designer's website is like a leaf on a tree: it is so common and so like the others, that no one can distinguish one from the next. Being noticed online (not to say in the real world) requires something more. This is where the smart designer will turn to the full range of social-networking tools: posting and responding to posts on design blogs and design Twitter accounts; or setting up their own blogs (like *ShellsuitZombies*), which, through featuring the work of other young designers, project a comprehensive awareness of themselves to the wider design world. We are creating an interconnected network of outlets, online and in print, that represent our design practice.

We do this because it is unrealistic to expect that an art director or client who we are interested in working with will have the time or the interest to spend the time trawling the web for every new job that we've done, whereas they might well be interested enough to hook up to your Twitter feed (where you can post links to your new work) or take a feed from your blog.

This organisation of a web presence is a two-way street, with design companies whose work we like creating networks of outlets for their own work and opinions. In creating these networks, these companies generously leave us information that we can use to focus our publicity on contacting them. This kind of trawling of the sites frequented by the people we want to work for is a serious matter, a task to be done regularly and methodically. Do it right, and we can hear about the competition of our dreams that will be judged by our industry hero; fail to do it, and we might as well sit in a basement counting the bricks on the wall for all the benefit we'll get from our expensive design education. For example, the Design 21 social network (www.design21sdn.com/), which is run in connection with UNESCO, is a key resource for designers who wish to do social design practice. If that's you, then you should be haunting this site. We have to immerse ourselves in, and keep ourselves informed of, the comings and goings of the small social world we wish to join.

Setting up a web presence isn't a matter of putting up a website (a shop if you like), but a matter of informing people where you are (telling people that there is a shop and letting them know where to find it). When a designer posts to a forum, they should make sure that there is some way of linking back to their site. When a designer wins a competition or a juicy contract, they should, at least, promote it on their own website. A designer should set up their blog as an RSS feed. RSS is a subset of .XML that basically establishes a permanent pipeline between the blog and the user's blog reader. In this way, whenever a designer has something to report, they can be sure that it will appear on the right people's computers. It is also the responsibility of the designer to keep up with the changes in the social networking landscape that might affect their business: if everyone they need to talk to has moved to a different platform, then they need to be there too.

Note on blogging and the law: The law in the United Kingdom covering blogging and libel has recently changed. A blogger who uses their blog to attack someone else may be guilty of libel. The defence appears to be if the blogger has previously included enough *backstory* to provide a context to the reader that justifies the comments they make. Just be careful.

Competitions are a great resource for designers wishing to make a name for themselves. As always think carefully about the type and reach of the competition you are going to spend your time on. The principle should always be that you need to get the biggest benefit for the least expenditure of your resources. That said, there seem to be more competitions for graphics appearing every week, and it can be tremendously time consuming to do the round of on- and offline resources to keep yourself up to date. To this end, I would suggest harnessing the power of a good search engine. I have Google set up to send me, for my students, a digest of 'graphic design competitions, graphic communication competitions, graphic arts competitions' every week.

In this way, I need to spend a minimal amount of time addressing the task of sorting through a million pages of rubbish to find the gold.[10]

Find a competition; look at the previous winners; see if you can see a trend that you might design for. Look up the design judges and see the sort of work they produce: don't copy it, but take note of any personal obsessions and professional approaches that appear in the course of their work; these can be a way into the judge's mindset.

Lastly, and perhaps most importantly in this digital world, lose some shoe leather walking the streets to make personal contact. Designers are people too (apparently this is true of clients as well). People like people; and it is all too easy to in this wired world to forget that. A good designer will make sure that they can do the rounds of past clients and future prospects on a regular basis. Just popping by and dropping off samples of your new work is a tremendously powerful publicity tool. Don't be mistaken and think that every visit will result in work: it won't. What will happen is the chances of your getting a job go up, even if only because the person you're visiting becomes curious to see how you work, or because they give you a lead on a job with another designer to get rid of you.

Arrange days when you can get into the city; do this a month ahead of time to get cheap fares. Contact all the people you would like to see and politely ask them if they have time to talk and see your work (many won't have the time; don't be disheartened, because the few that say 'yes' are worth it). Dress smartly, get your work looking its best, stick your mints in your pocket and go out there and sell yourself, as a designer and a person. Listen carefully to any titbits of information that come your way when you're visiting: they may be directly relevant or merely industry gossip. But even industry gossip is useful to have (giving you something to talk about at future visits).

Follow up on even the most tenuous positive reactions, send samples in the interim and include the people who were positive on your list for a future visit.

DOING PRO BONO

Pro bono is a Latin term and is a contraction of the longer term, pro bono publico, which means an act done for the good of the people (literally 'for the good of the public'). In English, it has come to mean a professional who does free or charitable work, in contrast with paid work. The right pro bono work is also an excellent way of establishing the right publicity for a young designer. Doing socially active work – the right socially active work – is both a benefit for the people being designed for and for the designer, who walks away with a great big lump of reputation. Once again, choose your causes wisely: choose them to make the right kind of public statement.[11]

Interestingly, if you look at many of the graphics blogs on the subject, it seems that some designers regard pro bono as some sort of tax dodge (the principle being that a designer might offset the time they spend doing charitable work against their tax liability). If you share this opinion, then please, for the love of all that you regard as important in the world, don't do it. The value in doing charitable work is in doing the right thing by others, and in being seen to be doing the right thing by those other designers who are likely to care about people who do the right thing. If either you or the designers you wish to work for aren't the types who are going to honestly care about serving social causes, then don't do pro bono work, because the mismatch between your work and the jobs you are asked to do will only serve to highlight the lack of care.

WORK TO PUT IN, WORK TO LEAVE OUT

This leads me to address the question of including personal work in a designer's promotional work. Personal work is only useful in publicity if it is brave work that a working designer would never normally be allowed to do.

1   If the work shows a technical innovation or ability that is beyond what the viewer would normally see in your work, put it in.

2   If the personal work is an endless reiteration of a personal style, leave it out (the work isn't telling the viewer anything that they haven't already seen in published work).

3   If you have mocked up work that looks like it was used in a real job, but wasn't, you should think carefully about leaving it out. This sort of work is often found on young designers' websites and smacks of a certain hopelessness. It seems to be saying, 'Look at what I could do if I were only given a chance.' The exception to this is found in point 1. If your version of the job shows a clear innovation that the real product doesn't, then it can stay.

4   Student work is fine for a time: designers will understand that those people fresh out of university have little choice. But, first, make sure that the work is excellent and brave (i.e. something beyond what the industry would feel able to tackle) and, second, make sure that the student work is replaced as soon as it can be by real jobs.

5   Don't put work in that is likely to upset the intended audience. I'm not saying dumb down your work, but I am saying sending a church group your design for a club compilation is just thoughtless. It *will* be read in the wrong way; it *won't* get you the job. Be selective.

6   Never, ever, include bad jobs. Even if the client was a major international player, if the job stank, don't put it in. You can make reference to the job in your publicity material, but don't include the work. Seeing bad work for a good client is confusing to future clients and will give the wrong impression.

TREATING THE PROCESS OF PUBLICITY AS THE MAINTENANCE OF A REPUTATION NETWORK

Reputation networks are a technical way of describing the ways in which opinions about the members of a society are formed and evaluated by the members of the society. So, in a class at school, there will be a constant process of evaluation and re-evaluation of the reputations of all of the classmates, by all of the classmates. This process of evaluation will automatically generate a set of reputations. If an individual behaves badly, the other members of the class will pass round the news of the bad behaviour, and, as a result, the reputation suffers. In classical business terms, it is said that, 'good reputation results from continuously fulfilling quality promises'.

I talk about 'maintenance' because, in my head, I think of a reputation as being like a garden. Gardens require constant, low-level inputs of work: do a bit every day and you have a beautiful garden; leave it too long between interventions and you have a jungle; this is a perfect description for the constant care and attention that your professional reputation needs.

Like it or not, designers *will* generate reputations by simply working as designers, which is why the process needs control. Do a good job, but behave like a prima donna, and a designer will be building a reputation as a good designer but a bad person: this type of designer will start to be avoided by other designers unless their specific skill set is needed. Do a job faster than expected, and the reputation quickly forms that you can save jobs that are running out of time; this sounds like a good thing, but the designer's clients will come to rely on that speed, and the designer may well get trapped in a cycle of increasingly crazy deadlines.

As you will be building a reputation anyway (by being a practising designer), then you should probably be doing what you can to control the process. Some of this comes under the general heading of publicity and keeping in contact. Some of it comes under the heading of putting out messages about your practice that you think that you and your practice can support. For example, don't say things about your practice that can't be evidenced by your practice, because the gap between the spin and the reality will undermine your reputation. Equally, if a graphic communicator does something unique and remarkable in their practice, they would be crazy not to highlight it – drawing people's attention to it with text and image (or video) in their blogs and their print samples, making play of it on their website and entering competitions that specialise in that strength. For example, a good typographic designer should submit work to the International Society of Typographic Designers (ISTD) and get their membership award (thus being entitled to put the letters MISTD after their name): the award is, in itself, a nice thing to have, but, in particular circles, it acts as a sign (in a semantic sense) of quality that builds the right kind of reputation.

An example that pleases me personally comes from a couple of student designers I know: Ben Marsh and J.K. Roach. Ben and J.K. did some lovely design work for a notional line of condoms intended for young men. These game-themed condoms were witty and charming and graphically sharp. As well as showing the client (in this context, the staff), they took some excellent studio shots of the packs and then seeded the shots into the blogosphere. They did the job so well that, about a week later, I found their work appearing on several blogs, including the AOI-owned international tech blog *Engadget*. A little bit of extra work, and Ben and J.K. got their work in front of millions of people across the planet.

OTHER THINGS TO CONSIDER IN GETTING AND KEEPING A CAREER

Being involved in the *right* projects

To a large degree, the way an individual graphic communicator is perceived by the rest of the industry is defined by the projects they are involved in, and it should be obvious that certain projects generate stronger positive messages than others. This leads to the inescapable conclusion that a clued-in graphic communicator should be planning the projects they take.

That said, most of us tend to indulge in a degree of drift in our working lives: we get distracted by all kinds of secondary stuff (fun, relationships, children, holidays, etc.). This is OK, this is normal, but do yourself a favour. Take some time, once or twice a year, and consider what you want to achieve and run a quick audit on the sorts of project that might take you a bit closer to your goal. Hopefully, your job will provide you with the opportunities you are looking for. If you find that this isn't the case, doing a bit of freelance or running personal projects can provide you with what you're looking for in your perfect portfolio. Having a job and planning a career are not the same.

Free press

I don't mean 'the free press' as in the local free papers that get thrust through your letterbox at unpredictable intervals, I'm talking about any free press exposure that you can manage to achieve. Once again, the trick is only to spend time and resources on press that is credibly going to be seen by the right industrial practitioners or potential clients. This kind of thinking is behind most of the contributions made by designers to the design press. It is well worthwhile for a designer to spend time establishing contacts to get their artwork in the gallery section of a magazine, or to have a feature article about them on a credible design blog. Following the same rationale, the press you get from doing pro bono work might give you tangible benefits in establishing a reputation with the right people; so, while the principal motivation for doing charitable work will be the benefits it brings for others, there is nothing to stop you getting some press attention from your good work. Getting some free press is often as simple as sending out a formal press release – a few words and some high-resolution photos in an easily accessible digital form – to any magazines, blogs or papers that you care about. The press needs to be fed constantly, and busy news editors might just be intrigued enough to follow up a press release.

The difference between the free press, paid-for advertising and blogging should be seen in terms of gaining reputation benefits by associating your own work with the reputation of the press outlet you choose. If you managed to get your work in the *Loughborough Echo* (my local paper), that might make your family happy and give you some tangible benefits when taking your Foundation portfolio round to degree interviews. A piece about you in the *Birmingham Post* is more significant than one in the *Loughborough Echo*, because the *Post* has a daily circulation of over 100,000 readers, and the *Echo* has about 18,000. The benefit is still not substantial, because the *Post* is still a regional paper, with a tight geographical distribution. Get a piece about yourself in *Computer Arts* and you're starting to make some noise, because the magazine is international and holds all the content online as well as on paper; more importantly, its readership is, by definition, interested in the visual. A piece, even a tiny piece, in *Design Week* or *Eye* is important stuff: you now have access to designers all over the planet, who are all in a position to give you access to interesting work. A quarter-page feature about you in *Eye* is going to get you more work than a full-page advert.

This thinking is one of the reasons that D&AD's New Blood is such an important event. The press surrounding the event is (in my opinion) sometimes more useful than the awards themselves. A young designer who can get themselves on the D&AD press releases will probably find their work appearing in *Creative Review*, *Digital Arts* and many other outlets.

Websites: personal

Every designer should have a web presence: a MySpace, Facebook, Twitter or blog account isn't enough on its own. Every designer should have a website that acts as a gallery and showroom for their work: a good-looking (and simple) website that gives interested people a quick and easy way to look at good-quality samples of their work. This is a bottom-line position for a working designer.

Now, it must be said that many blogs have become highly customisable to a designer with a basic knowledge of CSS, and some designers like to use an existing blogging engine (such as Tumblr) to carry the burden of their publicity. Don't do it. The blog is a great tool for engaging with your readers on a regular basis, but it fulfils a different function from a gallery website. Blogs are typically searchable, but the search relies on the reader knowing what they're looking for. A designer will get the greatest benefit from a website that allows for undirected browsing, like a stroll round a great shop, where a potential client can stumble on an unexpected treat. So, use both tools, in coordination, to do the job of publicity: the website to give a first point of contact and an overview of your work, and the blog to keep the client in touch with the breaking news.

There isn't the space here to go into much depth about website design here, but here are some 'must have' points to consider. A designer's website must have:

- **Good meta tags**. Meta tags are hidden pieces of information in the 'header' of a web page (if this makes no sense to you, talk to a web designer). The tags can describe the content of your page for web crawlers (code that feeds search engines); they can carry keywords about your pages and authorship information; and they can say when the page was last updated – all things that the big search engines such as Google and Bing are very interested in. A website that only carries the meta tags generated automatically by the HTML editor is going to be overlooked and lost in the mass of other designers' sites. To learn more, look online; there are many good sites that offer free information about meta tags, what they are and how to make them work.[12] Don't subscribe to services that offer to boost your page ranking: the big search engines guard their search algorithms (code) very jealously. Their bottom line depends on being honest middlemen between the searcher and the searched for. If they find a company has developed a way to reliably spoof the system, then they change the system. It's as simple as that.

- **Good keywords**. In addition to the hidden use of keywords in meta tags, it is a good idea to include keywords for individual images and blocks of text that you want people to see. For example, if you've won a competition, you should add the keywords '"competition name" competition winner' to your pages' meta tags, so that search engines can index you as the winner. You should also add a text about the win to your front page with the keywords 'competition', 'winner', 'the name of the competition', and the year. Pictures of the winning design should also be tagged (using the <alt> tag), and include the keywords in the caption. In this way, we have a self-referencing system of tags and keywords that allows search engines to capture our details correctly and then that allows a user to skip through the stuff they don't want to see and find the stuff they do.

- **Good images** (but not too good). Use the clearest images you can; if possible use a good image editor to optimise them for your web page and, where you can, optimise them to the right colour model (see Chapter 13). However, don't ever put in images that are of such high quality that an unscrupulous visitor could steal your work. More cautious designers might consider *watermarking* the images they put up (see the box). Both Photoshop and GIMP allow you to embed text (metadata) about the image and its author in the image, which is useful in itself, but doesn't protect the image from theft off your website. Although visible watermarking does alter the image, you might well think that the protection it offers is worth it. It's a decision that every designer has to make for him- or herself. Tricks such as scripts that protect against copying and downloading won't be effective, as most OSs have screen-capture applications that defeat the point of the exercise.

- **Good layout**. I almost feel like I'm cheating by putting this in, but it is a pretty important factor when considering how legible the individual images will be on the page. Cluster too many small thumbnails together and you are forcing your viewer to spend forever checking out every image, just in case it's the one they're looking for. Add to this the habit of running strong patterns behind the images, and you have a recipe for an unreadable page: there are good reasons for many top designers using black or white web pages to display their content. So, just because it's a website for you, doesn't mean that you have to design it as anything other than a good piece of graphics.

WATERMARKING

Watermarking is a method of varying the luminosity of some of the pixels in an image to include data that identify the image as being the author's property. Both Photoshop and GIMP can do this easily. Photoshop comes installed with a limited copy of a commercial watermarking utility called *Digimark*, which invisibly encodes ownership details in the image in such a way that it can't be removed by simple tricks such as cutting and pasting. The full Digimark tool does an excellent job but costs enough that it might be out of a young designer's reach, but there are a number of free tools that can make a discrete, but visible, watermark in GIMP, and, if you're a bit technical, you can knock up a Photoshop action that does the same (I tried, and it took me about five minutes to make one that, at the touch of a button, leaves my name in the middle of any image I choose) (see Figure 17.1).

FIGURE 17.1
Samples of various watermarking techniques: tonal inversion, lightening and hue variation

Websites: other

Let's take a moment to consider the benefits of having your work carried, commercially or for free, on other people's websites. If the website is prestigious, *Creative Review* for example (www.creativereview.co.uk/), the association being made between your work and its history of reporting the excellent in visual communication is a powerful publicity tool. What if you are offered a place on a website that is less exalted? A worryingly large number of both free and paid gallery sites seem to have near zero quality control on the design work they display, and these should be avoided. A designer might assume that any exposure is good exposure at the start of a career (following the principle that there is no such thing as bad publicity), but the assumption is wrong. A rock star who sits around in the evening in their local library, instead of attending glittering events at the hottest clubs across the globe, is degrading their public profile: the cultural codings of the sign 'library' (signifying old buffers reading the newspapers on rainy days) has negative connotations when contrasted with the sign 'rock star' (excitement, music, youth facing glamour and rebellion, with undertones of sexual excess and drugs): one sign sucks the power right out of the other. In the same way, an edgy designer who carelessly places their gorgeously dangerous and witty work on a web page with other people's Photoshopped fantasy princess or Ibiza-style Hed Kandi ripoffs[13] is looking to have their work contaminated by the company it keeps. For an example of what I mean, you might do worse than look at the typography gallery at *Designflavr*, which contains some decent examples of work but is pretty well uncurated, presenting the tightly controlled letterform sample with the same seriousness as an interestingly incoherent word mess. So, although it is always fun casually to sample *DeviantART*, you won't be making much of a visual impact against the rest of the goodies displayed. Be picky about the places your work appears and the company it keeps. If your work will be displayed in a way that lets it shine, then do it; otherwise give it a miss.

Websites: paid

Even more worrying are online 'agents' and galleries that promise to put your work in front of thousands of clients across the globe and actually enter you into an eternal bidding cycle against other designers who are all desperate for work. Really, try not to get involved. There are plenty of reputable employment agencies out there that specialise in design jobs and are being paid by the client looking for a designer, not by the designer. Register with them and get some decent working experience.

'Bid sites' such as peoplebythehour.com worry me: although doing nothing illegal, the nature of the site is such that design rates for jobs will be forced down, with better designers being forced out, and the fees being dropped through the floor. I look at much of the paid sector and see it as another argument for designers to form design groups and coops, where they can club together to buy in the expertise to build a web presence that truly does the job of representing them.

Although there is nothing wrong with paying people for publicity and to find work, this is a task better suited to professional agents and agencies who have the contacts and the resources to do the job right. A good agent (especially for illustrators, photographers and videographers) is a wonderful thing to have backing you up. They'll have a professionally designed website built for only one function, and that is to sell your talent.

Agencies

Agencies are a part of the design economy that is frequently ignored. So, while writers often have agents, as do footballers and people selling property, designers often fail to consider that there are companies out there that do nothing except join the right designer in blissful harmony with the right client, and all that they ask for in return is between 25 and 35 per cent of the fee.

Some designers bridle at the thought of having to give away some of 'their' money to agents. Personally, I think that agents have an honourable and worthwhile role: they get designers jobs that the designer would not normally get access to (I knew of an agency that specialised in finding holiday and sickness cover for magazine art directors. How would a designer ever stumble across work as niche as that?). A good agent will never ask for money up front, and will only take a percentage of the jobs that are paid for. The more work they find for you, the more money they get, and, if you find work without their help, then you keep the fee, because they've not rendered you any agency.

The downside is that many agencies will only take on designers (illustrators, editorial, videographers, photographers, etc.) with experience in the sector. The rationale is that they hope to get a reasonable return on their investment (in you) and need to be able to see a career professional that they can work with.

Contact emails: bulk mailers (spam is rude!)

Contact emails (and letters) are statements of intent. Their narrative should be one of a designer's interest in making a working contact with a specific organisation for a specific reason. You can't do this with a random email campaign. You end up with a blatant form letter that inadvertently insults the reader with its hopeless lack of specificity.

There are software tools that address this problem and that allow for the sophisticated insertion of *variables* which give a pretty good simulation of a meaningfully personal email communication (they are called 'bulk mailers'). You can do everything, from mail merges in your word processor, to inserting complex text and image variables in *InDesign*, to using a tool such as *MaxMailer*. Just because you can do something like this, does it mean that you should? Personally, I can think of a tiny number of circumstances where using a bulk mailer is the right thing for a designer to do when communicating with their clients. Christmas and New Year messages would be one use where a generic but personalised communication might be appropriate. For the rest of your communications, I would strongly suggest taking the time to communicate personally with your clients. An impersonal communication sends the wrong message; a faked personal communication is just a little insulting. On the day you find that you have just too many clients to keep in touch with, I would suggest hiring an admin who can do the grunt work for you.

Getting a first job is tough; getting the next one is tougher. Make a plan, make keeping in touch as much a part of your working life as the graphics you make and you should be able to find job after job, until you get to that magical point where you find yourself to be part of the design establishment.

NOTES

1   I suspect this is one of the reasons that, if you do an image search on 'design lecturer', you get a mass of very well organised images of people looking suspiciously trendy, smart, engaged and abnormally well groomed: the lecturers in question are all design professionals who know the importance of 'putting on the best face', which is the essence of publicity.

2   To see chaos in action, get some form of pendulum – a conker or a yo-yo for example – and let it fall into a natural rhythmic swing. This swing is one stable 'state'. The distance and range of the swings are predictable. If you give the weight a little whack to one side while it swings, you disrupt the stable state. The swings will, temporarily, become largely unpredictable, and this unpredictable swinging is a chaotic state. The range and even direction of the swings are unpredictable from one swing to the next, but eventually the weight will fall into a new stable state.

   The changes made by technology in the last couple of decades and the consequent social changes sparked by technology have been like a series of shocks to the previously stable state of the graphics industry. What the industry currently is and what it can do are completely unpredictable, which is both wonderful and scary. The shocks aren't over either, and as such the chance of a predictable career path for graphics workers in the next couple of decades seems unlikely.

3   If you're confused, the 'V' stands for Virgin.

4   Though in the past, I've used relabelled beer to get music industry reps to attend gigs. A&R men at record companies are famous for their love of free drinks, and so a few crates of lager with nicely redesigned labels worked a treat.

5   As the young Uruguayan Fede Alvarez found out when his excellent 'giant robots blow up lots of buildings' short film, *Ataque de Panico* (*Panic Attack*), got him a $30 contract from Sam Raimi's Ghost House Productions.

6   I worked with a designer who had charted her entire future around her intention to be a mother and designer. To this end, she had methodically furnished herself with a portfolio of skills that would allow her to turn freelance, at a high level in her chosen sector of the design industry, at a

time of her choosing, so that she could freelance and parent at the same time. An attitude that is admirable in its clarity and focus.

7   A low-level job can seem like a creative cage.

8   If you start off doing dull, provincial work, it becomes harder for you to get better work later, because you have nothing to show future employers.

9   Contact methods need to be as specific as possible; other design-industry workers won't be happy to receive generic mailers.

10 This is very simple to do. Go to: www.google.com/alerts, enter your search term, decide on the frequency with which you want the search to be run and the class of site to be searched, and give them an email address to send the results to you.

11 Unless you have any personal cultural or political position that you want to support. In which case, you must, of course, support it. Just make sure that the design work you do is reported.

12 I like the W3Schools.com site.

13 With all respect to Jason Brooks for serving a genuine social need, and long may he keep serving it.

CHAPTER 18

The future

To understand the future of graphic communication, it is useful to think first about the past: to understand why designers did what they did in the past. Designers are often so close to the means of production that they begin to think that the way that they do things is both *natural* and *right*, when it is nothing of the sort. Strangely enough, this confusion applies equally to those who love the graphic media of the past and those who love the media of the future. Many designers (and quite a few design educators) talk about craft in ways that venerate it, commenting, 'Isn't it a shame that the craft of this or that medium is being lost to the current generation of designers?' ('because', they say, 'there is clearly a purity in hand-printed letterpress that well-set type made in InDesign or Quark cannot supply').[1] For these folk, everything is shiny in the rear-view mirror; they live in a world of rediscovered glory, of work made better by seeming to be old. Work of the past, for these people, is always better than work of the now or the future.

Just as dangerous are those who think that graphics can only live on the bleeding edge of technology. Too often we hear people taking the *next-big-thing* stance, especially in design. They only acknowledge the quality in work if it is novel. For these people, only the new is good: 'social media are better than a poster, e-books are superior to books', they would claim – both are better because they are newer.

A curse on both of them! Both these schools of thought are asking you to invest in a style, an idea, a small set of media choices; they are selling you a mean slice of the design cake. Both are retailing trend as design, not design as a way to change the world. Both of these stances are dead ends that you should avoid, because those selling these lines must be either dishonest or dumb as a post. We need to see why these stances are unhelpful to working designers.

A designer needs to be focused on the now, by which I mean the actual life choices and physical constraints of the user. These are the conditions that will dictate the success or failure of the design. A medic in a war zone is unlikely to appreciate that the bandage they are about to use is screen-printed on Manila paper, or that it is made of a specialist form of a new synthetic polymer. They will, however, care that it is clearly labelled, is designed to be used with the minimum of fuss and that it works.

Designers who champion specific media choices are making the business of graphics a matter of style, trend and mode. In fact (as Victor Margolin says), it is a matter of process played out in society, an intersection of the process and the culture. Technology does not exist in isolation, it does not come into existence without a social reason: it operates within a cultural framework. Technology emerges from the sea of the social and finds its relevance in the social. Technology is semantic, it is a set of codes that are culturally significant: technology cannot ever be neutral.

Gutenberg didn't start the print revolution with the intention of altering the media landscape: he was too much of a businessman for that.[2] He was aiming at cutting the cost of producing Bibles, with the simple intention of selling them cheaper than the *scriptoria* could.[3] Gutenberg had a history of interesting business schemes. He came from a family that had business interests in metal-working (gold, coining, etc.), worked in gem polishing and is said to have been familiar with the copperplate printing of playing cards. As a result, he took a whole raft of pre-existing technologies, technologies that were well understood (a wine press, casting metals, paper, inks, etc.), and turned them into something that, in that specific time and place, made both cultural sense and (more importantly for Gutenberg) money. In other times and places, there would have been no need for Gutenberg's work (people needed Bibles), in other places there would have been no resources (Gutenberg had access to wine presses and metal casters, paper and ink). At this specific time and place, a social need meets the means to answer the need.

Print historian Nigel Roche (of the St Brides Print Library) points out that there is a ratio between the cost of working with old media technology and the cost of working with new media technologies that, when it is right, marks the uptake of the new technology. A handwritten Bible would typically take a year to produce. Roche explains that, when Gutenberg could produce a book for a quarter of the price of one from the scriptorium (a manual copying shop), printing swiftly took over from hand rendering as *the* way to publish. The change to a print design rather than handcraft came from the combination of the technology and a social opportunity, not from any desire to be new.

However, once he had his first press, and then when Schöffer took it over, the press took on a new set of codes. Presses turned books from being an idea of knowledge being handmade and rare (as in the scriptoria) into books being knowledge as available and consumable. Society places a meaning on technology. It places limits on how or when it may or may not be used.

I mention this to show that our childlike enthusiasm for technology, *any technology*, is not the future of graphic communications, the future of media. We can favour any technology of production, any medium we like. We cannot expect that medium to work for all people, in all places, at all times. People are different and will respond in ways that are bounded by their culture. In the same way, the history of the subject is not a history of technology, but a history of the social application of technology. The technology is only meaningful within a specific social context. Designers who draw the right connection between a medium and its cultural meaning are on to a winning formula.

So, what does this connection between media technology and culture mean to us as designers? It means *everything*. Technologists (scientists and engineers) are often not good at understanding the social dimension that their work inhabits. They are mad Darwinists, throwing novel technology into the field in an evolutionary game of Russian roulette, with no concept of how it will affect the world. They create, without thinking about the effects of the creation. From their universities and laboratories, they form spin-off companies to exploit their wonder devices commercially, which die because no one cares: the technology does not fit with the society. Equally bewilderingly, many pieces of technology are taken up to form a living part of the

POINTING AT COMPUTERS

The computer mouse was invented around the end of the 1960s. Look at representations of computing in the media of the 1960s and 1970s and you won't find a single mouse (or any form of pointing device at all). If you look at the cockpits of the *Millennium Falcon* in *Star Wars*, the controls look like the inside of a contemporary airliner – the computers are controlled with little flick switches. Why would this be? Because this is what the world at the time thought technology looked like: lots of switches and lots of lights. The viewer wouldn't have believed you could fly anything with a screen and a mouse.

Now today, we can go down to our supermarket and buy *bargain* mice, children's mice, trackballs, wireless, optical, one-button, two-, three- or five-button mice. They are everywhere. My phone has a trackball built into it, as have kiosk computers, some phoneboxes and sundry haptic variations. Thirty years ago, we didn't know what a mouse was; twenty years ago (in one of the *Star Trek* movies), we laughed at the crew of *The Enterprise* for thinking a mouse was an audio mike; now, being able to use a mouse is a fundamental life skill that requires no explanation. A child could do it.

The mouse as a device is much the same as it ever was; the social meaning has changed.

world, gaining meaning and value in a culture. I suspect that when Shuji Nakamura invented the world's first (usefully bright) blue LED in 1993, he wasn't intending them to be used to illuminate the undersides of modded cars driven by young men in baseball caps, but they were. This is what the philosopher Don Ihde calls *multistable design*: that strange phenomenon of users finding applications for technology that had never been anticipated by its inventors.

By contrast with the world's technologists, graphic communicators are very good at playing meaningfully with the social dimension. Designers are very good at seeing the fit of technology and society. Designers (industrial and communication) apply technology to fit social needs. Let's not forget that technology does not have to mean *high technology*; technology can also mean historic or current industrial technologies. A graphic-design response to a brief should always be a synthesis of the following elements: message, medium and meaning. Whether we are talking about an AR or a letterpress document, we should be witnessing the end result of a designer considering how a medium finds meaning in a society.

The message

+

what the message means to those who need to get the message

+

a medium that is sympathetic to the message
(at very least), preferably a medium that carries a meaning of its own that will reinforce the message

=

a successful job.

There are media that are entirely appropriate to a particular audience and media that are inappropriate; there are no universal good or bad media; full stop, end of discussion.

This leads us back, from theory, to the real world that designers have always had to inhabit. Designers in the past had narrow choices of production technologies open to them, whereas we inhabit a wonderland of design toys that are not just available but are also cheap and accessible. When we couple the range of new technologies now open to a designer with the industrial might of China and the developing world, we can get things produced that are wildly extravagant in historical terms but perfect for their intended audience. By my side, as I type, is a swing ticket (a clothing tag) taken off my eldest daughter's new school tracksuit trousers (£3 from Primark). The swing ticket is printed in full four-colour on both sides and it's silver foiled with a ribbon riveted to it. That's a lot of print processing and hand-finishing for a £3 pair of trackies. In the world of media plenty, however, such excess makes design sense. When designers *can* make anything, they have to think very hard about what they design. The designer of the swing ticket has understood what it takes to sell to a teenage girl.

This is not an original observation; smart people, paying attention, have always understood that 'things' have different values or mean different things, in different times and places. The philosopher Spinoza defined this relationship for us in the seventeenth century. In contrast to the prevailing absolutist views (my religion good, yours bad, etc.), Spinoza didn't believe in things being 'good' or 'evil' in themselves: he believed that things were 'good' and 'bad' in combination. The difference is not marked by the individual characteristics of things but by the way they relate to each other. Spinoza used the example of poison combined with a person; I'm going to follow his lead. Botulinum toxin is not 'evil', but it is very 'bad' in combination with you and your food. However, in combination with you, a syringe and your facial muscles, it becomes a *botox* injection and (I'm told) a good thing.

Spinoza talked of combinations that increased a person's (or a group's, or a whole culture's) *ability* to act. He regarded these combinations as good. These were called *joyful passions*. So, for Spinoza, a society that respected the individual's right to liberty was *good*, in that it enabled the whole of the society to act, not just the individual.

By contrast, a combination that reduces the person's (or group's, or culture's) ability to act is bad: these combinations are called *sad passions*. Spinoza would argue that slavery is *bad*, because, although it increases the ability for some to act, it reduces the ability to act for the society as a whole.

If we apply Spinoza's *sad passions* (the bad combinations) and his *joyful passions* (the good combinations) to thinking about graphics, technology and society, we can start making some sort of headway when considering the future of the industry.

Posters were *the* medium of choice for delivering loud, polemic and broad public messages, because they had the following positive characteristics. Posters:

- are cheap (once the initial set-up is taken into account);
- have a high visual distinctiveness (they stand out from the environment);
- are location independent (the message does not depend on the place); and
- are stylistically transformative (the presence of the poster changes the meaning of the environment).

In the context of the nineteenth century and the early twentieth century, they made perfect sense as the medium of choice for those seeking influence over, and communication with, those who needed to be swayed. The combination of big splashy message delivered at the same time, in public, to lots of people was, in communications terms, a joyful passion. The combination of public message and public audience worked a little bit of magic in the world.

Film and television have taken over some of the purpose of the poster, because they have similar characteristics (low cost, visual distinctiveness, location independence and stylistic transformation) as a medium of influence, but with differences that make them even more effective in some circumstances. Posters are a public medium, they are read and reacted to in public, but television is private. This private means of address is, by contrast, the medium's great strength. Television can deal with and discuss things we are only comfortable engaging with in private. Posters cannot show an unclothed human body in public on a poster (Sophie Dahl and the Opium perfume advert, for example), but designers can talk about STDs and safe sex on TV. We see soap operas, where private issues can be talked about, privately, but in common with the rest of the viewing audience.[4] We see advertising and political communication following suit: adverts blend with soaps and music video, politicians talk in hushed tones, as if they were sitting on the other side of a dining table from us, not in a studio a hundred miles away. These media work by creating a community in which we all share.

At the same time, the poster does not die, it just takes on different meanings. When the television becomes official, the poster takes on a new role as the way the unofficial – be it a gig poster or a call to protest – is broadcast to the public.

In the same way now, a whole raft of communications technologies intended for private communication become public, political (and sometimes commercial) media. Mobile phones (invented to help doctors in rural Finland) become a medium for organising protests. Social media become everything from charity fund-raising tools to a means of sexual predation. The Internet stops being a military command, communication and control system and becomes a way of ordering pizza or downloading homework sheets. Objects, media and ideas become things that they were never intended to be and, in turn, become platforms for other unintended creations. This effect is what the philosopher Don Ihde calls *multistable design*. Ihde says (2008, p. 130): 'I have, secondly, noted that technologies are frequently variably culturally embedded. The same technology may be used very differently and even mean very different things in two different cultural contexts.'

A multistable design is exactly what I have been describing to you: an object or idea crafted for one purpose, but then used by people for another, and coming to mean something completely new. There is nothing we, as designers, can (or indeed should) do about this. Cultures will use technology in any way they see fit: we cannot design *at* people and demand that they respond to our communications in one, and only one, way. Instead, we do our best as designers to design for the needs of our users, while watching out for those user-generated multistable designs, looking for ideas on how we can improve our own work.

It helps to think of these patterns of *use* as *ab-use* – not in the sense of an act that damages something, but rather as *use* in an unofficial, unapproved and abnormal way. These ab-uses are never accidentally made; they always mean something, they are always *significant* (in a semantic sense), and these meanings are by definition important to the culture of the user. (Otherwise, why would they bother doing some-

ACADEMIA.EDU

Social media serve many purposes, but the simplest purposes are those of sharing information about your life with your friends and making new friends: in short, they're about networking, being able to track the activities of friends, acquaintances and enemies. Academics have been using social media for all sorts of business-related purposes, tweeting and blogging away about their work for years, but it was all on a rather ad hoc basis. Like high school, the academic world is heavily dependent on reputation. Social-media developer Richard Price understood this. Academics and their home institutions all have websites about their research, and they go to conferences to talk about their work, while blogging, emailing and tracking each other like teenagers on Facebook. Understanding this, Price developed a social-networking tool for academics: www.academia.edu (go online and look your lecturers up). Academia.edu currently has over 200,000 academics using it on a regular basis, doing business and promoting their reputations like mad.

thing different?) The modded lights on a car are ab-uses of both the blue LED technology and the electrical system of the car, but not accidents, and they are full of meaning to the modder and the people the modder cares about.

The ways that people interact with and adapt the world leave smart designers valuable clues that they follow to improve the design. If a designer sees people take the timetable they have just carefully designed and watches the users continually flipping them from front to back in an effort to read the outward and return times, then they know that they have made a design mistake.

If a designer sees a group of people using a form of medium in a way that is different from its intended function, then they would be well advised to incorporate this use in the design.

Smart designers do just this. The US Army had all sorts of image problems, recruitment was down, and the recruitment standards kept being lowered to keep the active strength of the army up. This was a problem for an organization as dependent on integrated high technologies as the US Army.

In an ideal world, the US Army wanted to recruit young people who were: technically adept, smart and tactically experienced. Was this an unrealistic objective? The answer was no, it was just a communications problem, a problem the Army solved through the development of a very sophisticated, cross-platform, first-person, multiple-player computer game called *America's Army Online*. The military were very clear in their own minds that the game was a 'strategic communication tool' (Davis, 2004), which makes it squarely a graphic-communication issue.

Players from any part of the globe form squads of US soldiers and engage in online missions using standard US weapons and equipment. The rationales of the game are intended to represent the soldier's life as it is:

> That the game be played absolutely straight, as an honest representation of the service especially regarding ethics, codes of conduct, and professional expectation, and extending to accurate depictions of hierarchy, missions, weapons, equipment, uniforms, settings, discipline, tactics, procedure – in short this was to be a game a platoon sergeant could play without wincing.
>
> (Davis, 2004, as quoted by Neiborg 2004)

As a result, the designers of the game built a very successful communications bridge with the specific demographic with which they wanted to engage: young, intelligent, tech savvy and not averse to the idea of shooting people. It was important for the US Army that the game be an honest representation (in the client's view) of life as a soldier (action, yes; but weeks spent in barracks' drill, no), but also that the game made such a life appealing.

Whatever the morality of the idea, the design works; personally, I can tell you that playing the game was lots of fun and, more importantly, is reported to have been a great help in recruitment terms. Davis (as cited by Neiborg) states that, 'the game was cost effective – about 0.3% of the Army's recruitment budget – yet was . . . the Army's most effective medium for reaching young Americans'.

For me, *America's Army Online* is a clear indication of where graphics can go: not as a medium (I don't think we should become code engineers, perish the thought); not even as an approach (*America's Army Online* is propaganda, and, although I am ready to admit graphic communicators are often employed in advertising, I do not think that advertising and other forms of propaganda are necessarily our duty and destiny as designers); no, I believe that *America's Army Online* is an indicator of the future because it demonstrates a process. A process that exists outside technology and media, but is driven by an intelligent understanding of a user's culture and society. The thought processes behind *America's Army Online* could equally be driven to produce a letterpress page or a new set of drug packaging. The designers had identified a trend built of technology and society and followed it through to a successful communication-design solution.

How would a designer learn of these trends? Well, apart from the active research process looked at in Chapter 5, new research tools have appeared that designers would have never had access to before. The media researcher and code explorer Lev Manovich has built a computer system, modelled on the *data analytics* used by big companies such as Amazon to follow buying trends, to analyse trends in culture; he calls this process *cultural analytics*, and he uses it to extract very fine detail about changes in cultural taste and application that are directly applicable to design. Manovich talks of observing 'real-time cultural flows around the world'. He is intent on observing culture (on a very large scale), in real-time, as it happens. Manovich says:

> Imagine a visualization that shows how other people around the word remix new videos created in a fan community, or how a new design software gradually affects the kinds of forms being imagined today (the way Alias and Maya led to blobs in architecture).
>
> (Manovich, 2008, p. 3)

Designers would be looking at a resource that measures the global flow of tastes and preferences that make up large cultural groups as they happen. An invaluable tool: one that is unlikely to provide the kind of fine-grain information that a working graphic communicator will need, but one that might be able to provide some really useful tools for future research.

Currently, this takes place in Manovich's space-age CALIT2 installation at the University of California San Diego (look it up: the place has to be seen to be believed), but he believes that, eventually, these sorts of data visualisation might be carried out on PCs and smartphones.

There are also some interesting applications of social research as practised by viral marketeers. They carry out a specific search, working their way up the chain of people actively involved in a culture in order to find the *alpha user*: that user who all members of the user culture look to for advice on what is cool and uncool.

You, the reader, might well ask if this awareness of the social and the cultural doesn't lurk behind all current design practice? To which I would reply that it should, but is frequently absent. Too often we look for, and are rewarded for having, the 'neat idea' and the 'cute concept'. We see design magazines and blogs full of fun ideas that have received design awards from fellow graphic practitioners but that do nothing (or that are actively unhelpful) in the world. Don't get me wrong: many cool ideas turn out to be unexpectedly effective, to the surprise of both the designer and the user. This is because designers are frequently soaked in the culture they live in. But this is not a predictable phenomenon, and we would not be wise to build a career on it.

Let me show you a counter-example to the fine work done by the *America's Army Online* designers, but one born from the same US military cultural context. In the run up to the Second Gulf War, the US military produced a set of playing cards that carried, on the reverse side, images of various members of the ruling military and government party in Iraq. The idea was that these would be distributed to soldiers on the ground, so that, if they came upon one of these bad types, they would be able to identify them and take them into custody. Because of the contrast between the function of the medium (gambling and playing games) and the seriousness of the environment (a full-scale engagement), the end result of the exercise was to make the whole thing look casual and a little bit dumb. There was a disharmony in the exercise that undermined the design of the artefact.

WHAT DO WE DO ABOUT THIS?

Future trends

I'm not claiming that the following list of trends is exhaustive, nor that I have some sort of crystal-ball vision into future trends, but this list contains some interesting trends for the next few years that a creative and brave graphic communicator might wish to play with. Broadly speaking, all of these technologies are what are known as *disruptive technologies*, which means they are technologies that disrupt the current, accepted ways of doing things and have the potential to remake cultures. They share the characteristic of changing the cost-to-user relationship. Put simply, they make it possible to speak more specifically, to smaller numbers of people, for a much lower cost.

Items in the list may spark secondary items (these are indented). All of these technologies are available now. None of them is science fiction. Most of them are desperately in need of good graphic design to make them relevant to end-users.

Paper-like displays (now). Seen on an e-book reader. If it is monochrome (as opposed to colour), it is quite likely to have an eInk Inc. paper-like display. The display is a sheet of material with many thousands of microscopic spheres embedded in the surface. The spheres have a black side and a white side and can be switched, singly or in groups, from one to the other. This is a very-low-power process, which means these displays are great for uses that are remote from mains-power supplies. eInk displays can produce very fine digital text. However, they produce poor-quality black and white images and cannot usefully display video. This is not always going to be the case: there are a multitude of companies developing paper-like displays that can do both colour and video. Paper-like displays add value to a design by tapping into several basic functions of the human visual system. By introducing motion, colour and potentially sound, designs using e-paper can attract attention automatically. This opens up the following opportunities for designers:

- **Active book and magazine covers** (now). In 2008, *Esquire* produced an e-paper cover, or, to be more honest, a small segment of a cover that flickers from black to white and then swaps. The design is uninspiring, but the possibilities are wonderful. Imagine your magazine design, all movement and colour, sitting on a shelf of static covers. How could they compete?

- **Active point of sale/point of purchase** (now). A couple of years ago, the Xbox game *Jade Empire* had an e-paper POS. It used colour overlays over an e-paper base to produce colour images that can shift from light to dark. The effect is striking.

- **Active packaging** (mid term). It is possible to print electronics, including simple chips and batteries, on commercial printing presses. This means that packaging could be made to display a range of image and video. The content could be made locative (it knows where it is and responds); it could even be made responsive to contact: imagine a box for a child's toy that starts talking to a child when picked up. How would you design packaging that moves and responds?

- **Active mapping** (now, kind of). Smartphones can do maps. Linked to GPS, they can tell us where we are. This is nice, but, without a data connection to supply us with the map data, all we know is that we are somewhere on a pale-grey grid, and, compared with a traditional map, the screen is really small. Now imagine a full-size map, say a metre square, that could tell you where you are, adjust the position of the map to the direction you are facing, and display variable levels of mapping information: now tourist information, now industrial, now environmental. No problem! The University of Arizona is working on systems like this for the US Army.

- **Active signage/wayfinding systems** (now). From sale signs in Japanese department stores to road signs that activate in response to road conditions, these are some of the earliest applications of paper-like displays. But this in no way means that there is any lack of opportunities for an imaginative designer to apply creative solutions aimed at making the environment easier to understand for the traveller. Imagine a sign on a tube station that not only tells you that the Central Line is *this way* when you are standing on the Northern Line platform at Tottenham Court Road station, but that tells you that the next eastbound Central Line train will be arriving in five minutes and you'd better hurry.

This is not a fantasy; this is something that is being done, will be done more often and is big business. The makers of the BlackBerry smartphone, Research In Motion (RIM), have recently patented the idea of billboards that are active and responsive to the flow of traffic. When the traffic is flowing freely, the billboards show designs that are data light: big bold images, snappy text; when the traffic is slow, the display will be data rich: video, packaging shots, driving information (where to go and buy the product). What kind of graphic-design skill set will this sort of medium require? The bold, eye-catching qualities of the poster designer, the story-telling skills of the video director or the interactive expertise of the HCI designer?

Magazines/magazites[5]/webzines (now). Now, in many ways, this is strongly connected with the paper-like displays section above, as traditional magazine content is being shifted by the global players in the magazine industry to e-book readers. This is often a pretty flat affair, with functionality limited to some minor reformatting and the ability to jump from page to page. But it need not be so. It is entirely possible to make magazines massively interconnected (like a wiki, with every term being linkable) and formatted on the fly. Take a look at the *Guardian*'s award-winning web presence, which is almost there and has a high degree of interchange between print, online and e-book material. You can see a beautiful design strategy being enacted here, one that maintains the paper's core function (reporting the news) while elegantly not confining itself to any media form, and extending itself into blogging and video reporting.

Computer games (now). Two- and 3D environments, including first-person shooters (now) and *in-game advertising* (IGA), which place various forms of adverts and product placements inside the game space, and *advergaming*, a dreadful word invented to describe games as adverts (such as *America's Army Online*): there are lots of possible ways of using game construction technologies for communication purposes. Imagine an interactive game space to teach numeracy, or a tax website that you can walk through in order to fill in your tax returns. Logically structuring data in 3D space offers many potential advantages when working with a group of users who are used to working with such environments, which is pretty much every person who has ever played a computer game, used an Xbox or picked up a Game Boy. Where are the information designers building William Gibson's virtual information spaces (look it up)?

Virtual environments (now). Not only does advertising exist within virtual environments such as *Second Life*, but the owners (Linden Research Inc.) actively encourage a variety of advertising schemes. Once again, although there are technically interesting tools such as pay-per-click posters (they link the user direct to a site), the actual visual design is crude and unimaginative. Such environments need good communications designers to build good graphic solutions for the users.

FIGURE 18.1
A poster in *Second Life*

Augmented reality (now). AR is a compromise between the original visions of VR (psychedelic wonderlands that turned into *Second Life*) and the desire to make the world easier to understand for people who needed to know. Whereas a VR requires insanely powerful processors to generate the graphics and high-bandwidth data connections to feed it, AR is a simple graphical overlay on top of a live camera image. As all smartphones are equipped with at least one camera and are data-connected out of the box, they represent a ready-made environment for AR software to run on: no new equipment needed (this is another case of multistable design, where a device – in this case a phone – is drummed into service to do something it was never intended to do).

AR turns your smartphone into a window into a modified version of your world, showing content placed at specific GPS coordinates by other people. The big news about AR is that it operates on the basis of layers or channels. You only see the channel that you subscribe to. So, a public building may be marked by official signage in one layer visible from any phone, but your phone may also carry a news-agency tag linking to a news story about the building; another may link to a Wikipedia history of the building; and yet another may link to a piece of guerilla tagging (a kind of virtual graffiti), invisible to anyone not carrying that channel.

This layering of information makes for an incredibly rich playground for designers working in all kinds of graphic enterprise.

- **AR protest** (now). There is a digital anti-censorship protest in Turkey that is both witty and rather intelligent. The protestors have used Google Maps/ Earth to form a virtual protest march, obscuring the downtown Taksim Square of Istanbul with little digital protestors. As Taksim Square is the tourist centre of the city, and so likely to be Googled by foreigners, the pro- test potentially addresses those outside the country who are likely to be able to put pressure on the Turkish government without upsetting the locals. If you use an AR client such as Layar in the Taksim Square area, all you will see is protest. Nice thinking.

- **AR advertising** (now). There are AR advertising companies, such as Brightkite in the United States, that put locative adverts on to systems such as Layar. The idea is that, when you are out and about and using your AR client, you will stumble across one of Brightkite's customers. It's a great technology, but not one being applied very imaginatively. For me, as a designer, the sad thing is the dullness of the graphics applied, both aes- thetically and conceptually. We need good designers to make users' eyes pop out of their heads, and to make their hearts skip a beat.

- **AR wayfinding** (now). There are many commercial wayfinding solutions in AR, but again the implementations are rather lacklustre. All of them need some intelligent design applied to them.

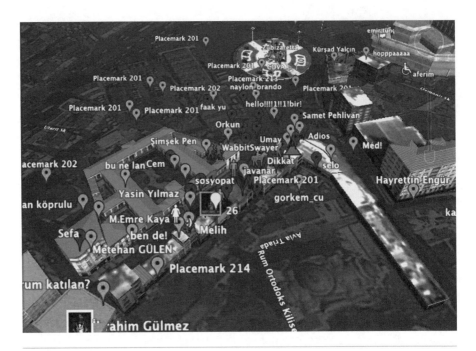

FIGURE 18.2
Taksim Square virtual protest

Locative media (now). If you have a wirelessly networked device, you will be, to some measure, involved in locative media. Google automatically checks the location of the wireless or phone connection you are using against its records of known wireless and cellular information (the Google Streetview vans sampled wireless location data at the same time as they took the photos – Google knows where you live). Then, a Google service called Google Local feeds you results based on your location. If you are using a GPS-equipped smartphone, the combined information from the GPS and the wireless location data can give a faster and more accurate fix on your position (eGPS). In short, because advertisers now know your location, within about 30 m anywhere on the earth's surface, they can give you very specific advertising information.

So far, this has been mainly about advertising, which is obvious, because that is where the money is, but there are some interesting indications about the possible uses that graphic communicators might make of locative technologies. Much of this has been covered in preceding chapters, but I want to make a plea to remember the user when you design. It is entirely possible to combine locative media with other technologies to start making some deeply responsive design. It is possible to deploy a design once, but to combine elements that are so specific and responsive to local need that people will embrace your message as their own. Where once a regional version of a television advert would be produced (you would see the same actor, with a London accent in the south, a Manchester accent in the north and a Scots accent in Scotland), it is now possible to produce a design that is specific to a town or even street level.

Rapid manufacturing (now). There is a second industrial revolution happening right now. Where the first was about huge factories, sometimes the size of towns, the second industrial revolution is about small manufacturing: about manufacturing a few objects at a time for people who want them, not a million for people who might want them in the future. These rapid-manufacturing (sometimes called rapid-prototyping) technologies have some very interesting applications for designers.

1   These machines work directly from digital models in a way that is analogous to printing. You design something on-screen, you hit a button and make one, ten or a hundred.
2   Because the technology has low set-up costs, it means that models or other 3D artefacts can be made pretty cheaply, in low numbers.
3   The technology exists to work in a number of materials – plastics of course, but also metals, wood, stone, glass, etc. – and in multiple materials.

Suddenly, graphic designers have a way of making 3D characterisations, or prototypes of artefacts, as a way of cheaply engaging with end-users. You no longer finish your project on child health by showing drawings of your characters to the clients; you can give them real models, perhaps even jointed toys, to play with.

Mash ups (now). The media theorist and artist Lev Manovich once claimed that we live in a 'remix culture'. When he said it, it was only really true of those with high levels of technical skill and access to some pretty high-powered equipment. But I like to think that Manovich was looking to the future, for now we truly are living in a remix culture. This has been the case for some years in music, where sampling and remixing has been easy and cheap to do. Now, it is happening in video (look at YouTube) and exists in potential in print (through scanning and resampling existing material). The technology is out there, and mash-up designs will work because they are using semantically familiar and relevant codes that have been proven to be effective. But be warned: this kind of sampling is almost certainly in breach of copyright law, and, where the directors of the *Green Lantern* movie seem undisturbed by a thousand fan-made videos, composed of material stolen from other movies and made in the spirit of hope and impatience, other big commercial ventures (I'm thinking of a chain of fast-food restaurants here) are not so forgiving and have spent large amounts of money pursuing those who have used their intellectual property.

Variants on this genre include *mechanima*, which is to say, films that are made by using the avatars from computer games as digital actors. The original for this genre was *Red vs Blue*, a series of films (still being added to) about how boring it is being a soldier in the *Halo* series of games. Once again, the communication works because the viewer understands the context of the original media and so understands the point of the new communication.

Successful examples are few and far between at the moment, with most mash ups being fan-made horror shows of loud music and bad editing; however, there are some moments of interest such as *9/11 VENDETTA past, present & future* (www. filmsforaction.org/film/? Film=198&Title=9/11_Vendetta:_Past,_Present_&_future), a short film that combines news footage with samples from the film *V for Vendetta* to make some very pointed comments about the political uses of fear. This is a project that undoubtedly involves copyright infringement and is a little rough around the edges but that presents graphic communicators with an interesting template for future actions.

Digital reworkings (now and the future). Now, this is not the same as a mash up; it is the next stage on from a mash up, where cultural property (intellectual property) is used to make a work, but where everything else is provided by the creator. This might sound like counterfeiting, but is normally made for reasons other than profit and often as a matter of love. In 2003, long before the current generation of *Batman* movies, an American film-industry professional called Sandy Collora made an 8-minute live-action film called *Batman: Dead End*. The film features a hat-trick of copyright infringement by having Batman and the Joker meet the Alien and the Predator. Collora made the film, not for money, but to build his reputation as a film director. In 2005, in Finland, a group of five friends enlisted the help of a hoard of sci-fi fans and their parents' living rooms to make a parody of the *Star Trek* films. The acting in *Star Wreck: In the Pirkinning* is pretty awful, but having said that, the makers of the film have managed to produce a feature-length movie with good production values that can be downloaded for free from the net and that is distributed on DVD by Universal Pictures. The technology to make and distribute sophisticated media projects has diffused so widely that there is little to stop young designers with heart and imagination from thinking big. Reworkings can take many forms – film, games, interactive media, print, even packaging – as long as they form a coherent communication bridge between the designer and the user.

FAN MADE

Without wanting to point the finger at sci-fi fans, there is a massive sub-culture of *Star Trek*, *Star Wars*, *Buffy* and other fan-made films. Although they are generally made for love and traded, some of these films are commercial and, in the case of *Star Trek Phase II*, it is actively supported by the heirs to the Gene Roddenberry estate. Personally, I rather like *Stone Trek*, a cross between *Star Trek* and the *Flintstones*.

DESIGNING FOR FUTURE TRENDS

What a study of design for communication in the past shows us about graphic communication for the future is that, despite the changes in technology, the core features of graphic communication remain the same: we stand between those who need to send a message (but can't) and those who need to hear a message (but aren't).

The scale of the message has changed, because, where we once needed to speak to a million to make economic sense of the job, we can now speak to just tens of thousands (but the right ten thousand). The new technologies let us make a shift from being steelworkers to clockmakers: both work in metal, but one deals in bulk, raw products, and the other makes work that is small, detailed and active. Now, this should not be read as an excuse for producing parochial work. In a world as media savvy as ours, users will expect work to be both local in reference and international in quality. No, communication designers have the ability to engage in a subtle yet effective way with our users, producing quality designs that use the appropriate graphic language – not just print and paper, but video and steel, plastic and code, print and light. The only prerequisite is that they speak clearly to those who need to hear.

NOTES

1   Rubbish! I learned to hand print; I had nitric-acid burns from etching for a year. There was nothing magical about the medium.

2   Bill Gates didn't start Microsoft with the intention of changing the world; Tim Berners-Lee wasn't trying to change the whole structure of human communication, he just wanted to swap ideas with colleagues. Gutenberg did much of the development of printing as a method of getting money out of financial backers.

3   A scriptorium was a copying shop where both lay priests and clergy would spend their days copying out the scriptures by hand, as a commercial operation.

4   The longest running soap in the world is the BBC's *The Archers*, which started as a conduit for agricultural advice, based on the principle that advice from the government might be acted on when received as part of a narrative, but not when put on a flyer or poster.

5   Credit to Emma Webb, who invented the term.

Bibliography

Baldwin, J. and Roberts, L. (2006) *Visual communication from theory to practice*, AVA, Lausanne.

Barnard, M. (2005) *Graphic design as communication*, Routledge, London.

Barthes, R. (1977) *Image–music–text*, Fontana, Glasgow.

Bayer, H. (1999) 'Towards a universal type', in Beirut, M., Helfand, J. and Poyner, R. (eds), *Looking closer*, vol. 3, AIGA/Allworth Press, New York, p. 61.

Belkofer, C.M. and Konopka, L.M. (2008) 'Conducting art therapy research using quantitative EEG measures', *Art Therapy: Journal of the American Art Therapy Association*, 25(2): 56–63.

Bernard, M. *et al.* (2001) 'The effects of font type and size on the legibility and reading time of online text by older adults', presented at the *Conference on Human Factors in Computing Systems*, Association for Computing Machinery, pp. 175–6.

Bierut, M. (2002) 'A manifesto with ten footnotes', in Bierut, M. *et al.* (eds) *Looking closer 4*, AIGA, Alworth Press.

Bolter, J.D. and Grusin, R. (2000) *Remediation: understanding new media*, MIT Press.

Buchanan, R. (1992) 'Wicked problems in design thinking', *Design Issues*, 8(2) (Spring,): 5–21.

Camerer, Colin F. (2003) Introduction to *Behavioral game theory: experiments in strategic interaction*, Princeton University Press.

Cole, B. and Durack, R. (1972) *Railway posters 1923–1947*, Laurence King Publishing, London.

Dadich, S. (2004) 'What you see is what you get', *The New York Times*, 4 October, p. A19.

Davis, M. (ed.) (2004) *America's Army PC game vision and realization: a look at the artistry, technique, and impact of the United States Army's groundbreaking tool for strategic communication*, US Army and the Moves Institute, San Francisco.

De Lange, R.W., Esterhuizen, H.L. and Beatty, D. (1993) *Performance differences between Times and Helvetica in a reading task*, John Wiley & Sons Ltd, pp. 241–8.

Dennett, D. (2006) *Breaking the spell: religion as a natural phenomenon*, Penguin (Penguin edition 2007).

Dwiggins, W.A. (1999) 'A technique for dealing with artists (1941)', in Bierut, M. *et al.* (eds), *Looking Closer 3*, AIGA/Alworth Press, New York, pp. 84–92.

English, L.D. (1998) 'Children's reasoning in solving relational problems of deduction', *Thinking & Reasoning*, 4(3): 248–81.

Fulks, M. (n.d.). Gestalt: Figure/ground. *Apogee Photo Magazine* (retrieved 5 October 2008, from: www.apogeephoto.com/mag2–6/mag29gestalt.html).

Garland, K. (1963) *The first things first manifesto*; available at: www.kengarland.co.uk/KG%20published%20writing/first%20things%20first/index.html.

Garland, K. (2000) *The first things first manifesto 2000*; available at: http://maxbruinsma.nl/index1.html?ftf2000.htm.

Gaver, B., Dunne, T. and Pacenti, E. (1999) 'Cultural probes', *Interactions*, 6(1).

Goldman, K. (1997) *Conflicting accounts: the creation and crash of the Saatchi & Saatchi advertising empire*, Simon & Schuster, New York.

Habermas, J. (2001/2007) 'Truth and seeing', in Preliminary studies in the theory of communication action and Theorising communication, p. 450.

Haill, C. (1998) 'Posters for performance', in Timmers, M. (ed.), *The power of the poster*, V&A Publications, London, pp. 26–71.

Hall, S. (1991) *Culture, media, language: working papers in cultural studies, 1972–79*, Routledge, pp. 124–7.

Hartman, S. (2008) 'Shepard Fairey: An interview with the artist', design:related, 23 July (retrieved 5 October 2008, from: www.designrelated.com/news/feature_view/32).

Hatchuel, A. and Weil, B. (2009) 'C-K design theory: an advanced formulation', *Research in Engineering Design*, 19(4): 181–92.

Heer, J. (2003) 'Chip Kidd', *National Post*, 12 September; available at: www.jeetheer.com/culture/kidd.htm (accessed 18 April 2010).

Hegarty, J. (1998) 'Selling the product', in Timmers, M. (ed.), *The power of the poster*, V&A Publications, London, pp. 220–31.

Horn, G.F. (1976) *Contemporary posters: design and techniques*, Davis Publications, Worcester, MA.

Ihde, D. (2008) 'The designer fallacy and technological imagination', in *Ironic technics*, Automatic Press, p. 20.

Jonassen, D.H. (2000) 'Towards a design theory of problem solving', *ETR&D (Educational Technology Research and Development)*, 48(4): 63–85.

Judd, D.B. (1953) 'Color in business science and industry', *Applied Spectroscopy*, 7(2): 90–1.

Kipphan, H. (2001) *Handbook of print media: technologies and production methods*, Springer Verlag.

Kress, G. and van Leeuwen, T. (1996) *Reading images: the grammar of visual design*, Routledge, London.

Luhman, N. (1996) *Social systems*, Stanford University Press.

McClurg-Genevese, J.D. (2005) *The principles of design*, 13 June (retrieved 5 October 2008, from: www.digital-web.com/articles/principles_of_ design).

McDonagh-Philp, D. and Lebbon, C. (1993) 'The emotional domain in product design', *The Design Journal*, 3(1).

Mcluhan, M. (1964) *Understanding media: the extensions of man*, McGraw Hill, New York.

Manovich, L. (2008) *Software takes command*, available free online at: http://softwarestudies.com/softbook/manovich_softbook_11_20_2008.pdf.

Margolin, V. (1989) *Design discourse: history, theory, criticism*, The University of Chicago Press.

Mills, M. (1994) 'The (layered) vision thing', in Bierut, M., Drenttel, W., Heller, S. and Holland, D.K. (eds), *Looking closer: critical writings on graphic design*, Allworth Press, New York.

Nardi, B. (1998) 'The use of ethnographic methods in design and evaluation', in Helander, M., Landauer, T.K. and Prabhu, P. (eds) *Handbook of human–computer interaction*, second edition, Elsevier Science B.V., p. 362.

Neiborg, D.B. (2004) 'America's Army: more than a game', in Eberle, E. *et al. Transforming knowledge into action through gaming and simulation* (CD-ROM), SAGSAGA, Munchen.

Norman, D.A. (2002) *The design of everyday things*, Basic Books.

Pink, S. (2007) *Doing visual ethnography*, second edition, Sage Publications.

Popovic, V. (2004) 'Expertise development in product design – strategic and domain-specific knowledge connections', *Design Studies*, 25: 527–45.

Salisbury, M. (2000) *Art director confesses: 'I sold sex! drugs & rock 'n' roll'*, RotoVision, Crans-Prè-Céligny, Switzerland.

Schenk, P. (1991) 'The role of drawing in the graphic design process', *Design Studies*, 12(3): 168–81.

Shapiro, P. (2008) *Obama's posters: Message in the image. American Thinker*, 15 April (retrieved 28 September 2008, from: www.americanthinker.com/blog/2008/04/obamas_posters_message_in_the.html).

Simon, H. (1973) 'The structure of ill-structured problems', *Artificial Intelligence*, 4: 181–201.

Stukuls, D. (1997) 'Imagining the nation: campaign posters of the first postcommunist elections in Latvia', *East European Politics and Societies*, 11: 131–54.

Thorne, C. and Bennett, S. (2010) *A user's guide to design law*, Tottel Publishing.

Tschorn, A. (2008) 'Typography: the character issue', *Los Angeles Times*, 30 March (retrieved 5 October 2008, from: http://articles.latimes.com/2008/mar/30/image/ig-font30).

Updike, J. (2005) 'Introduction' in *Chip Kidd: Book one: Work: 1986–2006*, Rizzoli International Publications, Inc., New York.

Ward, C. (1999) *Information visualization: perception for design*, second edition, Morgan Kaufmann.

Wild, L. (1994) 'On overcoming modernism', in Bierut, M. (ed.) *Looking closer*, Allworth Communications, Inc.

Wood, P.K. (1983) 'Inquiring systems and problem structures: implications for cognitive development', *Human Development*, 26: 249–65.

Wright, M.I. (2003) *You back the attack! We'll bomb who we want!*, Seven Stories Press, New York.

Wright, M.I. (2004) *If you're not a terrorist then stop asking questions!*, XLibris, Xlibris.com.

Yi-Luen Do, E. and Gross, M.D. (1996) 'Drawing as a means to design reasoning', presented at *Artificial Intelligence in Design 96: Workshop on visual representation, reasoning and interaction in design*, June 1996, Stanford University, available at: https://services.brics. dk/java/courseadmin/ITVAP/documents/getDocument/drawing+as+means+to+design+ reasoning.pdf.pdf?d=37269.

Index

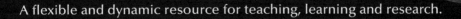